2005

The Dignity of Resistance

Women Residents' Activism in Chicago Public Housing

The Dignity of Resistance chronicles the four-decade history of Chicago's Wentworth Gardens public housing residents' grassroots activism. This comprehensive case study explores why and how these African-American women creatively and effectively engaged in organizing efforts to resist increasing government disinvestment in public housing and the threat of demolition.

Roberta M. Feldman and Susan Stall, utilizing a multidisciplinary lens, explore the complexity and resourcefulness of Wentworth women's grassroots organizing – the ways in which their identities as poor African-American women and mothers both circumscribe their lives and shape their resistance. Through the inspirational voices of the activists, Feldman and Stall challenge portrayals of public housing residents as passive, alienated victims of despair. We learn instead how women residents collectively have built a cohesive, vital community; have cultivated outside technical assistance and organizational and institutional supports; and have attracted funding – all to support the local facilities, services, and programs necessary for their everyday needs for survival, and ultimately to save their homes from demolition.

Roberta M. Feldman is Professor of Architecture at the School of Architecture and the Co-Director of the City Design Center at the College of Architecture and the Arts, University of Illinois, Chicago.

Susan Stall is Associate Professor of Sociology and Women's Studies at Northeastern Illinois University.

Cambridge Series in Environment and Behavior

General Editors: Daniel Stokols
                     Irwin Altman

An Introduction to Ecological Psychology
Allan W. Wicker

Culture and Environment
Irwin Altman and Martin Chemers

Inquiry by Design: Tools for Environment–Behavior Research
John Zeisel

Environmental Evaluation: Perception and Public Policy
Ervin H. Zube

Environmental Problems/Behavioral Solutions
John D. Cone and Steven C. Hayes

People in Cities
Edward Krupat

Human Territorial Functioning
Ralph Taylor

Work Places
Eric Sundstrom

Public Space
Stephen Carr, Mark Francis, Leanne G. Rivlin, and Andrew M. Stone

The Dignity of Resistance

Women Residents' Activism in Chicago Public Housing

ROBERTA M. FELDMAN

University of Illinois, Chicago

SUSAN STALL

Northeastern Illinois University

PUBLISHED BY THE PRESS SYNDICATE OF THE UNIVERSITY OF CAMBRIDGE
The Pitt Building, Trumpington Street, Cambridge, United Kingdom

CAMBRIDGE UNIVERSITY PRESS
The Edinburgh Building, Cambridge CB2 2RU, UK
40 West 20th Street, New York, NY 10011-4211, USA
477 Williamstown Road, Port Melbourne, VIC 3207, Australia
Ruiz de Alarcón 13, 28014 Madrid, Spain
Dock House, The Waterfront, Cape Town 8001, South Africa

http://www.cambridge.org

© Cambridge University Press 2004

First published 2004

Printed in the United States of America

Typeface Palatino 10/12 pt.   *System* LATEX 2$_\varepsilon$ [TB]

A catalog record for this book is available from the British Library.

Library of Congress Cataloging in Publication Data

Feldman, Roberta M.
The dignity of resistance : women residents' activism in Chicago public housing /
Roberta M. Feldman, Susan Stall.
p.   cm. – (Cambridge series in environment and behavior)
Includes bibliographical references (p.) and index.
ISBN 0-521-59320-4
1. Women in community organization – Illinois – Chicago – Case studies.   2. Community
leadership – Illinois – Chicago – Case studies.   3. Public housing – Illinois – Chicago –
Case studies.   4. African-American women – Illinois – Chicago – Case studies.
I. Stall, Susan. II. Title. III. Series.
HQ1421.F45   2003
363.5'85'0977311–dc21   2003041960

ISBN 0 521 59320 4 hardback

For the women of Wentworth Gardens,
who taught us the dignity of resistance

Contents

Foreword by Sheila Radford-Hill   *page* xi

Preface and Acknowledgments   xv

PART I. INTRODUCTION

1. Struggles for Homeplace   3

PART II. WENTWORTH GARDENS' HISTORIC CONTEXT

2. U.S. Public Housing Policies: Wentworth Gardens'
   Historic Backdrop   25

3. Memory of a Better Past, Reality of the Present: The Impetus
   for Resident Activism   59

PART III. EVERYDAY RESISTANCE IN THE EXPANDED
PRIVATE SPHERE

4. The Community Household: The Foundation
   of Everyday Resistance   91

5. The Local Advisory Council (LAC): A Site of
   Women-Centered Organizing   115

6. Women-Centered Leadership: A Case Study   151

7. The Appropriation of Homeplace: Organizing for
   the Spatial Resources to Sustain Everyday Life   179

PART IV. TRANSGRESSIVE RESISTANCE IN THE PUBLIC SPHERE

8. The White Sox "Battle": Protest and Betrayal   213

9. Linking Legal Action and Economic Development:
   Tensions and Strains   257

10. Becoming Resident Managers: A Bureaucratic Quagmire   295

PART V. CONCLUSIONS

11. Resistance in Context   341

Epilogue   352

Appendix A: Timeline of Wentworth Gardens Resident Activists'
Key Initiatives   356

Appendix B: A Demographic Profile of the Resident Community
Activists Interviewed, 1992–1998   358

References   359

Index   377

Foreword

Sheila Radford-Hill

I first arrived at Wentworth Gardens in the spring of 1982. I took the number 24 bus from downtown Chicago and got off at 35th and Wentworth Street, right in front of the old Chicago White Sox stadium, Comiskey Park. I walked the few short blocks past Tyler's Restaurant, past the grocery store, past Progressive Baptist Church, past T. E. Brown Apartments, past the senior citizens center, and through the modest neighborhood filled with homes that were well past their prime. As I walked, I was struck by the sense of neighborhood that these people of meager resources had somehow captured like lightning in a bottle. The easy familiarity and gossipy love that neighbors have for each other would lead me right to the office of the Wentworth Local Advisory Council (LAC).

As a trainer/organizer for Designs for Change (DFC), an education advocacy organization, I had the mission of organizing parents of special education children so that they could actively challenge the special education policies at their school. The neighborhood school was the Robert S. Abbott Elementary School, a once proud elementary school named for the famous founder of the *Chicago Defender*. Sadly, the memory of Robert S. Abbott was tarnished by a school plagued with low achievement and a disproportionate number of special education–identified students.

With the support of the Wentworth LAC, I visited the development frequently and confirmed what a DFC analysis of the school's enrollment patterns had shown, namely, that children from Wentworth Gardens were being inappropriately placed in special education classes. In addition, they were being educated in a setting that was becoming increasingly segregated because of the district's policy of busing children from other schools in the region to the Abbott School. In other words, Abbott had become a dumping ground where children were receiving inferior education services and, in many cases, were inappropriately referred for special education. Under federal law, children receiving these services were entitled to a "free and appropriate education"; through research it became increasingly clear that the school's practices violated these rights. As the parents became increasingly aware of the situation at Abbott, they discovered that the school district was indifferent to their plight. To make matters worse, the school's long-time principal was not an advocate for the children at Abbott: He was complacent about underperforming teachers and condescending to the parents, many of whom were poorly educated.

In the winter of 1983, the parents wanted change. At their request, I helped them organize a parent action against a regular education teacher who had become mentally incompetent to teach her class. After repeated attempts to get the teacher removed, the parents felt that some form of direct action was the only option left to safeguard their children's right to an education. None of the parents had ever done anything like this before; they were scared but resolute. They did not turn back even when the principal threatened to have them arrested for trespassing. On the appointed day, the parents commandeered a vacant classroom, and, with the permission of each child's parent, they moved the students to an empty classroom and demanded a substitute teacher. The protest was meant to pressure the principal and the district to put children before union work rules. If these authorities could not remove the *teacher from the class*, the parents could remove *the class from the teacher*.

Within 24 hours a substitute teacher was provided and the mentally incompetent teacher had been transferred to the central office. For more than a year after this action, the parents continued to collect and analyze data about Abbott school; some testified at the teacher's dismissal hearing; others became school activists, and, in 1988, with the passage of Chicago School Reform, they became members of the Local School Council (LSC).

When I left DFC and got a job at the Chicago Area Project (CAP), the residents again requested my help. My assignment was to provide technical assistance to their organization. This assignment also involved organizing the residents. This time, the intransigent bureaucracy was the Chicago Housing Authority (CHA), and the purpose of organizing the residents was to pressure CHA to repair neglected and dangerous conditions in the development.

Along with the struggle to repair Wentworth Gardens before it fell down around the residents for lack of investment and blatant neglect, there was the struggle to establish an independent organization to better serve their needs and the struggle to save their dilapidated homes from the City of Chicago and the State of Illinois partnership that financed a new White Sox park. The neighborhood south of 35th Street was destroyed by this stadium redevelopment scheme.

As the organizer involved in these struggles, I helped the residents form Wentworth Residents United for Survival, the South Armour Square Neighborhood Coalition, and the Wentworth Resident Management Corporation. I worked with residents to plan the overall strategy and several of the tactics discussed in this book. The tactics were often confrontational, but the strategy made use of and sought to preserve the community-building spirit that characterizes Wentworth Gardens. For these people, community building is an act of resistance: a commitment to join together out of the needs of people, to work together as neighbors, and to overcome the real and present danger of annihilation.

Through these struggles, I learned that the *heart of grassroots organizing* is resistance. Resistance is a moral response to the significant human misery heaped on marginalized people at the hands of inept, insensitive, complacent, and often corrupt bureaucracies. I learned that *the soul of grassroots organizing* lies in its insistence on human dignity for all people. These women taught me that *grassroots movements require both heart and soul*.

This book captures the story of women who simply refuse to accept institutional arrangements that dehumanize and degrade them. The intensity of this research is fueled by the researchers' commitment to placing the community action of the resident leaders in Wentworth in the context of the struggle for human dignity. In this instance, the research documents the struggle against timid and inept housing policies. These policies take place, in turn, within the larger context of changes in the U.S. economy that have accelerated the decline of low-income neighborhoods. The unequal distribution of economic prosperity has produced increased economic isolation and social distress among people in poor communities. Economic deprivation, toxic political representation, exploitative institutions, and austere social conditions are the forces that work against decent housing and sustainable development for the residents in Chicago's public housing.

The residents of Wentworth Gardens understand these realities, but they are not interested in organizing *around issues*; they want to save their homes and their neighborhood. Organizing in this community is a lopsided struggle for a place at the decision-makers' table, a place that is rightfully theirs because the residents share a vision of what their community should be.

The older leaders are effective representatives of this vision because the neighborhood they desire is as real to them as the reality of the neglected physical spaces is to those of us who do not live there. Their collective vision was formed from the memories of the neighborhood these women first called home. The love of home and the love of their community brought them together and will keep them together despite bickering and occasional falling-outs.

The older generation knows that when your home is threatened, it becomes a place of insurgency, a place where community building and social action can foster empowerment. After 20 years of watching the people in this development from the perspective of a community organizer, I am struck by the fact that the younger activists have a harder time imagining what the community could be like if active residents made powerful interests accountable to their needs. These younger women have grown to understand the heart of grassroots organizing. The struggle continues for their souls; this book is a window into that struggle.

The research is designed to document the struggles of marginalized people not only to validate their knowledge but also to challenge society's prevailing insensitivity to the lives of the poor. Deep within the soul of grassroots organizing are a thirst for freedom that cannot be quenched, a hunger for justice that cannot be satiated, a will to succeed that cannot be denied, and a desire to build a legacy of change that will pass on to new generations. This book is about *the heart and soul of grassroots organizing*. Let it inform your understanding of how grassroots people in modest circumstances can become change agents on their own behalf.

All struggles are not won in the traditional sense; a recent visit to Wentworth reminded me of this. As I walked throughout the "Gardens" on a hot summer day in 2002, I was dismayed at the magnitude of the challenges ahead of the residents who are now in charge of managing the development. But as I watched the young people celebrate the beginning of a fully resident-managed development, I realized that many more hearts are waiting to be touched and transformed into grassroots activists. To these young people will fall the broader task of building the institutional capacity needed to safeguard promises grudgingly made by the power structure.

If America is to achieve economic and social equity, if America is to live the promise of democracy, its scholars, teachers, researchers, policy-makers, and citizens will need to learn from the wisdom and experiences of people working for change in their local communities. The well-researched case study presented by the authors of this book reminds us that those called to strengthen the resistance of the poor are rich indeed.

Preface and Acknowledgments

In the spring of 1987 nearly 400 people – public housing residents, housing activists, community organizers, housing professionals, and academics – gathered for the Women and Public Housing: Hidden Strength, Unclaimed Power conference at the University of Illinois at Chicago. The intent of this 2-day conference was to provide a public forum to highlight resident-initiated responses to entrenched social problems existing within public housing developments locally and nationally. There was the added hope that the conference participants could become a base for future organized actions. One of us, Susan Stall, was the coordinator of the conference. The other, Roberta Feldman, prepared the photodocumentary for the plenary session, "Sharing Our Homes, Sharing Our Communities." Representatives from Wentworth Gardens spoke in the session "Planning Our Communities to Resist Displacement."[1] Through the year-long preparation for

---

[1] The necessity for a conference on women and public housing was first proposed at the closing session of the "Women and Safe Shelter" Conference (April 25–26, 1986) by public housing residents and advocates. The conference was preceded by a series of organizing meetings held throughout Chicago in which public residents voiced their concerns, raised issues they considered important, and shared their knowledge of local initiatives. These community meetings culminated in the "Women and Public Housing" Conference (May 29–30, 1987). Local and national community activists living in and/or working with public housing explored such issues as leadership development, self-employment, resident management, and welfare reform in 25 conference sessions. Wentworth Gardens appears in the document that accompanied the conference, A *Resource Directory for Residents in Public Housing*, which identifies 130 on-site service providers and advocates for public housing residents and includes 12 case studies of resident activists (Hunt-Rhymes et al., 1987).

As a direct outcome of the conference, Susan Stall, as a community consultant, with a committee of public housing residents and resident advocates facilitated the formation of the citywide nonprofit tenants' organization, Chicago Housing Authority Residents Taking Action (CHARTA). (See *The New York Times*, June 2, 1991.) Several Wentworth Gardens residents worked collaboratively with CHARTA organizers.

this conference we became acutely aware of the essential roles that women residents living in Chicago Housing Authority (CHA) developments play through their organizing efforts to create and secure their communities. This was our first opportunity to become acquainted with women from Wentworth Gardens, and we have remained involved with Wentworth activists since that time.

Our initial visits to the Wentworth Gardens development were motivated by our intention to write an accessible account of the residents' past and present organizing initiatives for an audience of community activists and reformers (Feldman & Stall, 1989). As we grew to know the Wentworth resident activists better, we were struck by their creativity, camaraderie, and tenacity in the face of formidable challenges. We became increasingly convinced that it was important to offer an alternative portrayal of public housing residents – one that contests existing pervasive negative stereotypes.

As feminist action researchers we recognized our privileged social positions and the structural barriers to developing a complex understanding of the everyday lives of low-income women of color. As white women who live in safe and secure housing, we do not face the same day-to-day issues that Wentworth activists confront. As a result we sought to bridge the differences between us and the residents, and whenever possible to build reciprocal relationships that foster an exchange of trust. We were cognizant of our responsibility not only to reciprocate the Wentworth residents' contributions to our research, but to contribute to positive social changes in their community.

Shortly after we began our research at Wentworth, in 1989, Susan Stall was invited to organize and chair the Wentworth Gardens Resident Management Community Advisory Board. The tasks of this advisory group have been to advise and support the technical and organizing tasks of Wentworth's resident management board. Later Roberta Feldman worked with Wentworth Garden residents and their South Armour Square neighbors on a feasibility study for a new adjacent shopping center through conducting participatory design workshops.

Since the late 1980s, we have attempted to promote the efforts of resident activists by documenting and giving public recognition to their past and current organizing achievements in a variety of alternative venues. For example, we prepared an exhibit for the Chicago Peace Museum in Chicago that provided photo documentation and text describing community actions at Wentworth; served in an advisory capacity to the Field Museum's new permanent exhibit *Living Together: Sheltering Ourselves*, which features the Wentworth resident activist Mary Rias in the accompanying video; and contributed to the telecourse aired by PBS, *Women and Social Action*, which includes the Wentworth resident activists in a 1-hour segment,

"Low Income Women's Resistance."[2] In several instances, Wentworth Gardens residents have participated in conference and colloquium presentations with us.[3] Also, we have presented our slide documentation and observations of their activism in varied and multiple settings and for diverse audiences in the hopes that potential community supporters will

[2] The installation, "Community Builders – Wentworth Gardens Resident Activists," was in the *Supportive Housing and Protective Environments (SHAPE)* Peace Museum Exhibition, February 26–May 28, 1994. It was designed and executed by Roberta Feldman, Jack Naughton, Susan Stall, and Linda Hover-Montgomery and is now mounted in the RMC conference room at Wentworth Gardens.

The telecourse *Women and Social Action*, directed by Martha Thompson, was distributed nationwide (live feeds as well as videotapes) by PBS Adult Learning Services from 1994 until 2000. Susan Stall served on a multiuniversity advisory committee for the development of the telecourse from 1993 to 1994 and worked with Martha Thompson to orchestrate the video segment taped at Wentworth Gardens. The 1-hour segment "Low Income Women's Resistance" focuses on the organizing successes and challenges at Wentworth Gardens. The accompanying study guide, *Teleclass Study Guide: Women and Social Action* (Thompson, 1994), also describes and analyzes the activism of the Wentworth Gardens residents, both in the study guide section "Low Income Women's Resistance" and also in a reprint of one of our earliest articles, "Resident Activism in Public Housing, A Chicago Public Housing Development: A Case Study of Women's Invisible Work of Building Community" (Feldman and Stall, 1990). *Women and Social Action* is still listed on the PBS Adult Learning Services website (http://www.pbs.org/als/women_act/index.html). Videotapes of the course are still being distributed by RMI Media Productions, Inc. Also, it continues to air at several colleges and universities licensed to offer it on the Education Channel (http://www.educationchannel.org/html/Telecourses/womensocialact.html), and it is still in use at at several colleges and universities.

The Wentworth Gardens resident Mary Rias was one of four individuals featured in a video exhibition, *Living Together: Sheltering Ourselves*, which opened at the Chicago Field Museum in 1997. This exhibit instructs visitors about the diversity of urban homes and neighborhoods in the contemporary United States. Roberta Feldman served on the advisory committee for this exhibit from 1995 to 1997.

The Community Design Center at UIC provided some of the technical assistance to work on two reports requested by Wentworth. Both the research and the reports were conducted in partnership with the residents: *Wentworth Gardens Resident Management Corporation Community Housing Concerns Report*, which had the contributors Khari Hunt, Hallie Amey, Susan Donald, Wateka Kleinpeter, Roberta Feldman, and Erin Hayes (May 27, 1998), and *An Assessment of the Resources and Needs Available for the Development of a Child Care Program at Wentworth Gardens*, by Susan Donald, Erin Hayes, and Bianca Wilson (1998).

[3] Since 1988, one or more Wentworth Gardens residents have presented with us in five colloquium, or conference settings: "Women and Housing Activism" at the Radical Scholars Conference, Chicago, July 1988; "Getting to Know Our Neighbors – IIT and the Public Housing Community," at Illinois Institute of Technology, Chicago, December 1989; "When Housing Is Not Enough: Chicago Public Housing Residents Become Community Developers," Future Visions of Public Housing (An International Forum), Cincinnati, Ohio, November 1994; "Resident Management at a Chicago Public Housing Development," International Environmental Design Research Association (EDRA) Conference, Saint Louis, Missouri, March 1998; and "Women, Resistance, and Public Housing," Gender and City Spaces (A Gender and Women's Studies Lecture Series), University of Illinois at Chicago, September 2002.

learn of the challenges and successes of these Chicago-based community efforts. Finally, through both our roles on the RMC Community Advisory Board and our protracted involvement as researchers we have attempted, whenever possible, to serve as conduits for material and technical resources in the greater Chicago area.

This book would not have been possible without the friendships we have developed and the gracious assistance we have received from numerous women in the Wentworth Gardens development, and from several of their community partners. We are especially grateful to the women of Wentworth whom we interviewed for this study, who included us in countless meetings and events. It has been our privilege to be welcomed into such an emotionally warm and vibrant community. They have changed our lives forever.

In a project with such an extended time frame there are numerous individuals who we want to thank. The four research assistants who assisted us in this project each made a unique contribution. Quentin Stevens did essential research of the CHA archives and prepared materials for the design workshop at Wentworth Gardens. Nancy Hudspeth did excellent reviews of the history of public housing and resident management and contributed to our observational data. Both Lynne Westphal and Lynne Moch observed at countless Wentworth meetings and events; their field notes and their interpretations of their data gathering were invaluable. We are indebted to Brad Hunt for his detailed responses to our inquiries on public housing history and his detailed and knowledgeable review of our chapter 2. Both Pat Wright and Jim Chapman generously shared written materials, legal documents, and their memories of the organizing efforts at Wentworth that predated our own involvement. Gowri Betrabet participated in the community garden focus group and contributed her careful observations. Diana Solis's early photographs at Wentworth inspired our own attempts at photo documentation of the residents' activism. Elizabeth Michaels transcribed the majority of our interviews. Brenda Sherwood transcribed the audio of a videotape of a Wentworth event. Laura Swartzbaugh and Holly Pringley helped us organize our references. Kevin Stevens supported digital files of images. Jason Feldman generously donated his design expertise to create the cover, photo collages, and timeline.

Many other individuals collaborated with us in our efforts to share technical resources with the Wentworth Gardens residents. Craig Wilkins offered the residents real estate development seminars and finalized the shopping center design. Jack Naughton was the cofacilitator in the participatory design workshop. Michael Gellick and Jacques Chatain gave their time and professional expertise to prepare the architecture and engineering assessment. Jason Feldman contributed the design for the Wentworth RMC's logo and newsletter. Erin Hayes, Bianca Wilson, and

Khari Hunt partnered with residents on the needs assessment survey and implementation study of the day care training center. Both Lynne Westphal and Lynne Moch were genuine participatory researchers at Wentworth – actively engaged in several Wentworth organizing and fund-raising initiatives.

Our thanks to Irv Altman and Dan Stokol, the series editors. Irv has consistently provided ongoing support for this book, from its first conception as a book chapter to its present form. Martha Thompson and Judy Wittner read numerous drafts of each chapter over the past years and generously agreed, along with Jamie Horwitz, Randy Stoecker, and Lynne Westphal, to read and comment on the first draft of our manuscript. Also, Jennifer Gress's careful reading and detailed editorial comments provided a detailed guide during our revisions. Sheila Radford-Hill was a wonderful sounding board for our theoretical musings and offered enthusiastic and thoughtful support throughout this writing project. Conversations with Leslie Kanes Weisman, Terry Haywoode, Maurine Wood, Gail Radford, and Charlie Hoch offered useful ideas and encouragement along the way, and intellectual collaborations with Nancy Naples and Randy Stoecker helped us to refine our theoretical thinking.

We also want to recognize our respective universities and university centers for their support of our work. Through the University of Illinois at Chicago, Roberta Feldman received a Great Cities Institute Faculty Seed Grant and a Great Cities Institute Faculty Fellowship. From Northeastern Illinois University at Chicago, Susan Stall received a Committee on Organized Research Grant.

Finally both of us have certain people in our immediate lives who sustained us during this multiyear endeavor:

Roberta Feldman:
The staff at the UIC City Design Center – Tasneem Chowdhury, Elizabeth Kocs, Laura Swartzbaugh, and Jenna Robison – I am indebted to you for covering for me in the last throes of completing the book manuscript. Judith Kirshner, the dean of the UIC College of Architecture and the Arts, and Katerina Ruedi, the past director of UIC School of Architecture, I thank you for the gift of time to complete this project.

My greatest debt is to the ongoing support of my family: my memories of my father's words, "You can accomplish whatever you set out to do"; my brother Leslie's unyielding support of my goals; the love of my husband, Richard, who lifted my spirits; my son Scott, who provided uncompromising intellectual council; my son Jason, whose creative talent gave visual expression to the project, and whose nurturance filled the void; and Monica and Gabriel for the time this book has taken from our being together.

Susan Stall:

I owe a tremendous debt to my writing group colleagues and friends, Martha Thompson and Judy Wittner, for their unflagging support of me and of this project. Thanks to Laurie Danch, Gail Radford, Robyne Luzietti, Kathy Lorimer, Liz Brown, Kathleen Slobin, and Lissa Schwartz, who provided me with emotional support when my spirits and my confidence were dragging. My mother, Phyllis Stall, did not live to see the completion of this project, but her spirit lives on through the intensified support of my sisters, Patti, Julie, and Stephanie, and my brother, John. Finally, I am blessed to have Charlie Hoch and Gina Hoch-Stall in my life. The writing process does not bring out the best in me, but Charlie and Gina continuously nurtured me with food, humor, and their unconditional love.

PART I

INTRODUCTION

1

Struggles for Homeplace

> [Y]ou really just haven't seen how some people are living over here. We have potholes over here large enough for a small child to fall in.... And we have roof leaks. It doesn't make sense for somebody to be living like [this].
>
> Beatrice Harris, Wentworth Gardens Local Advisory Council president

The resident Beatrice Harris, one of the key figures in local organizing efforts at Wentworth Gardens, is speaking with great dismay about the abysmal living conditions of her "homeplace," a 422-unit low-rise Chicago Housing Authority (CHA) family development on the South Side. The time is the late 1980s, when Wentworth, as in other CHA developments, is beleaguered by two decades of underfunding and inept management. Daily life in CHA family developments is beset by inefficient and inadequate buildings and grounds maintenance, and insufficient social, recreational, and educational services to meet the residents' needs (see also Kotlowitz, 1991; Slayton, 1988; Venkatesh, 2000).

When we began our fieldwork in 1989, we too were struck by the deterioration of Wentworth Gardens' buildings and grounds. Signs of dilapidated and unsafe physical conditions were visible throughout the development. The brick building exteriors were cracked. The concrete overhangs were scaling, and large pieces had broken off. Lead paint was peeling, and lights in the public entries and stairwells were in disrepair. The concrete sidewalks, exterior stairs, and retaining walls had huge cracks and large missing sections or were missing altogether. Excavated holes exposing rusted, broken heating pipes with steam bursting out were common. Children's play equipment in each of the development's courtyards was dismantled, leaving behind fractured concrete and big crevices that posed hazards for small children; extensive expanses of dirt with only patches of grass covered the development's central court.

Despite the best attempts of residents to decorate and keep their apartments clean, interior walls and ceilings showed signs of water leaks and

3

mold. Deteriorated plumbing pipes and fixtures, roofs that had not been replaced, and brick walls that had not been tuckpointed since occupancy resulted in water damage in the apartments.[1] Gerry-rigged electric wires making up for inadequate electric service, exposed heating pipes, sewage backup in the sinks and toilets, and lead paint in the apartments created health hazards; so too did the periodic floods, and rats and feral cats in the basements.

Records showed that Wentworth's buildings and grounds were cited for over 1,000 building code violations. Virtually none was repaired. Deferred maintenance had become such a serious problem that, as of 1991, a CHA report claimed that approximately $11 million would be required to repair and raise Wentworth's physical plant up to standard (On-Site Insight, 1991).

Physical deterioration was not the only threat to the Wentworth community's viability. Less obvious to the onlooker, but equally important, children's recreational and educational programs were inadequate, and the on-site field house required renovation and expansion. Social services were inadequate given the residents' needs. Wentworth residents voiced the urgent necessity for adult job training, day-care and after-school programs, young adult recreation and employment, and drug rehabilitation programs. Police protection was less than adequate, although crime at Wentworth was a less serious problem than in CHA's other family developments. Also as in other low-income communities, Wentworth's neighborhood was underserved by retail stores.

The deteriorated conditions at Wentworth Gardens were common to public housing nationwide. Whereas housing reformers had high hopes for public housing in the United States at its inception in the 1930s, by the 1980s, most deemed it a failure. Critics and researchers generally have agreed that the pressing problems facing the federal government's public housing program at the turn of the 21st century are underfunding; concentration and social and physical isolation of poor minority families, typically in undesirable and inaccessible locations; inappropriate building designs (especially high-rise structures, and "nondefensible" public exterior and interior spaces); crime and vandalism; lack of tenant selection and income mix; and again, ineffective maintenance and management, and inadequate or inaccessible services and employment opportunities (for a review, see Bauman, 1994). Notably, Chicago's public housing, although having the third largest number of units in the country (Popkin, Gwiasda, Olson, Rosenbaum, & Buron, 2000), is considered "among the worst in the

---

[1] Tuckpointing is a process to replace and repair the mortar between the bricks of the exterior walls in order to prevent water from seeping into the interior of the building.

FIGURE 1. Upper left: East side of Wentworth Gardens along Wentworth Avenue showing two-story rowhouses in 1988 (photographer: Roberta M. Feldman). Upper right: Entrance to the Wentworth Gardens field house and CHA management office located on Wentworth Avenue in 1997. The balloons on the tree were part of Wentworth Gardens' 50th anniversary celebration (photographer: Susan Stall). Center left: Interior courtyard showing two-story rowhouses and three-story walk-up apartment buildings in 1988 (photographer: Roberta M. Feldman). Center right: Three-story walk-up apartment buildings in the foreground and two-story rowhouses in the background as seen from the west side of the Wentworth development in 1988 (photographer: Roberta M. Feldman). Lower left: Front entry of a three-story walk-up apartment building in 1988 (photographer: Roberta M. Feldman). Lower right: Wentworth's central courtyard in 1988 (photographer: Diana Solis).

nation – poorly constructed, poorly maintained, and extremely dangerous"
(Popkin et al., 2000, p. 1).[2]

Wentworth Gardens residents have not passively acquiesced to these
worsening conditions; rather, for four decades, starting in the 1960s, they
have been persistently engaged in sustained grassroots efforts to stem
the deterioration of their buildings, grounds, services, and programs. In
1988, however, Wentworth activists' resolve was pressed to its limits. The
Wentworth Gardens development was threatened with demolition, first
to make way for a new White Sox stadium; shortly thereafter, to comply
with federal pressures to demolish public housing units nationwide. The
U.S. Department of Housing and Urban Development (HUD) required a
viability test of all public housing in 1996, calling for unviable units to be
razed. In Chicago, this is the vast majority of units.

In *The Dignity of Resistance: Women Residents' Activism in Chicago Public
Housing*, we describe the history of Wentworth resident–initiated individual and collective actions to alter living conditions that have threatened
their housing's and their community's viability. *The Dignity of Resistance* is
foremost Wentworth activists' story of their daily struggles to meet their
own and their neighbors' needs for survival and to save their homes from
demolition. Second, it is an analysis of their resistance against increasing
government disinvestment in public housing and social services, and the
growing poverty in their community. It explains why and how Wentworth
resident activists, African-American women representing over 1,200 people, mostly low-income female-headed families, carefully and effectively
took on the responsibility for creating a better future for themselves and
their neighbors.

The central questions we address in this book are, What has motivated
Wentworth Gardens residents, individually and communally, to initiate
and sustain their involvement in grassroots efforts to improve and defend their home? What strategies have these residents used? What resources, both personal and collective, as well as outside resources, have
they needed? What have been the essential challenges and accomplishments of their efforts? We interpret the answers to these questions within a
resistance theoretical framework, especially focusing on the role that public housing has played in the expression and imposition of both "power"
and "resistance."

UNCOVERING PUBLIC HOUSING WOMEN RESIDENTS' ACTIVISM

For the general public and for policymakers, the role that Wentworth public housing women have played in saving their homes is unexpected. The

[2] Only New York City and Puerto Rico public housing family developments have more units
(Popkin et al., 2000).

popular images of public housing are of an embattled war zone (Garbarino, Kostenlny, & Durbrow, 1993). As early as 1958, the journalist Harrison Salisbury described New York's public housing as "human catchpools . . . that breed social ills" (Williams & Kornblum, 1994). In a 12-part series, the *Chicago Tribune* (December 1986) called its city's public housing "The Chicago Wall . . . a physical barrier of brick and steel and concrete that separates black from white, rich from poor, hope from despair" (p. 1); and the Public Broadcasting System's documentary about life in the largest CHA development, Robert Taylor Homes, *A Crisis on Federal Street* (aired January 6, 1989, in Chicago), depicted residents as both helpless and predatory, and their housing environment as irreparable. With increasing frequency, the media have supported the call for dismantling public housing.

Social science research focused on residents' experiences of public housing also tends to be unfavorable and most often concentrates on big-city high-rise developments. In William Moore, Jr.'s (1969), observations of life in a midwestern high rise project, he described a "vertical ghetto," where residents were "living on segregated 'islands of poverty.'" In his study of the Pruitt Igoe high-rise project in Saint Louis, Lee Rainwater (1970) called these towers "federal slums" and described "fractured social relations and pervasive fear of physical and emotional violence." Often cited studies of life in public housing depict residents as on the defensive, attempting to protect themselves from surrounding and increasingly internal human and physical threats (Newman, 1972; Popkin et al., 2000; Rainwater, 1970). More generally, social scientists typically characterize low-income people as helpless and apathetic victims of despair (reviewed in Kieffer, 1984; Naples, 1988; also see Rappaport, 1981). Although scholars refrain from "blaming the victim," they portray an oppressed, alienated, passive, and powerless resident population victimized by stigmatization, poverty, and racism.

In Devereaux Bowley's (1978) history of Chicago public housing, he criticizes the "paternalistic philosophy" of both social reformers and public officials toward the poor, in particular those living in public housing, noting:

The residents were treated like children, and the tragedy is that for some it was the self-fulfilling prophecy – they acted like children and were satisfied to have public housing and welfare policies control their lives. Public housing thus tended to perpetuate a permanent class of dependent people, unable to fend for themselves. (p. 224)

It is presumed that low-income people, and especially public housing residents, are incapable of forming and participating in active, productive community (Venkatesh, 2000).

Our research at Wentworth Gardens does not support these blanket generalizations about public housing residents or their experiences; nor does the research documenting the struggles of low-income women who have historically fought, and continue to fight, for safe and decent shelter and adequate services (see also Birch, 1978; Keys 1991; Lawson & Barton 1980; Leavitt & Saegert, 1990; Weisman, 1992; Wekerle, 1980). The sparse current research focused specifically on public housing residents' activism illustrates an alternative portrayal: Patricia O' Brien (1995) analyzed the persistent and energetic abilities of a dozen African-American women to manage their public housing development in Kansas; Myrna Brietbart and Ellen Pader (1995) described the prominent role Boston public housing's women residents played in the redevelopment of Columbia Point into the mixed-income Harbor Point development; and Jacqueline Leavitt (1993) documented women public housing residents' successful efforts in Los Angeles to provide their youth with a sorely needed playground. Other current research on public housing (Popkin et al., 2000; Venkatesh, 2000), although focused on other issues, similarly has noted the role women residents play in working to improve their developments. Even with these inquiries, public housing women residents' efforts remain largely invisible.

Feminist social science and empowerment scholars are challenging the invisibility of low-income women's grassroots struggles by broadening the standard conceptualization of politics. Patricia Hill Collins (1991) speaks about some of the problems with conventional researchers' portrayal of the political process, especially for African-American women:

Social science research has ignored Black women's actions in both the struggle for group survival and institutional transformation. . . . White male conceptualizations of the political process produce definitions of power, activism, and resistance that fail to capture the meaning of these concepts in Black women's lives. (p. 141)

Traditional research and dominant cultural portrayals of politics focus on the public, official actors and workings of government, not only ignoring, but devaluing, community-based struggles of people to gain control over their lives: struggles in which women traditionally have played major roles. In contrast, feminist scholarship elaborates upon the ways in which people's race, class, and gender account both for their community-based needs and also for the nature of their involvement in grassroots politics (cf. Bookman & Morgen, 1988; Feldman & Stall, 1994; Gittell, Ortega-Bustamante, & Steffy, 1999; Haywoode, 1991; Leavitt & Saegert, 1990; Naples, 1998a, 1998b; Stall & Stoecker, 1998; West & Blumberg, 1990). Feminist researchers recognize that poor and working-class women, and in particular women of color, cannot rely on culturally normative routes of electoral politics nor financial resources to work in their best interests; rather, they gain their power from the bottom up, through involvement in collective grassroots activism. In low-income and working-class neighborhoods women generally, although not exclusively, have struggled for better schools, improved housing conditions, and safer communities and have challenged urban renewal and downtown growth priorities to save and renew their deteriorating neighborhoods (cf. Gittell et al., 1999; Naples, 1998a). Similarly, in public housing developments across the country, women residents have constituted the overwhelming majority of grassroots activists, organizing for improved building and site conditions, social and youth services, employment opportunities, and the very survival of their developments.

Homeplace as a Site of Resistance

Despite the increased attention by feminist scholars to the political dimensions of grassroots activism, the physical settings in which, and often over which, power struggles are manifest are largely overlooked (Feldman & Stall, 1994). Grassroots activism is implicitly place-bound: That is, the networks of relationships and the activism that they support are located in and may involve conflict over places. Sheila Radford-Hill in *Further to Fly: Black Women and the Politics of Empowerment* (2000) argues for an "applied feminism" that both explicates, appreciates, and supports the community-building processes of low-income women and "affirms and reclaims communities as actual spaces or locations where groups of people build reservoirs of activism and love" (p. xvi). As Radford-Hill does, we propose that the foundation of grassroots activism in low-income communities not only is substantially locally based, but often is intimately connected to ongoing struggles for rights to and control over spatial resources to sustain these communities. At Wentworth Gardens, the struggles for spatial resources that house and support everyday life – from the spaces to house needed services and programs in their community, and more generally to the buildings and grounds of their development – have been central to the residents' community activism.

The starting point for our analysis is the work of bell hooks (1990) and her conceptualization of the role of the "homeplace" in the expression of both power and resistance in African-Americans' lives. In her chapter, "Homeplace: A Site of Resistance," hooks proposed that historically, African-Americans' struggles to make and sustain a homeplace and community provided more than a domestic service or the necessities for everyday survival; it also had a "subversive value" as a source of resistance. She observed:

Historically, African-American people believed that the construction of a homeplace, however, fragile and tenuous (the slave hut, the wooden shack), had a radical political dimension. Despite the brutal reality of racial apartheid, of domination, one's homeplace was the one site where one could freely confront the issue of humanization, where one could resist. Black women resisted by making homes where all black people could strive to be subjects, not objects, where we could be affirmed in our minds and hearts despite poverty, hardship, and deprivation, where we could restore to ourselves the dignity denied us on the outside in the public world. (p. 42)

Their dwelling, no matter how simple, was typically the only physical setting that African-Americans could, with some reliability, call their own (also see Rainwater, 1966). Yet, hooks also recognizes the central importance of the experiences of "at-homeness." Her descriptions of the "feeling of safety," "of homecoming" (p. 41) upon arrival at one's home, and of black women's central responsibility in constructing "domestic households as spaces of care and nurturance" (p. 42) are indicators of experiences that are central to conceptualizations of at-homeness (Buttimer, 1980; Cooper, 1974; Csikszentmihalyi & Rochberg-Halton, 1981; Relph, 1976; Seamon, 1979; Tuan, 1977). hooks, however, views these experiences not as ends in and of themselves, but rather as central to conceptualizing homeplace as political – the construction of a safe, nurturing place "where people can return to themselves more easily, where the conditions are such that they can heal themselves and recover their wholeness" (hooks citing Thich Nhat Hahn, p. 43) in "the face of the brutal harsh reality of racist oppression, of sexist domination" (p. 42).

In *The Dignity of Resistance* we illustrate the importance of considering the homeplaces in which, and over which, everyday power struggles to maintain households and communities are manifest. We explain that public housing residents' struggles for the material and spatial resources of their homeplace are a critical source of resistance in their lives. Furthermore, we introduce the concept of *space appropriation* in our theoretical analysis of resistance to elevate the importance of individuals' and groups' creation, choice, possession, modification, enhancement of, care for, and/or simply intentional use of space in grassroots activism.

Our conceptualization of the role of space appropriation in the expression of everyday resistance is grounded in the well known work of Foucault (1979). He proposed that cultural discourses about power are transformed into actual power relations in bounded space and architectural forms. Manzo and Wolfe (1990), in interpreting Foucault's work, proposed that places are not only the site of power, of the assertion of dominance; they are also the site of resistance: "[A]s power reveals itself it creates the possibility of resistance" (Manzo & Wolfe, 1990, p. 4). They extend Foucault's theories to interpret the ways in which places reflect both "the desires of some groups of people to reproduce the social order in which they are dominant" and "the attempts by those without such power to resist and survive in a way that is meaningful in their lives" (Wolfe, 1990, p. 3).

Wentworth Gardens activists' efforts, as do other women's grassroots organizing actions, problematize the conventionally defined distinction between public and private life. American culture has been conceptualized as separate public and private spheres that split the "public" formal economic and government work done by men and sited in urban public space, from the "private" work done by women and housed in the home and neighborhood (Saegert, 1989; Tilly & Scott, 1978).[3] Women of color and low income women, however, have expanded the boundaries of caring for families beyond the private household into the expanded public sphere as they raised and nurtured children in extended family networks within communities struggling for survival (Collins, 1991; Stack, 1974). Through their grassroots organizing, they similarly have extended "the boundaries of the household to include the neighborhood," ultimately to "dissolve the boundaries between public and private life, between household and civil society" (Haywoode, 1991, p. 175).

Women resident activists are industrious individuals who initiate collective actions to create and sustain their community and homeplace and to engender efforts to redress social and economic inequalities and injustices. In our research analyses we have identified two modes of Wentworth women resident activists' resistance: their ongoing efforts of *everyday resistance* in the expanded private sphere and the extension of their efforts into *transgressive resistance* in the public sphere.

Engaging in everyday resistance, Wentworth resident activists have organized and participated in grassroots efforts to protect their community against the deterioration of the physical environment and social services necessary for everyday life. These women have drawn upon critical skills and strategies that they have cultivated through the everyday routine activities of maintaining their households and communities, that is, activities necessary to the "'social reproduction' of individual households as well as the social arrangements they make to protect, enhance, and preserve the cultural experiences of all members of the community" (Feldman & Stall, 1994, p. 192; see also Morgen & Bookman, 1988; Naples, 1988; Stall, 1991; Stoecker, 1992).[4] The importance of women's social reproduction work inside the home has been empirically documented and argued to be "a source of struggle and social change" (DeVault, 1991; Luxton, 1980; Hartmann, 1981); however, only recently has women's social reproduction labor in the community been recognized as a type of political organizing and resistance (Morgan & Bookman, 1988; Haywoode, 1991).

---

[3] The dominant ideal of family life in the mid-19th century, the "cult of domesticity," idealized and confined women's activities to the domestic private sphere. It sought to "protect" women and children from the corrupting influences and unsafe conditions of the public sphere by containing them in a safe, private haven (Cott, 1977). It is noteworthy, however, that African-American, Latina, and Asian-American women were excluded from the dominant ideal of the family and rather were treated as units of labor (Glenn et al., 1994).

[4] Social reproduction is a concept that was developed by feminists as a critique of Marxist theory's neglect to elaborate upon the notion of social-reproductive activities in the reproduction of labor power and its role in effecting historic change (Brenner & Laslett, 1986; Harding, 1981). Social-reproduction activities include the care of children, housework, the maintenance of physical and mental health, cooking, personal services, and education.

To confront the increased scale of the problems they have faced and the increasing political and economic power of the actors with whom they have engaged, Wentworth activists' have extended their resistance beyond the boundaries of their neighborhood and into the public sphere. Engaging in transgressive resistance, resident activists have instigated organized efforts and have created organizations to defend their community and homeplace against threats to its survival, and to assert their rights and protections as equal citizens in the polity. They have learned skills and strategies and have drawn on professional assistance to meet the requisites of these public sphere struggles. In resisting the destruction of their homeplace and community, Wentworth activists have contested the dominant ideologies of their identities as poor black women and defied the boundaries that separated them from the white male–dominated public sphere.

TELLING THE STORIES OF WENTWORTH GARDENS RESIDENTS' ACTIVISM

As feminist action researchers we employed a method of research inquiry that is change-oriented. We wanted to balance the portrayal of public housing residents that has overwhelmingly emphasized residents' deviance or their hardships and victimization. Instead of offering generalizations about the experiences of all Wentworth Gardens residents, we chose to focus our research on a core group of committed activists engaged in multiple and interconnected organizing efforts.

Both action and feminist research are interdisciplinary approaches that challenge the classic research paradigm with its emphasis on value-neutrality and objectivity. A major goal of action researchers is to "contribute . . . to the practical concerns of people in an immediate problematic situation" (Rappaport, 1970, p. 4). In a complementary, but more politicized manner, feminist researchers purport to engage in "research *for* women rather than *about* women" (Allen & Baber, 1992). The intention of feminist research is not merely to describe women's lives, but to "begin to draw attention to the political and social struggles of women" (Small, 1995, p. 946). Feminist researchers stress the importance of utilizing knowledge to initiate social changes that will contribute to the positive enhancement of women's lives.

In *The Dignity of Resistance*, we also have attempted to explicate the practical concerns and issues in the lives of the Wentworth activists and whenever possible to contribute to their positive resolution (see preface). Furthermore, it was our intention throughout this research process to challenge stereotypes about public housing residents, to expose and carefully analyze their accomplishments and the enormous challenges they confront, and to provide a more public forum for these heartening activists' voices.

With our focus on practical problems embedded in a particular setting, we have, as the majority of action researchers have, utilized a sociological case-study method (Small, 1995). We wanted to uncover the many decades of residents' grassroots activism preceding our entry into the field as well as their current organizing efforts. The case study method has proved to be the most effective means to investigate process (Becker, 1966), facilitating the explication of the historical causal process behind a particular event (Platt, 1984). The qualitative case study has allowed us to glean understandings of the "interconnected nature of people's actions, their relationships to others and the places they live, and the changes that occur in all of these over time"[5] (Saegert, 1989, p. 313). In particular, we used a multiple method approach (Castells, 1983; Henig, 1982), including interviews, focus groups, observations, and archival research to gain a breadth of understandings and greater reliability in our findings.

We conducted open-ended individual interviews with key Wentworth activists, 23 in total, who were active in organizing efforts during the 9 years of our field research. Using a snowball sample, we questioned the few activists we knew from our initial meetings with the residents to provide us with the names of other key Wentworth activists. Most of the interviews were conducted between 1992 and 1996.[6] We also had follow-up interviews with several of the activists to investigate their understanding of the events that had transpired since our first interviews.

A biographical narrative approach (Naples, 1998b) guided our interviews with each resident: an overview of the resident's family, educational, work, and residential history; a description of her life at Wentworth Gardens including her degree of connectedness with other residents and her level of satisfaction with living at Wentworth over time; an exploration of her community activism including the inspiration and motivations for her community work, and the particular actions she took; her understanding

---

[5] We recognize the limitations to the generalizability of the case study methodology. First of all, grassroots resident activism is dependent on organizing efforts and key individuals that are tied to particular persons and places; hence, the specific conditions surrounding efforts at a specific time and place may not be similar in all low-income settings. We hope that the findings of this inquiry encourage further investigations with other public housing communities, as well as studies that compare the experiences of resident activists with those of residents who choose not to participate in grassroots organizing. The need remains to conduct further in-depth case study research as well as more quantitatively oriented studies offering statistical strength, and sample and site representativeness, to elaborate upon and corroborate the ways in which low-income women of color struggle to transform their housing environments into viable communities.

[6] We interviewed the activists in the offices in Wentworth Gardens or, in a few cases, in their apartments. Each of the interviews lasted 1 to 2 hours. All interviews were audiotaped, transcribed, and coded. At the end of each interview residents were asked whether they wanted to be identified by their actual name or by a pseudonym. In all but one case, the actual names of the residents are used.

of current community problems; and her interests and hopes for the future of Wentworth Gardens. Nancy Naples (1998b) explains the advantages of this in-depth interview approach for the study of grassroots activism:

The biographical narrative approach offers a powerful method through which to explore the shifts in political consciousness and diverse political practices over time without artificially foregrounding any one dimension or influence. . . . Political activism is influenced by the dynamics of gender, race, ethnicity, class, and political culture that can only be understood through an embedded analysis that foregrounds local practices and individual perspectives. (pp. 8–9)

Again, as feminist, action researchers we valued the collaboration with resident activists and the community partners. Stephen Small (1995), in his overview of action-oriented research, recognized "the interdependence between the researcher and those researched" and the importance of "reducing the distance between the two" (p. 947). Models of action-oriented research share the assumption that both the researcher and the collaborator possess a distinct expertise and knowledge that are crucial for effectively engaging in the action research process (Susman & Evered, 1978). According to Small, "While the action researcher brings to the research process theoretical knowledge, experience, and the skills of conducting social science research, the participant collaborators bring practical knowledge and experience about the situations that are being studied" (p. 942). To gain a richer understanding of specific collective initiatives from the activists' viewpoints, we had expanded conversations (i.e., three focus group interviews) with residents who were central to these particular organizing efforts: the early Resident Council, laundromat, and grocery store; the community gardens; and the South Armour Square Neighborhood Coalition.[7] Additional collaborators in this research project were six technical assistants who worked closely with the residents on one or more organizing efforts. These individuals were also interviewed to assess their history of involvement and level of commitment to Wentworth Gardens, specific details about their involvement, and their observations and interpretations of the residents' community activism.[8]

As participant observers, but also to reduce the distance between the researcher-researched roles, we regularly attended meetings and events at Wentworth Gardens. Together with our three research assistants, we were active participant observers in over 100 on-site resident meetings, training sessions, workshops, and celebratory events from 1992 through 1998.[9]

---

[7] Group interviews were audiotaped, transcribed, and coded.

[8] We identified these technical assistants through our observations and knowledge of Wentworth activists' initiatives. All technical assistants' interviews were audiotaped, transcribed, and coded.

[9] With the graduate students Lynne Moch, Lynne Westphal, and Nancy Hudspeth, we were active observers from 1992 through 1998 and recorded observations of 114 meetings and

Attendance at these numerous meetings, as did the focus group interviews, greatly expanded the number of resident activists who contributed to our research findings. Also essential to our study were data collected from a resident-conducted needs assessment survey sponsored by the Wentworth Resident Management Corporation (RMC) and a child-care program assessment, also by the RMC. Last, we consulted demographic data sources (e.g., CHA reports and census data); court documents; historical archival documents including CHA newsletters and residents' newsletters; and reports from the news media. We officially concluded our fieldwork in 1998, and all data about the Wentworth residents (e.g., their ages and length of time in the development) and the physical state of the development, unless otherwise indicated, refer to that date.

In this case study of public housing women's activism, we developed our interpretive framework through the qualitative method of grounded theory (Glaser & Strauss, 1967). This method of theory development relies on a data collection process that is controlled by emerging theory; in fact, it generates theory through the reciprocal processes of fieldwork and theory building. The researcher inductively builds up a systematic theory that is based on, or "grounded" in, the observations. This means that the researcher simultaneously "collects, codes, and analyzes . . . data and decides what data to collect next and where to find them, in order to develop . . . theory as it emerges" (Glaser & Strauss, 1967, p. 45; Huberman & Miles, 1994). Thus, initial decisions for theoretical data collection are based on a general problem area, rather than a preconceived theoretical framework, in this instance, an examination of the myriad ways that Wentworth women participate in grassroots activism to build community and appropriate their homeplace despite severe obstacles to their success. The importance of the grounded, qualitative interpretive method is that data can be obtained on ambiguous or contradictory areas of social life that cannot be easily tapped by more restricted data collection techniques or with a preconceived theoretical framework. Our theory building method also has the advantage of studying the experiences of particular people in particular places supporting ecologically valid interpretations consistent with transactional approaches to environment–behavior relationships (cf. Altman & Rogoff, 1987; Proshansky, 1978; Saegert, 1989). This position contends that it is only possible to understand human behavior in the context in which it occurs.

We bring an interdisciplinary approach to both inform and broaden the development of our theoretical concepts and our theoretical

events. Comparison of our own field notes with each graduate student's notes allowed us to assess the reliability of the observations Field notes were analyzed for recurring themes and patterns. We attended other community events, particularly celebratory occasions, solely as participants, typically taking photographs.

framework. We have found that to represent and understand Wentworth Garden women's voices and actions adequately, we could not rely solely on a limited number of concepts nor on a narrow theoretical framework. For example, central to our research observations and interpretations are insights from environment and behavior studies, sociology, women's studies, community psychology, and urban planning. Without the development of this multidisciplinary interpretive lens, we would have missed the complexity of Wentworth women's resistance.

Who Are the Wentworth Gardens Activists?

Wentworth activists are predominantly older, long-term residents, a core of 20 to 30 women that has fluctuated over four decades of resident activism. The 23 activists we interviewed are African-American women who range in age from 26 to 79 years.[10] Most of these women were married, but now, more than half were either widowed or divorced. All were mothers, with an average of four children. (See appendix B for detailed resident activist demographic characteristics.) Fifteen were "older-generation activists," with an average age of 65 years, compared with the eight "younger-generation activists," averaging 39 years. This generational difference was recognized by the residents as well, who identified the older-generation activists by referring to them as "Mrs." followed by the last name and to the younger generation by their first names.

All older-generation activists, except one, were born in the South, the majority to sharecropping families. Most migrated north as adolescents or young adults for "a better life" in the 1940s, the 1950s, and the 1960s. They derived some benefits from the northern demand for labor needs during World War II, the postwar boom economy, and later the burgeoning economy of the 1960s. The women's common pattern was to finish their education in the South, move up to live with a relative in Chicago, find a job, and meet their future husband, marry, and form their own household.[11] This generation found work in small factories, laundries, and dry cleaners and as service workers in hospitals, cooks in restaurants, and housekeepers.

---

[10] A few of the residents also had some Native American heritage in their ethnic background, and in one case Creole. Also, one of the resident activists, Ella Fitzgerald, moved out of the development into her daughter's home shortly after we interviewed her in 1994.

[11] "During the 1940s, 1.6 million blacks left the South, to be followed by almost 1.5 million during the 1950s" (Payne, 1995). Of the black migrants between 1910 and 1960, 87% settled in seven states – New York, New Jersey, Pennsylvania, Ohio, California, Illinois, and Michigan (McAdam, 1982). One of the Wentworth activists moved north before World War II, three during the wartime period, seven after the war in the latter 1940s and 1950s, and two in the 1960s.

The older- and younger-generation activists differed in educational attainment: More than half of the older generation did not progress beyond the 9th grade. In the segregated South, where educational and economic opportunities were limited for African-Americans, the school calendar revolved around the cotton season. Most black children were not in school when they were needed in the fields (Payne, 1995). Also, formal education for rural black children ended in the ninth grade; thus black youth would have to travel to a large town or city in order to obtain a high school education. It is not surprising, therefore, that less than one-third of the older activists had attained a general equivalency diploma (GED) or high school diploma.[12] In contrast, among the younger-generation activists, all but one had attained a GED or high school diploma. A few activists in both generations had had some college education.

Unlike their older counterparts, the younger-generation activists either were born in Chicago (four of the eight) or left the South at birth or before they were 6 years old. Compared with the older-generation activists who had lived in Wentworth Gardens considerably longer – in 1998, 31 years on the average – the younger-generation activists had resided in Wentworth for an average of 12 years. As a result, the housing experiences of these two generations differed greatly. Unlike the older-generation activists, who had experienced Wentworth in the 1950s through the 1960s, when it was, according to them, "beautiful," the younger generation confronted deteriorating buildings and grounds when they moved into the development from the 1980s through the early 1990s.

The older-generation activists also first lived in Wentworth Gardens at a time when there was greater stability in the lives of the resident families. The result of change in federal rent structure policy in 1969 was that many two-parent working families moved out of CHA developments, including Wentworth Gardens. By 1997, there was an employed family member in only 15% of the CHA households (CHA, 1997). The younger-generation activists had to raise their children in a setting with much more challenging social problems than those experienced by the older generation. Crime, attributed primarily to drug dealing street gangs, had increased dramatically in CHA housing beginning in the late 1970s, as in public housing in other major U.S. cities (Popkin et al., 2000). By the late 1970s teenage pregnancy was on the rise across the nation, but particularly in low-income communities.[13] Families were increasingly headed by single

---

[12] Most of the older activists were in schools in the South in the 1940s and 1950s. In 1940, the median number of years completed by black women was 6.1, rising to 7.2 in 1950, 8.5 in 1960, and 10.2 in 1970. In contrast, for white women the median number of years of school completed was 8.8, 10.0, 11.0, and 12.2, respectively (Rodgers-Rose, 1980).

[13] Teenage pregnancy is not only an issue in low-income communities. The United States leads the Western world in the rate of teen pregnancy. Informed estimates suggest "that of the approximately 11 million unmarried adolescent females who are sexually active, about

females.[14] Like their older counterparts, all of the younger activists are mothers, but the majority have never married.

Although both generations of activists have a history, if even a short one, of volunteering for community activities and organizations, the younger-generation activists are much more likely to have secured paid positions as a result of their volunteer work in Wentworth Gardens.[15] The reasons are primarily differences in age and education. Whereas most of the older activist residents have retired from paid employment, the younger activists are attempting to map out a career path for themselves. Understandably, their involvement in grassroots activism is motivated not only by their desire to improve their homeplace, but also by the need to secure paid employment. Also, the younger-generation activists, because of the greater number of years of schooling, were more likely to have learned the technical skills required for the job opportunities within the development, particularly through the RMC.

Where Are the Men Activists? Women resident activists explained that through the early 1970s there were men who volunteered and served as leaders in the Resident Council and in other community efforts; in fact, two of the husbands of the older-generation activists we interviewed were volunteers. By the later 1970s, with the increased absence of men as husbands and engaged fathers in public housing, this pattern changed. The reasons for the absence of adult male role models and activists in lower-income communities like Wentworth Gardens are numerous and interrelated. The economic transformations in the United States that began in the 1970s included the vast expansion of service sector employment at the expense of the manufacturing sector. Thousands of well-paid manufacturing jobs were lost (Wilson, 1996). For the minority poor and working classes, in general, unemployment had increased because of plant mechanization, closings, and relocations. The urban black population did not have the necessary education or transportation

1 million become pregnant each year" (Crooks & Baur, 1999, p. 396). Approximately 95% of unmarried adolescent mothers elect to keep their babies; as many as 80% of this group drop out of school, and many do not return to the classroom. "Faced with the burden of childcare duties and an inadequate education, teenage mothers are highly likely to be underemployed or unemployed and dependent on welfare services Furthermore, low education levels and limited employment skills severely limit the efforts of these young mothers to obtain economic independence as they move beyond their teenage years" (Crooks & Baur, 1999, p. 396).

14 Until 1960, 80% of all black children lived in families with both parents. By 1977, less than half of all black children lived with both parents (Rodgers-Rose, 1980). In CHA developments, by 1972, only 6% of children lived with both parents.

15 Two of the 15 older-generation compared with 6 of the 8 young-generation activists secured paid work through their volunteer efforts.

access to take advantage of white-collar jobs in the urban periphery. As a result:

Lodged in the unskilled, service, and operative sectors, they experienced far greater job attrition than other demographic groups in the 1960s. (Venkatesh, 2000, p. 45)

Current census data show that the rate of national unemployment for blacks is twice the rate for whites. This increase in black male unemployment or underemployment has resulted in a rise in marital discord and divorce (Sidel, 1992).[16] According to Ruth Sidel (1992), "There is little question that the unemployment of black men has had a direct impact on the rise of black female-headed families" (p. 109). In addition, federal welfare regulations require that welfare support benefits be awarded only to single-parent households, not to intact but struggling families; as a result, poor householders may postpone, avoid, or break up a marriage in order to secure the benefits necessary to survival.

It is not surprising, then, that Wentworth's core activists are predominantly women. Economic disruptions and federal welfare regulations coupled with changes in public housing rental guidelines have penalized intact working-class families. Increasingly in the United States, public housing has become a "distinctly gendered urban problem" (Spain, 1995). Although the first public housing leaseholders were overwhelmingly male-headed families, in Chicago public housing, in 1991, 85% of the families listed a woman as the primary leaseholder (CHA, 1991); by 1997, the percentage was up to 94% (CHA, 1997). In fact, the feminization of poverty (see Pearce, 1978, 1983) was first identified in public housing (Kivisto, 1986). Since more women and female-headed households are found in the lowest income categories, they therefore are likely to require subsidized housing (Leavitt & Saegert, 1984; McClain, 1979–80; National Council of Negro Women, 1975). As noted by Leslie Kanes Weisman (1992):

The extent to which American women of diverse racial backgrounds are unable to find adequate shelter, and therefore depend on public housing, is a bitter comment on the prevalence of women's poverty. With the exception of the Federal Housing Administration (FHA) and the Veteran's Administration (VA) programs, federal housing programs are essentially women's programs. (p. 106)

[16] In her book *Women and Children Last*, Ruth Sidel (1992) examines the nature of the mothering role versus the fathering role in our society. Only partly biological, the "special nature of the mothering role" is contrasted with the "tenuous" relationship of the fathering role. For men their primary importance in the family is still as a breadwinner; thus for men, unemployment or underemployment is far more devastating than it is for women. Particularly in a racist society, an unskilled black man who is unable to play the traditional father role often walks away rather than daily confront his own failure (also see Liebow, 1967).

Wentworth Gardens public housing women residents' decades of resistance to their increasing poverty, the deterioration of their homeplace, and the threats to their community are part of a broader history of low-income women's struggles to resist societal inequities and injustices that threaten their survival. An understanding of these and other acts of resistance, and of the conditions that both foster and obstruct such actions, is necessary to make visible the nature of political action in low-income communities. Local and federal housing policies have been unable or unwilling to provide ample quantity and quality of housing for low-income people (Birch, 1985). Deep cuts in existing federal and local housing programs, landlord abandonment, real estate development, and gentrification have resulted in a further decrease in the supply of low-cost housing. Public housing women's collective actions, therefore, will become increasingly important as shrinking resources and new political conflicts continue to threaten the availability and viability of the homes and neighborhoods that they depend on for the necessities of daily life.

OVERVIEW OF THE BOOK

To provide the context of resident activists' struggles, we begin part II, "Wentworth Gardens' Historic Context," with chapter 2, the history of public housing nationwide and in Chicago. We examine the powerful and diverse political, economic, and cultural factors that have contributed to the apparent current failure of the U.S. government's public housing program. More particularly, we describe the changes in government policy and regulations, underfunding, and mismanagement that have resulted in public housing's deteriorated material conditions and inadequate social programs and services. In chapter 3 we discuss how these changes in Wentworth's viability, in particular in contrast with its better past, have motivated Wentworth women residents' activism.

Parts III and IV describe Wentworth activists' everyday and transgressive resistance to save their homeplace. The chapters in these sections are organized in a loose chronological order; but because various actions overlap and some continue over many years, an effort may be introduced before it is elaborated in a later chapter. To assist the reader, we have included a timeline of the activists' key initiatives over the course of their activism (see appendix A).

Part III, "Everyday Resistance in the Expanded Private Sphere," in particular, examines Wentworth women's strategies to improve the viability of their homeplace and sustain their community. We describe how resident activists have organized and participated in grassroots efforts within the expanded private sphere to increase the social cohesiveness and solidarity among their neighbors and to enhance local residents' daily lives by augmenting local services and programs. In chapter 4 we explain how the "community household" provides the foundation for *everyday resistance* at Wentworth Gardens. We illustrate how the residents activists' creation and participation in the extension of the family network to nonblood relations in the development link the organization of domestic life and grassroots organizing. In chapters 5–7 we describe Wentworth activists' initial years of organizing, from the early 1960s through the early 1980s, when they concentrated their efforts on providing necessary programs and services and the appropriation of spaces to house these activities. Chapter 5 explores how the caretaking work of the community household has become formalized through the residents' "women-centered organizing," the predominant organizing strategy Wentworth activists used in these early decades. We explain how, through the on-site Local Advisory Council, activists have made creative and vital organizing contributions to provide youth programs and services, tenant security, and fund-raising. In chapter 6, we explain how participation in women-centered organizing necessitates the development of a particular form of leadership. Chapter 7 analyzes how, through their appropriation of space, residents were able to house needed on-site services effectively.

The Wentworth activists' efforts to improve and sustain the viability of their development became increasingly difficult when the Wentworth development was threatened with demolition, first by the Chicago White Sox, then by HUD and the CHA. In response to this threat, Wentworth activists broadened their everyday resistance to include transgressive resistance. Part IV, "Transgressive Resistance in the Public Sphere," examines the tenuousness of Wentworth's residents' rights to safe and decent shelter and the strategies activists used to save their development from destruction. In chapter 8, we describe how Wentworth activists expanded their organizing efforts to include confrontational organizing as they attempted to save their homeplace and their surrounding neighborhood from demolition to make way for a new White Sox stadium. As the necessity for neighborhood retail services became more acute, in chapter 9 we examine how Wentworth activists worked with technical assistants, broadening their efforts to include real estate and economic development to plan for a critically needed retail shopping center. Ultimately, with CHA plans to raze the vast majority of Chicago's public housing developments, chapter 10 describes the activists' 9-year effort to take advantage of a federal resident management development program to save their development from the wrecking ball.

To conclude *The Dignity of Resistance*, in chapter 11 we revisit our findings and theoretical framework to critique current government public housing policies. In the epilogue, we briefly describe Wentworth Gardens' situation at the time we completed the book.

PART II

WENTWORTH GARDENS' HISTORIC CONTEXT

U.S. Public Housing Policies

Wentworth Gardens' Historic Backdrop

The U.S. federal government's assisted housing program was belated, irresolute, and very limited in extent (Vale, 2000). Compared with most other industrialized nations, America's 20th-century public housing programs were insubstantial. Currently, less than 2% of Americans live in government subsidized housing developments, while rates of these other nations are at least 10 times higher. This small percentage of units cannot be explained by the lack of need for affordable housing. Estimates of the homeless and the underhoused – those living in dilapidated or severely crowded conditions – vary from the federal government's statistic of 5.3 million families (HUD, 1999), to 50 million reported by the Low Income Housing Coalition.[1]

The U.S. government's reluctance to become involved in public housing is deeply rooted in the American political system (Jackson, 1995; Nenno, 1996). Federal housing policies, on the whole, have favored the private real estate industry (Jackson, 1995). Initially government programs encouraged homesteading through the direct provision of land and, more recently, home ownership through tax incentives, especially of single-family dwellings.[2] Today, subsidies given through tax abatement for home ownership mortgages far outweigh the cost of all federally subsidized public housing programs (Jackson, 1985).[3]

When the federal government finally did get involved in supporting public housing, it left little choice for the residents. In particular, the government determined where projects were sited, what types of households were eligible for tenancy, and what the income and race of the occupants would be. Federally assisted housing programs also determined the types

---

[1] Reported at the Low Income Housing Coalition national conference, 1998.
[2] E.g., Land Ordinance of 1785, Homestead Act of 1862.
[3] Homeowners may deduct the interest on the mortgages of their primary home from their gross income when calculating their federal income tax.

of housing and recreational and social services available to the residents. Public housing became an unintended testing ground for theories of architectural form and neighborhood structure, and their capacity to influence human behavior and personal morality. The government did not, however, provide adequate funds to assure ongoing adequate buildings and grounds maintenance and social services and programs. Because of government policies that regulated tenants' incomes and rent structures, rental income did not generate adequate funds for operating and maintenance costs; nor did the government adequately finance the difference. Despite these shortcomings, public housing remains one of the only affordable housing options for the very poor in the United States.

CONTROVERSIAL ORIGINS

Advocacy for federally assisted housing support has been a long, ongoing struggle accompanying the urbanization and industrialization of the United States. The unprecedented numbers of migrants, mostly unskilled from both the rural South and other countries, transformed every major American city (Wright, 1981). Because of erratic and low-paid employment, and resultant poverty, most of these migrants were obliged to live in deplorable housing conditions in segregated ghettos in the inner cities. In Chicago, for instance, by the early 1920s and 1930s, approximately one-third of the city's population was poor and living in overcrowded, dilapidated housing; moreover, efforts to improve the quality of housing through city regulations, inspections, and enforcement had proved ineffective to eliminate residential crowding, unsanitary conditions, and disease (Bowley, 1978).

The Depression provided the impetus for the first federal public housing programs, but the early 20th-century American housing movement – a loose coalition of social workers, labor leaders, economists, lawyers, and municipal officials – created the intellectual and grassroots support for its acceptance. Women at the forefront of the housing reform movement, notably Edith Elmer Wood, Catherine Bauer, Helen Alfred, and Mary Simkovitch, sought to dispel the conventional wisdom that blamed the poor for their deplorable living conditions (Wright, 1981); rather, they attributed the poverty, disease, and demoralization of the urban poor to the deplorable physical housing conditions of the urban ghetto. Wood conducted the first national survey of housing conditions in 1919 to collect evidence to support their claims. The survey found that approximately one-third of Americans lived in substandard housing, and one-tenth in "conditions which are an acute menace to health, morals, and family life" (from Wood's 1919 book, *The Housing of the Unskilled Wage Earner*, cited in Birch, 1978, p. 133). These findings demonstrated that people lived in slums because they had no alternative housing options; the private housing market had failed to provide low-cost, decent housing supportive of family life. Transforming these conditions was the key to curing the ills of the ever expanding city and the social problems related to urban poverty (Vale, 2000; von Hoffman, 1996; Wright, 1981).

Wood argued that the housing problem demanded social justice – housing that met families' needs, for example, proper plumbing and heating, and adequate fresh air and light, all at a cost that low-paid workers could afford (Birch, 1978). She, and the other women leaders in the housing reform movement, called for federally financed housing to "uplift the poor" by freeing them from the dangerous and indecent "slum" living conditions.[4] To gain acceptance for a comprehensive program of slum clearance, housing loans, construction, and code enforcement, women housing reform leaders founded housing lobby groups; sought the support of influential women's organizations, national labor, education, public welfare, religious, and veterans' groups, and housing officials; and led efforts to organize grassroots support among tenement dwellers, resulting in petition drives and public testimony to the U.S. Congress.[5]

The real estate industry in the United States, however, remained adamantly opposed to government subsidized housing, fearing both loss of revenues and government control (Vale, 2000; von Hoffman, 1998; Wright, 1981). Waging a public opinion battle, they depicted public housing as dangerous – a "road to socialism" – an erosion of American values of self-sufficiency and individual dignity (Wright, 1981, p. 222). Early housing reform efforts were stymied by the dominant cultural portrayal of poverty as a personal moral failing, prevented by hard work. In the United States, a person's dwelling has been construed not as every citizen's right, but rather as individually owned property to be earned through personal initiative (Nenno, 1996; Vale, 2000). This ideology is well captured by Clare Marcus Cooper (1974):

America is the home of the self-made man, and if the house is seen (even unconsciously) as the symbol of self, then it is small wonder that there is a resistance to the State's providing houses for people. (p. 438)[6]

---

[4] The term *slum* was defined by the federal government as "any area where dwellings predominate which, by reason of dilapidation, overcrowding, faulty arrangement or design, lack of ventilation, light or sanitation facilities, or any combination of these factors, are detrimental to safety, health, or morals" (1937 Housing Act, sect. 2.3).

[5] Edith Wood participated in the National Public Housing Conference founded in 1931 by Mary Simkovitch and Helen Alfred. Wood also founded the Labor Housing Conference in 1934 and was instrumental in founding a third lobby group, the National Association of Housing Officials, in 1933. The AFL-CIO and the American Association of University Women, the National Association for the Advancement of Colored People, the American Association of Social Workers, the National Conference of Catholic Charities, the American Legion, the United States Conference of Mayors, and the National Institute of Municipal Law Officers were supporters of a permanent federal housing program (Fisher, 1959).

[6] Before the 1980s, in the field of environment and behavior, the term *man* or *men* was typically used generically to include men and women.

According to Gwendolyn Wright (1981), "It was desperation that brought about the first programs of federally financed, publically owned housing for the poor" (p. 220). The economic hardships of the Great Depression created the political climate favoring the government's first intervention in the private housing industry. Unemployment was distressingly high: Fifteen million people were out of work and 4 million families were on federal relief (Wright, 1981). The Depression resulted in the creation of the "deserving poor": laid-off workers whose misfortunes were not of their own making (Mitchell, 1985). It also resulted in hardships for employees in the housing industry; one-third of the jobless were in building trades (Birch, 1978; Listokin, 1990; Wright, 1981). Nationwide, members of the banking and construction industries pleaded for and were granted federal intervention and assistance, beginning in 1933 (Bowley, 1978).

Since the first federal housing program, public housing starts have fluctuated, explained by political pressure exerted by crisis conditions – in addition to the Depression, World War II and its postwar housing shortages, and the urban riots of the 1960s – as well as by the political leanings of the majority government[7] (Nenno, 1996). The federal public housing programs not only have provided affordable housing, but have been a vehicle, as well, for federally funded employment, public health programs, and federal action on civil rights (Vale, 2000; Wright, 1981).

THE OPTIMISTIC YEARS: EARLY PUBLIC HOUSING PROGRAMS

When the U.S. Congress drafted an employment bill in 1933, the national housing lobby groups finally achieved their goal. They were instrumental in securing provisions that launched public housing (Birch, 1978; Von Hoffman, 1998). The 1933 National Recovery Act and the subsequent 1937 Wagener Steagall Act legislated slum clearance and "decent, safe and sanitary" housing for families who could not afford market-rate apartments (cited in Birch, 1978, p. 141). Early public housing programs are typically depicted by housing research and the media as temporary housing for upwardly mobile working poor families. This "original vision" was used by housing proponents, such as Catherine Bauer and Elizabeth Wood, to promote the program to a skeptical Congress, but the actual federal policy

---

7 Federal housing assistance has been characterized by starts and stops: changes in goals, programs, and funding, with some programs lasting only 6 to 8 years, allowing little time to develop efficient processes and practices (Nenno, 1996). The government's public housing programs have lasted 2 to 6 years and have ranged from financial subsidy of new construction to debt service support, subsidy of below-market interest rates, direct cash grants to families to meet their housing needs, tax benefits to housing investors and developers, and housing block grant programs.

was not directed to this goal; rather, it was viewed as permanent housing.[8] Fifty local housing authorities were created in 30 states (Fisher, 1959), and over 160,000 public housing units were developed nationwide before 1945 (Bowley, 1978; von Hoffman, 1996).

Not surprisingly, the housing industry vigorously opposed the implementation of the 1933 Housing Act, arguing that the government was entering into competition with private real estate developers. To address the industry's concerns, the U.S. Congress shaped the 1937 Housing Act more stringently to assure that there would be no increase in the overall supply of housing units (Schill, 1993). Specifically, an "equivalent elimination" provision required that for every unit of public housing built, a unit of slum housing must be demolished, resulting in no additional low-cost housing units despite the growing need[9] (Fisher, 1959). Moreover, limits also were placed on construction costs, reduced from the average of $6,200 for housing built under the 1933 Housing Act to no more than $4,000 under the 1937 act (Schill, 1993). Operating costs also were to be kept to a minimum.

Most public housing projects were built in cities near the downtown in low-income blighted or abandoned areas, where cheap land was readily available through purchase or condemnation (Spain, 1995) and where resistance to public housing would be minimized[10] (von Hoffman, 1996). Existing patterns of racial segregation in these communities were sustained by a federal authority's Public Works Administration Neighborhood Composition Rule (NCR) requiring that a housing project not alter the racial character of the existing neighborhood (Bratt, 1989; Fisher, 1959). After World War II, attempts to locate public housing developments in outlying neighborhoods encountered stiff, sometimes violent resistence. Although the federal rule was no longer in effect, the federal government did not intervene in local disputes over public housing site selection (Hirsch, 1983;

---

[8] Personal communication with Brad Hunt, Ph.D. student in history, University of California, Berkeley.

[9] The equivalent elimination requirement was enforced extremely liberally. The removal of housing for any reason – not just slum clearance – was counted. Few local public housing authorities were forced into clearance to meet this provision (personal communication with Brad Hunt, Ph.D. student in history, University of California, Berkeley).

[10] Initially the federal government used the powers of eminent domain – the taking of land for public purposes – to acquire the land for the projects. The federal government built and owned the units, which were administered by local agencies. In 1935, the U.S. Court of Appeals declared the federal use of eminent domain unconstitutional (Birch, 1978; Fisher, 1959; Listokin, 1990). State courts, however, decided in favor of the constitutionality of states' and localities' use of eminent domain powers (Schill, 1993), thus pushing for decentralization of the public housing program and creation of local housing authorities (McGuire, 1962). The 1937 Housing Act gave the local authorities responsibility for all public housing development and management (Listokin, 1990); the act remains in effect today.

von Hoffman, 1996). Racism continued to dominate the site selection process in U.S. municipalities.

In addition to the race of the tenants, household characteristics were controlled by federal government regulations. Tenancy was not open to any family unable to afford housing in the private market; rather, the federal policy restricted eligibility to the working poor: "actual families, excluding lodgers or unattached individuals . . . responsible tenants, chosen in order that every family accepted for consideration is capable of paying the rent and has a satisfactory character" (Fisher, 1959, pp. 164–165). Thus, the "unworthy poor" – those without employment and unable to pay rent – were not eligible; nor were households not considered "families" (e.g., singles, single-headed households, nonrelated adults).[11] Tenant screening, to assure that an applicant had proper housekeeping and behavioral standards, also was used by local housing authorities to select as well as evict tenants. Because there were no uniform federal rules or procedures regarding the lease conditions established at the federal level, a local housing authority, for instance, could terminate any tenant's lease without a detailed explanation or hearing. Most public housing leases until the 1960s were month-to-month (Schill, 1993). Eligibility for public housing was a privilege, never a right.

The rents charged to tenants, similarly, were established by federal regulations. Initially, as in the private market, rents were based on apartment size. Rents were determined and collected by local housing authorities with the provision that they were adequate to cover the housing management and operational costs, and to repay the federal government's construction debt. Beginning in 1941, however, the federal administration changed its policy and encouraged local authorities to use a graded rent based on a percentage of a household's income (Birch, 1978). As a result, rents became inadequate to cover operating and maintenance costs, and long-term replacement, especially as the buildings aged.

Racial Discrimination and Segregation in Chicago Public Housing

In 1937, Chicago established its housing authority, the CHA. Elizabeth Wood, executive secretary of the CHA at its inception, and Robert Taylor, the first African-American chairman of the board, provided the leadership to set the stage for the authority's subsequent policies and regulations over the next several decades[12] (Popkin et al., 2000). Through their influence,

---

[11] It should be noted that the overriding goal to serve the interests of the slum dwellers was undermined by these eligibility criteria; most did not have the financial resources, required family structure, or the right citizenship to be eligible for the replacement public housing (Fisher, 1959).

[12] Elizabeth Wood, before her appointment as executive secretary of the CHA, had worked as the director of publicity for the Home Modernization Bureau, was a caseworker with

the CHA charted its course to provide decent housing for the poor, in particular, to serve the lowest-income population federal regulations would permit.[13] Wood was committed to replacing slum housing with better apartments and neighborhoods, but the housing would be modest for people with modest means:

Our idea is to build a community that is raw, unfinished, and let it ripen and mature as people live in it. We try to match the simplicity of a workingman's neighborhood. Then we encourage people to finish their own homes, to do things to suit themselves. That's the American way. (Kahn, 1941, citing Wood, p. 1)

Wood and Taylor also supported racial integration but ultimately were unable to affect the racial composition of Chicago's public housing because of both federal regulations and Chicago's city council (Popkin et al., 2000).

The first three Chicago public housing developments, constructed between 1935 and 1938, were built in white communities in blighted or industrial neighborhoods. A total of 2,572 units were built.[14] All of the tenants, other than 26 black families at one development, were white[15] (Bowley, 1978). Government efforts to meet the housing needs of Chicago blacks were insignificant. Only one pre–World War II public housing development, Ida B. Wells Homes, was targeted for black families in 1934, but it was not dedicated until 1941 (Bowley, 1978). The CHA chose the site, located in the Black Belt but near its borders, to be built exclusively for black tenants. Land acquisition was delayed by neighboring white property owners to the east and south, who ultimately took legal action to stop the project. The suit was lost, and the CHA finally expedited the 1,662-unit development.

United Charities of Chicago, headed the staff of the Metropolitan Housing Council, and was executive secretary of the Illinois State Housing Board (Meyerson & Banfield, 1955). Robert Taylor was secretary–treasurer of the Illinois Federal Savings and Loan Association, which encouraged black home ownership, and worked as manager of the Michigan Boulevard Garden Apartments, an early philanthropic housing development for low-income families (Bowley, 1978).

[13] All housing authorities did not set such goals. For example, the housing authority in New York City historically sought a wider tenant income mix, in part because of demand from a wider income group.

[14] The first three public housing developments in Chicago that were developed by the Federal Public Works Administration but managed by the Chicago Housing Authority (CHA), were incorporated in 1937. These three developments were the Jane Addams Homes (1,027 units), the Julia C. Lathrop Homes (925 units), and the Trumbull Park Homes (426 units).

[15] The CHA interpreted the federal Neighborhood Composition rule literally, allowing 26 black families to rent in the Jane Addams Homes because this was the number of black families who had lived in the housing demolished to build this development. In response to the threat of a lawsuit initiated by the black community, the number of black families was increased to 60 in the late 1930s, but all were segregated in one section of the development (Bowley, 1978).

Chicago's black community was understandably distressed by the lack of government support for their housing needs, which were the most desperate of all of Chicagoans' (Hirsch, 1983). The first wave of black migration from the rural South, encouraged by both increased demand for industrial workers and the reduced number of immigrants entering the United States during World War I, increased the black population in Chicago from 30,000 at the turn of the century to nearly 250,000 by 1930 (Philpott, 1978). Racial hostilities directed against their migration were overt; for example, in 1917, *Chicago Tribune* headlines described the "SWARM" of "DARKIES FROM DIXIE" and begged, "Black man, stay South!" (cited in Philpott, 1978). In fact, the *Tribune* offered to help pay the way for any blacks who wanted to return to the South but got no takers. With the end of World War I, and the return of the veterans, racial hostilities remained high. Because of the acute housing shortage, whites viewed blacks as competitors for housing, and racial clashes over housing, as well as transportation, employment, and recreation, became daily occurrences. Blacks families were restricted to living in black neighborhoods, suffering discrimination in the quantity and quality of housing available for rent or purchase.

Racially motivated housing discrimination had segregated black families in what was called the "Black Belt," a spatially isolated area on Chicago's South Side (Philpott, 1978). With the post–World War I migration, the Black Belt increased in size by expanding its borders, with a smaller community established on Chicago's West Side. White immigrants could and did move from their entry ethnic neighborhoods when they could afford better housing; blacks did not have that option. They were restricted to the small number of segregated communities through racial zoning ordinances, restrictive covenants, and redlining.[16] In addition, if African-American families tried to move out of black ghettos, frequently

---

[16] Racial zoning ordinances in the early 20th-century Chicago regulated the racial composition of neighborhoods by who could rent or purchase a home in a locale. The U.S. Supreme Court struck down racial zoning in 1917 (Philpott, 1978).

After the U.S. Supreme Court outlawed racial zoning ordinances, real estate boards and property owners' groups increasingly used racial covenants, a contractual agreement between property owners in a given area that none of them would allow a "colored person" to occupy, lease, or buy his property, as a legal way to keep blacks out of their neighborhoods. During the 1920s and 1930s, many large businesses, prominent individuals, and the Chicago Real Estate Board sponsored a covenant campaign to prevent blacks from buying or renting property in Chicago's white neighborhoods, and many suburbs as well (Philpott, 1978). These racial covenants remained in effect until they were forbidden by the U.S. Supreme Court in 1948 (Hirsch, 1983).

Redlining refers to real estate financial investors' practice of drawing red lines around geographic areas in which they will not give loans. This practice was outlawed in the federal 1968 Fair Housing Act, but enforcement has proved difficult.

intimidation and violence were used to contain them (Philpott, 1978). In the spring of 1917, the Chicago Real Estate Board formulated a code of ethics to control racial integration, an agreement not to sell or lease property to a black family on a block that was less than 25% black. The board, however, had no ability to enforce the code. "Blockbusting" – selling to blacks in a white neighborhood, then cashing in on the panic of Whites who wished to sell their homes and flee the neighborhood – became a common practice. The realtors would purchase whites' homes inexpensively, then resell them to blacks at much higher prices (Hirsch, 1983). Blockbusting resulted in considerable wealth for many realtors; however, sustaining racial segregation through this means proved beyond the control of the Chicago Real Estate Board. A new campaign was implemented to organize "owners' societies in every white block for the purpose of mutual defense" (Philpott, 1978, p. 164). These property owners' associations became the middle-class equivalent of gangs, whose sole purpose was to keep blacks out of their neighborhood. The associations employed a variety of tactics: newspaper publicity, mass rallies, blacklisting of realtors, boycotting of merchants, and intimidation of black residents. When these methods failed, they resorted to violence on a scale previously unknown. It became commonplace for mobs of 50 to 200 white protestors to terrorize black households that were outside the concentrated black neighborhoods, vandalizing, burning, and bombing their homes and inflicting personal injuries. But blacks defended themselves, resulting in the infamous Chicago race riot of 1919 that enveloped the city, leaving 38 dead and hundreds injured (Philpott, 1978).

Severe overcrowding and high rents in the black ghetto were the norm (Hirsch, 1983). Two-thirds of the black population in the 1930s lived in "kitchenette" apartments paying rents two to three times higher than those in comparable white communities (Philpott, 1978). According to the CHA (1943):

The intense [housing] shortage [for black families] has resulted in exploitation by landlords. A given quality of accommodations is nearly always rented to a Negro at a much higher rate than it would be to a white family. The Negro group is the lowest paid in the city, yet it is forced to pay a higher percentage of its income for rent, and receives much less for its money. (p. 16)

To maximize profits, real estate owners divided thousands of large single-family homes and apartments into small rental units, typically a single room with either minimal kitchen equipment (e.g., a gas plate in a closet) or use of a common kitchen, a bathroom shared by several families, and no central heating, gas, and electricity (Hirsch, 1983). Public health in the black community also suffered as a result of crowding and poor sanitation; for instance, child mortality rates and the number of tuberculosis cases were much higher than in the city as a whole[17] (Hirsch, 1983).

The second wave of rural southern black migration, which began in the 1940s, drew even larger numbers of black families to the North to meet the demand for industrial workers created by World War II. In Chicago, the increases were dramatic, from 278,00 blacks living in Chicago in 1940 to 492,000 in 1950. The housing shortage for families of all races was pressing; the housing needs of black families continued to be the most "dismal"[18] (Hirsch, 1983). A 1943 report issued by CHA found that of the blacks then living in Chicago, none was "living in standard conditions" (p. 14):

Negro housing needs which, as everybody knows, are the worst in the city. Areas available for Negro occupancy are walled in by deed restrictions so that the increase in population (an estimated 10,000 a year) within the limited areas is resulting in terrific overcrowding and all the other evils that result from an intense shortage. (p. 14)

Supporting the Defense Effort: The Development of Wentworth Gardens

During World War II, social welfare programs including public housing were reduced in favor of defense housing efforts – homes for war workers[19] (Nenno, 1996). In Chicago, the CHA implemented four housing projects for war workers that originally were planned for low-income residents (which after the war were converted back to low-income housing)[20] (Bowley, 1978). As a result of pressure from the Chicago black community and the support of Elizabeth Wood, the CHA had sought sites for two of these developments

---

[17] Poor health also could be attributed more generally to low income and to poor access to health care.

[18] Minimal housing had been constructed during World War II since labor and resources were diverted to the defense effort and the federal defense housing program was inadequate. When the war ended, the housing shortage was exacerbated by the large number of returning veterans, and by physically dilapidated housing stock that had been worsened by age and overuse (Hirsch, 1983).

In the Black Belt, during World War II, overcrowding became endemic, with estimates of 375,000 blacks living in housing equipped for 1100,000 people (Hirsch, 1983). The percentage of black families living in crowded conditions (more than 1.51 persons per room) rose from 19% in 1940 to 24% in 1950.

[19] The federal housing program was converted to a defense program by the Lanham Act of 1940 (McGuire, 1962). The federal government also supported the hasty construction of 195,000 temporary dwelling units built near war industries or military bases nationwide for war workers (Atlas & Dreier, 1994; Bratt, 1989).

[20] The four public housing developments converted to war worker housing were Francis Cabrini Homes (586 dwelling units), Lawndale Gardens (128 dwelling units), Bridgeport Homes (141 dwelling units), and Robert H. Brooks Homes (834 dwelling units) (Bowley, 1978).

that would allow for racially integrated developments[21] (Bowley, 1978). Two projects were specifically planned for defense housing in Chicago; Wentworth Gardens was one of these two developments.[22]

Named after "Long John" Wentworth, a former Chicago mayor (CHAT 1948), CHA, in conjunction with the Federal Public Housing Authority, planned to build Wentworth Gardens for black war workers (Bowley, 1978). Construction, however, did not begin until 1945 and was not completed until after World War II. The Wentworth Gardens development was changed to low-rent housing, with veterans given preference.

At the time, the Wentworth Gardens site was at the periphery of the Black Belt. Although the CHA wanted to integrate the project, the day applications were taken, thousands of blacks lined up, in comparison to the few whites who showed up and quickly left.[23] "The Tenth Year of the Chicago Housing Authority" (September 30, 1947) report proudly announced its occupancy:

Wentworth Gardens, the tenth permanent low-rent housing project for low-income tenants, was completed and fully occupied by June 1947.... More than 2,100 people live in the project. (p. 16)

Wentworth Gardens was built on an isolated site on the southern edge of the Armour Square neighborhood approximately 2 miles south of Chicago's business district. The 16-acre site was in a primarily industrial area. The site was selected from a list of six submitted by Elizabeth Wood to the commissioners (CHA Official Minutes, September 11, 1944). Originally this site had been proposed by housing reformers in 1935 for a federally funded project, but federal officials rejected it, fearing violence from the nearby white communities. By the time the site was selected, there were fewer objections, because it had been absorbed by the expanding black ghetto.[24] Wentworth was one of two sites determined to be the most

---

[21] In particular, Cabrini and Brooks Homes were planned to house both white and black tenants. The tenant mix, however, was not equal; rather Cabrini Homes was planned to be 20% black tenants, and Brooks Homes, 80%. Upon occupancy, whites were unwilling to move into a predominantly black development; hence, Brooks was occupied by only black tenants. At Cabrini, the black quota ultimately was relaxed, with 40% of the tenants black (Bowley, 1978).

[22] The other development was Altgeldt Gardens. The Federal Public Housing Authority held ownership of both developments until 1956, when they were transferred to CHA (Bowley, 1978).

[23] Personal communication with Brad Hunt, Ph.D. student in history, University of California, Berkeley. Hunt drew this information from an interview with Jim Fuerst, former CHA statistician.

[24] This information was learned from a personal communication with Brad Hunt, Ph.D. student in history at the University of California, Berkeley. Hunt drew this information from Arthur Bohmen, Elizabeth Wood, & John Fugard, "A Housing Project for the Southside of Chicago," May 24, 1935, in PWA Housing Division Files, Box 94, Folder H-1402, Record Group 196, National Archives II, College Park, Maryland.

suitable, largely because it required minimal demolition of structures (Bowley, 1978). The site had been used as a baseball park, first by the White Sox, a white team who used the open field until 1910, when they moved into a stadium, and later by a black baseball team.

Wentworth Gardens' site planning and building design were similar to those of the earlier public housing built nationwide (Franck, 1995, 1998; von Hoffman, 1996; Wright, 1981). Public housing design was influenced by a mix of the early 20th-century Anglo-American models of community design and European modernist architectural traditions. Housing reformers, architects, and planners, including Bauer, championed these new formal building and site planning models not only because of aesthetic preferences, but because of their beliefs that this model would create a better living environment, one, especially, that stood in sharp contrast, in both image and function, to the urban slum.

The early public housing site planning perspective was adapted from the British Garden City model and its interpretation by American town planners: a discrete, residential development whose goal was to restore small "community sociability" and "moral character" (Franck, 1995; von Hoffman, 1996). This perspective hoped to enhance community life by open spaces for recreation and socializing free of the impact of the automobile. Low-rise residential buildings were arranged in rows and around semi-enclosed courtyards in a "superblock," combining several city blocks into one large area. Buildings faced away from the street toward the interior of the development, with shared outdoor landscaped spaces for common use. The development boundaries were reinforced by the surrounding streets and the inward-oriented buildings. Formal and spatial coherence, achieved through uniform site and building design standards, was intended to create a sense of order and common identity for the development. Adapting the streamlined, functional style of the European modernist international school of architecture, American architects located buildings on the site to maximize exposure to the sun, ventilation, and densities believed optimal to promote public health. Repetitive patterns of low-rise buildings, all of uniform design, were used not only to create the image of order, but also to provide efficiency and economic utility.

Wentworth Gardens adhered to the modernist site planning and architectural principles of its time.[25] Wentworth was built at a density of 26 dwelling units per acre, and a cost per unit of $4,234.[26] Originally four square city blocks, buildings were arranged on the superblock parallel to the city grid. All the buildings were arranged around interior shared

---

[25] The development was designed by the architects Loebl and Schlossman (Bowley, 1978).

[26] Data provided by Brad Hunt, Ph.D. student in history, University of California, Berkeley. He drew the data from a CHA development cost statement.

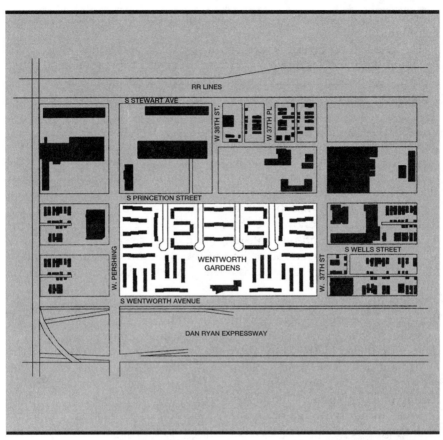

FIGURE 2. Wentworth Gardens' site plan.

landscaped areas: 28 two-story rowhouses were arranged in parallel rows facing common, interior lawns; nine three-story walk-up apartment buildings were arranged in Us surrounding children's play equipment; and all of the building clusters were organized around a prominent centrally located green space. All outdoor space was intended to be shared; there were no private back or front yards. As in many of the developments of its time, a community building flanked the east side of the central green.

All the rowhouses and walk-up apartments were made of the same materials and had the same appearance: standardized masonry construction with red brick exteriors, "punched" windows, and flat roofs. Details were kept to a minimum except for flat concrete shelters overhanging the front doors of all the buildings (which also acted as balconies for the adjacent apartments) and glass block above the front doors of the walk-up apartment buildings.

The unadorned exteriors adhered to the early modernist style while keeping building costs down. According to the CHA (September 30, 1947, report), Wentworth's design sought "to secure certain advantages while adhering to the principle of economy which is necessary in public housing" (p. 17).

Wentworth's apartment designs also followed the modernist principles of efficiency and economy and minimal housing design standards, hence the modest room sizes and compact arrangement. Finishes were minimal and masonry surfaces were painted and heating, plumbing and electric services exposed. Wentworth apartments were relatively identical, varying only in the number of bedrooms. Wentworth Gardens apartment sizes were as follows: 28 three-room units, 254 four-and-one-half-room units, 84 five-and-one-half-room units, and 56 six-room units. They all had a fully equipped (according to the standards of the time) eat-in kitchen, one bathroom, a living room, and two to four bedrooms (CHAT, 1948).[27]

While the CHA adopted the early modernist site planning and architectural design principles to reinvigorate family life, little effort was given to evaluate the efficacy of these decisions. A small sample study (86 residents) conducted by the CHA (1950) sheds some light, in particular, on the apartment design of Wentworth and four other similarly designed CHA projects. According to the report, 70% of the units were "over occupied" – having one or two more individuals than intended by the federal public housing authority design occupancy standards – hence explaining many of the negative findings, primarily complaints about inadequate space for family activities, but also dissatisfaction with the minimal finishes.[28]

---

[27] The room sizes are as follows: The eat-in kitchen is 100 square feet for the apartment with the smallest number of bedrooms to 150 square feet for the apartment with the largest; the one bathroom is approximately 35 square feet; the living room averages 180 to 190 square feet; and one large bedroom averages 140 square feet, and one or more smaller bedrooms average 110 square feet.

[28] The specific findings were as follows: Storage space was inadequate in all rooms, as was the size of the eat-in kitchen (e.g., residents in the largest units had to stagger meals because of insufficient room); the eat-in-kitchen also served as a secondary living room (e.g., for studying and hobbies) because of the inadequate space in the living room and bedrooms for these activities. Residents complained about the drabness and hazards of the minimal finishes. Concrete floors created falling hazards and fatigue. The "drab" tan paint on all the walls in all the units was criticized. At Wentworth, the unpainted concrete slab ceiling was disliked. Sound transmission between adjacent apartments was a nuisance. First-floor tenants in all of the sample developments were concerned about their safety because of the absence of bars on their windows. The only reported positive finding for Wentworth residents was satisfaction with the balconies.

POST–WORLD WAR II PUBLIC HOUSING: CHICAGO'S URBAN
RENEWAL LEGISLATION AND FEDERAL HOUSING POLICIES

After World War II there was a burst of public housing construction nationally. While the federal government promoted middle-class home ownership through government-insured mortgages as the focus of its housing
agenda, public housing increasingly became the home of residents displaced by urban renewal efforts (Vale, 2000; von Hoffman, 1996).

Interestingly, Chicago's early 1940s urban renewal legislation established the framework for the federal government's post–World War II
urban redevelopment and public housing legislation (Hirsch, 1983).
Chicago's downtown business and institutional leaders began to formulate
a plan for the revitalization of "blighted" inner city neighborhoods based
on public land clearance and private redevelopment (Bowley, 1978; Hirsch,
1983). Their objective, supported by the mayor, was to stem the relocation
of the middle class to the rapidly expanding suburbs and sustain the city's
fiscal stability. To make their investment worthwhile, Chicago corporate
and institutional leaders sought to initiate redevelopment on a massive
scale. To do so, they needed to amass large tracts of land and minimize
the public's opposition. Two urban redevelopment bills were introduced
to the Illinois General Assembly, the Blighted Areas Redevelopment Act
and the Relocation Act, both adopted in 1947. These acts called for an expansion of the definition of eminent domain – the taking of private land
for public purposes. The plan allowed a public agency to acquire privately
owned land through the powers of eminent domain, clear the land at the
government's expense, and sell it to developers, but at a fraction of the
original cost. Chicago's business leaders proposed that this "one-time subsidy" would be recovered from the increased tax revenues produced by a
profitable project.

The business and institutional leaders also included public housing in
their urban renewal plan as a necessary means to provide dwellings for
low-income residents displaced by slum clearance, especially given the
severe housing shortage in the city (Hirsch, 1983). They understood that
low- income families living in these areas could not find affordable housing
elsewhere. They also sought to stem the possibilities for protests from the
potentially displaced families that might block a project. Most importantly,
business and institutional leaders guaranteed that key decisions regarding
public housing site location would remain in the hands of Chicago political
and business interests. The bills assured the City Council's authority over
site selection for more than two decades.

It should be noted that the implementation of the Chicago City Council's selection of public housing sites did not go smoothly. Racial concerns
dominated the site selection negotiations between the Chicago City Council and the CHA. They were fueled, in part, by racial riots in neighborhoods

experiencing pressures of racial change from white to black residents, and by CHA's post–World War II attempts to integrate public housing racially. Largely through the efforts of Elizabeth Wood and Robert Taylor, the CHA attempted to integrate three new temporary veterans' developments, but race riots broke out and thwarted their plans.[29] These riots were part of a larger pattern of racial conflicts in Chicago, as well as other U.S. cities. Racial conflicts and violence that followed the war through the late 1950s erupted over housing and employment and involved hundreds to thousands of white protestors. Severe housing shortages during and after the war restricted residential mobility for both black and white families. With the postwar suburban construction boom, many white families left the central city, but the blacks until the early 1950s remained in the existing ghettos, restricted by discriminatory government and real estate practices (Hirsch, 1983). Subsequently, blacks moved into the areas vacated by the whites. Not only did they not want to give up their privileged access to jobs and housing, they believed their individual rights were threatened by inappropriate, if not illegal government intervention (Hirsch, 1983). In Chicago in the late 1940s, a racially motivated bombing or arson occurred roughly every 20 days (Hirsch, 1983). The most infamous riot in a CHA development was witnessed at Trumbull Park Homes. In 1953 attempts were made to integrate this all-white development, igniting racial riots that made national headlines (Bowley, 1978). Whites' acts of violence at this development – harassment of black tenants, use of explosives, and large demonstrations – continued for a decade (Hirsch, 1983).

Elizabeth Wood's progressive views on racial integration were blamed for the violence, leading to her dismissal (Hirsch, 1983). Wood's departure resulted in the agency's dismantling of CHA's goals, although unrealized to date, to integrate and distribute public housing throughout the city. CHA's power was limited by placing the agency under the authority of the mayor and the City Council, who selected the relocation sites for the first postwar federally funded public housing primarily, although not exclusively, in existing racially segregated ghetto areas.

[29] Black families, accounting for 20% of the veterans in need of housing, were rented apartments in temporary public housing developments typically built in outlying middle-class white neighborhoods. The first veterans' development opened without incident, but black families who had moved into the second development, Airport Homes, located on the southwest side of the city, were threatened by mob violence within 2 weeks of occupancy (Hirsch, 1983). Other black families would not move into the development; ultimately it remained white (Bowley, 1978). A year later, in 1947, another serious riot occurred at another veterans' public housing development on the southwest side, Fernwood Park, where 4 of 52 families moving in were black. Rioters attacked black motorists in the vicinity to distract the police while other rioters stormed the development (Hirsch, 1983). It took 1,000 police 2 weeks to restore order, and 6 months for black families to reside in the development (Bowley, 1978).

In the years after World War II, Congress reactivated its public housing program with its most ambitious goals to date. The landmark 1949 Federal Housing Act called for "a decent home and a suitable living environment for every American family." In effect, however, following Chicago's lead, the federal government established public housing as a subsidiary of a broader, federal urban renewal policy. Major retrenchment in the federal role in housing was blocked by the strength and legacy of the housing reform movement (Nenno, 1996); however, downtown business interests, with their agendas of slum clearance and protection of the central business district, became the primary drivers of policy (Hirsch, 1983; Nenno, 1996). As part of a massive slum clearance program, the federal government authorized construction of 810,000 public housing units in 6 years – a goal, however, not achieved until 1972. To satisfy the private sector, the act also expanded the eligibility criteria for federally insured mortgages, opening home ownership, primarily in the suburbs, to more moderate-income, primarily white families (Jackson, 1985). The subsequent 1954 National Housing Act limited construction of new public housing to the amount needed for residents displaced by urban renewal efforts, although this provision was repealed shortly thereafter in 1955 (Flanagan, 1997).

To protect the private real estate industry further, the postwar housing acts also stipulated more stringent income eligibility requirements: Tenants' incomes had to be 20% lower than the income required to afford the lowest-cost housing in the private market (Meehan, 1979). If tenants' incomes rose above the maximum, they were obliged to move out (Fischer, 1959). These changes in tenant eligibility resulted in the exclusion and loss of many stable and upwardly mobile tenants. Families displaced by urban renewal and highway clearance programs, typically very low-income and racial minority families, were given priority for public housing units (Bratt, 1989). Concomitantly, urban renewal policies and federal highway projects disproportionately displaced urban blacks, leaving them few housing alternatives but priority status on the waiting lists for public housing (Vale, 1996; von Hoffman, 1996; Wright, 1981). Gweldolyn Wright (1981) explained:

Between 1949 and 1968, 425,000 units of low-income housing, mostly the homes of poor minorities, had been razed for redevelopment; and only 125,000 new units had been constructed, over half of which were luxury apartments. At the same time, highway construction projects eliminated minority neighborhoods, subsequently increasing the proportions of blacks applying for public housing. And housing authorities were required to give first priority to persons displaced by federal programs. (p. 234)

Meanwhile, white families were more likely to move out of public housing than nonwhites. The average monthly move-out rate between 1947 and

1957 was two to three times higher for white families than for nonwhite families (Fischer, 1959). Although the postwar period was a time of general economic prosperity, white families benefitted more than racial minorities. Segregation and isolation of the urban minority poor were further assured by "white flight" to the suburbs, as noted, supported by the expansion of the federally insured mortgage program. As the white middle class, as well as industry and employment, moved to the suburbs, racial discrimination and gender bias in education and the job market left those with fewer educational opportunities and marketable skills, hence lower incomes, behind in the inner cities (Schill, 1993; Spain, 1995).

In Chicago, the massive scale of the urban renewal programs resulted in a deluge of displaced residents' making application for public housing (Venkatesh, 2000). The CHA abandoned its goals for mixed-income developments – that is, unemployed and working families – to give priority to the very poor, displaced families. Sudhir Alladi Venkatesh (2000), however, notes that CHA could have taken a different strategy:

> The Housing Authority could have adjusted to the influx by relocating black applicants across the city, but to preserve the status quo in accordance with the wishes of city political leaders, the agency did not offer black applicants immediate available housing units in white neighborhoods. (p. 40)

Instead, displaced black poor residents were given only two choices: living in segregated public housing developments or remaining on the waiting list for public housing for an indefinite time.

As a consequence, U.S. public housing increasingly became the home of poor minorities. For example, at the end of World War II, 26% of public housing tenants nationally were racial minorities; by 1960, they were approximately 50% of the tenants (Spain, 1995). By 1950, the income of public housing residents was 64% of the national median (Atlas & Dreier, 1994). But the increasing percentage of women-headed households was viewed with the greatest alarm. Deemed "problem families," they were depicted as lacking a commitment to monogamous values and living "unregulated lives" (Spain, 1995). In Chicago, the statistics were even more dramatic. In 1948, 60% of CHA residents were racial minorities, increasing to 86% in 1960, and so-called broken families were 27% of those living in CHA housing in 1948; the percentage had risen to 48% by 1960 (CHA Statistical Report, 1948–1984).

The critics of post–World War II federal housing policy equated urban renewal with minority removal (Wright, 1981). Mary Nenno (1996) argued that the designation of a "slum" requiring urban renewal often referred to any area, not necessarily a blighted neighborhood, containing minority populations. In Chicago, virtually all public housing built in the 1950s through the 1960s was built in black communities and occupied by poor black families[30] (Hirsch, 1983; Popkin et al., 2000). Of the 33 public housing developments built after World War II through the mid-1960s, all but one were built in existing black ghettos on the South or West Side.[31] Not only were poor blacks segregated and isolated in vast public housing developments; widespread slum clearance effectively blocked the growth of working-class black communities in these previously expanding black neighborhoods (Popkin et al., 2000). Through their influence on the City Council, Chicago's downtown and influential white communities had prevailed (Hirsch, 1983). It is noteworthy, however, that the siting of public housing units in predominantly black communities has been attributed to black politicians, who sought to retain their constituencies, as well (Venkatesh, 2000).

THE "BOLD EXPERIMENT": HIGH-RISE PUBLIC HOUSING IN CHICAGO

During the 1950s and 1960s, the construction of high-rise public housing developments dominated in Chicago, as it did in other cities such as New York, Philadelphia, and Saint Louis (von Hoffman, 1996). Purportedly to save money while developing as many units as possible, Chicago chose high-rise construction, in particular, extremely large developments (Popkin et al., 2000). From 1955 to 1963, the CHA constructed 21,000 units; only 2,000 were not high-rise complexes.

The CHA built "almost a solid corridor of low rent housing" for 30 blocks along State Street and nearby streets in the original Black Belt (Hirsch, 1983, p. 243, citing the *Chicago Tribune*, December 24, 1958). Further exacerbating the isolation of this vast area of public housing, these new developments were cut off from the surrounding neighborhoods by new expressways and expanding subway lines. The most infamous, the Robert Taylor Homes, with 4,415 units in 28 16-story high-rise buildings, was the largest public housing development not only in Chicago, but, at the time, in the world (Bowley, 1978). The Taylor Homes are located directly southeast of Wentworth Gardens, across the Dan Ryan Expressway. All of these high-rise public housing developments were intended for large families with children; 75% percent of the units in these buildings had three to five bedrooms to accommodate large families (Bowley, 1978).

[30] By the mid-1960s, of the 33 public housing developments approved in Chicago after World War II, 25 were located in census tracts where the black population exceeded 75% (Hirsch, 1983). Six of the seven remaining developments were located in census tracts undergoing racial transition.

[31] Of the 33 developments built between World War II and the early 1960s, Cabrini Green was the only large-scale complex that was not built in an existing black ghetto. It was built in an Italian "slum" neighborhood just north of Chicago's downtown adjacent to an existing, older CHA rowhouse development (Bowley, 1978).

As in the design of earlier public housing, European modernism prevailed.[32] Rather than low-rise buildings, post–World War II U.S. architects and public officials favored Le Corbusier's influential model of high-rise buildings standing in an orderly pattern in vast expanses of greenery (von Hoffman, 1996). Le Corbusier's visionary plans for redesigning the city with "towers in the park" provided a powerful image for modernizing the aging urban landscape. Supporters who had advocated these designs sought to replace the disordered, deteriorated slum with "bold and comprehensive" modern planning; for instance, the influential housing reformer Elizabeth Wood called for such "innovations in city development" (Wood cited in Bowley, 1978, p. 65). Through standardization of these high-rise developments, and the production of large numbers of units, modernist housing designers also sought to provide a well designed, efficient, and economical dwelling, especially in contrast to slum housing. The CHA favored high-rise developments because construction costs were less than those of low-rise housing.[33] This argument, however, was shortsighted because the maintenance costs of high-rise developments were estimated at more than two times greater than those for a comparable low-rise development (Bowley, 1978).

In Chicago, high-rise public housing initially was greeted with optimism. For instance, Venkatesh (2000) reported that the first Robert Taylor Homes residents in Chicago were pleased with the considerable improvements over their prior homes (Venkatesh, 2000). The dwellings were not crowded, and each unit had its own kitchen and bath. Grounds were attractively landscaped, and social and recreational programs were an improvement over those previously available. At the time, the CHA had adequate funds for maintenance and worked to screen tenants to maintain a stable tenant mix (Venkatesh, 2000).

With time, difficulties in the design and construction of high-rise public housing surfaced. These isolated environments of stark repetitive high-rises contributed to the stigma associated with public housing developments (Hirsch, 1983). Rather than creating a positive image in contrast to the surrounding slums they were replacing, these developments came to underscore the role of public housing developments as stigmatized "warehouses for the poor" (Hirsch, 1983; von Hoffman, 1996).

---

[32] Dearborn Homes, with 800 units in 16 high-rise buildings and occupying only 10% of the site with vast open lawn areas, set the precedent in 1950; it was followed by Henry Hormer Homes (920 units completed in 1957), Stateway Gardens (1,684 units, 1958), Cabrini Green (3,019 high-rise units added to the existing rowhouse development in 1958–1961), Rockwell Gardens (1,112 units, 1961), and the Robert Taylor Homes (4,415 units, 1962) (Bowley, 1978).

[33] CHA also noted savings in land costs. These costs might have been realized if the developments had been built on small sites, but most high-rise public housing developments were built on vast areas of land that could have accommodated nearly the same number of units in low-rise housing, including sufficient outdoor recreational space (Bowley, 1978).

As the prior low-rise public housing developments had been, the massive high-rise developments were designed nationwide without the input or subsequent evaluation of the intended residents. According to Alexander von Hoffman (1996):

[T]he supporters of highrise redevelopment simply assumed that modern structures would transform the low-income people who were streaming into America's large cities. . . . Explaining long-standing policy in 1965, the chairman of the Chicago Housing Authority Charles Swibel declared, "Families who must or want to live in the inner city will have to learn to live with the high-rise building." (p. 11)

The developments, however, did not have adequate facilities, such as recreational and community spaces, to meet the needs of the residents, especially the large numbers of youth; nor were there adequate facilities and programs in the surrounding neighborhood. Chicago's failure, in general, to provide and maintain sufficient educational, recreational, and employment opportunities for low-income youths in the city gave public housing youths no alternative to their developments' facilities and programs (Venkatesh, 2000).

The difficulties of supervising children as well as the higher incidence of criminal activity in high-rise compared with low-rise public housing developments have since been well documented (Bowley, 1978; Jacobs, 1961; Newman, 1972). Research has shown that high-density, high-rise dwellings and large expanses of undifferentiated outdoor space constrain informal social controls, where residents can recognize each other and watch out for their neighbors' safety and deter vandalism (Newman, 1972). Elevators, stairwells, long hallways, and superblock arrangements also decrease surveillance opportunities by residents and police. Providing for and supervising children's activities are complicated by the lack of immediate access to the outdoors and the difficulty of accommodating children's recreation in the galleries and the great expanses of open, outdoor spaces without play equipment (Jacobs 1961; Newman, 1972). Moreover, the dominant cultural norms in the United States about appropriate housing for child rearing are not tall building complexes (Feldman, 1994), but rather single-family and other low-rise, low-density residences.[34]

The implementation of these huge developments also was beset with other serious problems. The federal authorities held down subsidies while local housing authorities compensated by increasing the number of units per building and skimping on basic amenities and building safety features (von Hoffman, 1998). In Chicago, CHA built 11 high-rise developments

---

[34] Although it is possible to raise a family comfortably and effectively in a high-rise building – as many families choose to do in our largest cities – it has been conventionally accepted in the United States that high-rise developments are not the best choice of building type for large families.

between 1950 and 1969, according the Susan Popkin and her colleagues (2000), all at a substantial cost, but poorly built:

> The cost was tremendous – about $20,000 per unit in 1960 dollars. The politically connected developers, who used cheap slab construction, shoddy materials, and poor workmanship, allegedly siphoned off huge sums of cash to line their own pockets. (Baron, 1969, p. 13)

Critics agreed that this "bold experiment" had failed: High-rises were a poor design decision (Bowley, 1978; Franck, 1995; Jacobs, 1961; von Hoffman, 1998). As early as the 1950s, some housing reformers and planners expressed qualms about what Bauer condemned as supertenements:

> The public housing project therefore continues to be laid out as a "community unit" as large as possible and entirely divorced from its neighborhood surroundings, even though this only dramatizes the segregation of charity-case families. Standardization is emphasized rather than alleviated in project design, as a glorification of efficient production methods and an expression of the goal of decent, safe and sanitary housing for all. But the bleak symbols of productive efficiency and "minimum standards" are hardly an adequate or satisfactory expression of the values associated with American human life. (Bauer, cited in Bowley, 1978, p. 128)

Despite the vocal opposition to high-rise developments and the damning empirical research, it should be noted that this architectural model is not solely nor necessarily primarily responsible for the purported failures of public housing. There is empirical evidence suggesting that some public housing residents are satisfied with living in high-rise developments if assured proper building and site maintenance and management, adequate social and recreational services, and personal security for themselves and their families (Metropolitan Planning Council, 1986; Vale, 2000; von Hoffman, 1996). The assumption of idealistic housing reformers, architects, and planners that public housing design, whether high- or low-rise, can alone solve the social problems associated with poverty, however, is simplistic. This environmental determinist position – that the form of the physical environment determines people's behavior – does not take into account interacting social, economic, and political factors. For instance, in Chicago, the difficulties public housing residents have experienced are not solely attributable to the high-rise form of public housing; rather, they also are the result of the segregation and concentration of poor black families in inner-city public housing "second ghettos" (Hirsch, 1983) and other racially discriminatory practices that impacted on poor African-Americans' educational and employment opportunities (Bowley, 1978, Hirsch, 1983; Smith, 1999).

THE TROUBLED YEARS IN PUBLIC HOUSING: THE 1960S–1990S

By the middle of the 1960s, the problems in Chicago's public housing, as in many other major municipalities, had become acute. In Chicago, opposition to CHA's massive, racially segregated, and in particular, high-rise developments peaked in the 1960s, fueled by the civil rights movement (Bowley, 1978). Whereas in the past residents had turned to local relationships with CHA housing management to pressure for improved housing conditions, they now turned to the civil rights movement for social justice and equity (Venkatesh, 2000). In 1966, Dr. Martin Luther King, Jr., and the Southern Christian Leadership Conference led massive protest marches in the city.[35] They succeeded in pressuring Mayor Daley and other civic and governmental leaders to accept an agreement to seek enforcement of open housing legislation and to promote racial integration in the Chicago metropolitan area. The agreement also contained provisions ending the concentration of high-density CHA public housing; instead, midrise (eight stories maximum) multifamily housing would be built on scattered sites, and families with children would occupy only the first two floors.[36] A 1968 federal housing act and a decision by the U.S. Supreme Court added regulatory and legal support to prohibit racial discrimination in housing rentals or sales throughout the nation. In the following year, 1969, in the landmark *Gautreaux v. Chicago Housing Authority* lawsuit, a federal judge found that the CHA had practiced racially discriminatory site selection and tenant assignment[37] (Bowley, 1978). Since this decision, a court-imposed comprehensive plan has dictated the scale and location of new CHA rental buildings to promote racial integration and to lower housing density.[38]

---

[35] The Christian Leadership Conference had established the Chicago Freedom Movement to fight racially motivated housing discrimination (Bowley, 1978).

[36] This agreement served to halt construction of new high-rise projects that had not been previously approved, but it was not applied to construction of new public housing outside Chicago's black ghetto.

[37] The summary judgment found that 99.5% of CHA family housing was located in all-black neighborhoods or those neighborhoods in which the racial composition was changing to predominantly black families. CHA family housing was occupied by 99% black occupants. In addition, the CHA had imposed racial quotas in four predominantly white projects (Bowley, 1978).

[38] Specifically, new housing would be built in areas with 30% or less black population; no single development could house more than 120 persons, or 240 under special circumstances; no development could aggregate more than 15% of the total number of housing units in a census tract; last, no family units for children could be located above the third floor of a building (Bowley, 1978). The *Gautreaux* decision resulted in 8,000 units in private market apartments and 2,000 scattered CHA sites. A *Chicago Tribune* study (Martin & McRoberts, December 8, 1998), however, reported that the CHA sites were located in only 10 wards, all but one with overwhelmingly minority populations.

While considerable gains had been made in prohibiting racial discrimination and the concentration of the poor in mass high-rise housing developments, the CHA remained responsible for attending to its aging and poorly maintained existing housing stock. Deterioration of the buildings and grounds of all the developments, low- and high-rise buildings alike, was visible. CHA had made efforts to respond, but they had not anticipated the personnel and resources necessary for physical upkeep (Venkatesh, 2000). CHA personnel rallied for the authority to press the federal government for renovation funds, but the CHA bureaucracy moved all too slowly.

Public housing finances nationwide were in disarray, inadequate to cover operating costs, let alone deferred maintenance (Meehan, 1979). As previously noted, the initial federal housing legislation, the 1937 Housing Act, required that tenant rents cover operating expenses. No provisions were made for long-term maintenance. Beginning in 1940, rather than using apartment size to set rents, the federal government encouraged rents to be set as a function of tenant income. As tenant income in public housing developments across the nation dropped, rental income decreased, but costs for operating and maintaining public housing continued to rise. In response, the federal government, in the 1965 Housing Act, authorized very modest rent subsidies to cover the shortfall for operating expenses. HUD also began a modernization program, granting local housing authorities funds for deferred maintenance of their buildings and grounds; yet these subsidies were too little, too late (Listokin, 1990). CHA, for instance, received $27 million in 1968 for modernization, hardly adequate to impact deferred maintenance costs.

All the while, housing authorities were held captive by the changing political climate in Washington, D.C. Operating budgets were reduced by millions, often without warning (Venkatesh, 2000). To compensate for this shortfall, housing authorities across the nation raised tenants' rents, in some cases astronomically, to pay for operating costs (Meehan, 1979). Rents of 50% of income were not uncommon. Some public housing residents were paying as much as 75% of their income for rent. Protests ensued, and rental strikes put several local housing authorities at the verge of bankruptcy. In response, the federal government legislated a series of acts and regulations to give priority to the neediest households, and between 1969 and 1971 Senator Edward Brooke's sponsored federal housing act amendments capped rents at 25% of the tenants' incomes (Popkin et al., 2000). Subsequent regulations required public housing authorities to rent to families in greatest need. The ceiling on rents also was eliminated. There was a gradual surge of working families, unwilling to pay higher rents for often deteriorating units, who abandoned public housing for lower-rent apartments in the private market. The consequence was that the economic mix of residents living in public housing dramatically changed.

The successful protests against rent increases galvanized public housing residents across the nation to organize to demand fair treatment from housing authorities. Up until the late 1960s, for example, local housing authorities' management and eviction rules were not regulated and often functioned arbitrarily.[39] Encouraged by the civil rights movement and the antigovernment climate of the late 1960s, and with the support of public interest legal services, tenants' organizations challenged local housing authorities for basic tenants' rights (Atlas & Dreier, 1993). One of the first victories for the tenants occurred in 1967 with a court ruling that the Little Rock, Arkansas, housing authority could not refuse occupancy to a family with out-of-wedlock children (Spain, 1995). Because of the number of court rulings across the nation in favor of the public housing tenants, local housing authorities were required to establish protocols for accepting and rejecting applicants, and evictions required a fair hearing and documentation (Schill, 1993). Unfortunately, although in theory this was a victory, in actuality, many housing authorities were so poorly managed, as the CHA was, that they simply gave up tenant screening and evictions entirely; in fact, CHA managers said that they had no power under the new federal rules.[40]

Subsequently, also as a result of the rent strikes and other organized protests, residents demanded and won the right to participate in their local management decisions. The federal government, beginning in 1970, required housing authorities to establish guidelines for residents' roles or lose federal modernization funds. In Chicago, in fact, the CHA had failed to act on this federal mandate for 4 years until, when threatened with loss of these funds, they established democratically elected tenant Local Advisory Councils (Venkatesh, 2000) (see chapter 5).

Continuing to Spiral Downward: 1970s and 1980s

U.S. public housing in the 1970s and 1980s fared no better. New construction of federally subsidized housing had been halted, yet the federal government continued to be responsible for millions of units in large family housing developments, buildings that housed the majority of the federally assisted housing population. These developments continued to suffer from poor management, building and grounds deterioration, and inadequate services. In Chicago, for instance, housing maintenance was in

---

[39] Resident behavior was regulated typically through a system of fines for minor infractions such as littering, loitering, and petty vandalism. Tenants objected to the fines because they could become both a hardship for low-income families and a source of arbitrary management. Also, public housing tenants could still be evicted without a hearing.

[40] Personal communication from Brad Hunt, Ph.D. student in history, University of California, Berkeley.

such "deplorable" condition – "The conditions scream out for attention" (McCabe, October 10, 1979) – that the CHA Board of Commissioners ordered an investigation. The CHA, without adequate funds either to renovate or to replace the units, began to leave apartments vacant in the most deteriorated buildings, typically in high-rise developments (Popkin et al., 2000). Beginning in the late 1970s, Chicago public housing experienced a dramatic rise in crime. As in public housing in other major U.S. cities, criminal activity was primarily gangs' drug dealing (Popkin et al., 2000). Public services including police, schools, and sanitation also became increasing inadequate, and the neighborhoods surrounding CHA developments lacked services and stores, as well as jobs.

Because of the change in tenant eligibility and rent requirements, and economic downturns, the number of very low-income tenants in public housing was increasing even more dramatically than in the past. By 1988, the average income of public housing households was one-fifth of the national average (Atlas & Dreier, 1993). By 1986, 60% of public housing families were on public assistance (National Association of Housing and Redevelopment Officials, 1986). Minority tenancy nationwide (nonwhite and Hispanic) had increased to 78% by 1984 (60% black households, 24% Hispanic); minority tenancy increased in the largest public housing authorities most dramatically to 93% (Focus, 1985). By the end of the 1980s, three-quarters of all public housing households were headed by women, and only one-third had an employed head of household (Spain, 1995). Nearly one-fifth of public housing residents had an income less than 10% of the median for their local area (Popkin, 2000). There were no significant changes in the public housing household characteristics in the 1990s (Epp, 1996).

Again, in Chicago, the statistics were even more dramatic. In 1980, residents moving into public housing earned only 30% of CHA's income limit for residency. Minorities, primarily African-American, were 95% of the tenants, and single-headed households had risen to 71%. (This later figure would be higher if the 13% elderly had been excluded in the CHA's calculation.) By 1991, the median income of Chicago public housing families was $6,000 (Popkin et al., 2000).

CHA: "The Worst Managed Housing Authority in the Nation"

In 1982, federal officials gave the Chicago Housing Authority the "dubious distinction" of being "the worst managed housing authority in the nation" (cited in Venkatesh, 2000, p. 113). Maintenance had virtually lapsed, and increasing numbers of units, because they were uninhabitable, were boarded up. To make matters worse, in 1987, the federal government slashed the nation's public housing budget by 87%. By the end of the decade, CHA reported that $1 billion was necessary for deferred maintenance. CHA was receiving 10,000 new work orders per month and more than 30,000 orders remained unfulfilled, with some tenants' requests many years old. Remarkably, despite this state of distress, Chicago public housing had long waiting lists: in 1980, approximately 13,000; by 1984, nearly double, 24,000.

Notwithstanding the fiscal constraints imposed by the federal government, Chicago's public housing was suffering from mismanagement and corruption (Venkatesh, 2000). Although CHA's buildings and grounds were in abysmal condition and the authority claimed a deficit of $33.3 million, $50 million slated for repairs remained untouched in low-interest bank accounts (Popkin et al., 2000). The authority had no strategic plans, neither short- nor long-range, to attend to the fiscal and physical problems of their public housing stock (Venkatesh, 2000). The housing authority's debt was staggering. By 1978, CHA owed at least $34.4 million to vendors, contractors, and utility companies; rather than attending to current and differed maintenance, the agency cut this budget while increasing spending on administrators' and midlevel managers' salaries. Critics uncovered shady investment decisions and disbursement of high-paying contracts benefitting CHA board members and friends. The city was implicated, failing to prosecute the CHA in its court for thousands of building code violations. CHA's mismanagement came to a head when media reports circulated that the CHA had failed to renovate and fill vacant apartments because of a secret plan to vacate empty high-rise complexes to make way for future demolition and resale of the land to private developers (Venkatesh, 2000). From the early 1960's, CHA's executive director was "a crony" of the then mayor, Richard J. Daley (Popkin et al., 2000, p. 13). Despite ample evidence of malfeasance, the chairman of the CHA board remained until he and the rest of the board were forced by HUD to step down in 1982. In December 1987, HUD declared CHA "severely troubled" (Venkadesh, 2000, p. 118). A federal judge placed the CHA in receivership until HUD located a new management team.

Questioning Public Housing "Viability": The 1990s

To contend with its deteriorating family housing stock, in 1989, Congress established the National Commission on Severely Distressed Public Housing to explore contributing factors, identify remediation strategies, and develop a national action plan to eliminate distressed conditions nationwide. Although the number of troubled projects had been estimated as much higher by its critics, the commission identified only 6% of the total public housing units as severely distressed (Epp, 1996).[41] Not surprisingly, the

---

[41] Throughout the 1980s, the federal government funded several studies that disputed the notion that the public housing stock was in poor physical conditions and cited only a small percentage of housing units (4–6%) that exhibited "chronic problems" (Epp, 1966). Instead,

commission also found that historically, the modernization (renovation) needs of older public housing buildings had been underfunded. It is note-worthy that the federally funded modernization programs, put in place after the commission's report, were, once again, grossly underfunded – a $2–$3 billion budget for modernization nationwide per year compared with estimated costs of $21.5 billion (Epp, 1996). The impact on improving the physical conditions, management, and operations of distressed devel-opments hence was small. In Chicago, because of CHA mismanagement, many of these funds were not spent, explaining, in part, why the deterio-ration of CHA's housing stock is among the worst in the nation.

In 1994, the Congress commissioned a national viability study to assess the comparative costs of renovation versus direct assistance to households through rental vouchers in their family developments.[42] Approximately 100,000 public housing units, most in high-rise developments, failed the viability test.[43] Again Chicago stands out: The CHA had the largest num-ber of units that did not meet the viability standards for rehabilitation (Richards, August 23, 1998). It is noteworthy that Wentworth Gardens was not among these developments.

Chicago's particularly poor performance on the viability test was only one of the problems faced by the CHA in the mid-1990s. Because of its ongoing mismanagement and a new series of scandals including the em-bezzlement of much of the CHA's pension funds, the federal government seized the agency in 1995. It was not until May 1999 that the city resumed control (Washburn & Garza, May 28, 1999).

In the 1990s, across the nation, political and public support for public housing had waned: Public housing was now viewed as a waste of taxpay-ers' money. The beginnings of this downturn in support could be found two decades earlier, in Saint Louis. The architecture award – winning high-rise Pruitt-Igoe housing project, although occupied only since the mid-1950s, had become uninhabitable. The indelible image of the dynamiting of the

---

the studies asserted the vast majority of public housing stock was in good condition, re-quiring only minor renovations. The commission studied the number of families living in distress, rates of serious crimes in the development or the surrounding neighborhood, barriers to managing the environment, and physical deterioration of buildings. In addi-tion, they noted that institutional abandonment of such basic services as police and fire protection, health care, education, employment, and youth programs was common in the severely distressed sites. These findings echoed a 1979 U.S. Department of Housing and Urban Development study of public and social services, which had found that police and fire protection, employment information facilities, recreation, health care, and day-care facilities were typically unavailable or of poor quality in the most troubled developments (Spain, 1995).

[42] The viability test applied only to developments with 10% or greater vacancies.

[43] A Metropolitan Planning Council report critiqued the viability study, stating that it system-atically underestimated the cost of vouchering out tenants and overestimated the costs of building rehabiliation (cited in Hendersen, May 29, 1998).

first Pruitt-Igoe buildings in 1973 became the symbol of the failure of the federal public housing program (Meehan, 1979; Spain, 1995).

THE PRIVATIZATION OF PUBLIC HOUSING

The federal government's retreat from support of public housing as a solution to the problems of urban poor families began two decades before the dynamiting of Pruitt-Igoe – as early as the mid-1950s. Rather than continuing to subsidize large projects for low-income families, the federal government began to devise alternative programs emphasizing subsidized housing for, once again, the worthy poor, in this instance the elderly. Instead of targeting new funds to house poor elderly – who did indeed need housing assistance – in 1956, the federal government legislated a program to redirect substantial federal funds slated for family housing to construction of assisted housing for the elderly. The government also mandated that the elderly have priority admission to public housing[44] (Meehan, 1979). In Chicago, over the course of 17 years, until federal financing was phased out in 1976, 9,667 subsidized units for the elderly were built in 46 developments, the largest senior housing program in the nation (on a per capita basis) (Bowley, 1978).

Beginning in 1959, the government sought to get out of the business of housing development and management through privatizing public housing. Three below-market interest rate subsidy programs were legislated over 10 years – the federal Housing Acts of 1959, 1960, and 1968 – to encourage private financing of low- and moderate-income rental housing. Federal loans were given to private developers to build, own, and manage publically subsidized housing developments (Listokin, 1990; Bratt, 1989). Because of public opposition, however, these subsidized developments also were located typically in lower-income neighborhoods and geographically isolated, or otherwise undesirable locations (McGuire, 1962). Ultimately, the federal government's target to subsidize 6 million rental units was unmet, and only 2.6 million rental units had been constructed by the end of a 10-year period (Nenno, 1996). As part of these programs, a total of 143 projects with approximately 20,000 multifamily rental units were built or rehabilitated in Chicago[45] (Bowley, 1978).

In 1973, the federal administration placed a moratorium on new construction of public housing, stating that the time had come for better alternatives to house the nation's poor. The solution was a voucher program

---

[44] With the 1956 Housing Act, a special premium of an additional $500 per room was granted for construction of elderly public housing (Bowley, 1978). This premium was paid because elderly housing, typically one-bedroom apartments, is more costly per square foot to construct than the conventional three-bedroom apartments in family housing.

[45] The developments ranged from 6 to 803 units, most in high-rise buildings located on Chicago's South Side, West Side, and north lakefront (Bowley, 1978).

that would provide federal subsidies to low-income households renting housing in the private market. This form of privitization of public housing purportedly would produce cost savings: Rental allowances would provide equivalent housing to government-owned developments, but at a lower cost. The program began in the mid-1960s with a very modest demonstration project and expanded through the 1990s to include 1.4 million households nationwide.[46] The 1974 Housing and Community Development Act solidified the voucher program with the Section 8 rental assistance program legislation. As in the past, this program was originally targeted to aid the working poor but was altered in the early 1980s to serve more disadvantaged households (Bratt, 1989; Listokin, 1990; Nenno, 1996). Initially the Section 8 program was targeted to households earning 50% to 80% of the local median annual household income but was lowered in the early 1980s to households earning less than 50% of the area median. The federal government funded the cost of the difference between a specified cap, a federally determined fair market rent, and 25% of the tenant's household income. Initially, the Section 8 vouchers could be applied to construct and rehabilitate new housing or provide rent subsidies for existing housing. Within a few years, the federal government revised the program to include only housing vouchers for existing rentals in the private market, which increasingly became the dominant form of federal housing assistance to the poor.[47] CHA had more than 22,000 households receiving vouchers, second in the nation only to New York City (Lynch, June 23–July 6, 1998).

Although the rental voucher program may appear to provide a good solution to the poor's housing problems – in particular, by giving poor households the option to live where they prefer – it has not functioned as intended. The program's fundamental assumption – that the private market will provide adequate housing for low-income families – is flawed. Households receiving vouchers often have difficulty finding a satisfactory apartment, for instance, one that is in close proximity to job, or in an otherwise desirable neighborhood. Landlords do not have to accept vouchers, despite the Fair Housing laws. Discrimination against racial minorities and families with children is still an obstacle to many rental voucher recipients (Smith, 1999; Wright, Zalalem, deGraff, & Roman, 1997). The fair market

---

[46] The first pilot rental voucher program, targeted to residents who could qualify for public housing, was legislated by the Housing Act of 1965 (Bowley, 1978). In Chicago, by 1975, 3,000 households had participated in the voucher program; the majority were the low-income elderly (72%).

[47] Overall the 1980s resulted in a precipitous 74% decline in federally assisted housing from 299,811 units in 1980 to 78,767 units in 1989. Although Congress did not totally abandon support for new housing construction, support for private market vouchers increased from 36% in 1980 to 80% in 1989 (Nenno, 1996).

rent established by the government often is lower than the local market rate for comparable housing, again restricting families' housing choices to low rent neighborhoods with housing that is as dilapidated as the public housing alternatives. Moreover, the availability of voucher rental assistance is vulnerable to federal legislation, which can reduce both the number of vouchers and the time frame for the assistance.[48]

Ambitious Renewal or Devolution in Public Housing

In the 1990s, the U.S. federal government made a major shift in housing policy while maintaining an emphasis on privitization. The intent has been to reform public housing, in particular by stressing tenant "self-sufficiency" programs and redevelopment of the most troubled public housing. The new federal programs, Homeownership and Opportunity for People Everywhere (HOPE), emphasize home ownership for low-income families through the sale of public housing and publically held single-family properties to residents; the redevelopment of distressed public developments into "smaller-scale, economically mixed housing that is an anchor for neighborhood renewal"; and the support of resident management of government-owned housing[49] (HUD, 1996, cited in Smith, 1999, p. 49; see also Nenno, 1996). Within the first decade of the 21st century, the federal government plans to sell 50,000 public housing units to tenants and demolish another 100,000 units that did not pass the 1994 national viability test[50] (Smith, 1999).

The HOPE program, like its predecessors, is a "bold new experiment" executed with no evidence of whether or not it will improve the lives of current public housing residents or provide adequate housing for those people who cannot afford housing in the private market. There is considerable debate about whether the programs are an ambitious renewal or the devolution of government-owned public housing – "a rhetorical smoke screen that masks a more powerful rationale for getting the Federal government out of the business of maintaining a permanent stock of housing for the very poor" (Smith, 1999, p. 49).

What we do know is that local authorities have begun to demolish public housing units in large numbers, primarily high-rise developments. The

[48] Section 8 vouchers have other limitations, which are due to governing regulations. They are granted for only one year and households have only 60 days to find housing.
[49] HOPE also included programs to house the homeless and bonuses and tax credits for states and localities that remove regulatory barriers to affordable housing (Nenno, 1996).
[50] The demolition and the resulting decrease in the number of federally funded public housing units were made possible by congressional repeal, in 1995, of a one-to-one replacement regulation requiring that any demolished federally funded public housing unit be replaced by another public housing unit. The one-for-one replacement regulation was added to the 1937 Housing Act in the 1970s (Henderson, May 29, 1998).

HOPE VI program allows local public housing authorities to decrease the percentage of units in the new developments that serve extremely low-income households (30% or less of the median household income for the city or county), if they provide the displaced families with rental vouchers. The exact percentage reduction and ultimate income mix of the redeveloped housing have, as of yet, not been established by local authorities and the federal government.

Despite the CHA's ambitious redevelopment plan, a key question remains: Where will the thousands of displaced residents who call the projects home go? Although the city pointed to rental vouchers as the solution, the media and public housing residents, as well, have their doubts. Critics of the rental voucher program express caution when the government equates tenant-based voucher assistance with public housing units (Smith, 1999; Wright et al., 1997). Harold Henderson (May 29, 1998), a journalist for the Chicago *Reader*, spoke directly to the dilemma:

No doubt, a voucher is a "housing opportunity" – and many CHA residents are happy to take one and leave – but when the chips are down and the market is tight, you can't live in it. That's the problem. Section 8 vouchers build no new homes, especially no affordable ones with two or three bedrooms. (p. 18)

Henderson reported that public housing residents are similarly concerned about the reliability of Section 8 rental vouchers; also, many do not want to move. Although some residents worked with the CHA on its redevelopment plan, many residents, such as virtually all of the Wentworth Gardens resident activists, were unsupportive and were concerned about their housing security. They would prefer to remain at Wentworth if their housing conditions and management improve.

In Chicago, the housing options available for public housing tenants who have been "vouchered out" are very restricted, most often into housing that is as dilapidated and communities that are as segregated as those they left. According to the *Chicago Tribune* (August 23, 1998), the residents are "Out of the Hole, into Another":

As the Chicago Housing Authority begins dismantling such pillars of poverty as the Robert Taylor Homes and Cabrini Green, thousands of families face the question: Will they wind up in conditions as poor and disadvantaged as the ones they left? (p. 1)

The CHA admitted in a 1997 report to HUD that the "existing Section 8 units are located overwhelmingly in impacted areas, far from employment growth centers" (cited in Henderson, May 29, 1998, p. 18). Rather than encouraging the deconcentration of racial and ethnic minorities (one of the goals of the voucher program), displaced CHA residents with vouchers find rental housing primarily in poor, minority neighborhoods[51] (*Chicago Tribune*, April 28, 1999). Even more problematic, the findings of a study completed by the UIC Voorhees Center (Wright, 1997) documented that the private market in Chicago could not absorb all of the households that would be displaced when all the public housing units planned for demolition were razed. In the Chicago six-county region, there are approximately two low-income families for every affordable housing unit (Wright, 1997).

AN UNCERTAIN FUTURE

In 1998, when we completed our fieldwork, there were 1.3 million dwelling units of government-owned public housing for families and the elderly, only 11% of which were built after 1990 (Epp, 1996). There were more low-income housing units built and managed by private developers but subsidized through government loans and insurance than there were government-owned public housing units: 1.9 million compared with 1.3 million apartments (Listokin, 1990). Although public housing apartments represented less than 2% of the nation's total housing supply and 4% of the nation's rental stock (Atlas & Dreier, 1993; Spain, 1995), it constituted 34% of the affordable housing stock for extremely low-income families (Smith, 1999). Even with the pressing need for affordable housing for the very poor, programs for new construction have been insubstantial, with more units demolished than built.

Reformers' hopes for "decent, safe, and sanitary" housing for low-income Americans have been dampened by government resistance to enter the business of public housing, business interests' opposition, and racial and class discrimination. Not all those involved in the design, development, and management, however, have been negligent, as aptly noted by Venkatesh (2000):

Designers thought that high-rises would free the poor from urban ills, not compound their hardships, and their faith was grounded in the science of urban planning. Black politicians made the difficult choice of ghetto public housing versus no low-income housing at all. Well before racist city official rejected their proposals to locate low-income housing in white communities, CHA officials had wanted to build public housing in ghettos to address local housing shortages. Later, CHA managers fought for the needs of their constituents while their budgets decreased, and politicians tried to infuse the housing development with law enforcement resources in a effort to increase household security. (p. 270)

---

[51] The *Chicago Tribune* (Richards & Martin, April 22, 1999) reported on Paul Fischer's study of approximately 1,000 families relocated from the ABLA Homes, Cabrini Green, and Robert Taylor Homes. He found that more than 80% were relocated in census tracts that were 90% black, and more than 90% of the displaced CHA tenants lived in census tracts where the median income was less than $15,000.

Despite the best intentions, the dramatic cuts in federal funding from the 1960s on hampered local officials' efforts.

At the turn of the 21st century, nationwide there is a severe shortage of affordable, safe, and decent housing for the very poor (Smith, 1999). Andrew Cuomo, former secretary of the U.S. Department of Housing and Urban Development, repeatedly stressed poor Americans' housing predicament: The number of low-income households requiring housing was at its highest, while the number of affordable housing units for these households continued to shrink (HUD, October 1, 1999). This is the most distressing fact of the turn of the century public housing policy: The number of government-owned public housing units is being reduced while the need for affordable housing, particularly among the very poor, is at an all-time high.

In the 1960s, public housing residents were increasingly burdened by deteriorating physical facilities and inadequate services to meet their needs. Now they are confronted with the potential destruction of their homes. At Wentworth Gardens, women resident activists are acutely aware of the decreasing viability of their development, but they, as well as many other Chicago public housing residents, have not stood by and ignored this threat to their development's viability. For over four decades, they have worked tirelessly to resist the political, economic, social, and physical realities that have shaped Wentworth's deteriorating conditions and, when also threatened, the broader South Armour community in which Wentworth is located. Our analysis of Wentworth resident activists' struggles to improve their housing conditions begins with the impetus for their actions: both their memories of Wentworth's better past, which guide their struggles, and the realities of the present, which challenge their ability to sustain everyday life.

3

Memory of a Better Past, Reality of the Present

The Impetus for Resident Activism

> We're not fighting for the status quo to keep these raggedy build-
> ings. . . . We're fighting to be able to stay in the community. . . . We've stayed
> there during the hard times. Now we're going to up and move now that
> they're going to redevelop it? That's insanity.
>   Wardell Yotaghan, a longtime resident of Rockwell Gardens CHA family
>   development and cofounder of the Coalition to Protect Public Housing,
>   *Chicago Tribune*, (McRoberts, June 20, 1997, p. 5A)

On June 19, 1997, "Juneteenth Day," over 1,000 public housing residents,
including several Wentworth Gardens activists, and their supporters con-
verged on downtown Chicago for a march and a rally to protest HUD and
local policies that threaten the very existence of public housing.[1]

> WE SHALL NOT BE TAKEN FOR GRANTED ANYMORE
> WE SHALL NOT BE MOVED
> (Flyer announcing "The People's March" to Protest Public Housing Policies, The
> Coalition to Protect Public Housing, Chicago, June 19, 1997)

Sponsored by the Coalition to Protect Public Housing, the event drew attention to the failure of government plans to improve the living conditions
for Chicago public housing residents, as well as current policies to remove
these very low-income residents from their homes. Instead, the coalition

---

[1] Juneteenth, the oldest African-American celebration, commemorates June 19, 1865, the date
when Texans got word that the Civil War had ended and former southern slaves were free.
African-Americans across the United States have been quietly observing Juneteenth for
more than a century. It is an official holiday in seven states, and there is now an organized
movement to push the holiday to national status. Dr. Ronald Myers, chairman of the national Juneteenth Observance Foundation in Washington, D.C., recently reported: "The
slave legacy must be dealt with and reflected upon in this country in a positive way.
The drive to make it a national holiday has served as a catalyst for participation and pride
in Juneteenth." (Glanton, 2002, pp. 1, 22)

59

called for a "Public Housing Contract" to give "guarantees to residents including the choice to remain in their redeveloped community and accountability that clearly states tenant and management responsibilities" (Coalition to Protect Public Housing brochure).

If we were to abide by the Chicago mainstream media and the nationwide media as well, we would conclude that public housing is an undesirable place to live. Dark portrayals of projects beset by violence, dilapidated structures, and joblessness are the evidence used to support the demolition of buildings in the most distressed CHA developments. At the time of Juneteenth Day, CHA had slated a total of 16,000 to 19,000 units for demolition within 5 years as part of HUD and CHA plans for public housing reform. The *Chicago Tribune* (1997) found wisdom in these plans, a satisfactory end to the "chaos and misery that seem endemic to the city's public housing."

Conventional wisdom presumes that residents living in the nation's most troubled public housing developments are trapped by poverty, dislike their developments, and would move immediately if given the opportunity. Tearing down troubled inner city public housing and converting developments into mixed-income communities are touted as serving the best interests of not only society, but residents as well (Vale, 1997). Yet some Chicago public housing residents are vocal in their expressions of anger and fear about the potential loss of their homes to redevelopment. Henry Horner residents took legal action to protest the Chicago Housing Authority's (CHA's) plans to raze their development. At Cabrini Green and ABLA, residents similarly have organized and pressed lawsuits to halt demolition plans.

The Coalition to Protect Public Housing was formed to oppose CHA's plans to demolish public housing (Henderson, 1998). They had no trust in CHA's promises to assure housing for the displaced residents; in particular, they did not trust that there would be adequate replacement housing in the private market, nor did they trust that rent subsidies would be provided by the federal government's Section 8 program. Wardell Yotagham, head of the coalition, explained their mission:

Any plan that don't replace the units, any plan that depends on Section 8, we will oppose them. Those plans will end up making people homeless. (cited in Henderson, 1998, p. 20)

Although there are no CHA-wide studies to assess residents' housing satisfaction and relocation preferences systematically, there are development-based studies that provide support for the coalition's contention that many residents would like to "change the face of public housing without changing the faces in public housing" (Coalition to Protect Public Housing brochure). A 1986 resident-conducted survey in three high-rise CHA developments, sponsored by the Chicago Metropolitan Planning

Council, found that most residents expressed the desire to remain in their development, although they indicated considerable dissatisfaction with their housing conditions. CHA also surveyed residents of three of its largest family developments, Henry Horner, Robert Taylor, and Cabrini Green Homes, as part of their redevelopment plans (Henderson, 1998). With the exception of those in Robert Taylor, the vast majority of residents stated preferences to remain in the redeveloped public housing developments or in replacement housing in the immediate neighborhood.[2]

Public housing residents' lack of desire to move is not unique to CHA housing. In his study of resident satisfaction in five public housing developments in Boston, Larry Vale (1997) observed that most surveyed residents indicated satisfaction with their public housing, even though they were distressed by "the devastating effects of drugs, disruption, and disillusionment that stem from concentrated poverty and unemployment" (p. 173). Interestingly, two-thirds of the residents expressed the desire to "stay put" – not only those residents with little chance of economic mobility, but also some who were upwardly mobile. Vale uses the concept of empathological place to describe the apparent conflicts in the surveyed residents' assessments of their public housing:

Rather than unambiguously evil environments, public housing developments serve as a source of empathy as well as a locus of pathology. For many residents, a housing project is what one might call an empathological place, a place where profound ambivalence is the ruling emotional response. Empathological places are those where the fear of remaining is counterbalanced by the fear of departure, where the ties of friendship are inextricably juxtaposed with the incursions of unwanted outsiders. (pp. 159–160)

Wentworth Gardens resident activists, too, have conflicted feelings about their development. As we will describe in this chapter, these activists, although they give due recognition to the very difficult housing problems they face, also believe that Wentworth is a "nice community." They want to remain in their housing and express considerable concerns about the

---

[2] At Henry Horner, one-third of the residents stated preferences to live in rehabilitated apartments in the development, and another third, in replacement housing in the immediate neighborhood. The last third preferred to live elsewhere in the Chicago region, if given Section 8 vouchers. At Cabrini Green, according to the executive director of CHA at the time Joseph Schuldiner, "Basically everybody wanted to stay," whereas at Robert Taylor Homes, most of the residents, 75%–85%, wanted to move (cited in Henderson, 1998, p. 18). These findings are not surprising. Cabrini Green is located on what is now prime real estate. Adjacent to the city's "Gold Coast," a neighborhood with the most costly real estate in Chicago, the area surrounding Cabrini Green is gentrifying, with costly townhouses built across the street. Cabrini Green has good access to shopping and mass transit, as well as employment opportunities. Robert Taylor, on the other hand, is geographically isolated in an area of concentrated public housing and is perhaps the most dilapidated of all the family developments.

potential loss of their development. How do we explain the activists' conflicted responses to their housing? How does this explanation provide a
context for understanding Wentworth resident activists' ongoing commitments to struggle to sustain the viability of their housing development?
Finally, how do we explain the disparity between conventional wisdom
and the pleas and actions taken by Wentworth Gardens and other Chicago
public housing residents and their advocates to save their developments
from demolition? We will find the answers to these questions in the words
of Wentworth Gardens' resident activists as they describe their residential
autobiographies, a migratory path that began for the majority of the activists in their childhood homes of poverty in the rural South, activists like
Lottie Weathersby.[3] In reporting the activists' descriptions, we have taken
care to site all of these women to assure that each person's voice is heard.

"*I'M HERE TO STAY*": LOTTIE WEATHERSBY'S COMMITMENT TO WENTWORTH GARDENS

Lottie Weathersby has been a Wentworth Gardens resident for over
25 years, and she has no intention of leaving: "I'm here to stay."
Mrs. Weathersby moved into Wentworth when her youngest was one year
old and her oldest was 20. Today, in her 60s, she lives in the same four-
bedroom rowhouse with her youngest daughter and two grandchildren.

In contrast to her expressed attachments to Wentworth, Mrs. Weathersby's memories of the places she lived in the past are "brutal." "I would
never go back," she explained in describing her intense sense of alienation
from her childhood home in Mississippi. She adamantly stated that she
would not even want to be buried there:

I told [a family member in Mississippi], ever since I been in Chicago you don't have
to save me a burial ground in this city [in Mississippi] 'cause I didn't even want to
go back to Mississippi then.

Born in a rural area in 1935, granddaughter of a slave, Lottie lived in
a household with 13 siblings in a five-room house – a kitchen and four
bedrooms, each with two beds. There was "no running water, no electricity,
no inside bathroom. All of that was on the outside." Her family's work life
was equally harsh:

We was sharecroppers. When it was hot last summer [a record heatwave in Chicago]
I often think about it. They talk about all the people that died in the heat last summer.
Those kind of days we were in the field chopping cotton and corn. It would be so

---

[3] In this chapter we are reporting the responses of only the 22 resident activists from whom we
obtained residential autobiographies. Thus when we say "all" of the resident activists, this
does not include the voices of those residents who were interviewed through an abbreviated
interview format or observed at community meetings and events.

hot in the field. And we were bare-footed. We didn't have on no shoes. We had to take a rake in front of us and dig a place to put our feet where we could step up and your feet wouldn't be so hot. At bean pickin' time, we picked beans; we picked cotton. I could pick at least thirty bushels of beans a day. I could pick 250 pounds of cotton a day, and walk home from the field; and walk and get my bath water; and get my bath and all that stuff . . . and get up the next morning at 5:00 and be ready to go to the field at 6:00 . . . it was a struggle. And we was working on . . . 60/40. . . . The White man got 60 percent.

After her marriage, Mrs. Weathersby's life in Mississippi continued to be harsh. In addition to raising a family and working as a domestic, she and her husband sharecropped in lieu of paying rent for a house. As in her childhood home, it had no running water or electricity:

I was more-or-less supposed to have been a housewife and mother, but I worked for White people doing their housework – cleaning the house, washing, ironing. After that I started to work in a chicken house picking up eggs. We would pick up like 6,000 eggs a day. . . . This was on the White man's farm. And in order for us to live in the house for no rent, I would work picking up eggs and they would pay me $30 a week 'cause I worked seven days a week. And they had another girl that was working with me, there was two of us. And they had two chicken houses. Each one of those chicken houses had 3,000 chickens apiece. . . . And we would have to put them [the eggs] through a little machine, which wasn't a big machine. We had to put them through there one by one, and wash them all each day.

In 1967, hoping to change her life for the better, Lottie Weathersby left Mississippi and her physically abusive husband and traveled north with her children to Chicago. Her work life was less of a hardship, but housing herself and her children proved difficult because of constrained housing options in the private market. She held several different jobs, as a factory worker or housekeeper. Although her income was considerably higher than she had earned in Mississippi, it was inadequate to pay all the bills. She and her eight children were living on the West Side of Chicago in a two-bedroom apartment. Because of the crowded conditions, the family used the enclosed but unheated back porch, even in winter: "It was cold, but we used it anyway." Yet, it was the rat infestation of the apartment that was the impetus to apply for public housing:

I was living . . . in an apartment that had rats – great big rats! My kids was terrorized by them. . . . I said, "I'm gonna find you all somewhere else to stay," and they said, "Okay," and I put in for [public] housing the day after Thanksgiving in 1972.

It was not until 1974 that Mrs. Weathersby was offered an apartment in CHA housing, first in a high-rise complex, then in scattered site housing. Despite the wait, she turned down both options. She emphatically stated, "I wanted nothing highrise" in particular, because the high-rise public housing developments had a bad reputation: "I had heard a lot about the highrises." She specifically noted that she was concerned for her smaller children's safety: "I didn't like moving into a highrise building because I thought about the elevators, the windows, and my kids being smaller at the time." The scattered site housing was an unaffordable option because the rent subsidy was inadequate.

Mrs. Weathersby would not agree to move with her children into public housing until she was offered a four-bedroom apartment at Wentworth Gardens. She explained:

[T]he leasing clerk from Wentworth called me and she told me, "I got an apartment I think you're gonna like" ... and when I came over here and I accepted this [apartment] and I thought this was beautiful. I didn't even bring my kids over to let them see it until I moved in, because I knew this was gonna be where I was gonna live.... My apartment was ready to be moved in – painted, waxed floors, new refrigerator, stove, everything. It was different from what it is today. My apartment, my yard and everything was ready to be lived in.... The grounds was beautiful. Nothing like they is now. They had flower beds in all four corners. The four corners was a beautiful sight.

Mrs. Weathersby also liked Wentworth Gardens' location because it was convenient, well served by stores and good public schools.

Mrs. Weathersby's highly critical appraisal of Wentworth's housing conditions in June 1996 was particularly relevant in comparison to her memories of Wentworth's better past. In contrast to its former well-tended buildings and grounds, the current housing conditions at Wentworth Mrs. Weathersby described as deplorable. Buildings and grounds have not been maintained, and her requests for repairs go unheeded:

I asked for new face board [in the bathroom] because my face board is falling off the wall.... The pipes under that is rotted out and is causing the water to run in.

In frustration, Mrs. Weathersby indicated that she would take matters into her own hands if necessary:

And if they don't do it, I'm not gonna worry about it.... I'm gonna take my rent money and I'm gonna buy me a face board and put it in my house and send them the receipt.[4]

Mrs. Weathersby didn't blame the on-site management; she believed the manager's "hands are tied" by lack of funds from CHA. It is not surprising that her hopes for improvements at Wentworth Gardens included "a lot of interior work. We need cabinets. We need paint."

---

[4] According to the Chicago Tenant Bill of Rights residents in buildings with more than four units may deduct the cost of repairs from their rent if the landlord fails to make the needed repairs within a reasonable period of time.

Mrs. Weathersby also was displeased with the newer residents, particularly in comparison to her long-term neighbors and friends in the development. She was concerned about the loss of some of these "old-timers," working residents who moved when CHA changed their rent policies and their rent exceeded the cost of a comparable apartment in the private market. Mrs. Weathersby: "Yeah well, when they [CHA] went into this rent thing about 30% of your income, a lot of people moved because their rent was coming up to like $700 or $800 a month."[5] Weathersby deemed the old-timers responsible caretakers of their housing: "Residents are supposed to care enough about where they live to think this is where I live, and this is what I'm gonna do to keep it clean." In contrast, according to Mrs. Weathersby, the newer public housing residents "don't do that"; nor do they adequately supervise their children: "A lot of things I don't like in the neighborhood is people not watching their kids, not knowing where their kids is going."

Although highly critical of the poor living conditions, Mrs. Weathersby was committed to working toward Wentworth's improvement. Motivated by her sense of duty to the community and guided by her memories of Wentworth Gardens' better past, as were other older-generation resident activists, she was committed to working on behalf of herself and her neighbors to improve her housing development:

There's just so much difference from then and now, and that's why we're working to try to get Wentworth back to where it used to be. All along the sidewalks on all of the exterior parts was beautiful. And this is why I'm working as hard as I'm working to try to get Wentworth back to look [as it did in the past].

Lottie Weathersby's residential autobiography is not unusual. She, like nearly all of the other Wentworth Gardens older-generation resident activists, and 3.5 million other blacks, was part of the second wave of southern migrants to the north. And, as they have for many of these hopeful migrants, children and grandchildren of sharecroppers, the prospects for economic advancement, and more generally an improved quality of life for many black migrant families, have fallen far short of expectations, leaving these families in a lifetime of poverty (Stack, 1974). Yet, Mrs. Weathersby's response to her unfulfilled aspirations, rather than "conditioned acceptance," has been to continue to work for the betterment of her and her neighbors' everyday lives.

Mrs. Weathersby speaks about Wentworth Gardens as a source of difficult challenges to her and her neighbors' everyday survival but

---

[5] The 1969 Brooke Amendment limited a public housing tenant's rent to 25% of the family's adjusted gross income (see chapter 2). In 1983, this figure was changed to 30% of the resident family's adjusted gross income (Listokin, 1990). As noted by Lottie Weathersby, this meant that increasingly working-class public housing residents, who were paying rents of $700 and $800 per month, could find better housing in the private market.

simultaneously a source of deeply experienced attachments. Although paradoxical, these apparent conflicting experiences of homeplace have provided the impetus of her activism. Her attachments to Wentworth help to explain her sense of responsibility and commitment to remain in Wentworth and her work to sustain Wentworth's viability, as her actions to improve conditions at Wentworth contest the current harsh realities of daily life in the development.

ATTACHMENTS TO HOMEPLACE

Theoretical conceptualizations of people's attachments to the places they call *home* – both their dwelling and their neighborhood – have garnered the interest of many disciplines and have been denoted by many terms.[6] Despite the diversity and complexity of the perspectives on *place attachment* – one of the more commonly used terms – there is some concurrence about its characterization and ongoing development (see, for example, Altman & Low, 1992; Feldman, 1988, 1990; Giuliani & Feldman, 1994). For most researchers, these attachments are conceptualized as complex, interrelated psychological and behavioral bonds with both the social and the physical environment of the home (reviewed in Giuliani & Feldman, 1994; Low & Altman, 1992).

Researchers have observed that throughout recorded history, the significance of the homeplace has exceeded the necessities of functional and material support for shelter and security. People develop a deeply experienced relatedness, both ideas and emotions, that bind them to their homeplace in ways that cannot be explained solely by the home environment's utility to meet survival needs. Feldman (1988), in drawing together the various perspectives on place attachment, explained the formation and function of these bonds as follows:

It is through purposeful "concentration" of the multiple routines of daily life in one location that homeplace is distinguished from its surrounds and endowed with significance and meaning. Homeplace becomes an enduring, tangible symbol

[6] Attachment to place has been considered in the literature on the phenomenology of daily life and place, community sentiments and identity, psychological perspectives on the role of place in the development of self-identity, residential stability and mobility, and perceptions of residential area quality, community participation, and others.

In addition to place attachment (Altman & Low edited volume, 1992; Fischer et al., 1997; Fried, 1963; Shumaker & Taylor, 1983; Taylor, Gottfredson & Brower, 1985; psychological bonds with home have been referred to as *community commitments or attachments* (Kasarda & Janowitz, 1974; reviewed in Fischer et al., 1977), *rootedness* (Relph, 1976; Tuan, 1980), *belonging* (Buttimer, 1980; Fried & Gelicker, 1970; Keller, 1968; Seamon, 1979), *sense of place* (Hummon, 1992; Relph, 1976; Tuan, 1980), *at homeness* (Dovey, 1985; Seamon, 1979), and related concepts, including *place-identity* (Proshansky, 1978; Proshansky, Fabian & Kaminoff, 1983), *spatial identity* (Fried, 1963), and *place dependence* (Stokols & Shumaker, 1981).

of the individual and social self, of the continuity of one's experiences, and of that which is valued by the inhabitants. (pp. 335–336)

Attachments to homeplace are experienced as an intimate sense of belonging, comfort, and being at ease in a locale, both in its material surrounds and in the social relationships formed in this locale (see Feldman, 1988, for a review of the empirical research). They are expressed through not only desires and actions to maintain one's residence in this place, but also a sense of responsibility and commitment to continue to tend for and take care of one's homeplace. It is important to note, however, that long-term involvement in a place does not necessarily result in positive attachments. As is evident in Lottie Weathersby's childhood experiences, profound alienation from a place may result from particularly negative experiences of a homeplace (Giuliani & Feldman, 1994).

Most scholars have focused on individuals' direct, focused involvement in their homeplaces; however, some researchers have noted the contributions of collective and culturally based experiences in the development of place attachment as well (Low & Altman, 1992). Place attachments may result from people's shared experiences in the home locale, place-embedded social relationships, and culturally shared meanings and activities associated with a dwelling and neighborhood.[7] For instance, researchers have found that meanings and experiences associated with past and present social relationships in homeplaces are as important in explaining place attachments as are the experiences in the material surrounds of home per se. Place attachments also connect people to their culture through ideas and material symbols that are associated with their past, present, and desired homeplaces. Through the development of place attachments, according to Low and Altman (1992), the home becomes "a medium or milieu which embeds and is a repository of a variety of life experiences, is central to those experiences, and is inseparable from them" (p. 11).

People do not necessarily develop attachments to their homeplaces; nor are all attachments experienced with equal intensity. Ample research has found, however, that women, minorities, lower-income people, and older and long-term residents are more likely to be more attached to the places they call home, and these attachments are experienced more intensely (reviewed in Saegert, 1989; Feldman, 1996). Women spend more time in and gain more satisfaction from the home, as well as take more responsibility for the care and personalization of the home setting. Lower-income minority people's social life is frequently focused on the neighborhood, and

---

7 Cultural ideologies about good and proper homes may inhibit or foster people's bonds with particular types of homeplaces (Feldman, 1996). For instance, cultural ideologies about appropriate types of places to live, such as the dominant cultural ideology that families with children should live in the suburbs and that women should have closer bonds with the home than men, are likely to affect people's bonds with their home environs.

they depend more on these informal interactions for their survival. Older people, too, are dependent upon the familiarity of their home environs and social networks to compensate for mental and physical decline. Long-term residency contributes to not only the familiarity of home environs and long held social relations, but also embedded, materialized memories of their lives and self and group identities. And these attachments are apparent even when the physical setting – both the dwelling and the neighborhood – may be physically distressed (Fried, 1963; Saegert, 1989).

As Mrs. Weathersby's were, all Wentworth activists' words and actions were filled with indications of intense attachments to this place they call "home". Their attachments to Wentworth are explained by their individual experiences and shared understandings of their residential past, present, and potential future. Whether their past homes were in the rural South and/or the northern black ghetto, Wentworth activists share memories of poor physical housing conditions resulting from lack of affordable housing and discrimination in the private housing market. They also share memories of Wentworth's "better days" whether through direct experiences or, for the younger-generation activists, through the recollections of the older generation residents – this earlier "beautiful" housing was compared to the places that they had lived in previously. Residents' memories of Wentworth's better past, especially in contrast to Wentworth's current conditions, as well as the lack of alternative adequate housing, explain Wentworth residents' attachments to their home – both its physical and its social environment – and the role these attachments play as primary motivators for Wentworth activists' hopes and actions for Wentworth's better future.

Constrained Housing Options in the Private Market

February [1947]: Crowd of 3,000 masses; first day application lists are opened for Wentworth Gardens; lists closed after second day with 3,500 applicants. Approximately 1,200 families expected to be eligible for the 422 living units in the project. . . . *June*: Wentworth Gardens fully occupied.

A CHA 1947 report to the mayor reported on the crowds of applicants for residency in Wentworth Gardens. The demand for public housing was not surprising. In addition to the lack of stable, sufficient income, discriminatory practices against blacks and large families with children in the private housing market restricted Mrs. Weathersby and other African-Americans to residency in Chicago's South and West Sides (as reported in chapter 2). Housing conditions were costly but often deplorable, as many families lived in crowded quarters and/or dilapidated buildings (Bowley, 1978). Despite similar racial segregation in Chicago public housing, in its early years it was considered a desirable housing option by black families.

For all of the Wentworth activists, many of whom were employed, housing in the Chicago private market generally exceeded their ability to pay. Their housing prospects were further constrained by personal and household hardships. The reasons Wentworth activists gave for needing affordable housing included lack of employment caused by family caretaking responsibilities (e.g., for children in the extended family or for ill family members), loss of employment, and family violence.[8] Many southern migrant black families experienced problems of instability, violence, and alcoholism (Friedman, 1968; Gelfand, 1975; Wood, 1982, all cited in von Hoffman, 1996). Such problems, along with serious illnesses, without the benefit of adequate medical care, hampered these migrants' abilities to hold steady jobs and remain safely in their homes.

As Lottie Weathersby did, Wentworth's activists, both the older and the younger generation, considered Wentworth Gardens to be an affordable housing option, particularly in contrast to the costly housing in the private market. In the words of the older-generation Wentworth activist and spiritual leader Janie Dumas, "the rent was very high" outside public housing. Mrs. Dumas moved into Wentworth in 1968 from Chicago's South Side with her husband, a postal worker, and her two children.

Evelyn Ramsey, as Mrs. Dumas had, applied to public housing as her only affordable option:

So I'm living on the west side, 3826 Gladys, and I had a nice apartment, with a basement . . . and everything. But I was on public aid, and I was payin' like, $331 for rent. . . . And then after the lease was up they was gonna raise the rent again. So basically the reason that I was able to survive was because at that time my grandmother was livin' and she was gettin' uh, SSI check. And I was gettin' food stamps and her SSI check, 'cause most of my check was, I think I was gettin 367 dollars and my rent was like $331 or something like that. So I had very little left.

Mrs. Ramsey, inspirational mentor to many Wentworth resident activists and mother of two children, moved into Wentworth in 1975. She, as two of the other activists had, explicitly mentioned that she preferred not to live in public housing but had no other affordable options – "I don't wanna live in no project." Public housing's negative portrayal in the media was her rationale:

I've always had this thing about, at that time they called it a project. . . . 'Cause you know, you hear so many, you hear so many strange things . . . that goes on there . . . in the news. . . . [But] I never did hear too much about Wentworth in the news. . . . So, its' just, you know, you perceive these ideas or, what it's like. . . . I'm forced to stay here because of my income.

---

[8] In the residential autobiographies of the 23 activists we interviewed, many volunteered the following reasons (at times more than one) for their lack of employment: family caretaking responsibilities, $N = 9$ (39%); loss of employment, $N = 6$ (26%); and family violence, $N = 3$ (13%).

Affordability was not the only constraint on Wentworth residents' private market housing options. Racial discrimination in the private housing market compounded the difficulties in finding improved housing other than in CHA developments.[9] When describing their prior housing, all of the women activists had lived in neighborhoods with solely or predominantly African-American families. None of the activists, however, mentioned being constrained in housing choice by race. It may be that racial discrimination in the housing market is taken for granted, and its mention was deemed unnecessary.

Wentworth women not only suffered from race and class discrimination; they also were disadvantaged in the private rental market because of discrimination against families with children, particularly large families. Beatrice Harris, a resident leader and president of the Local Advisory Council (LAC), explained that as her family grew to seven children, she "was moving around a lot," some nine times in her married life before moving to Wentworth in 1966:

It was really hard for a mother with children to find a place. If you go to an apartment, the first thing they say is, "How many children do you have?" You say, "Three." And they say, "No." I remember many a time in all of that moving, most of the time I had to go find the apartment because [her husband] was at work. And everywhere I'd go they'd say, "No children!" Some of them had the signs in the window. The law changed where they had to stop putting the signs in the windows, but they could still say no, and they were saying no. Many a time I use to cry, "Where is the babies going? What's going to happen to the children?"

Beatrice Harris explained that public housing was one residential option that did accept families with children.

With limited affordable options available in the private housing market, Wentworth resident activists often described their housing before they moved to Wentworth as unacceptable. Remember that Mrs. Weathersby decided to apply for public housing because of a rat infestation in her apartment. Dorothy McMiller, one of the original Wentworth volunteers in the resident-run on-site laundromat, moved into Wentworth with her husband and her three children in 1957, but they did so reluctantly. She, as did Evelyn Ramsey, "didn't never wanna live in a project." Dorothy McMiller was left with little choice because the housing she and her family

[9] In his book *The Poorhouse*, Bowley (1978) reported that although the Black population has traditionally experienced the greatest shortage of housing in Chicago, by 1976 the problem shifted from one of scarcity to one of affordability. Because middle-class black families out-migrated to neighborhoods and suburbs not previously open to blacks, in the 1960s and 1970s there was no longer a shortage of housing units in the predominantly black areas of the city. Black families now found an increase in vacancy rates in the traditional ghetto, but also a severe shortage of decent housing that Chicago's low-income population could afford.

lived in was in such poor condition that it compromised the health and safety of her children. Her daughter was seriously injured by an exposed heater in her South Side apartment. She explained that she needed to find a new place to live rather quickly:

[My daughter] was afraid [of getting burnt again], havin' nightmares and all like that. And every time I watched [I knew] I got to move away from the place.

A social worker at the hospital where her daughter received ongoing treatments assisted her in getting an apartment at Wentworth Gardens.

In addition to dilapidated, unsafe housing conditions, many resident activists had lived in overcrowded quarters before Wentworth, unable to afford an adequately sized apartment in the private market for their households.[10] Francis Mae Jones, a divorced parent of three children, was working various jobs – in a laundry, for a dry cleaner, and as a nurse's aide – but could only afford a one-bedroom apartment:

I was looking for a larger place...only had one bedroom. So somebody... recommended that I put in for the projects. I did.

She moved into Wentworth in 1975.

When they could not afford and find decent housing in the private market, several resident activists lived with family members before applying for public housing.[11] Susan Donald and her two children had been living with her father before moving into Wentworth Gardens in 1985:

Well to tell you the truth, [I lived with my] father, and uh, I didn't have a job and my education was very limited. And I stayed with him, and we weren't getting along.... I applied for low-income housing because I was on public assistance. And that took about six years before they [CHA] called me.

Desiree Davis was born and raised by her working grandparents on the South Side of Chicago. Married, with six children, she and her husband were employed, he as a janitor, she as a waitress, yet, their income was inadequate to cover all their living expenses. To make ends meet, they lived with a relative:

I used to live in my uncle's building. And my uncle passed. And I used to work for my uncle. I worked in a restaurant. Barmaid and I was a waitress. And uh, he was teaching us how to go into managing... the business. And after he had passed away.... I was on my own. I quit school [college].... That was the main reason, because of the income. So I put in for Section 8, for low income housing and this [Wentworth Gardens] is what came.

[10] Ten (45%) of the 23 activists we interviewed volunteered that they lived in unsafe and crowded housing conditions before moving to Wentworth.
[11] Five (23%) of the 23 resident activists we interviewed indicated that they lived with their relatives before moving to Wentworth.

Bertha McKinney and her three children were living in the attic of her mother's house on Chicago's South Side. She paid her mother rent and renovated the attic with her own money in order to make it as livable as she could:

[T]he attic was fine but I had too many babies for the attic! There were only two bedrooms up there. . . . Yeah, you know, up in Momma's attic.

She decided to apply for public housing because she needed more space, it was affordable, and it was "time to leave Momma." Seven years later, in 1982, her application came through for Wentworth.

I came here because I liked the way it looked. . . . And then I wanted to move by myself, and, so my mother always told me, get something that I could handle myself; and at the time, I could handle Wentworth. You know, with my own little ol' small rent that I'm paying.

"It Would Catch Your Eye When Coming Down on the Bus" (Bertha McKinney): Memories of Wentworth Gardens' Better Past

The roots of resident activists' shared positive attachments to Wentworth are found in their memories of Wentworth's better past (see also Saegert, 1989). It is true that Wentworth activists applied to public housing because of the obstacles racism, poverty, and discrimination against families, particularly single-parent families with children, placed on their housing choices, but they also were attracted to Wentworth Gardens, even though some were hesitant to live in public housing, because it was a safe and attractive housing option, especially before the 1980s. As explained by researchers interested in the reasons for household mobility, Wentworth activists were both pushed from unsatisfactory housing circumstances and pulled by more satisfactory alternative housing.[12] In fact, in addition to its affordability and adequately sized apartments for larger families, activists explained, Wentworth Gardens was exceptionally desirable, chosen over other alternative CHA family developments. The former CHA executive director Vincent Lane, who lived with his family across the street from Wentworth Gardens in the 1950s, concurred. Mr. Lane remembered, "I envied the kids in public housing," adding, "The best housing in the community was Wentworth Gardens" (cited in Atlas & Dreier, 1993).

Wentworth activists were most attracted to the type of housing available – townhouses and low-rise three-story apartment buildings, rather than high-rises, the other available type of family public housing. Several activists found the townhouse units especially desirable because they were most like single-family houses. This was true for Geraldine Scott,

---

[12] Rossi (1955) gives one of the earliest statements of this explanation of why families move.

who moved into a townhouse in 1990 with her seven children, and found
it to be "a God send," "just like a house."[13] Tecora Butler, a resident since
1977, particularly noted that her townhouse was like a home because it
had both a front and a back entrance and a yard:

I can walk right out of my front door.... I can walk right out of my back door.
I really likes that way you have two ways out.... I can get out there [the yards] and
plant me a few little greens and stuff and get little flowers and stuff together.

Decorative shutters added to the buildings sometime after construction,
according to the older-generation activists, also contributed to the image
of a home. The Wentworth activists' preference for the townhouse units
is not surprising. In the United States the normative dwelling type and
the dominant cultural ideal are the single-family dwelling (Hayden, 1984),
and the townhouse is the closest approximation as a multifamily housing
type in public housing.

Many Wentworth activists explicitly stated that they had rejected, when
offered, an apartment in a high-rise public housing development. Some
waited several years for an apartment in a low-rise development. Recall
that Lottie Weathersby would not accept living in a high-rise – "I wanted
nothing highrise." Reasons typically centered on the "bad reputation,"
violent crime, crowding, poor maintenance, and difficulties and safety
issues posed for child rearing. For instance, Juanita Brown, who has lived
in Wentworth since 1960, emphatically asserted that she would not live in
a high-rise:

It's too many people stacked up on each other. Okay, I was a young women when
they were building them [developments], all highrise. And I said then, "That's
trouble." You cannot stack too many people's in one place. You got trouble. And
honey, we've been having trouble ever since.

Dorothy McMiller applied for a low-rise CHA development but was offered an apartment at Stateway Gardens, a high-rise development located
near Wentworth east of the Dan Ryan Expressway. She declined because

I don't like heights. I wouldn't keep my kids in no [high-rise] – [it is] not good for
raising children. A place with just one door, no porch, no place for kids.

Marcella Carter also would not tolerate living in a high-rise development.
She vehemently stated:

In my opinion, they should knock them suckers down. They should blow [them
up].... You know I was looking on T.V. one time and I saw they ... put bombs
all around these, this big building [in Pruitt Igoe, Saint Louis] and they blew that
sucker up. They need to blow them big tall ones down. Fifty, sixty, some people that

---

[13] *Geraldine Scott* is a pseudonym for the one resident activist we interviewed who asked that
her actual name not be used.

living . . . on top [of one another]. . . . They're not doing everything in the buildings, and they're not making it decent for the residents.

In contrast, when offered a three-story walk-up apartment, Wentworth activists accepted, considering these apartments preferable to high-rise alternatives. Although the apartments are not large, all activists living in the three-story walk-up apartments found them ample to meet their space needs, particularly in comparison to their prior living arrangements. Barbara Andrews stated she liked her two-bedroom walk-up apartment because "I think because it's small and it's quaint. I mean, it is so, it is so cuddly. . . . I really don't need a whole lot of room for me and my [two] sons."

Other reasons the activists gave for requesting Wentworth Gardens over other public housing developments included that it was attractive, well maintained, and beautifully landscaped and in a convenient location.[14] The well tended grounds and gardens and a fountain located on the most visible corner of the development, 39th Street and the Dan Ryan Expressway, were unique characteristics of Wentworth and helped to explain the significance that residents attributed to these features when they described their initial attraction to Wentworth Gardens. When Beatrice Harris applied for public housing, she specifically asked for Wentworth Gardens, although she anticipated difficulties in getting in because it was "beautiful":

I use to live right down here where Sox Park is. . . . I would pass Wentworth and she [a friend] would say, "[T]his is a beautiful place"; and I said, "I hate to look at it 'cause I know I'd never be able to live in a place like that." I didn't know anything about it. It was just that it was so beautiful, and so I just felt like . . . how was I gonna get up in here.

As Mrs. Harris did, Tecora Butler, who has lived at Wentworth for over two decades, persisted in pressing the CHA until she was granted an apartment at Wentworth:

I had already, before I moved from the West Side, put in for [public] housing and they had sent me a number of places like Stateway. I didn't want that [high-rise development] and so I sent back [for another development]. . . . In passing we would see Wentworth over here and it looked so beautiful and so quiet over here. . . . In that corner up there they had . . . bunch a little flowers and stuff over there. . . . So I changed and I refilled my papers and, uh, put down Wentworth. And [it took] so long getting in here. I kept waiting and waiting; and I kept calling, calling. . . . They kept saying they didn't have nothing vacant. So I went and called them one day and I told them, I said, "They fixin' to condemn this . . . where I'm in . . . and I got to

---

[14] The frequency of reasons Wentworth activists volunteered for choosing Wentworth are as follows: preferred townhouse units, not a high-rise, $N = 9$ (41%); attractive, $N = 6$ (27%); well maintained, $N = 4$ (18%); landscaping, $N = 2$ (9%); location, $N = 2$ (9%).

have somewhere to go." I said, "Y'all don't have nothing that I can get down there [Wentworth Gardens]?" So the lady told me, "We don't have but one vacant." So they had after I saw her, they had that one all the time! . . . So I said, "Well, I'll take that."

According to Bertha McKinney, it was the gardens on all four corners and the decorative fountain that particularly drew her attention when she moved into Wentworth, in 1982, with her three children:

The outskirts of Wentworth were so beautiful they would catch your eye because they had, like, um, a statue or running falls. Like a little waterfalls right here on the corner.

For Mrs. Butler, Wentworth was not only eye-catching, but conveniently located as well, accessible to mass transit, schools, and medical facilities. Bertha McKinney agreed:

I mean, see, if I get on the train, I'm six minutes from the Loop [Chicago's historic downtown]. I could take Wentworth's bus and go to the Loop. I could take State Street bus and go to the Loop. . . . Because I'm right at Halsted little shopping area, Lake Meadows, the Loop . . . and I can take any of these buses. This bus right here will take me to Plaza.

As we have seen, Wentworth activists were drawn to this development over other CHA housing, in part, because it defied their negative images of public housing – "Oooh, it is so pretty!" (Faye Perteet). Even though Wentworth's architectural design is characterized by the repetitive, austere modern style that is distinctive of all CHA housing, it appears that the most prominent attractions of Wentworth were those design details that contributed to an image of home: its low-rise dwelling types were surrounded by attractive landscaping, and, most importantly, it was not a high-rise development.

Once Wentworth activists, particularly the older generation, moved into the development, they were not disappointed. Their memories of the development in its "better days" were quite salient – better physical and social conditions. There was general agreement among these residents that, in the past, Wentworth was a well maintained development with well cared for buildings and grounds, attentive management, strict policies regarding acceptable tenant behavior, friendly and helpful neighbors, and little crime. Wentworth activists especially remembered the well kept interior landscaping: "The lawns were nice; the grass was nice" (Marcella Carter), and there were ample benches for adult socializing and children's play equipment located throughout the Wentworth grounds. The organization of buildings around small courtyards with play equipment allowed residents the opportunity to supervise their children and maintain general surveillance over these common areas.[15] Mary Rias, a resident since 1965, explained how she, like her neighbors, would restrict children's play to the areas around the house, so that they could be properly supervised from the apartment windows and front door. Mrs. Rias remembered, "Well, . . . the kids could get out and play; they didn't fight."

As Mary Rias has, other older-generation activists have shared memories of a past when residents acted responsibly, adhering to appropriate child rearing and housekeeping standards. They remembered how well residents supervised their children and maintained their apartments, buildings, and landscaped areas. They also noted the strict CHA policies supporting such standards. According to Beatrice Harris:

It was such rules that if they found an envelope outside with your name on it and you hadn't picked it up, you had to pay a fine. They would fine you heavily, and honey, people was cleaning up and picking up, and they wasn't causing no problems. It was really nice.

Juanita Brown commented similarly:

The upkeep of your apartment, you keep that up yourself. You couldn't let your child empty the garbage. That was good. . . . O.K. When they come in and made inspection of your house, that mean they'd inspect the walls, the floors . . . do you understand. The sink, the cabinets, and all of this. And at that time those people knew to keep this up. You couldn't put holes in the walls. You couldn't let your kids ride the doors down.

Older-generation activists believed that CHA's strict tenant screening and housekeeping regulations attracted residents with proper standards. Ella Fitzgerald noted that the CHA checked that she was paying the rent in her private market apartment before granting her a lease in 1958; Beatrice Harris stated that when she moved to Wentworth in 1966, they asked for her marriage licence and allowed only working families to rent in public housing. Other resident activists agreed that altered CHA policies contributed to their current problems. Ella Fitzgerald observed, "They just move anybody in." Juanita Brown explained that, in the past, tenant screening and housekeeping regulations helped prevent this problem:

They [management] don't care who they put in here. It wasn't like that before. They would interview you; they would . . . [review] your record, they'd make trips to see if you're up keeping your place; and stuff like that. They would not just take it on your word. . . . See when I moved in here [in 1960], they [management] had rules and they [residents] abide by them rules. . . . When they stopped all this, that was the wrongest thing for them to do.

---

[15] Cooper, Marcus, and Sarkissian (1986), in their research-based design guidelines for housing with children, noted the importance of contained areas visible from apartments where children could play.

A well maintained development also was attributed to "cooperative" management personnel. Mary Rias remembered:

[When] management was better [in the past]. You could walk around and see what you wanted [repaired]. . . . Then I'd go up to the office and tell [management] . . . and get it fixed in one day.

The older-generation residents, such as Maggie Mahone, who moved into Wentworth in 1964, were on good terms with early managers and even looked back on a few of them with fondness:

Then it [good maintenance] had a lot to do with our management. We had managers here who really took pride in trying to help the neighbors. . . . We had Mr. Charles Gordon. He was a good manager. . . . Yeah, you know, you could go up to them and tell to them . . . what you wanted and they would try to help you.

When speaking about Wentworth's better past, residents recalled more than Wentworth's attractive, well tended physical setting; equally important was Wentworth's community life. Virtually all the older-generation residents spoke with great emotion about their interactions and bonds with their neighbors in their earlier years at Wentworth.[16] According to Maggie Mahone: "It was really nice when I moved here [in 1964]. The people seemed to be more together and more neighborly." Wentworth's friendly and supportive community life was attributed, in part, to the small size of the development. Younger-generation activists concurred that Wentworth's size was still a positive feature. Desiree Davis explained: "[I]t's not a large community. It's only 422 [units]." Carol Robinson observed, "It's such a small complex, that everybody knows everybody." And Marcella Bryant added, "If you don't know the parents, you know the children."

The small size of the development and related perceptions of neighborliness of its residents also were associated with the older-generation activists' memories of Wentworth's past as a safer community, with little to no crime. Janie Dumas explained: "It's a small place and, you know, I feel free here. . . . I feel that I'm not afraid." Dorothy McMiller noted that she did not feel the need to lock her doors: "Every year I used to go out of town and spend like a whole month and . . . no bars and no nothin' on my door. Just close my door . . . it just like I left it."

These residents' reasoning about the small size of the development and resultant neighborliness and feeling of safety and security corresponds to similar arguments proposed by housing researchers, in particular, McCarthy and Saegert (1979). Using the theory of social overload, they

---

[16] Two older-generation activists stated that initially they valued their privacy and had little interaction with their neighbors. With time, however, they developed neighborly relationships.

sought to explain the experiences of alienation and higher crime rates in high-rise than in low-rise housing, focusing in particular on public housing developments. They theorized that in higher-density housing, residents were unable to know all their neighbors and to discern strangers from residents; the large numbers of residents living in the building exceeded an individual's cognitive capacities for recognition. In contrast, in a low-rise development, it is possible to know all of one's neighbors, to develop neighborly social relationships, and to reach an accord about acceptable behavior.

Wentworth's activists' memories of a better past were the foundation of their deeply held attachments to the homeplace and community they called home. They provided a standard against which current conditions were assessed, and a standard to aspire to in their actions to resist the deterioration of the material surrounds of their homeplace.

"The Change Has Been for the Worse" (Juanita Brown): Wentworth Gardens Today

Juanita Brown, and the other older-generation activists, agreed that the conditions at Wentworth Gardens have deteriorated:

Tremendous changes. And the changes haven't been for [the] good. . . . The changes have been for the worse.

Unlike public housing built in the 1970s and later, Wentworth's dilapidated buildings and grounds cannot be explained by poor materials and construction; rather, they are due to age and lack of maintenance. In addition, decreases in funding for social and recreational services for CHA residents created further burdens on Wentworth activists' struggles to maintain the viability of their home. When they were developing the Wentworth RMC, resident activists called upon one of the authors, Roberta Feldman, to conduct an independent architecture and engineering assessment.[17] The report found that deferred maintainance had become a serious problem. The buildings were well constructed masonry structures but needed substantial renovation, including tuckpointing, roof repairs or replacements, and concrete repairs. Mechanical, plumbing, and electrical systems were beyond industry standards for useful life. Site conditions – exterior lighting, streets and walkways, parking areas, play areas, and landscaped areas – were in such bad condition that they posed physical hazards. The

---

[17] Roberta Feldman, through the City Design Center, was asked to arrange for an assessment of the viability of Wentworth's buildings and site for the Wentworth RMC. Feldman asked Michael Gelick, a professor in the School of Architecture at the University of Illinois at Chicago, to prepare an architecture and engineering report.

report also noted health hazards including raw sewage and feral cat and rat infestations.

The consultants' reports corroborated activists' assessments of Wentworth's poor present, physical conditions; yet the findings were hardly heartening. The older-generation resident activists' assessments were all the more poignant because they were described in explicit contrast to better past conditions. Marcella Carter remembered:

[W]hen I first moved in [Wentworth in 1972] it was beautiful. The lawns was nice; the grass was nice; the apartments were nice. . . . But, uh, now I don't like it because . . . the whole development looks terrible.

Wentworth's dilapidated buildings and grounds, unresponsive management and poor maintenance, crime, and inadequate social services were particularly striking. Furthermore, many of the difficult living conditions these residents sought to escape by moving to Wentworth were now the very problems they had to contend with: problems that posed risks to their health, safety, and security. In the early 1990s, Beatrice Harris spoke with considerable dismay about potentially dangerous physical conditions at Wentworth (see chapter 1), but potholes and roof leaks were not the only safety and health hazards. Juanita Brown added:

[L]ook we got lead in here. . . . Some apartments have roaches, rats and stuff like that. And unhealthy conditions.

Over the past five decades, the original laundromats, children's play equipment, and much of the other outdoor landscaping were in such poor condition that they were dismantled. Lucille Perry, who first lived at Wentworth as a child and returned as a resident in 1987 with her own children, observed:

[T]hey tore down the whole, the things [playground equipment] in the backyards for the walk-ups. We used to have swings and [seesaw] boards. . . . Yeah, they have took them. Now it's just a backyard with concrete in it. So the kids really don't have nothing to do now but play ball out there.

The play equipment described by Lucille was not even properly removed, leaving jagged ends of former pipes jutting up from the ground, presenting a safety hazard.

Marcella Carter puts the blame for Wentworth's dilapidated conditions squarely on the shoulders of HUD and CHA:

We don't have decent, we don't have sanitary, we don't have safe housing! 'Cause the housing inside the apartments need remodeling. That's the decent. Safe, sanitary . . . out there now, all the sewages in here is messed up and they smelling inside your apartment. What is coming up in my bathtub every morning, the water is coming up in there on its own; it can't be safe.... They promised safe, decent, sanitary housing, and I think they [HUD and CHA] failed us.

For Mrs. Carter, the solution is obvious:

Have them [CHA renovate the buildings] up into the '90s. Come out of the '40s, back into the '90s. Wentworth was built in 1945 so they still back there in 1945. They need to come up to 1990s.

She noted that without adequate government budgets for the repair of the buildings and grounds, Wentworth would continue to deteriorate.

In addition to the need for total building and grounds rehabilitation, resident activists have been especially frustrated by the on-site CHA management's unresponsiveness to their everyday repeated requests for improved maintenance. Carole Robinson, a resident since the early 1970s, asserted:

Definitely, the maintenance isn't good. People need kitchen sinks . . . they [CHA on-site maintenance] always say they don't have any.... [People need] screens. And they say, "Well, next week we'll put all the little screen doors up...." But they never do it.

Mary Rias complained that unlike in the past, requests for maintenance may take years:

[T]hey don't take care of them [the buildings] good a lot; like they used to.... [L]ike if I need something did to my house, I wouldn't have to wait no two years or three years.

Unlike the attentive, resident-friendly management of the past, current on-site management "don't care," assert Wentworth activists such as Juanita Brown:

You see, the managers that they've been getting ain't [good] . . . because they're there for a pay check. Now do I need to say more? I don't need to say more.... Because we used to have good managers that did their job.... Even the janitors, how can the managers say that the janitors ain't doing their job and the manager ain't doing his job?

Inadequate operating budgets and a sharp decrease in the number of janitorial personnel also are faulted for Wentworth's poor physical conditions. Mrs. Carter admonished:

They [janitors] don't have no supplies up there. They don't have no lawn mowers; they don't have nothing. The grass is growing up everywhere. So how you gonna sit up in the office and you doing your job and you don't have nothing up there.... Lot of the repairs can't be done because the working people don't have supplies.

Even when the buildings and grounds are repaired, activists such as Desiree Davis observed that often the work is done improperly:

[I]t's like when they had sandblasted the bricks, and, you know, and then they put the windows in. They have people to come in and do the job so rapidly, it's not properly done.[18]

Activists also expressed the concern that the repair and remodeling have been done without ttheir consultation. For instance, when Wentworth's central courtyard was renovated, the residents were not asked about their needs or interests. As a result, according to Faye Perteet,

They built a new playground up here but they built it for little, little kids . . . not the medium size kids, where they could go and swing or play and whatever.

Hallie Amey, president of Wentworth's Resident Management Corporation (RMC), expressed a related concern about the RMC's ability to maintain this courtyard space. She recognized that if the residents had played a role in its design, they might have developed a sense of ownership and pride in the courtyard: That is, they might have formed place attachments that would have motivated them to care for the courtyard. Research on participatory design, in which users play an active role in environmental decision making, supports Hallie Amey's contention. Francis and associates (1987), in a review of the literature, concluded that participatory design not only contributes to greater user satisfaction with the physical setting but enhances the likelihood of care and concern for the setting as well.

Apart from maintenance issues, resident activists were concerned about increased illegal activities in the buildings and on the grounds of Wentworth. Gangs and their drug dealings and drug use were the most prominent current crime problems. When asked what she liked least about living at Wentworth, Carol Robinson answered, "It's mostly like the gangs." Mae Francis Jones said it was drugs:

Well, the way the peoples are into drugs. . . . People is taking drugs. And that's something that [it] seems like I can't get over.

Activist parents were particularly concerned about keeping their children away from gangs and drugs. One younger-generation activist, Lucille Perry, explained, "My son never liked the projects because of gangs and different things, so we never did hang around here." Faye Perteet, also a younger-generation activist, was exasperated about the drug problem at

---

[18] New windows were installed in most of Wentworth's buildings in the early 1990s, but many did not fit properly or were not installed properly with appropriate trim and caulking.

Wentworth but believed that it was not very different anywhere else she could afford to live:

I mean I got tired.... Okay, I used to live on 71st.... Sometimes you could see the drugs actually, you know, exchanging.... And my kids would see that and I would try my best to keep them away from that. But I see, when I got out here [Wentworth], it's still the same thing; and I'm wondering, should I move again. And I'm like, no, because wherever I go, it's going to be the same.

Despite the concern among all resident activists about Wentworth's crime problems, statements of apprehension were frequently followed by remarks, like those of Maggie Mahone, an activist on security issues, that crime is worse in other CHA developments:

The kids are not so bad [at Wentworth] where you hear like in other [CHA] communities that they are doing a lot of shooting. Mostly, it's the drugs; that's the worse thing we have.

Bertha McKinney believes crime is committed by a very small number of Wentworth residents: "only one or two percent of little bad fellas or people that you have around." Wentworth activists' perceptions are supported by crime statistics that indicate that Wentworth has the lowest incidence of crime of all CHA family developments.

For many of the activists, crime at Wentworth also is less of a concern because of widespread social bonds among residents. According to Marcella Carter, "Everybody knows everybody," and this condition makes her less afraid of criminal activity at Wentworth Gardens:

I've been here so long that everyone knows me. So, I don't worry about crime too much. I don't worry about people breaking in my house. I don't worry about, if I come in at two or three o'clock in the morning somebody will end up behind me and knock me out.

Barbara Andrews was fearful when she moved in, but with time she found that she need not be because her neighbors watched out for her:

[M]y neighbors, they know that this is my first time living in a housing development.... This lady [neighbor]... come to the apartment, check up on me. If they see someone coming to my apartment that they're not used to seeing, you know, they'll kind of peep out of the peephole.... I like that because when I first moved up here I was scared. If I was out at night, I stayed where I was at. But I like it [now] because like, even the guys that hang out outside, they don't really know you but they know who should be in my apartment and who shouldn't. So, if anything happen, they pretty much aware. Because, if someone come over to see me and I'm not at home, they'll say,... "Barbara, who was that guy that was up knocking on your door last night?"... So if something ever happen, someone would know.

As Wentworth residents have, Rohe and Burby (1988), in their investigation of fear of crime in public housing, observed that residents' feelings of safety were related to their belief in their neighbors' intervention in difficult situations.

Irrespective of Wentworth's relatively lower crime statistics and residents' positive perceptions of lower crime rates when compared with other CHA developments, resident activists wanted safety and security improved. All believed that better and more consistent policing was necessary. Desiree Davis:

I don't like the people selling the dope.... I think it could be in control.... [We're] supposed to have police protection. You know, like I said, they might do it for a moment and then...they stop worrying about it anymore. It lasts a month and then it stops.

Resident activists also called for increased social service and drug programs. They associated crime at Wentworth with decreases in social services, especially activities for youth and drug prevention and rehabilitation programs. A decrease in social services, in general, was a central concern for the activists, who, as we will see in subsequent chapters, have attempted to fill the gaps.

The results of a Wentworth residents needs assessment survey completed in 1998 confirmed that in general Wentworth residents' assessments of their development were similar to those we found in our interviews with and observations of activists.[19] The survey findings revealed dissatisfaction with poor physical conditions, inadequate social and youth services, and poor management and maintenance.[20] But half of the residents who responded to the survey approved overall of the Wentworth community; Wentworth residents were generally satisfied with safety in their apartments and neighborhood, their apartment conditions when compared with

[19] In 1998, the Wentworth RMC board asked one of the authors, Roberta Feldman, to assist them in conducting a resident needs assessment survey. They sought to use the survey as a community organizing strategy and to identify Wentworth residents' priorities for action when the RMC assumed full management. The RMC board was a full participant in the study development and implementation. A committee was formed and worked with Feldman's research assistant, Khari Hunt, to design the self-administered survey. The committee determined the survey questions and their wording. Respondents were asked to rate the importance of and their satisfaction with a range of both positive and negative characteristics of the development. The committee distributed the survey to every household, with a request that an adult member of the household respond. Twenty-seven percent of the residents returned the survey to the RMC office.

[20] The indicators that were considered highly important and were rated as unsatisfactory were heat in winter, playground equipment, child care facilities, counseling and social services, RMC and LAC equal treatment of all residents, residents' knowledge of whom to contact when they have a management problem; maintenance staff responsiveness and quality of work, and residents' knowlege of the RMC's role in the community.

average living conditions, and residents' pride and participation in their community.[21]

"[A]IN'T NOBODY PUTTIN' ME OUT.": PLACE ATTACHMENT AT WENTWORTH

I care about where I live, and I want everybody here to feel the same way. This is our community. This is our home. . . . And I'm telling, ain't nobody puttin' me out. If you feel like that, you better get out there and do something. . . . I love this place, you hear me! I love this place. (Beatrice Harris, RMC community meeting, Field notes June 28, 1997)

With an emphatic "No!" the vast majority of Wentworth activists, when asked whether they had any mobility desires or plans in the foreseeable future, asserted their intention to remain at Wentworth.[22] Hallie Amey explained that even though she had other housing options, she chose not to move:

Now you see, I'm a senior citizen, and it's by my choice that I'm still in CHA cuz I could live almost anywhere now. I am retired and I have enough to live in a moderate place if I'd want to, but I choose to live there [Wentworth].

Resident activists understand that they have few, if any, better affordable housing options than Wentworth, yet they do not portray themselves as trapped. Quite to the contrary, when speaking about their realistic options, they state that they have no plans or desires to move because they like where they live. For instance, Evelyn Ramsey, who earlier shared that she was "forced to stay" in public housing because of income constraints, reported in another interview that only a wrecking ball would drive her out of Wentworth. As Mrs. Ramsey does, Desiree Davis refuses to move, stating that she will remain "until they tear it down."

Wentworth activists' words and actions were filled with expressions of homeplace attachments[23] (see Feldman, 1988, for a review of place

---

[21] Those indicators that received a high importance rating and were positively rated for satisfaction were apartment safety and security, neighborhood safety, resident pride in their community, apartments that meet average living standards, condition of apartment plumbing, potable water in apartments, residents' participation in volunteer activities, residents and community leaders work well together.

[22] Three activists maintained aspirations to own a "real house," but they recognized that their desire for the American ideal home – ownership of a single-family residence – was out of their financial reach. For example, Marcella Carter lamented, "If I could, if I had the money, I would buy me a house." Only one long-term activist explicitly stated that she wanted to move but could not afford an apartment in the private market.

[23] The frequency of volunteered indicators of attachment to homeplace are as follows: it is my "home," $N = 22$ (100%); it is my "community" $N = 22$ (100%); a sense of belonging, at-ease, and comfort, $N = 22$ (100%); sense of responsibility or duty to care for and maintain homeplace, $N = 22$ (100%); sense of ownership, $N = 8$ (36%).

attachment indicators). In addition to stating intentions to continue to live at Wentworth, the activists we interviewed expressed several other indications of deeply experienced attachments – both to the physical surrounds and to their neighbors. All of the activists called Wentworth their "home," a place in which they felt embedded, a part; comfortable and at ease. According to Desiree Davis:

It feels like home.... Like you're home. You know. Like you're in your own home. You can be yourself. Right, comfortable.

Several activists explicitly mentioned that they had developed a sense of ownership of their homes, despite their renter status. Lottie Weathersby explained:

And I feel if you've lived in a place and paid rent for twenty years you pretty well own that place.... I'm here to stay.

For the activists, Wentworth is not only their homeplace; it is also their "community." Even with their current difficult and unsafe housing conditions, and their warranted concerns about the future viability of Wentworth, resident activists still speak with conviction about the positive aspects of living at Wentworth, especially its supportive social life. The younger-generation activist Susan Donald states:

[T]his is one thing that I've always found fortunate about Wentworth: I think Wentworth has always had, it's always been close knit. You know, and the people still really care and love each other. You know, and they care about what happens. Because like I said, they watched these kids grow up. They were, they were here from the time they was crawling until the time they're walking around now.

According to all of the activists, community life not only remains the most positive quality of everyday life at Wentworth, but is a key source of their attachments to and their reason for remaining at Wentworth. Bertha McKinney:

[I]t's the people. Because, I guess if it was the housing, I would have been gone. But it's just like a big family here. In a lot of ways. [I know] just about everybody. And most all the children I know by names.

Janie Dumas concurs:

I like [everybody].... I know everyone in here, you know, most of them. So I'm just still here.

Marc Fried (1963), in his seminal paper "Grieving for a Lost Home," observed the "highly disruptive and disturbing experience" of so-called slum removal (p. 151). He described, through the poignant words of prior West End residents of Boston, their strong positive attachments to their former neighborhood and the "intense, deeply felt, and, at times, overwhelming" grief they experienced when an urban renewal project forcibly dislocated them from their community (p. 151). The West End was one among many lower-income neighborhoods that were razed in the name of urban renewal. As in the West End, residents of these neighborhoods were not consulted about these renewal plans; rather, they were evicted without the opportunity to return to the redeveloped communities because, typically, they could not afford the new apartments (Wright, 1981).

According to Herbert Gans (1962), who also studied the West End both before and after its redevelopment, this neighborhood was not a slum despite the somewhat dilapidated building exteriors and crowded living conditions. Rather, it was a vital ethnic community characterized by close social ties and strong psychological ties to the neighborhood. For the politicians and professionals who planned this urban renewal project, and the Boston public more generally, residents' understandings of their community remained invisible: "[A]ll of Boston was convinced that the West End was a slum which ought to be torn down not only for the sake of the city but also for the good of its own residents" (Gans, 1962, p. 287). Slum removal for the benefit of the residents without their consultation was not a new idea. From the mid-19th century on, social reformers sought to "uplift the poor" through slum clearance (von Hoffman, 1996; Wright, 1980). The satisfactions residents gained from living in these communities and the positive attachments they experienced remained opaque to outsiders, who saw only physical deterioration.

Vale (1997), in his explanation of why Boston public housing residents had no desire to move irrespective of their dilapidated housing conditions, drew similar conclusions:

Ultimately those who express the desire to stay on indefinitely in public housing are those who have lived there the longest and who have formed the most durable social attachments. They wish to stay not because of physical conditions or management efficiency, but because the place has become their home and neighborhood. (p. 168)

As Fried, Gans, and Vale had, we found that all of the Wentworth resident activists expressed their strong sense of being involved with and intimately psychologically bonded with a geographically based social group and that these social attachments largely explained residents' decisions not to move. Perhaps the most striking expression of Wentworth activists' attachments to the homeplace is not only their shared concern, commitment, and determination to remain at Wentworth, but their willingness to engage in the ongoing struggles necessary to make Wentworth a better place to live. Hallie Amey:

I feel like I have something to give to the community, and that's what I'm about. I do not plan to leave there at present until I've finished what I'm about doing now.

The relationship between place attachments and actions to improve one's home and neighborhood has been well documented. Community and environmental psychologists have observed that the greater the intensity of psychological attachments to places, the greater the extent of participation in neighborhood organizations (reviewed in Saegert, 1989). Susan Saegert and Helene Clark (1989), in their study of low-income women's actions to form cooperative housing in New York, also observed that residents who were attached to their homeplaces were more likely to engage in actions to improve their buildings, and these actions, in turn, contributed to an increasing intensity of place attachments to these homeplaces: That is, attachment to place is a developmental process. At Wentworth, similarly, attachments to place have motivated actions to sustain the viability of the homeplace, and through these actions, place attachments have grown in intensity, thus stimulating further resident activism.

Wentworth activists' actions to improve their development not only are motivated by their intense attachments to their physical and social environment, but are guided as well by their shared memories of Wentworth's better past and their hopes for its better future. Juanita Brown:

I hope to see it improve before I die. Hope to see, even just to put it back like it was when I moved in here. I would be happy, you know.

The younger-generation activists, who do not have their own memories of a better past, develop understandings through long-term activists' mentoring: Tecora Butler described how activists share their experiences of this past:

Yeah, we talk about . . . how it used to be and how it is now, the difference in it now and what it used to be.

These memories of a better past are not simply wistful longings for better days, but rather an impetus for and frame of reference to guide activists' present actions and future plans for the types of improvements they seek. Lottie Weathersby:

You know, there's just so much difference from then and now, and that's why we're working to try to get Wentworth back where it used to be. . . . And this is why I'm working as hard as I'm working.

Lottie Weathersby reminds us that it is through this hard work that Wentworth Gardens has become a reflection of the activists' attachments:

It's not where you live, it's how you live; it's how you keep up where you live.

It is through the activists' individual and collective efforts and stubborn hope that Wentworth Gardens has become a symbol of their forbearance.

Saegert (1989) cautions, however, that recollecting a better past and hoping for a better future may provide a guide for action but do not necessarily lead to action. Rather, in her study of low-income cooperative housing in New York City, African-American co-op residents who were not linked to their neighborhood through multifaceted social ties and activities and therefore did not have a context for effective action experienced a sense of futility. In contrast, those co-op residents who were intimately attached to and actively participated in the social life of their community did have a context to work collectively to improve their housing conditions.

As we will see in the upcoming chapters on the Wentworth activists' everyday resistance, for several decades, they have been building strong social bonds and organizing their community for collective actions to appropriate the material surrounds of their housing development to improve their and their neighbors' everyday lives. Yet older-generation activists, such as Ella Fitzgerald, recognized that it would not be easy to "try to get it back together like it was. It can be done. But it's gonna take some hard work." Resident activists remain optimistic that their hard work will pay off. Juanita Brown agreed:

I'd like to see Wentworth grow; and Wentworth gonna' grow too, you believe me. Wentworth is gonna get up and sparkle and everybody is gonna' be talking about it, and want to get into Wentworth.

Along with the other public housing residents who marched downtown on Juneteenth Day, Wentworth activists do not seek the status quo; rather, they want the choice to remain in their development, not as it stands today, but as it could be, as good as it was in the past. Jamie Dumas:

[A]s we go through and work together . . . it's gonna be a beautiful place and this place is gonna bloom up. Really, that's what I really see true here.

PART III

EVERYDAY RESISTANCE IN THE EXPANDED PRIVATE SPHERE

4

The Community Household

The Foundation of Everyday Resistance

> Everybody is like a family ... like everybody looks out for each other. ...
> Some people don't have a telephone; they'll let you use their telephones. ...
> You receive calls there or whatever. Anything that's needed you can always
> go to any of your neighbors and ask for it and get it.
>
> Monica Ramsey, Wentworth Gardens resident activist

Weather permitting, Mrs. Mary Rias can be found on her "front porch,"
a small slab of concrete in front of her townhouse apartment, sitting in a
worn lawn chair supervising the children playing in front. If not on her
front porch, she often can be found in her kitchen preparing meals, not
only for her family, but for her neighbors as well. Her apartment is located
next to the abundant community garden that she coordinated and worked
in for over a decade. For Mrs. Rias, the distinction between the space and
activities of her home and those of her development blur. Her caretaking
and nurturing roles in the private space of her home spill outside her doors
into the community, and often the needs of community members are met
within her home.

A mother of five children and grandmother of nine grandchildren,
Mrs. Rias moved into Wentworth on November 13, 1965, with her husband
and three children. She remembers the exact date of that move because, in
her own words, "I was so glad to get here." As nearly all of the more senior
activists had, she migrated to Chicago from the South, in her case rural
Mississippi. The oldest of 10 children, she had to quit school at the beginning of 10th grade to work in the fields. At 28 years of age she moved up
to Chicago to work in a succession of jobs – for a cleaners and in hotels and
restaurants, primarily as a cook. Mrs. Rias stopped her paid work in 1979
in order to care for her disabled daughter, who is now in her 30s.

A widow since 1988, with five grown children, and currently in her 60s,
Mrs. Rias "watches" up to 10 children every weekday during the
school year. These include two foster children who live with her, four

of her own grandchildren, and two grandchildren of another activist, Mrs. Hallie Amey. She also assumes the responsibility for any of the Wentworth children who are within view, whether to assist a child in need or to scold a child for misbehavior.

Mrs. Rias knows all of her neighbors and often spends her free time, in her words, "neighboring." This may include cooking for individuals in the community who are ill, such as her next-door neighbor, Lucille, or preparing food for large groups of residents for a neighbor's funeral or community event. Mary Rias equates her cooking with her special role in the Wentworth development:

I always cook for the residents. If somebody needs some food, I always cook it here. Everybody in here know me . . . from cookin'. . . . [W]hen peoples know you, and you can help peoples. People call me and ask me, "Can I have a cake? Can I have some food?" That just makes people know me.

In addition to her culinary skills, Mrs. Rias engages in other forms of informal helping including assisting senior citizens in the development with filling out CHA forms, running errands, and caring for them when they are ill.

As many other activists do, Mrs. Rias explains that her motivation for volunteering her time at Wentworth stemmed from her maternal concern; in particular, she wanted additional eyes and ears to watch out for her children:

I wanted to get involved because I had one boy, and I had four girls. And I wanted to get out 'cause my kids was growing up and when they do things, I say, "Well, maybe I know peoples and they can kind of tell me what they doin'."

But what began as a personal concern for her own children soon extended to a larger concern for her community:

I just like workin' in the community and I like workin' with people.

Mary Rias's informal helping within the Wentworth community has led seamlessly to her more formal community organizing efforts. She responds whenever she is needed. She began her organizing efforts when she took over for Mrs. Juanita Brown as the block captain for one of Wentworth's seven blocks. In addition, Mrs. Amey recruited her to work in the laundromat in 1984. Mrs. Rias volunteered 12 hours per week – 3 hours an evening, four times per week – and quit 4 years later only after her husband died and she had no one to share the care of her daughter. And for the past decade, Mrs. Rias has been working in Wentworth's summer food program "feedin' the children."

In recent years Mary Rias's organizing activities, along with those of the other Wentworth activists, have become more publicly visible. In the later 1980s, she participated in the South Armour Square Neighborhood

Association opposing the construction of the new White Sox stadium, and currently she serves on Wentworth's Resident Management Corporation (RMC) Board. Her roles, as chair of the RMC's Outreach Committee are to "help get the news out" and to get people involved. This recent work has served further to intensify her close bonds with her neighbors. She was clear that in an emergency she would feel comfortable in asking any of these neighbors for help, while always making herself available to assist them in any way she can: "We all just work together."

Perhaps Mrs. Rias's most important role in the community is her designation as the "keeper of the keys." Mrs. Rias:

I have all the keys. The key to the new [RMC] office, to the laundromat. And I had the keys to all the things over here. . . . So I have to get up runnin' every mornin'.

On several occasions, when we arrived at the RMC, the office was closed; but Mrs. Rias, watching the "goings on" from her window, arrived shortly thereafter to open the door. She would invite us in and, typically, call Mrs. Amey, the RMC president, with the announcement "They are here!" Her responsibility is an acknowledgment of her respected place in the community. She earned this responsibility through her years of trustworthy and caring service.

For over three decades, Mary Rias has been committed to and attended to the hard, routine work of creating social bonds in her community. She has worked to build relationships to solve concerns and problems shared by all Wentworth residents. Her participation, like that of other Wentworth women activists, is not elicited by outside institutions nor motivated by monetary reward; rather, it has been rooted in her personal relationships – her feelings of attachment and support within a caring community of involved residents – and her attachments to the physical place she calls home. Mrs. Rias has expanded her familial care and nurturance beyond the boundaries of the private sphere and space of her individual household to include the children of Wentworth, and community residents more generally. She has shared housekeeping and household managerial responsibilities and, at times, economic responsibilities typically associated with the family with her broader community. Mrs. Rias is a member of what Susan Saegert and Jacqueline Leavitt (Saegert, 1989; Leavitt and Saegert, 1990) have called a "community household."

THE COMMUNITY HOUSEHOLD

The activities of women in co-ops linked domestic life and cooperative organization. Leaders and tenants both likened the building to a family. . . . Women leaders knew that all tasks also involved the maintenance of communication and social bonds. . . . The constant attention, both of a physical and social nature, to repetitive and unending demands had much in common with housework. Although the leaders often complained of the incessant demands, they also took pride in their extended homemaking and saw the work as acts of nurturing. (Saegert, 1989, p. 304)

Jacqueline Leavitt and Susan Saegert (1990), in their research on a newly created New York City low-income co-op program, in particular in its implementation in the African-American community of Harlem, used the concept of community household to describe the link between the organization of domestic life and community organizing. They described the community household as "an expanding circle of connection and support, building on the life of the household, but linking its strengths with those of tenants' associations, neighborhoods, cities, and the nation" (p. 172). Saegert (1989) held that the "[c]ommunity household organization extends many of the modes of organization central to domestic life beyond the bounds of the individual household or kin group" (p. 312). Leavitt and Saegert (1990) found that the tenant leaders in the low-income co-op apartment buildings in Harlem were almost always women, the majority, African-American and longtime residents of their building and neighborhood. Women leaders used skills and strategies developed in maintaining their households and dwellings and their small family incomes to organize their neighbors within the co-op building.

Helene Clark (1993), in studying the progress of the co-ops first studied by Leavitt and Saegert, similarly found evidence of the importance of the integration of women residents' social life and organizational effectiveness. According to Clark, several years after their creation, the most successful co-ops "all had a high level of social integration and communication among tenants" (p. 134). When a building was at risk, residents relied on longstanding social ties to organize their actions at the building level. They also relied on shared knowledge about their neighborhood, based on its history, as well as common experiences of poverty and racism to guide their strategies and actions. The strong tenant co-op associations, rooted in rich social networks and a gender-based response to home and community, were essential to the success of the co-op venture.

While Leavitt and Saegert (1990) recognize that the organization of domestic life is an important backdrop to the structure and development of the community household, they do not explicate the linkages between domestic and collective life. Our analysis begins where theirs left off. We describe how the essential work of creating and cultivating social bonds is constructed in the community household. We elaborate upon the community household model to uncover how women's work in extended family networks – of mothering and the work of kinship – is expanded beyond the confines of the nuclear family to include unrelated children, youth, and adult neighbors in the Wentworth development. We then explain how social linkages between domestic life and collective life are made through cooking and sharing food, neighboring, and information sharing. More generally, we will show that the community household serves as the foundation of everyday resistance; we also discuss some of its limits in addressing activists' concerns.

Expanding the Extended Family Network

At Wentworth Gardens, the creation and nurturing of dense, supportive, and cohesive social networks are rooted in women activists' experiences of domestic and social organization. Networks are shaped by the skills and experiences of older black women residents who migrated north from the rural South and who have lived in Wentworth for many years, some for decades. The domestic housekeeping (e.g., rearing children, cooking family meals, doing the laundry, and grocery shopping), norm setting, and conflict resolution skills that these women residents often developed as girls, and then later as mothers, are employed to build social relationships in their community.

For the women activists in Wentworth, the development functions as an extended family network. To support and sustain the social life of the community household, activists care for and about its nonrelated members as if they were their own children and kin. At Wentworth Gardens, the community household members include all of the resident activists and other residents who have entered into relationships with them, especially those they assist. Resident activists describe Wentworth Gardens as a "family community." When speaking about youth in the development, they refer to "our children" or "daughters of our community." And in turn, senior activists may be affectionately called "Mother" by unrelated residents. This community household is inherently place-based, its spatial domain defined by the geographic boundaries of the development – with the exception of prior residents who remain members of the household through frequent visits.

In the Wentworth Gardens development, the organization of the community household begins with women's traditional roles in the work of kinship and, when focused on children, mothering. Although not inherently linked to biological sex, this work is derived from a "socially constructed set of activities and relationships involved in nurturing and caring for people" (Glenn et al., 1994). This work of community othermothering and the work of community kinship are grounded in an ethic of care and provide an important foundation for Wentworth women's community activism.

Community Othermothering. At Wentworth much of the work of the community household is directed toward children by women whom we refer to as "othermothers" (Collins, 1991), community household members who feel and take the responsibility for the care of all of the children in the community. The conditions that create and support othermothering, according to Patricia Hill Collins (1991), are rooted in experiences of slavery. Collins observed:

[T]he African-American cultural value placed on cooperative child care traditionally found institutional support in the adverse conditions under which so many Black women mothered. (1991, p. 120)

Specifically, the structure of networks of bloodmothers and othermothers, developed during slavery, survived emancipation in the rural South, ultimately to be brought north by black women migrants from the South.

Black motherhood, according to Patricia Hill Collins (1991), "consists of a series of constantly renegotiated relationships that African-American women experience with one another, with black children, with the larger African-American community, and with self" (118).[1] Central to black motherhood are women-centered networks of bloodmothers and women who help shoulder mothering responsibilities: othermothers (Collins, 1991, p. 119; see also Troester, 1984). Othermothers can include extended family members, "fictive kin" (Stack, 1974) who informally adopt a child, or neighbors who care for one another's children. Othermothers in the past and today not only provide for community-based child care, but draw on the expanded domestic organization to build community institutions and fight for the welfare of their children (Collins, 1991). Building on Collins's work, Nancy Naples (1992) describes "activist mothering" as a broadened understanding of mothering practices "to comprise all actions, including social activism, that addressed the needs of their children and the community" (p. 448).

In Wentworth, the acceptance of the role of women as othermothers allows women activists to "treat biologically unrelated children as if they were members of their own families" (Collins, 1991, p. 129). A vivid example of the power of the othermother is evident in a brief examination of the life of Faye Perteet, a younger-generation resident activist at Wentworth Gardens. The youngest of 11 children, Faye's mother died in childbirth when she was 5 years old, and by age 13, Faye had become a ward of the state. Moved from the conflict-laden home of her father in Robert Taylor public housing to a foster home, she recalled meeting her first "othermother":

[A]fter I left home and I went to the foster home. The lady there that I call my mother now, took care of me until I turned about ... sixteen or seventeen. ... [S]he took me in as one of her daughters.

---

[1] In her book *Black Feminist Thought*, Patricia Hill Collins (1991) develops an Afrocentric feminist analysis of black motherhood. Her analysis is meant to challenge both white feminist analyses with their limited angle of vision on race, and those of black male scholars who refuse to see beyond a glorification and sanctification of black motherhood.

Also during this period Faye met another woman, a Young Women's Christian Association (YMCA) employee, Alberta McCain,[2] who became another othermother, providing Faye with emotional and material support during her adolescence. Faye:

So, you know ... she was like *another mother* [emphasis ours] to me because every weekend she would take us home with her. ... We would play in her house and she would comb my hair and ... sit downs and have talks. ... But, I really miss her ... because ... when I left the YMCA, I didn't really actually keep in contact with her. And then when I did finally you know, get back with her, it wasn't long after, she died.

The continuity of othermothering in Faye's life is evident in her explanation of why she would like her foster "mother" to live with her and her children at Wentworth:

I want her to come over here with me but she got two great-grandchildren and she wants them; she raises them. And I'm like, you can bring them with you, I mean, you know. So I was thinking about getting a four bedroom, I have a three bedroom now. And I'm thinking about getting a four bedroom so she can come and live with us. And my kids know that she's not my real mother, but they still consider her their grandmother, 'cause that's all they know, you know.

Now in her 30s, Faye, in addition to raising her own three daughters, because of her past experiences with othermothers, has shaped her expressed concern and care for the youth at Wentworth. Faye expressed both a general concern for youth and more specific care for one particular Wentworth youth:

And the kids around here like, some of them ... I take as my own kids, you know. ... I have this young lady, that, well she's a child. Before she went down South and stayed with her father, she used to come to my house and ... everyday, she spends the night, mostly everyday. Her mother's on drugs and we used to feed her. She used to, you know, call me her *second mother* [our emphasis], and everything. ... [I]n a way it made me cry.

As an activist in the RMC, Faye has worked closely with organizers such as Mrs. Hallie Amey and Mrs. Marcella Carter, who provide inspirational guidance to her in her organizational work but also are othermothers to her own children:

Then Miss Amey and Miss Carter and them ... inspired me a little bit to you know, care for people. She [Mrs. Carter] comes by my house sometimes and takes my kids out to lunch or dinner or whatever.

[2] Alberta McCain was a resident activist at Dearborn Homes public housing at the time we initiated our study. She eventually served as the president of the Dearborn Homes Resident Management Corporation until her death in 1990. She was active outside her development as an officer of CHA Residents Taking Action (CHARTA) and also served on Wentworth's RMC Community Advisory Board.

Faye Perteet, Mrs. Carter, and Mrs. Amey, as well as other Wentworth community othermothers, base their actions on an ethic of care and responsibility connected to relationships, rather than on a morality of individual rights (Gilligan 1977). As Collins (1991) explains:

Community othermothers' actions demonstrate a clear rejection of separateness and individual interest as the basis of either community organization or individual self-actualization. Instead, the connectedness with others and common interest expressed by community othermothers models a very different value system. (pp. 131–132)

Black women's ethic of care is built on years of mothering work in their family and the expanded private sphere of the community (see also Gilkes, 1980). Additionally, scholars who have examined the history of black communities have identified a rich helping tradition that children learn as part of their African cultural heritage, a heritage that is strongly associated with the black religious tradition. Researchers observe that African-Americans are more religiously observant than other Americans and that their religious tradition is distinct in its encouragement of the intertwining of religion and civic engagement. This is not surprising when we consider that in the African-American community, the church is the oldest and most resilient social institution and has traditionally been the only black-controlled institution within a history of racial oppression (Putnam, 2000, p. 68). Moreover, Cheryl Gilkes (1985) has estimated that across the various black religious activities, women make up 75% to 90% of the participants.

Nearly all of the Wentworth activists, in discussing their early histories, shared that they had been "raised in the church," and most are still church members and active in a local congregation. Several resident activists mentioned that their parents', most often their mothers,' activism or ministry in the church was an important model for their own church and community work. Activist resident, Ella Fitzgerald, stated, "Church is my home." She recalled that not only her mother, but "all the mothers" in the Mississippi town where she was raised, were involved in the church.

Community othermother, Juanita Brown, also had parental role models of church- and community-involved parents. Born in the South, Mrs. Brown and her family migrated north to Chicago when she was a child. Growing up as the middle child of 12, Juanita Brown described her childhood years as "the most happiest, happiest life, because I came from a big family, and a beautiful family." As a girl, Juanita Brown took her turns caring for the younger children and the household, "which was no problem because, as I say, it was the way we was raised." Mrs. Brown first learned about community work from her parents, who taught her the importance of taking responsibility to care for one's neighbors. Her mother and father were active church members. She recalls that her mother played an essential role in fund-raising to secure a larger church: "[M]y Mama, she did a lot . . . she helped to build this church." Her parents also were actively engaged in assisting those in need in their immediate neighborhood:

I was brought up on 29th and Dearborn. . . . Down there by those projects [Dearborn Homes]. And I can remember them helping peoples that needed help: peoples that was in trouble; peoples that you know, needed food; or there was burnout [fire]; or someone passed.

A grandmother of eight and mother of four, Mrs. Brown has been a Wentworth resident since 1960. The ethic of care and religious tradition of helping others that Mrs. Brown learned as a child she now extends to the youth in Wentworth, treating biologically unrelated children as her own. Mrs. Brown shared:

I have a neighbor that has a handicapped daughter. I help her out. And when she's not there, I get the bus, wait for the bus, bring her daughter in. If she hungry, I feed her.

Recognized as a community othermother by other Wentworth residents, Mrs. Brown often is asked to attend to the needs of neighbors' children:

They [mothers] ask me if I see their children; would I tell them to go in the house and make them stay 'til they gone – they went to the store or they went here or there. O.K.

Because of Mrs. Brown's attentiveness to Wentworth youth and the respect she has for the "younger generation," she believes that they, in return, have respect for her:

My interest is with the young people. . . . And I talk to them. . . . You gotta talk to them like a human being. . . . They understand that. . . . 'Cause I say, "Go to school. Don't waste your life like this [hanging out], you know. You gotta get somewhere high in life, but you can't get there without an education. O.K." That's my whole manner of talking to them. . . . Some of them say, "Thank you, Miss Brown. . . . " That's a way you can win them over, for respect. And every last one of them that hangs out there, they respect me. . . . If I'm gonna give you respect, you give me respect. And they do that.

All of Wentworth activists, whether older or younger generation, function as othermothers in the community. They, as do othermothers in other African-American communities, challenge academic practices that fragment social life and create false separations between the family and the community, mothering and activism, and social reproduction and productive work. In introducing women as community othermothers we are challenging narrow definitions of mothering that point only to its biological and legal expressions.

The Work of Community Kinship. In addition to their traditional domestic roles, women typically have been responsible for the work of kinship (di Leonardo, 1987), a concern about and care for sustaining and supporting relationships with blood relatives and those related by marriage. Motivated by an ethic of care for people outside their family, and rooted in a religious tradition that values community involvement, African-American women activists extend the private sphere work of kinship to their social relationships in the community (Saegert, 1989): what we call *community kinship*. Haywoode (1991) explains, "Extended families and friendship ties are important elements of community life. It is women who build and maintain these relationships; they become the human links in a chain of relationships, concern and social life" (p. 175). The work of community kinship involves responsibilities and social networks that are broader and more diverse than conventional ideas of neighboring. This work begins in building interpersonal neighboring and helping relationships; the work of community kinship extends neighboring to build social cohesiveness among all members of the community household.

The work of kinship within the community household may include creating informal social service networks to providing support for the ill, the shut-in, and the aged; lending money; remembering birthdays; sharing holidays and celebrations; and in other ways establishing and cultivating relationships. Essential to the strength of the community household is the principle of generalized reciprocity – helping someone out without the expectation that you will get anything immediately in return – but with a confidence that sometime in the future either that individual, or someone else, will return the favor. Generalized reciprocity is key to the work of kinship and the establishment of relationships of trust (Putnam, 2000).[3]

We began this chapter with the words of Monica Ramsey, who stated that at Wentworth, "everybody looks out for each other"; indeed, Wentworth activists, as community household members, call upon each other for assistance, as well as others in an even larger network of neighbors and friends in the development. They have established a network of social exchange through the people they assist, who, in turn, provide assistance to them in times of need (see also Stack, 1974).[4] The following are a few specific examples:

---

[3] The proposed importance of generalized reciprocity is adapted from Robert Putman's (2000) argument that the principle of generalized reciprocity is the "touchstone" of social capital (pp. 134–137).

[4] In *All Our Kin*, Carol Stack's (1974) participant observation study of black families in "the Flats," an inner-city midwestern neighborhood, we are introduced to an extensive exchange system among the mostly single women raising children on public assistance. Through her research Stack became aware of "the alliances of individuals trading and exchanging goods, resources, and the care of children, the intensity of their acts of domestic cooperation, and the exchange of goods and services among these persons, both kin and non-kin" (p. 28).

Juanita Brown gives generously of her time and scarce resources to help her neighbors:

They'll [neighbors] say, "Let me have this." . . . If I got it, I'll let them have it. . . . Sometimes . . . we may run a little short of anything before we go to the grocery store or something like that. We're supposed to help each other. That's the way I see it. . . . Anybody in trouble in my building, I'm there. Gonna be there, see what I can do.

Tecora Butler, who was quite active in the church in the small southern town she originated from, now "ministers" to residents in Wentworth Gardens by phone calls to the sick and cooking for and attending to the families of those who have lost loved ones. She described how she participates in community kinship work:

Well, sometimes, you know, just anybody that needs help, [we help] if we can help them. Like this one lady lives in the third apartment from mine. She is kind of sick. . . . Like I go down there laughing and talking, and call her on the phone and talk with her. And if we're cooking something, we always take her food down there. . . . If somebody pass [dies] in the neighborhood, like Stewart – ain't been long before she lost her son – we got out in the neighborhood and took up a little offering and stuff.

And, in turn, Mrs. Butler relies on her neighbors. For instance, she and her neighbors keep watch over what is going in their immediate neighborhood to assure each other's safety. Mrs. Butler:

If I hear of anything going on around the house at night, even if I hear her [neighbor's] door open up late at night, I call her and find out who it is. . . . She do the same thing [for me].

Her neighbor has her key and her son's telephone number in case of an emergency. Mrs. Butler: "Matter of fact, I gave her a key to my door and I got a key to her door."

As it does for Juanita Brown and Tecora Butler, for Bertha McKinney, the work of community kinship also means "looking out for each other." Bertha shared that Wentworth residents monitor the "comings and goings" at the development, including watching each others' apartments when people are away. In an emergency, she related that there are "plenty peoples I could call." First on her list would be residents, Mrs. Marcella Carter, Mrs. Evelyn Ramsey, or her own sister. She also might call upon one of "my little man friends" in the community:

I could maybe look out of that door and one of my little man friends that's down there. I tell them, "Well, come on and take me." Just about any of them out there I [could] ask. I remember once my baby fell off this bicycle and cut his arm. And so the fellas saw him running in, so they came up. "Do you need us to take him to the doctor?" So, it's just good help around. I guess that's why I stay around here. Good, friendly, and they look out for your kids.

Maggie Mahone, a well respected Wentworth activist, has willingly extended support, including financial aid, to her neighbors in times of need without the assurance or expectation that this support would be reciprocated, for instance, even to a new neighbor that she hardly knew:

I like the neighbors, you know. And...I think they all like me....And I try to help...anybody as much as I can....I have a neighbor right here...you know...when you move into a neighborhood, long time before you know this one and that, but she knew me. And any time she wanted something, she would always come to me. She would come to me and borrow money. And you know, it's just like, the first time for everything,...sometimes you be kinda hesitant about it; but she would come to me and wanna borrow money; but I have it. I loaned it to her whether I get it back or not. But she always paid me back. And, right now, she doesn't have a phone, so she come in and use my phone....Anyway that I can help anybody, I do it.

Members of the community household at Wentworth also are quick to come to each other's aid in time of crisis. Lottie Weathersby explained:

When somebody dies I think I'm the first person called. And I do things for them, like...I try to attend the funerals and things....I try to be as supportive to everybody as I can.

When needed, phone calls are made by Mrs. Amey, Mrs. Ramsey, Mrs. Harris, or others in the Local Advisory Council (LAC) office, and collections are taken up to help cover funeral costs. When Mary Rias lost her husband a few years ago, residents rallied to support her. The aid they provided was very vivid in her mind:

When my husband passed...the people ran to help me. You would never have thought...Gave me money, food...[help with] clean up....But everybody helped me. 'Cause I didn't have that much insurance with my husband. I was just lost. And they told me, don't worry about it, and I didn't....Didn't have money to bury my husband.

For years Mrs. Rias's care giving was based on the principle of generalized reciprocity. Now the residents' assistance, particularly with her husband's burial costs, was a meaningful, but unexpected, pay back for the years of community service that she and her husband had provided to the Wentworth community.

In all of our observations, irrespective of whether they occurred during an official meeting or at informal gatherings, we witnessed Wentworth activists making arrangements to help one another, celebrating a life passage or holiday, and more generally, providing emotional support in difficult times. Tangible signs of the work of community kinship are obvious in all of the Wentworth community spaces. In the LAC office and laundromat, for instance, there often was a birthday card or a condolence card to sign for one of the resident activists or one of their immediate family members; newborn baby and graduation photographs, congratulatory cards, and children's drawings are pinned to the walls. Also, we observed that residents with developmental disabilities or afflictions such as Alzheimer's disease, rather than being shunned, are welcomed into social settings, and, when possible, are given appropriate social tasks to perform to affirm their membership in the community household.

It is through the recognition of life passages and achievements, and the exchanges of goods and services that the Wentworth activists extend the boundaries of their immediate families to include the community household and the residents of the larger Wentworth development. By acting as community othermothers and engaging in the work of community kinship the activists both create and reproduce a dense social network. Over a period of time, through these repeated exchanges, the activists both manifest trustworthiness and in turn place extensive trust in each other, thereby further encouraging the norm of generalized reciprocity within the community household (Putnam, 1993). These activities also serve another fundamental purpose: By helping the developmentally disabled, the elderly, and the infirm to remain in Wentworth Gardens, rather than being placed in segregated or custodial care, the activists are helping to ensure the richness and the diversity of community life (Haywoode, 1991, pp. 176–177).

Linking Domestic Life to Collective Activities

Domestic activities are essential to building and maintaining family networks. Cooking and sharing food and sharing information about everyday life, which often results in establishing agreed upon norms for behavior, are all domestic activities essential for sustaining the family network. These domestic activities are similarly essential to building and sustaining the community household.

Cooking and Sharing Food

So everybody gets to meeting, then I cooks cornbread.... I can make a nice pot of greens and cornbread. And that's another thing that gets you hooked up too ... that's another way I think I met Mrs. Amey. We was having some kind of potluck dinner or some sales or something, and I think I cooked a couple of sweet potato pies. And that's how we began to get together, and everybody got to cooking something different and we sitting around and meeting.... Because, you know, everybody can relate to food. (Mrs. Bertha McKinney)

Preparing and sharing food are central domestic activities that bind individual Wentworth residents to the community household and serve as a context for community organizing (also see Clark, 1994). As Bertha McKinney, a resident at Wentworth since 1982, astutely observed, "Everybody can relate to food." Many of Wentworth's core activists make a contribution to the development and engage in community building through the cooking and exchange of food.

All of the Wentworth activists learned or practiced their cooking skills through preparing meals for their families, but for some of these women, their skills also were cultivated through their years of working in food service and, for a few, in the creation of their own food business.[5] For example, Mary Rias applied her job skills as a former cook in a hotel and restaurant. Evelyn Ramsey also had restaurant work experience that she applied to preparing enticing dishes in the Local Advisory Council office for one occasion or another. As a young adult, with an eighth-grade education and $4.80, Mrs. Ramsey left her grandmother's home and moved to Memphis. For 2 years she supported herself through restaurant and child care work. Not surprisingly, when she moved to Chicago in 1973, besides occasional factory employment, she primarily worked in food service at Woolworth's lunch counter and later a seafood restaurant as a "head" waitress. Mrs. Ramsey boasted:

I've always been a great waitress. I waited tables and worked, ran a couple of restaurants until I moved over here.

While living at Wentworth, between 1973 and 1988, Mrs. Ramsey supported herself by preparing dinners in her home and selling them, first in a local bar, later to other small businesses. Subsequently, she obtained her current employment in the Wentworth LAC, where she is often seen preparing food for a community event or an ill or elderly Wentworth resident.

For Janie Dumas, the sharing of food is intimately tied to her sense of religious duties to assist her neighbors. Among the Wentworth resident activists, Janie Dumas has been the identified spiritual leader. Often providing the opening and closing prayers at meetings and community events, she makes no distinction between her spiritual work and her work in socially reproducing the community household. Born to missionary parents, Mrs. Dumas began her own "ministering" for "the Lord" by bringing together several families in her Wentworth home for meals and prayer:

I call my work as a mission, you know. I would . . . [bring] maybe three families. . . . We didn't have much food. And we would have like, we'd get seven dollars together. And they would get their money and bring it to the house; and I would go and get a pot of greens and things; and I would call those families over to my house. And we would pray; and we would all sit and eat. And we did it twice a week or once a week, you know.

Throughout her residency at Wentworth, Mrs. Dumas has ministered to those in need, both at Wentworth and in other Chicago West Side and South

---

[5] In the late 1980s, the RMC of LeClaire Courts, another low-rise public housing development in Chicago, creatively built on their residents' cooking skills to develop a resident-run business, a catering service.

Side communities. She has distributed food to the homeless, has passed out clothing collected by Chicago churches, and has visited and prayed for the ill in nearby churches and hospitals. The food she distributes, at times to as many as 60 people, is prepared in her kitchen at home. She has paid for most of the costs she has incurred "out of my little income," sometimes taking her "last dime" to do so.

Feeding children also is one way many Wentworth activists extend their community othermothering to community children, making the connection between domestic and collective life. Much of Mrs. Dumas's community organizing has involved children. She began her "ministering" to children when she moved into Wentworth. She started by informally organizing activities not readily available to Wentworth's youth. For Mrs. Dumas, food is central to the way she cares for and nurtures neighborhood children. For instance, in the Spiritual Development Center she created in one of the basements of Wentworth's walk-up apartment buildings, she has served children lunch once a week, again assuming most of the cost:

I'm gonna help the children making up the soup and sandwich down there. And they sit and they could eat. They could sing, whatever, you know.

Mrs. Dumas explained that she could not do otherwise, because the children are hungry:

Cause a lot of kids, they running around and they homeless. I say, I'm gonna open up and have beans and some bread or something, and make some rice or something for them, you know. Not no charge, you know. I just . . . like to do this for my heart. . . . And I'll be blessed for it, you know.

Cooking is a way to satisfy hunger, but it also is an essential way to become connected to other people. According to Bertha McKinney, she met Evelyn Ramsey, her block captain and the first person to encourage her to become active in the community, "in the yard in block four." They developed their friendship around the preparation and sharing of food:

[T]hen her [Mrs. Ramsey's] little friend lived next door to me. So, with her little friend living next door to me, she introduced us and we'd all sit around and she'd cook up a pot of this and I'd cook up a pot of that . . . We played spades together. Sit around and eat watermelon or something, and just laughing and talking. And that's how I got started. . . . Yeah, most likely, I was probably sitting somewhere talkin' to Miss Ramsey.

Mrs. McKinney then met Mrs. Hallie Amey by sharing impromptu meals outside the old LAC office. It was Mrs. Amey who cajoled her into her current volunteer work in the laundromat and store:

And if I'm sitting up in that LAC office with Miss Ramsey, you'll run into Mrs. Amey. Because see, she's in and out of this office too.

Finally, food preparation and sale are one key way Wentworth activists raise funds for many of their community programs and services. Bertha McKinney explained that her involvement with the LAC continues to be food-related: preparing meals and treats for annual community events, that also often serve as fund-raisers:

[W]e had a little Fun Fest outside, and we'd all get together there, yeah.... Well, I just help them out a little bit at the Fun Fest, you know. Because they sell little items like snowballs and all that. When I help, I do a little stand for them. Stand around and sell snowballs or something. Whatever they need me for. And like, if we get together and have to have dinners or whatever, I help cook.

Mardia Earving, to raise the necessary funds to renovate the space and repair or purchase equipment for the Wentworth community store, prepared and sold food, paying for the supplies out of her own pocket.

Both Kenneth Boulding (1981) and Lloyd Warner (1963) speak of the significance of gift giving to the basic integration of the community. Warner (1963, p. 142) points to the "latent feelings of solidarity, unity, and interdependence, that is evoked by gift-giving." In support of this point, Boulding (1981, p. 4) argues that a gift – a grant made out of benevolence – "involves an identification on the part of the giver or donor who parts with the gift with the welfare of the recipient [community member or entity] who gets it." Through their contributions of food supplies, their food preparation, and more generally their time, resident activists such as Mrs. Ramsey, Mrs. McKinney, Mrs. Dumas, and Mrs. Earving create social bonds with others as they themselves become more tightly attached to and integrated into the community household.

Gossip: Sharing Information

What may appear to the casual observer as idle chatter, or time-wasting gossip, is really the process of building a network of social exchange, information sharing, informal contacts, and the creation and affirmation of social integration and cohesion. It has a practical value and more than practical value, it may become a form of self consciousness for women. (Haywoode, 1991, p. 173)

Outsiders to a group or a community are not able to appreciate the significance of sharing information, what is commonly called "gossip," especially in the way that an insider can (Heilman, 1976). As suggested by Gluckman (1963), gossip is not idle "chatter": Rather, "The outsider cannot join in gossip" because "gossip does not have isolated roles in community life, but is part of the very blood and tissue of life." In fact, once group membership is established and individuals are organized around "the fairly successful pursuit of common objectives," one contributor to the sustenance of these relationships can be an interest in the group's gossip: That is, "Friendship leads to gossip," and gossip also leads to friendship (Gluckman, 1963, as reported in Heilman, 1976, p. 153).

Gossip is a central part of neighboring and organizing at Wentworth Gardens. It provides an opportunity for women "to think out loud . . . the means by which they explore their obligation to sustain life in the midst of difficult conditions" (Kaplan, 1982, p. 548). It is through "gossip sessions" that relationships are once again formed and solidified, essential information is exchanged, organizing plans are formulated, and community norms are established (Heilman, 1976).

Mrs. Tecora Butler gossips on a regular basis, often with resident activists, strengthening her social integration and cohesion with the individuals in the community household:

I know just about all of them [neighbors]. . . . We get out sometime and we all sit out there and visit. They be out in the garden walkin' and talkin'. It's a couple that I go to their house and visit. . . . We just sits down and laughing, talking, and I go to Mary's [Rias's]. . . . I be over there . . . and she likes to be in the kitchen cooking and doing different things. And me and her just sits around there just laughing and talking about you know, just things in general.

In addition to creating the sociability evident in the above exchange, gossip functions to disseminate local neighborhood news and information. Often talking about "things in general" turns into discussing organizing issues or problems at Wentworth. Desiree Davis explained:

We socialize on the porch. . . . We may talk about the upkeep of Wentworth. Then try to find out . . . what they [resident activists] trying to do at Wentworth; and I try to encourage them to come to a meeting and find out for themselves.

Gossip sessions can further evolve into attempts to problem solve and make plans to take specific actions. Bertha McKinney elaborated:

We mostly be talking about Wentworth. Mostly every day you have something going on in Wentworth. . . . We talk about maybe the security, or the paper on the ground, the broken glasses, the nasty hallways, or a hole here and there . . . or this dumpster has been turned over. Just all kinds of things we sit there and discuss. . . . They might be sitting around talking about well, we gonna do the yards today; or we gonna get somebody to come in for, you know, to organize for the dance; or we gonna have a fund raiser; . . . or Miss Smith's door fell. We gotta figure out a way we gonna help her get this back up. So, but that's mostly all we sit around talking about little Wentworth business.

The exchange of everyday information not only bonds activists to each other, but allows for the exchange of information about Wentworth activists' organizing efforts with each other and other Wentworth residents. Mrs. Lottie Weathersby:

My neighbors rely on me for everything. . . . All of my neighbors rely on me for information coming from CHA, from the LAC, from the RMC.

Norm Setting. Gossip also serves as one means to establish group norms for behavior. It is through the regular exchange of views about individuals and events at Wentworth that standards of "proper conduct" are established. Ideally, the norms for appropriate behavior are shared by members of a household. Traditionally it is the mother who provides guidance and supervision to assure that these norms are followed. In the community household model, norm setting is expanded beyond the domain of the family into the community (Clark, 1993; Pardo, 1998). As resident activists participate in social exchanges, community norms are negotiated and renegotiated. Engaging in the construction of community norm setting is a means to assert informal social control: an attempt to establish a safe and stable neighborhood for all residents.

As in cooking, Wentworth's children and young adults are the activists' primary consideration when discussing, constructing, and attempting to enforce community norms. For instance, an adult male youth worker described how, through gossip, Wentworth activists engage in an "informal screening" of youth that can operate as a check on destructive youth behavior:

There's a screening to the point where . . . residents keep track of everything that's going on. . . . They know everybody in the area. "That's the so and so boy, or that's the so and so girl," and they [the youth] know who that is. So they know it would be shameful for them to be part of something that would be embarrassing to themselves and their families. Therefore they wouldn't do any crime in the area. . . . They have little fights and something like that . . . but as far as a gang activity . . . they don't have it here.

All of Wentworth activists share concerns about delinquency prevention and readily discussed their efforts to steer neighborhood youth in the "right direction." This includes not only working actively to keep the children "out of [criminal] trouble," but teaching them to be considerate of others and to uphold what the activists consider to be proper behavior. In her description of an exchange with youth at a summer holiday gathering, Mrs. Evelyn Ramsey provided evidence of how a conversation with her sister alerted her to the need to engage in community norm setting:

We got some young men that call themselves gang bangers. . . . [L]ike fourth of July . . . we barbequein'. . . . And they said, could they hook up [their music] here? I say . . . "I have no objection to you hookin' up . . . but, nine o'clock, you got to cut the music off." And my sister came by and she said, "Do you hear the lyrics to that music they playin' out there?" I say, "No, I don't know the lyrics to this rap and stuff." . . . So she said, "You just listen . . . that's not fit for kids or nobody to listen to." So I go outside in the field. . . . They playin' this. . . . Burn . . . uh, don't put no water on it, let it burn. . . . And she say, "Do see what I mean?" I say, "Yeah." And she say, "That is degradin'. . . ." So I walk up to the young man and I say, "Look, that's all right for you all in your house, [not out here].... You got little bitty kids out here and dancin' on that."

This interaction could have escalated into an altercation with the youth but instead was defused because of Mrs. Ramsey's actions and reputation as a community othermother and her prior social contacts with these young men:

[T]hey changed the music. And I told 'em, I said, "In 30 minutes you're gonna have to unplug it because we got seniors and we got peoples that works.... So I go out down there and told 'em, I say, "You're gonna have to turn the music down." So they, they turned the music down.

For members of a community household, correct behavior is established not as a compromise between self-interested individuals, but through practical reciprocity in a network of relationships (Ackelsberg, 1988; Haywoode, 1991). Mrs. Ramsey explained:

I treat 'em [the youth] nice.... You let 'em up in your house.... [They] come and say, you gotta a sandwich? If I got some I try to make 'em a sandwich. If they come in use your phone I say, "Use the phone, not to socialize with." But, in the meantime, I treat 'em like they're young mens. And I get the ... respect from 'em.

Because Mrs. Ramsey treats these youth with respect, she in turn has earned their respect and their assistance. For instance, she noted: "If I go out, I pull up out here and I got a car full of groceries, somebody's gonna come up [to help me]." Moreover, Mrs. Ramsey, since she has expressed a willingness to share the use of her car with youth in the community, has no concerns about and has had no problems with theft:

I don't lock my car. I never have. I've had four new cars since I've been livin' in here. I never had my car taken or anything did to it. I leave it. I get groceries and stuff in my car. They don't take it. 'Cause when I bought the car, I called them and told 'em. I say, "This is my car.... If you wanna a ride, you ask me. If you gotta a license ... I might even let you drive it. But otherwise stay out of it. It belongs to me so you pass the word up." Never had a problem yet. So, it's, it's a lot of times that's the way that you treat young folks.

For Bertha McKinney, her relationships and knowledge of the youth at Wentworth garnered through her active participation in the community household also act as a measure of security, especially when she is working in the basement store alone. She shared that because of working in the store, she knows "just about everybody":

And most all of the children I know by names. Because they in an out of the store.... So know a lot of them.... Know their apartment numbers too. [Laughs].... I know where they are.... See, I'm very sharp-minded. I pick up on things.... You gotta know where the people ... live. And just like I'm in the store, where I learn faces and names simply because you never know who gonna come in there on you. . . . You got to, you got to be observant like that because if you don't you're lost. You got to know, like if you have strangers coming in and out of your store, so you ought to know who they are. And what house they come from.

A year before we spoke to Bertha McKinney, the store was robbed by someone in a mask. Although not working at the time, Bertha argued that if the robber was a resident, a mask would not have prevented identification. She explained that she knows not only individuals' faces and names, but also their body shapes, the shoes they wear, and even the way they walk:

Because, if some young men was to come in the store, I know just as good who they are because I'm sitting there looking in the mirror and I can tell the way they walk who they are.

Wentworth activists not only assume the responsibility of setting community norms, they are conferred with the privilege and the power of publicly criticizing others in the Wentworth development, particularly those who fall short of what they consider "proper conduct." They have garnered respect and a reputation for trustworthiness as community othermothers and through the work of community kinship (Gilkes, 1980, p. 223; also see Collins, 1991). The norms established by Wentworth activists, however, are not agreed upon by all Wentworth residents. Increasingly the activists must contend with social problems that extend far beyond the boundaries of the community household and the efficacy of the social bonds they have created.

Limits of the Community Household

For its members, the community household is a source of social support and community organizing. Outsiders may perceive it otherwise. Activists report that they know some Wentworth residents view them as a clique, believing that they use their influence to obtain special favors and resources for their members.

Despite the consistent efforts of the Wentworth Gardens activists to expand membership in the community household, and to extend their community othermothering to a range of residents in the development, most Wentworth residents are not embedded in the Wentworth Gardens community as both the older and the newer generation of community activists are. In fact, the majority of the activists expressed their concerns about newer residents who do not care for their children, their apartments, the Wentworth grounds, and so on. For instance, Mrs. Lottie Weathersby noted that youth are not being properly directed by their own parents, "A lot of things I don't like in the neighborhood is people not watching their kids, not knowing where their kids is going." Mrs. Evelyn Ramsey is also concerned about the disintegration of the family that she sees around her:

The grandparents is too old and tired. And the parents is drugged out and don't care.... [I]t's just the situation where our kids is just, I don't know, fallin' by the way. I don't know why they fallin'.

The activists can no longer expect that their shared norms about building and site upkeep – concerns about the maintenance of common hallways and yards and about vandalism – will be respected by other residents. Lucille Perry addressed some of these issues:

[T]he teenagers coming in and urinating and what not in the hallway. And, the kids constantly playing in the halls and breakin' the lock off after they [maintenance personnel] put it on. That's the newer generation that moved in the building; you know, like young girls, really too young to have their own place.

And Faye Perteet, while explaining that she is willing to extend herself to the Wentworth youth, added a caveat: "I'm here, like I said, I'm here for any child that wants to listen to a grown-up." Elijah Anderson (1990), in his study of inner-city Philadelphia, observed similarly that the exodus of working-class blacks "has diminished an extremely important source of moral and social leadership within the black community." He found that the senior statesmen and stateswomen, such as the older-generation activists at Wentworth, are still there, but in dwindling numbers. The community "mothers" who acted as the eyes and ears of the neighborhood have become "overwhelmed by a virtual proliferation of 'street kids' – children almost totally without parental supervision, left to their own devices" (pp. 4, 69, 72). Anderson's (1990) research conclusions can also be applied to Wentworth Gardens:

As family caretakers and role models disappear or decline in influence, and as unemployment and poverty become more persistent, the community, particularly its children, becomes vulnerable to a variety of social ills, including crime, drugs, family disorganization, generalized demoralization, and unemployment. (p. 72)

Over the past two decades, the moral authority of the community household members in Wentworth has been threatened. Community othermothers no longer can assume that their public admonishment of delinquent youth will be welcome or even acknowledged. Activists cannot depend upon shared community norms to engage in effective moral persuasion, when, for example, drug dealers, who do not share the activists' community norms, flaunt their illegal activities. Mrs. Harris's anger and frustration are evident in her account of some of the activists' attempts to "clean up" Wentworth:

I'm hoping that maybe some kind of way we can change these [negative] images around here [at Wentworth]. We're working on it.... These guys that use to hang around here all the time when we was having meetings and they out there talking about their [drug] money. . . . We had to call the police to come and get them away from this [LAC] office. We would go there, "Look, get away from this office. . . . Ain't nobody want to hear this and see this."

Calling in a third party, the police, to exercise coercive enforcement would not have been the resident activists' first choice and is problematic for several reasons: It is less efficient and more unpleasant than voluntary cooperation, built through establishing relationships of mutual trust (Gambetta, 1988). Because these drug dealers operate outside the social bonds and community norms of the community household, and thus outside its moral suasion, their "cooperation" can only be obtained through force, assuming appropriate and fair enforcement measures.

CONCLUSIONS

Much of Wentworth activists' time and ongoing efforts are spent creating and sustaining their community household. Within this household, community is an extension of the private sphere, organized to build and maintain social relationships and resources. Wentworth activists build community relationships in ways that are similar to those used in building family relationships, by creating a safe and nurturing domestic sphere–like setting where they can identify and discuss issues of mutual concern. They build communities in small groups, very much like their households. Women's membership in these place-based social networks contributes to a sense of solidarity, and their unique offerings, such as cooking and the work of kinship, contribute to a sense of significance – both essential components of a cohesive social fabric.

We have seen how Wentworth's community household allows for the development of reciprocity, trust, and community norms among residents. The social relations between friends and neighbors are created and nurtured through "a nonmonetary exchange of goods and services" (Leavitt & Saegert, 1990, pp. 173, 181). These exchanges and the cementing of relationships provide the support for household members and neighbors in the development in times of need.

The members of Wentworth's community household demonstrate a clear rejection of separateness and individual interest as the basis of participation. In fact, the connectedness with others and common interest expressed by these women model a very different system of ethics. These community othermothers demonstrate a generalized ethic of care and accountability for all the residents in the Wentworth development who respond to their outreach efforts and concern. They are able to apply their religious beliefs and religious institutional attachments in furthering a tradition of helping others.

At Wentworth, the creation of the community household is at the core of resident activists' engagement in everyday resistance. Recall hooks's (1990) contention that African-Americans' historic struggle to create and sustain a safe and nurturant home and community does more than provide the necessities of everyday survival: It is a source of resistance to challenge the societal obstacles of racism, classism, and sexism that impact on their daily lives:

> Black women resisted by making homes where all black people could strive to be subjects, not objects, where we could be affirmed in our minds and hearts despite poverty, hardship, and deprivation, where we could restore to ourselves the dignity denied us on the outside in the public world. (p. 42)

As we will see in upcoming chapters, Wentworth activists have used their community household as the base for their activism. Effective community organizing at Wentworth Gardens, as in other low-income, minority neighborhoods, is underpinned by social cohesiveness among residents (Ackelsberg, 1988; Clark, 1993; Saegert, 1989; Stall & Stoecker, 1998; Wekerle, 1996). As observed by Saegert (1989): "Supportive social relationships are the ground out of which cooperative efforts to take control over critical areas of people's lives grow" (pp. 312 – 313).[6] Essential to this social fabric are the "warm and caring aspects of the construction and maintenance of interpersonal relationships" (Daniels, 1987, p. 409) that contribute to a feeling of social solidarity. Equally important is the support of social solidarity, a "we-feeling" that "encompasses all those sentiments which draw people together and support mutual regard and respect (sympathy, courtesy, gratitude, trust and so on)" (Clark, 1973, p. 404) and provides a sense of significance, an individual's experience of status and achievement, a person's belief that she or he has an important role to play in the community. This "social glue" (Saegert, 1989) that holds Wentworth resident activists together is not simply the backdrop of their local struggles, but rather forms the foundation for sharing concerns and problems about their development, for devising strategies for local action, and for

---

[6] Perkins, Brown, and Taylor (1996), in an analysis of studies seeking to predict participation in grassroots organizations from several cities, find further support for the relationship between an integrated community social life and community organization participation. They found that neighboring, involvement in religious and community organizations, and community-focused ideas and values (e.g., organizational efficacy, civic responsibility, and community attachments) were consistently and positively predictive of participation. They also found that measures of two psychological constructs presumed related to participation – locus of control and internality – were not consistently predictive.

Furthermore, they found that African-Americans participate more than whites with similar income levels. They explained this finding in light of the greater discrimination and higher rates of social, economic, and environmental problems experienced by blacks as well as the likelihood of fewer informal connections to power: "Both of these disadvantages make grassroots activity more necessary in minority communities" (p. 90).

sustaining themselves, their households, and their community through adversity.

Social assets, or the "social capital" of low-income communities, facilitate cooperation and mobilize solidarity but are typically overlooked, especially in a society that places the highest value on economic assets. Robert Putnam (1993), the scholar who has most popularized this concept, defines *social capital* more specifically as the features of social organization, such as networks, norms, and social trust, that facilitate coordination and cooperation for mutual benefit (p. 67). Putnam (2000) distinguishes two forms of social capital: *bonding social capital*, which solidifies ties between people within a preexisting group in a geographic locale, and *bridging social capital*, which links the group with others outside the immediate group within the geographic locale and beyond its boundaries. Bonding social capital is vital to undergird reciprocity and mobilize solidarity; bridging social capital is better for "linkage to external assets and for information diffusion" (pp. 22–23). Richard Couto (1999) examines how people in poor communities rely on community social support as well as more formal organizations such as philanthropic social service organizations and churches not only for their survival, but as the basis for community organizing for social change. Similarly, contributors to Warren, Thompson, and Saegert's (2001) edited collection illustrate that social capital can contribute positively to communities' quality of life and enhance community revitalization efforts.

For the Wentworth Gardens residents, the cultivation of bonding social capital, cohesive and supportive relationships within the community household, is essential to everyday resistance; yet, in order to thrive, the community household must build outward, engaging in community organizing efforts to broaden its scope developmentwide. They must formalize the work of community kinship and othermothering to create bridging relationships with people and organizations outside the Wentworth development (Leavitt & Saegert, 1990, pp. 172–173). If we apply this process to one example, Wentworth's youth, community othermothers engage in a type of "familism," providing youth with nurturance, structure, and norm setting. But to access the staff, funding, organizational, and other resources necessary for organized youth programs, Wentworth activists must orchestrate and cultivate bridging social capital, relational linkages external to the community household, as well. In the next chapter, we explore "women-centered organizing," one organizing mode Wentworth activists use to extend their relational linkages, especially in and through their Local Advisory Council.

5

The Local Advisory Council (LAC)

A Site of Women-Centered Organizing

Often when you walk into the LAC office, after the screen door slams, there is something cooking. You may be invited to sit awhile, have a cup of coffee, share your news, or stuff envelopes with an announcement of the latest community event; or you might stop in the office to make a phone call, or sign up your child for a field trip. Mrs. Beatrice Harris, the LAC president, after chatting with you about your family, might ask you to stay awhile and help organize an upcoming barbeque for the development; or Mrs. Hallie Amey, a former LAC secretary, may stop in to talk with Mrs. Harris, first to ask about her health, followed by a strategy discussion of how to solve the basement flooding in the LAC operated on-site laundromat and convenience store. For example, in one two hour visit in late March, 1996, the discussions and work included: details of an upcoming Easter Egg hunt for the children; Mrs. Evelyn Ramsey musing about her need to get away for a break; one of the youth events and the Youth Council election results; the state of the coffee (it was very old); the Women for Economic Security (WES) program; post office jobs; flyer preparation by a volunteer for a CHA-initiated communitywide event, with Mrs. Amey providing personal feedback; and debates about how the food donations for the event should be organized, what people outside the Wentworth Gardens community should be invited, and which resident will call and invite a local politician to attend. There was quite a bit of planning work conducted in this short period of time, but it was done amidst joking, story telling, and many phone and interruptions. There was also a vast array of visitors to the office in this same two hour period: CHA employee, Tim Goosby, and a Park District employee looking for youth for a sports program; senior resident, Edna Nolan, for a visit and a cup of coffee; Lottie Weathersby, to place phone calls, one to the local Alderman's office about the LAC obtaining car stickers for parking during White Sox games, and the other to a teenage girl to make flyers; and several other residents to ask questions and/or to share information. (Field note observations, March 1996)

Since 1971, the Local Advisory Council (LAC) office at Wentworth Gardens has been the focal site of the community household, a place where the "official business" of the office and the everyday activities of the community household are integrated. In fact, from the early 1970s until the late 1980s, Wentworth's LAC was the sole on-site organization that worked to address the residents' concerns and problems surrounding daily survival.

At the LAC, much of the business of CHA–tenant relationships is conducted by elected resident representatives. For instance, the latest versions of tenant leases and tenant regulations are kept here. Flyers from CHA Maintenance that alert tenants to hot water shut offs and boiler repairs were first demanded by, and now are sent out of, the LAC office. LAC workers are responsible for organizing youth trips, sports teams, and the summer children's food program, supported by the CHA or not-for profit organizations. LAC community workers have run the Local School Advisory Council elections for Abbott School, the local elementary school, and the yearly summer CHA youth employment programs. For adult residents, activists working through the LAC also organize social services, job training, and employment services offered by governmental agencies and not-for-profit organizations.

For the development as a whole, the LAC activists organize grounds cleanups, food and clothing distributions, crime prevention programs, as well as celebrations and ritual events. The LAC is the place where residents obtain information on what is happening in the development, or in the CHA or, more generally about government programs that may have an impact on their lives. In addition, the LAC Service Committee is responsible for oversight of the resident-run laundromat and convenience store.

Equally significant, the LAC is the hub of Wentworth's community social life. Housed near the middle of the development, upstairs from the grocery store, the LAC office is where residents, from preschoolers to seniors, come to obtain and share information about the "goin's on" at Wentworth; to gain and give social support and to engage in friendly and at times heated conversations; and to plan parties, celebrations, and other social events. There is also much informal helping that takes place here: collections for resident funerals, arranged visits to hospitalized residents, phone calls made for residents without a phone, answering children's questions, sharing information about jobs, and counseling tenants with personal problems (for example, to prevent eviction or to enter a substance abuse program). Clothes and food drives originate in this office, as does the regular distribution of government food surpluses.

Wentworth's LAC serves as a focal site of everyday resistance, a place where community household activists transform the values and skills they have learned in sustaining their own families and their community household to organize their broader community around survival needs. It has been a key site of *women-centered* community organizing, as the extended domestic structures of the community household are linked to larger collective, formal organizing activities. It is the place where the creation and cultivation of both bonding and bridging social capital are seamlessly combined. Through the participation of resident activists, relationships are built between the residents who work in the office and those who visit, and new leadership is cultivated through these social bonds and the everyday business affairs of the office. The LAC is also where Wentworth activists extend their social bonds beyond their development to bridge with individuals, organizations, and institutions outside the Wentworth community. These bridging relationship are particularly germane at Wentworth, a community isolated geographically, politically, and economically from powerful societal actors. The creation and maintenance of bridging social capital have been integral to Wentworth activists' meeting their organizing objectives and affirming their social legitimacy. These outside relationships are crucial from the earliest stages of organizing, as observed by Saegert (1989), connecting "emerging community households to the resource allocation process of the broader society" (p. 313).[1]

WOMEN-CENTERED ORGANIZING

Community is not just a place or an attitude; it is a "dense network of overlapping social and geographical connections that ground individuals in both a sense of place and in a sense of social solidarity" (Haywoode, 1991, p. 172). In the Wentworth Gardens community, effective resident activism is underpinned by the social cohesiveness of the community household (Clark, 1993; Saegert, 1989; Stall & Stoecker, 1998; see also Ackelsberg, 1988; Wekerle 1996). Stall and Stoecker (1998) point out that a cohesive social fabric does not develop spontaneously; it must be constructed:

Someone has to build strong enough relationships between people so they can support each other through long and sometimes dangerous struggles. . . . This process of building a mobilizable community is called "community organizing." (p. 1)

Community organizing is the ongoing process of developing and maintaining social relationships, identifying issues, mobilizing around those issues, and building an enduring organization (Alinsky, 1971; Stall & Stoecker, 1998). At Wentworth, both social bonds within the community and social bridging to individuals outside the development are cultivated through women-centered organizing – the craft of building and maintaining an enduring network of people who identify with common ideals and can act on the basis of those ideals (Stall & Stoecker, 1998). The social construction of

---

[1] On the basis of a study of women-led/women-focused organizations in nine states and interviews with nearly 150 women leaders, Gittell, Ortega-Bustamante, and Steffy (1999) describe community programs that create both bonding and bridging social capital – a mix of "advocacy, organizing, service delivery, and development" (p. 78).

community is largely the work of women who, through their day-to-day labor – their fund-raising, clerical work, provision of specific services, and planning and execution of local events, parties, and celebrations – not only "weave the fabric of community life" but provide an "expression of neighborhood solidarity and resistance" (Haywoode 1991, pp. 175, 177; see also Gittell & Vidal, 1998).

Distinct social constructions of gender in our society mean that, for women, community relationships include social bonds crafted through routine activities to support social reproduction, such as child care, housekeeping, and shopping (DeVault, 1991). Similarly, community activism frequently is a response to the social reproduction needs of their community, especially of their own children and of other children in the community. Women-centered organizing is distinguished not only by gender. Women's social class, race, and ethnicity also contribute to specifying women's housing and support service needs, and the nature of their involvement in grassroots activism (reviewed in Morgen & Bookman, 1988; see also Naples, 1998a; Pardo, 1998; Saegert, 1989; Stoecker, 1992). Low-income, minority women intertwine the means and ends of their domestic life and their community-based social relationships with community organizing because of the history of their reliance on these skills and strategies for their survival. As Gilkes (1980) argued:

The reactions to oppression and to the social consequences of racism are an important part of Black culture and social organization. . . . As one explores the situation of Black women known for their hard work, one discovers . . . a system of routine activities organized around coping with and eliminating the problems of oppression. (p. 220)

Low-income minority women span the conventionally defined public and private spheres, working primarily in the expanded private sphere to organize around supporting the everyday needs of their households and communities.

In this chapter, we analyze the ways in which the both the LAC's physical setting and its activities blur the distinctions between the private and public spheres of life. We examine three LAC focus areas – youth programming, tenant security, and event planning – to illustrate the multiple ways in which Wentworth activists elaborate upon and formalize their work of othermothering and community kinship to organize programs and services at the development level. We cite examples of the ways in which these activities are supported by and build bonding and bridging social capital to support residents' organizing efforts. In particular, we closely examine the community organizing work of four Wentworth women activists who have been integral to the effectiveness of the LAC's programs. Through this examination, we attempt to capture the detail of their work to provide a better understanding of women-centered organizing, especially the skills and "never-ending" hard work necessary to orchestrate developmentwide programs and recruit new and younger activists to carry on the craft of organizing. We also explore the problem of activist burnout, the toll of the endless work of women-centered organizing. We end with a brief glimpse at the cultivation of younger-generation Wentworth organizers. To provide a context for this analysis, we begin this chapter with a short history of the establishment of the LAC in CHA family developments and, more specifically, in Wentworth Gardens.

ESTABLISHING WENTWORTH'S LAC

In Chicago, the LACs were wrestled out of struggles between the residents and CHA, a reticent partner in supporting resident participation. In the summer of 1970, the CHA, responding to a national HUD mandate to increase resident participation, created the Central Advisory Council (CAC), a 38-member group representing 19 family housing developments. The CAC had slated tenant elections for November 1970 to elect tenant representatives from the developments (1 for each 50 residents), but these elections were canceled when HUD officials were informed by a "dissident" CHA tenant's organization, the Chicago Housing Tenant Organization (CHTO), that the CAC had not defined the role of the tenant representatives. A HUD administrator warned the CHA that they would halt the approval of all future modernization grants until the "scope of authorities and responsibilities of tenant participation" were clearly enumerated. Through a series of meetings with CHTO, a democratically elected resident advisory council and their distinct responsibilities were established (Honchar, February 12, 1971).[2] Resident participation in management of their developments was a major victory for public housing residents.

The LACs were officially created when a Memorandum of Accord was signed in 1971 by the CHA and the Central Advisory Council. However, the CHA implementation of the LACs proved difficult for developments like Wentworth, where there was already a viable Resident Council (see the timeline in appendix A).[3] According to Hallie Amey, who had served

---

[2] The Central Advisory Council would shortly become an umbrella group of residents who are presidents of the LACs in each of the 19 developments.

[3] This was the second Resident Council in Wentworth Gardens. Earlier there was a viable Resident Council in the development in the late 1940s through the early 1950s. This first Resident Council is described in a CHA publication as working with the manager, "to obtain increased community agencies' services for project families. In accordance with the Authority's program for developing community relations, the plan is to utilize Wentworth social space for activities not only for residents, but for other families in the surrounding area" (CPMT, 1948, p. 11). This council was terminated at Wentworth when the treasury monies were misappropriated by one of its officers.

as the first president of the Resident Council in the late 1960s and who has worked with the LAC since its inception, there was "no clarity in the beginning" differentiating the responsibilities of the two organizations, which appeared to be chartered to do the same things. Mrs. Amey remembered "strife" and a "continuous rift" between the LAC and the Resident Council that eventually "began to get ugly." Mrs. Amey:

[A]fter the dissension became...where it was just so noticeable and, you know...confusion between the presidents [of the two councils]....It just wasn't necessary to volunteer and have that much friction goin' on.

With no indication that the Resident Council would eventually have to disband, Mrs. Amey decided to be active in both groups and was elected an officer, the secretary of Wentworth's LAC. Mrs. Amey stated, "The best you could do at that time was just attend those meetings and do the best you could." Further conflict resulted because of pay inequities. Unlike the LAC officers, who received small hourly stipends for attending official meetings, the Resident Council officers received no remumeration. Ultimately, the Resident Council was disbanded. Mrs. Amey learned a lesson from this unfortunate situation that she would apply nearly 20 years later when there was a similar rift between the LAC and the newly forming Wentworth Gardens Resident Management Corporation (see chapter 10).

Across the 19 Chicago family public housing developments, opinions have been mixed about the effectiveness of the LACs. Minimally, LACs at each CHA family development are made up of residents who hear each other's complaints and pass them up through the hierarchy to the Central Advisory Council (CAC), the overarching organization of CHA-wide LACs, ultimately to the CHA. The LACs also are involved in social programming in their developments, and some have taken advantage of job training and economic development opportunities. At its best, the LACs can function as a "mediating structure" – a distinct sphere of social activity existing between the family and the state (Couto, 1999), in this case, the resident household and the CHA. The LAC's local leaders, through the support they receive from nonprofits, foundations, and government agencies, increase and improve the resources they need for socially reproducing their community and countering the abuses of CHA and its representatives.

This ideal is often not the reality, and LAC offices vary in their accomplishments, the competence of their officers and staff, and their level of volunteer participation (Grimes, 1983). Although the LACs are the "official" organization representing CHA residents, some residents complain that they do not represent their best interests. Complaints include the LAC's lack of real authority to deal with pressing issues, disputes about the way LACs use their budgets for social programs, and suspicions about nepotism, for instance, in the LAC presidents' choice of full-time clerical workers and the means by which city jobs for CHA residents are filtered exclusively through the LACs.

Although it has not been immune to criticism, Wentworth's LAC has been, and continues to be, effective. Mrs. Hallie Amey, who served, in 1970, as the first Wentworth representative to the Central Advisory Council (CAC), explained the contribution of the continuity of community workers:

We are fortunate here because so many of us were already community-based workers before the LAC came in. That's the difference [in Wentworth Gardens]. Mrs. Driver was a community-based worker, Mrs. Harris, Mrs. Carter, and many, many more before the LAC came in.

Volunteer workers are essential to the LACs effective functioning. Some of the office staff is paid by the CHA – the president and one staff member – but most of the workers are unpaid. The comments of Melvin Spring, a former volunteer, then a paid employee through the Chicago Area Project, a nonprofit social service organization, underscores the importance of these volunteers:

There are a lot of volunteers in the [Wentworth Gardens] neighborhood; and that is really what helps. . . . [W]hen you have a lot of part time volunteers . . . and you have a successful ratio of [part-time to full-time] volunteers; because if everyone works to full capacity then they wouldn't be able to take care of their own family. . . . The residents stay [in the LAC office] sometimes to 7:00–8:00 p.m. . . . Three or four people will gather together and do things as we speak, all of them preparing something; or . . . something happens in the area . . . some boy broke a window or something, so they get in touch with the family so it won't occur again . . . or have to take care of someone who doesn't belong in the neighborhood.

Core activists called on their friends and newer residents to work with them at the LAC, and its leadership all were hard-working and respected community volunteers before they assumed paid LAC positions.

Even though the LAC's formation was formally dictated by the CHA, Wentworth's extant community household and its cohesive social networks that predated it created the basis for a successful mediating structure. The LAC was built upon these long-standing networks of social involvement and interdependency. Its effectiveness was dependent upon the community household members' commitments to continue to live in Wentworth Gardens, where these social networks had been created and nurtured (see also Clark, 1994). The Wentworth resident staff and volunteers, in their everyday business tasks and informal helping at the LAC, also bridged the expanded private sphere of daily life with agencies and organizations outside their development – the CHA management and personnel, local schools, and nonprofit organizations including the Chicago Area Project.

THE INTERSECTION OF THE PRIVATE AND PUBLIC
SPHERES: THE LAC OFFICE

On walking into the LAC office, it is immediately evident that the distinction between private and public space and private and public work is blurred. The physical manifestations of official business and informal social activities are intermingled.

The office is in one of the centrally located three-story walk-up apartment buildings in the Wentworth development. It is apparent that the LAC office is a converted two-bedroom apartment unit complete with a kitchen – no major renovations were made to the apartment. The LAC's main entrance opens into a kitchen with a working stove and two refrigerators, one oversized. The kitchen may be full of boxes of government surplus foods that are distributed from this office or leftovers brought by one of the residents to share with anyone who visits. Evelyn Ramsey, the LAC office clerk, often has something cooking on the stove for a community event, a family in distress, a snack for an LAC meeting, or an extended family dinner. Wandering comfortably back and forth between her own apartment kitchen, across the hall, and the LAC kitchen, Mrs. Ramsey clearly sees each space as an extension of the other, as are the personal and public uses of these spaces in her everyday activities.

Every square inch of the office space gets used. Mrs. Ramsey's office, the former living room, is set up with two workplaces – an old desk, assorted filing cabinets, and a new computer stand – all covered with new and old business equipment, papers, mail, personal belongings, and children's toys and books, including Mrs. Ramsey's grandson's electric car. A worn couch in the room is not spared; its surfaces are spread with flyers, a book, a big pink stuffed animal, and on at least one occasion, a small child asleep while his mother attended a meeting. The rest of the furnishings are a hodgepodge of styles, several apparently donated from residents' homes. One lamp is modern with a black plastic design; another is a living room table lamp with a white pearly shade. There is a wall clock, styled after a wristwatch, big and gold. The door between this front office space and the kitchen has a jerry-rigged bar across it with a blue cloth, which acts as a screen to keep the heat and smells of the kitchen separate from the work spaces.

A bulletin board on the wall leading to the hallway that goes to the back rooms is full. On one visit it included a picture of a newborn, flyers advertising upcoming youth events, and other new and old announcements, including one on how to get birth certificates (e.g., for enrolling children in school). The back two former bedrooms have been converted into one large meeting room, which houses a long table, additional office equipment, a computer table, bookshelves with textbooks and encyclopedias, more bulletin boards, and a worn sofa. The long table serves as a work space, a place to visit both during and between meetings and event planning and a place for neighbors to share a meal. It too is covered with papers, forms, and so on, including, in one instance, a petition to contest the U.S. Congress's bill to raise public housing rent. When there is no meeting in the room, children may sit on the sofa being tutored, watching TV, or sleeping, waiting for their mother to pick them up; or, as on one occasion, it may be piled high with clothing for distribution to Wentworth residents.

Although the LAC office was not originally built to house business functions, and funds have not been adequate to furnish it fully with business furniture, the space has been adapted for the official duties of the LAC. It is a comfortable and comforting space, perhaps, in part, because of the "homelike" furnishings, the domestic brick-a-brack, and personal belongings. Comfort most importantly is due, as we observed during all times we visited the office, to the affection and care shared among the staff and volunteers, and the respect and concern extended to residents and visitors who stop by.

The LAC office is not only a work space, but a place to visit and meet friends and to plan community parties and social events. Wentworth's LAC functions as an essential free space. A concept identified by Evans and Boyte (1981, 1986), *free spaces* are social settings, particular types of places located in the community where people can develop "a deeper and more assertive group identity," where "ordinary citizens can act with dignity, independence, and vision." They are voluntary associations that exist between individual private lives and large-scale institutions and can include "religious organizations, clubs, self-help and mutual aid societies, reform groups, neighborhood, civic, . . . and a host of other associations grounded in the fabric of community life" (Evans & Boyte, 1986, pp. 17–18). Rooted in the fabric of community life, these spaces function in a relatively open and participatory manner. Couto (1999) argues that "free spaces" offer a "tangible form" and are "an important political dimension of community-based 'mediating structures'" (p. 129). Although it is a CHA-mandated organization, Wentworth's LAC is able to maintain a certain autonomy and to operate effectively because of the rich array of volunteer workers who operate in and around this free space.

Working on-site, grassroots activists are deeply connected to their community and see it as an integral part of their own lives. In women-centered organizing there is a real concern about involving and developing people – social relationships, skills, leadership, and a sense of possibilities (Evans & Boyte, 1986) – not just programs and services. Terry Haywoode (1991) argues that "[w]omen are powerful community organizers because they see the relationships developed in organizing as a deep personal commitment and an important social relationship" (p. 181). Their work in the community is informed by their own intimate experiences with poverty, with child rearing, and with violence; they understand the urgency of meeting human needs and improving their declining neighborhoods.

Mrs. Evelyn Ramsey is one of these committed community organizers. When you enter the clutter-filled rooms of the LAC office, Mrs. Ramsey is likely to be the center of activity. In her sixties, Mrs. Ramsey is no stranger to hard work, nor to the impact of racism and poverty. Born to sharecroppers in rural Mississippi, she lost both of her parents when she was 8 years old. Her father was burned to death in the fields in a racist act of violence, and her mother died giving birth to her 12th child. She and her 10 siblings were then raised by her 60-year-old competent but strict paternal grandmother. This othermother, the efficient manager of an extended household of 18, coped by carefully directing the work of each of her grandchildren. The fifth of 11 children, Mrs. Ramsey described herself as a "tomboy," who "ran in the pack with the boys...the leader of the pack." She resented her grandmother's harsh child-rearing practices and her "whippin' days" and eventually left home after completing eighth grade at the age of 13. Mrs. Ramsey made her way north in 1956, and in 1975 she moved into Wentworth Gardens. After four prior moves in Chicago, she sought the affordability of a public housing apartment. Admittedly, Evelyn Ramsey was attracted to Wentworth Gardens, not to public housing. In fact, as other residents she had quite negative feelings about "the projects." Even after she moved with her two daughters into Wentworth, Mrs. Ramsey maintained her negative beliefs about people who lived in public housing. It was not until after her first formal volunteer involvement in the grocery store, three years after she moved in, that she changed her opinion.

It was Mrs. Amey who first introduced Mrs. Ramsey to community work, but it was Dorothy Driver, a former LAC president, who recruited her for her current LAC position. According to Mrs. Ramsey:

[Dorothy Driver was] a big-mouthed, business person, excellent bookkeeper, very detail-oriented. Miss Driver didn't like meetings.... [W]hen she was in the office it was business.... [She] sent Mrs. [Beatrice] Harris to all the meetings.... She was a wonderful person. I think a part of me died when Miss Driver died.[4]

Three years before she gained her present position in the LAC, Mrs. Ramsey was seeking a bigger apartment for her family – her two daughters and her new grandchild. Mrs. Driver, then the LAC president, and Mrs. Amey recommended to the CHA management that Mrs. Ramsey move into the

---

[4] Dorothy Driver died in 1986. She was one of the most well respected of the Wentworth activists. An enlarged photo of Mrs. Driver, placed in the interior entryway of the first Resident Management office at Wentworth, remains there, in what is now a community activity center.

vacant apartment across the hall from the LAC office. Mrs. Ramsey explained the advantages:

I moved down here 'cause I'm a big mouth; and when I see things I'm not afraid to report it all.... And Miss Driver said, "Okay ... that Ramsey moved across there, that way she'll be able to watch out, 'cause they kept breakin' in the store [located in the basement of the building] and stuff like that." She [Mrs. Driver] said, "They not gonna go by Ramsey breakin' in the store."

Now there is a well worn path between Ramsey's busy three-bedroom apartment and the crowded LAC office.

Mrs. Ramsey, as do other community organizers in Wentworth, both paid and unpaid, lives and works in the Wentworth community. She receives a wage from CHA and is expected to keep the office open for business during "official" hours; yet, the actual hours Evelyn Ramsey spends tending to "resident business" cannot be easily calculated because they far exceed her official clerical duties and paid hours of employment.

Much of Mrs. Ramsey's work involves attending to the needs of the Wentworth residents and their children. For instance, the LAC serves as the emergency contact number for working parents of children at Abbott School. When the children of these parents are ill either Mrs. Ramsey or Mrs. Harris must retrieve them. Mrs. Ramsey also receives and responds to emergency calls from the residents, whether she is at the office or her home. She is often seen dashing out the door to visit a sick resident or to tend to building problems. Mrs. Ramsey observed:

I have peoples call me twelve and one o'clock at night.... And I've gotten up to help peoples sweep water at night [when their apartment floods]; or gotten up to make calls, because maybe the person didn't have a telephone, to take somebody to the hospital. They [the residents] say, "Called 911, and they didn't come." They didn't have any carfare to get to the hospital. And then they get to the hospital and they don't keep 'em, and they call you back at three o'clock in the mornin', and you get up, go back.

It is nearly impossible for activist residents, such as Mrs. Ramsey, to rest, let alone take a "vacation" from work while remaining in the development. According to Mrs. Ramsey:

[Y]ou cannot have vacation.... And for this weekend I went up to Milwaukee and stayed a couple of days.... Because, if you stay over there [her apartment], they [the residents] know I'm there, and they walk in and out. If they need anything, they expect you to do it.

Yet, in describing the rigors of her "job," Mrs. Ramsey harbored no resentment about these demands; rather she expressed gratitude:

But you know what...? I'm so thankful to be able to have a car and have transportation. And to be able, you know ... to help somebody.

In her interrelated roles as LAC clerk and community household member, Evelyn Ramsey is repeatedly called upon and responds to the daily impact of racial discrimination and economic inequality on Wentworth residents' lives, whether in terms of insufficient building maintenance, inadequate public services, or lack of a telephone or money for transportation. Mrs. Ramsey's activities and comments support Cheryl Gilkes's (1988) study of wage-earning African-American community workers. In her research, Gilkes found a blurring of professional activities and community activities among the women she interviewed: "The early-morning and late-night phone calls, a permanent feature of their 'typical day,' reveals the ways in which their 'work' extended beyond the boundaries of a 'job'" (p. 57). In fact, for these black women community workers, their work was "part of a total lifestyle" (p. 59). Women-centered organizers are not paid professionals from outside the community; like Mrs. Ramsey, they typically are rooted in local networks and are closely linked to those with whom they work (Stall & Stoecker, 1998).

Youth Programming in the LAC: Extending Community Othermothering

To organize their community, Wentworth activists develop and utilize bridging social capital with individuals in outside groups, institutions, and organizations and, at times, across organizations. Private sphere concerns and objectives guide the types of relationships they develop to support resident activities and services. In fact, most LAC-sponsored formal resident-initiated service programs have been accomplished through the organized efforts of individual residents and the outside relationships they have garnered. Activities and services for the youth of the development are of particular importance.

Wentworth Gardens has been characterized as a "children's city" (CHA, 1947). Forty-five percent of the resident population are below 18 years of age, and of these children, more than half (56.5%) are below 10 years of age (CHA, 1997). Thus it is not surprising that youth are a major focus of Wentworth's women-centered organizing efforts. The LAC provides access to resources needed for LAC staff and volunteers to expand upon their community othermothering work.

The monies and support for youth programming are acquired through funds directed from the CHA to the LAC, other government monies secured by the LAC through grant applications, and services from nonprofits such as the Chicago Area Project (CAP). Wentworth activists have worked hard and have been very effective in securing these outside resources, in particular, utilizing their bridging social capital: that is, through the relationships they created with individuals in these organizations. For instance, in the late 1980s, as a result of activists' relationships with CAP personnel, the LAC gained a Volunteers in Service to America (VISTA) worker, a 2-year federally funded position, through CAP. Resident Marcella Bryant, a Wentworth resident, was hired to fill the VISTA position, in particular to work with delinquent and predelinquent youth in the Wentworth community.[5] At that time she was one of five VISTA workers in Chicago, and the only VISTA position located in Chicago public housing.[6] As part of her VISTA youth work, Marcella collaborated with Mrs. Maggie Mahone on augmenting an existing Youth Council. The LAC organized this program in 1981 to provide a creative outlet for Wentworth youth. Marcella explained:

> Our gangs are not really as intense as they are in other neighborhoods.... [I]t's not that bad over here. Most of the time we are trying to take care of our own little problems.... But it's the gathering, and all teenagers like to get together and what they call "hang together." You see we were trying to create [improve] ... the Youth Council, which just has the concept of trying to get them to come inside and spare some of that energy on the inside creating ideas on something they would like to do; and having fun ... and learn something rather than standing around.

There is agreement among the activists that children and youth need to be constructively engaged in order to keep them out of gang-related "trouble." At Wentworth, programming directed to children, teens, and young adults has included sports programs, numerous field trips, after-school tutoring, a Big Brother and Big Sister program, a teen pregnancy prevention and drug awareness program, a Youth Council, a Boys Girls Club, and a Step-Up Work Apprenticeship Program.

Although many of the resident activists have worked with youth in various formal programs over the last four decades, the individual most closely associated with youth programming at Wentworth Gardens is Mrs. Beatrice Harris. A grandmother in her early sixties, Mrs. Harris, in addition to raising her own seven children, has helped to rear her daughters' children. Originally from Mississippi, she was living in the Armour Square neighborhood north of Wentworth before she moved into the development in April 1966. Mrs. Harris began her work as a volunteer in the community as a Parent–Teachers Association (PTA) vice-president at Abbott School even before becoming a Wentworth resident. Employed by the CAP, she also serves as the LAC president. More recently, she was elected to the Resident Management Corporation's (RMC's) board and is chair of the

---

[5] Marcella Bryant first served as a bridge between the Wentworth Gardens community and Abbott Elementary School, which her children attended. She also served as the vice-president of Abbott's Local School Improvement Council. Her prior volunteer work both in Wentworth and at the school helped her to secure the VISTA position.

[6] Marcella also bridged with other VISTA workers citywide, since she met with them on a weekly basis, taking important knowledge about citywide youth problems and programs back to Wentworth.

RMC's Youth Committee. Mrs. Harris aptly explained, "I have volunteered all of my life since I've been here." It is true that she is centrally involved in most of the community projects at Wentworth Gardens. Like those of other resident activists, her story conveys how women-centered organizing is motivated by attachments to the community household and the Wentworth development she calls home. It illustrates how othermothering is extended from the household into the community through neighborhood institutions and organizations (see also Pardo, 1998).

For Mrs. Beatrice Harris, her roles as mother, grandmother, president of the LAC, and CAP community worker are all intertwined. In speaking of her paid half-time work with CAP, Mrs. Harris shared:

I like the job because it kept me right here with my kids and I was kind of able to keep up with them and the problems they was having. I was able to deal with them because all of it was related in with my work.

Beatrice Harris further explained that she identifies herself primarily as a "youth worker," a community othermother sharing the responsibility to care for all of the children in the development. For example, in the 1970s, when Mrs. Amey first served as a community outreach worker for CAP but was based at Stateway Gardens, Mrs. Harris volunteered to organize youth events at Wentworth.[7] Periodically CAP would send individuals to the development to work with Wentworth youth at the Wentworth field house, but according to Mrs. Harris, there "was hardly anything going on." In response, Mrs. Harris organized different types of youth activities:

I was taking children on trips and we would organize trips and things. We were holding parties and things for them and in the evening time [when] we had no programs within the community, other than Park District, that was going on.

Mrs. Harris has been a paid half-time CAP employee in Wentworth Gardens since 1979. In this position, she works through the LAC with the support of CAP to provide counseling, social events, and leadership development as part of "youth guidance," yet, she not only delivers CAP services and programs but builds relationships with this organization that assist in furthering her own organizing goals and those of other Wentworth activists (also see chapter 6).

Mrs. Harris elaborated on her more recent work with CAP:

This is a program that we are working on right now. We have about three people [part-time youth workers] who have been coordinated through CAP. We have youth counseling. We have young people that we give them things to do. Like last night,

---

[7] Stateway Gardens is another CHA family public housing development, a high-rise development located east of Wentworth Gardens across the Dan Ryan Expressway. In the 1970s, Stateway and Wentworth were managed by the same management office located at Stateway.

we had a skating party for the smaller kids. They [youth workers] charge them 25 cents. They sold popcorn as a fund raiser and sold food . . . they made $22.00. Last week they had a little sock hop up at the [Abbott] school and made thirty-some dollars. . . . It gives the young people from ages thirteen to seventeen something to do instead of being out here in the street.

In line with CAP's delinquency prevention goals, Mrs. Harris strives not only to provide good times and constructive outlets for the youth participants, but to support their personal growth, especially to expand the children's visions of their options in life:

They [CAP] also have a tea every year that's . . . with the young people. . . . We have our dance group . . . they [youth] go to different places. . . . It's pretty good . . . and that comes from us working with them [youth] in the community. . . . These are the things that youth guidance is all about, to give the young people a direction, something to do to give them a better outlook on life. . . . And you got to let them know that you got to get up and try to do something for yourself.

Another CAP program she encourages introduces youth to a range of career opportunities:

We have a Youth Conference every year. . . . [I]t's getting so large. . . . Last year had about 30 young people [at the conference] that went from our community. And what we do is get taffy apples and M&Ms [candy] and we have the kids sell a box. And that box does not pay for their ticket, but at least it makes them feel like they bought their own ticket. . . . This year they are going to be $14.00. . . . [T]he kids are so excited about it. . . . There's so many other communities that bring kids too. What the conference is about is we have keynote speakers there from the Bar Association; we get people from AT&T; we get people from UIC [University of Illinois at Chicago]; and doctors. . . . And you pick whatever . . . you are interested in . . . and let them tell you about this and how you can get into it, and how you can better yourself. . . . They have young people from different schools . . . that was on the panel and they was telling about their accomplishments in high school. . . . It would make the younger kids see what they were doing . . . and it might inspire them.

CAP's Wentworth program is run out of the LAC office; however, to expand programming, Mrs. Harris also strategically appropriates other Wentworth spaces and works with other youth workers, including the Park District in the field house, after-school programs at Abbott School, the Boys and Girls Club located in a Wentworth garden apartment, and, since the 1990s, the original RMC office. Additionally she organizes field trips to sites outside the neighborhood. Here Mrs. Harris describes some of the wide ranging program opportunities for youth she organized in early 1991:

We have an after school tutoring program, we have modern dance, we have cooking, sewing, arts and crafts. We have a small place here [in the LAC office] where we work so we can take our work to the school, to the Park District, to the Boys and Girls Club, wherever.

[W]e took them [the youth] to the park, the Park Academy, that was in February.... They loved it.... In July, we take about 30 kids to the Historical Society to a workshop for the youth on a Saturday morning. And they [Historical Society]...do all of the chaperoning. They hold the workshops. They feed them and do all of that.... [T]he fireman took them around and showed them all of the things and had a little show for them, with them coming down the ropes and all of that.... In the summertime we get a lot of free tickets for the kids and we take them to baseball. We have some Little League teams in the summertime.... We have playoffs that we do with CHA, and we have sports-a-rama every year. It consists of the little bitty kids and the larger kids.

When necessary, Mrs. Harris also works with children one-on-one to provide direct and effective youth assistance. Here she described one such intervention:

One girl appeared at the Park District that runs the modern dance class.... She was very enthusiastic about the program.... And we would buy the little tights and things, and they would dance out on the field...and she loved it. And we arranged [through CAP]...to send her to a dance school downtown.... [W]e paid for it and she's a very good dancer.

As a community othermother, in all of her interactions with children, whether as individuals or through the programs she organizes, Mrs. Harris communicates with the children that they are cared for beyond their immediate families:

And see we do these types of things, you take them on trips and things and give them little outings to make them feel that somebody cares about them and maybe that would help them.

Yet, Mrs. Harris recognized both the successes and the limitations of the youth programs and services she organizes, for instance, in describing the CAP program:

[W]e work with children. It's [CAP] a juvenile delinquency prevention program. You can't prevent problems sometimes, but sometimes you can. There have been a lot of children that have came through this program that we see that have did wonders. There have been a lot that have come through and it didn't do anything. They always teach us down there at the [CAP] meetings that you can't save the world. If you save two or three of them, you've done wonders; and the thing is you just don't stop.

Even effective women-centered organizers, like Beatrice Harris, however, cannot meet all of the needs of youth at Wentworth. Mrs. Harris understands that one organization, such as CAP, cannot solve all of the community's problems. She recognizes that she must bridge to, and network with, other organizations and organizational programs to augment resources

to engage in community organizing effectively. Yet, CHA and other government programs are being severely curtailed, largely by political and
economic decisions made outside the activists' control. Because of recent
cutbacks in federal funding for these programs, resident activists constantly struggle not only to expand youth program funding and offerings,
but to maintain the youth programs they have created. The Wentworth
Gardens field house, for example, while it is open, remains in disrepair.
It stands in stark contrast to the new field house in Armour Park, located
four blocks north of the development at the edge of a historically white
ethnic community. This well equipped facility remains unofficially off-
limits to African-Americans (see chapter 8). To add to the difficulties, in
December 1998, the Chicago Park District downgraded the Wentworth
field house from a "park" to a "playground," resulting in a significant loss
of staff and programming. Moreover, after-school programs were eliminated when Abbott School's Local School Advisory Council voted to cut
back funding for late hour janitorial services. These cutbacks have had a
major impact on the ability of Wentworth's women-centered organizers
to expand upon the LAC and CAP program offerings, frustrating their
attempts to help youth negotiate a safe passage from childhood and adolescence to adulthood (Dryfoos, 1998).

Also discouraging and challenging is having to work closely with a
mismanaged bureaucracy such as the CHA, whose motto might well be
"Enormous changes at the last minute." The LAC is the resident liason
with the CHA, and this bridging relationship is a close and problem-laden
one. Since so many CHA programs go through the LAC office, the office
is always brimming over with a variety of forms that need to be filled out,
sent out, or filed. To compound their work, the forms may arrive late or
be lost or routed incorrectly.[8] Over the course of our observations, CHA's
timeline for notification of activities, including completing the forms, often
required a 24-hour turnaround time, or even less. Geraldine Scott, who has
worked in the LAC office, describes this problem:

[T]he LAC does have a lot of programs and things that come through their hands
and by me being there now [working in the office], I understand CHA could do
stuff at the last minute. Last minute they'll call, "Uh, we gonna do this and do
that. Could you bring thirty kids or something? . . . " And so, the LAC has a responsibility. You know, you gotta get out, and you gotta find these kids. . . . You
know, they got somethin' and they wanna see if three residents wanna [go]. Now,
which three residents do you choose and things like that. So, it's, it's kinda a hard
thing.

---

[8] We observed a CHA staff person who was dropping off forms for an annual youth event
on Friday; the forms were due the following Monday. The LAC office was to have received
them earlier, but they had been delivered incorrectly first to Wentworth's CHA management
office.

On one of our visits to the LAC office one spring day, Mrs. Harris explained that she was spending the whole day doing paperwork – filling out forms:

Seems sometimes the job just is paperwork. We have to fill these out once a month. The white forms, we fill these out . . . are due twice a month. These were due Friday, but I only just got them Friday since we were in Springfield [the state capital].

Finally, equally distressing to activists are those residents who are not directly involved in community-building activities, but are suspicious that the activists, as "insiders," are gaining special rewards and excluding other residents from their "clique." Both Lottie Weathersby and Geraldine Scott shared that they had heard negative comments, in particular about LAC activists, before they became involved there. Geraldine:

I heard all the horror stories about the LAC. . . . It's like, some people, you know, you talk to your neighbors around here, and people that's been living here, they'll tell you all, "Up there, they're all for themselves, you know. All they do is look out for their family. They do this, they do that." You know, and you hear all the neighborhood gossip and stuff. You know, you hear all the negative things before you hear the positive things. . . . You could never please everybody. . . . So, it's, it's kinda a hard thing. And people that don't really know . . . they see it as favoritism and stuff, you know. . . . [Y]ou're not gonna satisfy everybody, no matter how fair you try to be.

One limit of bonding social capital is that these strong in-group loyalties can also create strong out-group antagonisms (Putnam, 2000, p. 23).

Although the accusations of other residents are discouraging to Wentworth organizers, activists such as Beatrice Harris are clear that their organizing efforts will not be deterred by rumors or nonactivists' negative feelings about them or other community organizers:

[I] feel that I don't care what you think about me I'm just here. I mean I'm working and this is what I want to do. This is what I like to do.

Tenant Security: Formalizing Community Norms

Wentworth residents have been active in organizing to ensure their and their neighbors' safety and security. Guided by the same objectives that govern their more informal community norm setting, activists seek to encourage other Wentworth residents both to maintain community norms of acceptable behavior and to adhere to CHA rules and governmental laws. They have approached this goal through multiple means, including activist representatives working with the 9th District of the Chicago Police Department; organizing Block Watches; forming a resident Tenant Patrol; establishing Security Committees, first in the LAC, later in the RMC; and most recently, forming the CHA Tenant Patrol.

Mrs. Maggie Mahone is the resident activist most recognized and responsible for organizing around security issues. Born in Alabama to sharecropping parents, Maggie Mahone and her younger brother were raised by an othermother, her mother's sister, after her parents died when she was 8 years old. She graduated from the ninth grade, worked as a cook in a hotel in Mississippi, and in the late 1950s moved up to Detroit, where she met her husband. Maggie Mahone moved into Wentworth with her husband and her 5-year-old daughter in 1964. Now in her early 70s, a widowed grandmother of four, Mrs. Mahone still lives in her original apartment on the first floor of a three-story walk-up apartment. She has a close relationship with her daughter, Francine, and her grandchildren, who, until recently, also lived in Wentworth.

Maggie Mahone has been active directly or indirectly in every major initiative at Wentworth since the mid-1960s: the laundromat, the grocery store, gardening beautification efforts, and other resident support programs.[9] For example in 1973, she and nine other Wentworth residents (including Beatrice Harris and Hallie Amey) participated in a "leadership class" provided by the Citizens Information Service of Illinois. The residents developed a Community Resource Book, in which Mrs. Mahone included information on local civil rights and human rights organizations. She has been an officer in the LAC and the RMC and a president of the Park Advisory Council and is a member of the Silver Blades, a group of eight senior women, all but one of whom live in Wentworth Gardens. In addition to her housekeeping jobs on the South Side of Chicago, her Wentworth organizational work claims about 20 volunteer hours per week. Mrs. Mahone explained that she spends the majority of this time on development security issues.

After Mrs. Mahone settled into Wentworth, it did not take her long, 2 or 3 months at most, to become active in Wentworth's community organizing efforts. Mrs. Mahone explained that it was Mrs. Amey who first encouraged her to participate:

[Y]ou know Miss Amey with that little charming smile. . . . She came by that day and knocked on the door and said, "Good morning, how you doing?"

It was Mrs. Amey who connected Mrs. Mahone with the local police. In 1964, Mrs. Mahone began attending the monthly meetings with the 9th Police District Police commander. Mrs. Mahone found these meetings to be very informative:

[T]he District Commander would tell us all the things that happened within that month's time. Like if there was an arrest made over here at Wentworth Gardens or

---

[9] Mrs. Mahone also was involved in the PTA and worked as a classroom volunteer at Abbott School, which her daughter attended. She served as a Girl Scout leader, as well, for 10 years.

who got shot, and who was robbed, and you know different things like that. He'd bring us up on the different things that would be happening at the stations.

Mrs. Mahone sustained an active role with the 9th District Police Division, utilizing her knowledge and relationships with police officers to work for Wentworth's security.[10]

In 1975, she became a "beat rep" in a city-sponsored community policing program. The Chicago Beat Representative Program was operated through block clubs and area meetings to increase community participation in neighborhood security and to facilitate communication between the beat officer and the residents in the officer's target area.[11] As a beat rep, Mrs. Mahone represented Wentworth at the police district level, attending monthly area meetings. In this role she both received information about crime patterns in the area and was given the opportunity to share Wentworth residents' security concerns with the police. Mrs. Mahone described how this communication took place:

[There is] this community relations sergeant in there taking notes. If you have a problem in your backyard with kids drinking beer and what time this is happening, he's taking notes and he'll put men to work on that.

Mrs. Mahone spearheaded the first efforts to organize Block Watches in Wentworth's seven blocks; however, residents were hesitant to participate. Mrs. Mahone:

When we were working on that [Block Watch], I have forms at home to fill out. If you wanted to become a member of the neighborhood watch, you'd sign your name. And then after I got these filled out, I'd take them back to the beat rep office . . . and the rep coordinator . . . would get the signs to go into the windows that [said], "This is a neighborhood watch and we call the police."

Since only a few residents agreed to place signs in their windows, this organizing effort was not successful, although efforts to establish Block Watches still are under way under the auspecius of the RMC.

Mrs. Mahone has consistently reported any illegal activity she has witnessed over the years – in fact, one youth called her "Mrs. FBI." Yet, she understands that many residents may be afraid to participate in a

---

[10] In 1973, because of her active role with the 9th District Police Division and involvement in Wentworth security issues, Mrs. Mahone delivered a "citizen rebuttal" to an editorial on a citywide controversy that involved an allegation of police brutality on a local major television news program. Mrs. Mahone felt it was important to challenge publicly "[t]he prevailing opinion in this section of the district . . . [that] most of the police officers in the 009 District were hard core racists" (*Community Police News*, September 1975, p. 4). For her support she received a commendation letter from the Chicago Police Department's deputy superintendent.

[11] By the late 1980s, the beat rep program had been terminated.

neighborhood security program such as a Block Watch, even to call the police, because they fear retaliation from known offenders:

[T]here are so few people that will call the police if you see something. But I do call the police if I see something happening that shouldn't be happening. As long as they're [offenders] not bodily harming me, they can say anything they want to, and it don't bother me. So I'm not afraid to call the police.

Mrs. Mahone's observations were supported by another resident, who, although she also has been active in working on security issues in Wentworth, admitted that she herself is fearful to call the police:

[If] I call the police, then when you finish talking to them . . . they tell them [the offender] who called. I live alone. I live by myself. I can't afford nobody trying to break [in]to my house. . . . So I keeps my mouth shut.

Mrs. Mahone suggested that some residents also might not call the police because they think the police will not respond. This poses a dilemma for third-party enforcement. To be effective, the third party must be trustworthy; but when it is a representative of the state, the safeguards against the abuse of power may be weak or missing. In Chicago and other major cities in the United States, the police have often been cited for misuse of power either by underreacting – selectively underserving certain populations – or by overreacting – engaging in police harassment, for example, (North, 1990).

Police nonresponse has not been Mrs. Mahone's experience, although she admits that she is very persistent:

I get very good service from the police department because I'm determined. If I call them or something and nothing happens, I'll keep calling.

Mrs. Mahone explained that she also has the advantage of knowing the police at the station:

And then when you go to the meetings you get to know the policeman, and the commanders, and the sergeants, and you know who to ask for when you call. I might call and say, "Let me talk to Officer Edwards, or whoever."

This advantage could be viewed as a disadvantage by residents who fear being labeled as police collaborators. Mrs. Mahone, on the other hand, insists that she is not fearful of the consequences of her community security work:

People ask me if I'm afraid to be out there. No, I'm not, as long as they know you're not afraid. Sometimes you might be afraid, but you don't let them know it. . . . One day I went into the basement [store] and there was a group sitting on the porch. . . . [W]hen I walked past, one of the kids said, "She ain't nothing but a policeman." So I just turned around and looked at every one of them, and you could see the guilty one. So I just looked at them and they turned around and went on home. By that, they knew I wasn't afraid of them.

In addition to challenging youth when it is necessary, Mrs. Mahone has worked with other activists to engage Wentworth youth in programs that steer them away from delinquent activities; "to try to service the youth so they wouldn't get into too much trouble." In the summer of 1988, for instance, Mrs. Mahone worked with Marcella Bryant, then the VISTA worker, to create the first Wentworth Junior Police program. Before that summer, Wentworth had no youth police programs, although the 9th District Police had started programs in other neighborhoods in their district. Marcella explained how the program was organized:

[T]he Junior Police program . . . meets every Wednesday at 4:00 at the park district field house and we have like about thirty kids and the ages range from thirteen and under. We have different things such as alcohol and drug awareness. We have books and stuff that we read about; and I have like parent volunteers; and we have one of the 9th district police, Officer Carter, who's the neighborhood relations [police representative].[12] He comes over also and works with the kids every Wednesday. . . . Every week he's there. . . . [T]hen we have a woman [police officer] who calls and supplies us with films; and comes out and talks to the kids concerning gangs and crime . . . to prevent them at a young age from getting involved with a lot of crime; or understanding the fact that if you do this crime, the punishment that is behind this crime. So they [the kids] bring all kinds of questions to the meeting with Officer Carter, and we have a nice time with the children. . . . It works very well.

To encourage the youth to keep attending meetings, Wentworth activists organized social activities that were integral to the meetings.

The organizing of the Wentworth Junior Police Program is an illustrative example of the bridging social capital that is central to effective community activism. For instance, the prior social relationships of Mrs. Mahone, Marcella Bryant, and Officer Carter were useful in taking advantage of a juvenile delinquency prevention program, effectively bridging the Wentworth community and the 9th District Police Department.

As Mrs. Mahone and other activists have worked toward a safe and secure environment at Wentworth, their efforts have become increasingly difficult in the last 10 to 15 years. Mounting unemployment and underemployment are associated with the increase in drug abuse and drug dealing in the Wentworth development; so, too, is government disinvestment in

[12] Officer Carter was described by Mrs. Mahone and other activists as a local police officer who worked especially hard to establish a close relationship with the Wentworth Gardens residents. As an African-American, he was a role model for the young men in the development and would participate in community events outside his designated work hours.

housing in general, and in youth programming more specifically. These obstacles have presented challenges to Wentworth organizers seeking to curtail crime in their community. Maggie Mahone, in her current work with the CHA Resident Tenant Patrol and as chair of the RMC's Security Committee, knows all too well the difficulties these obstacles pose. For instance, when she holds regular "security meetings," she invites only a select, trusted group of women to protect their personal safety: the members of the security committee, the manager, and the CHA police. Mrs. Mahone:

[We] sit down and we talk about drugs and things like that; and you can't talk about drugs with just anybody; you have to be careful. So that's why I don't want too many people in the security meetings.

Irrespective of these challenges, Mrs. Mahone and other Wentworth residents continue their women-centered organizing to stem crime in their development. In the spring of 1998, 19 older-generation activists, including Maggie Mahone, graduated from a Senior Citizen Law Enforcement Academy held at the Wentworth field house. Also noteworthy is the recognition that Mrs. Mahone received for her organizing efforts in September 2000 – a citywide award from the 9th District Police Department for her "volunteer efforts to maintain a safe community in Illinois." By formalizing community norm setting, Mrs. Mahone and other activists have encouraged adults and youths to become collaborators in accepting and communicating community behavioral norms and to participate in wider crime prevention efforts. Mindful of some of the limitations of their "partners," they continue to bridge with CHA's Tenant Patrol and Chicago's Community Policing Program, attempting to mobilize city, state, and federal resources to work for a safe and secure development.

Event Planning: Enlarging the Work of Community Kinship

With the increasing difficulties of maintaining safety and security at Wentworth, enlarging the work of community kinship to bolster the morale of activists is crucial to sustaining vital social relationships within their development. As with community othermothering and norm setting, Wentworth women activists extend and formalize the work of community kinship to expand their bonding social capital. At Wentworth Gardens, women organize numerous parties, celebrations, and yearly ritual events through the LAC – an Easter Egg Hunt, the summer Funfest, the Back-to-School party, the Halloween and Christmas parties, a Wentworth resident reunion, and periodic award banquets paying tribute to residents who have worked tirelessly in the community. Through their women-centered organizing of these LAC-sponsored events, they contribute to a sense of social solidarity among all involved.

FIGURE 3. Upper left: Wentworth women resident volunteers cooking for a community event (photographer: Susan Stall). Upper right: The Wentworth Local Advisory Council (LAC) office reception area – Mrs. Lottie Weathersby on the phone and Marcella Bryant standing in the doorway (photographer: Diana Solis). Center left: The LAC president, Beatrice Harris, with youth in the LAC office (photographer: Diana Solis). Center right: Wentworth children performing at a community event (photographer: Susan Stall). Lower left: Wentworth residents dancing in the central courtyard at a community event (photographer: Susan Stall). Lower right: Members of Wentworth's CHA Tenant Patrol and other activists in front of the Field House celebrating Wentworth's 50th anniversary (photographer: Susan Stall).

In her study of elite women volunteers, Arlene Kaplan Daniels (1985) developed the concept of *sociability work* to capture a distinct and important form of labor, particularly apparent in the activities of women engaged in the planning and execution of community events. These "parties" are essential components of women-centered organizing because they elicit both the attention and the allegiance of participants, build a sense of community spirit, and promote generalized reciprocity and a sense of community responsibility. Daniels explained:

Sociability provides an avenue for collective representations . . . to be reaffirmed. The party is a collective representation that asserts [community] membership.[13] Collective representations are activities that become meaningful symbols to an entire group. . . . These symbols are strengthened and reaffirmed through repetition. (pp. 372–373)

The yearly community events organized by Wentworth activists are integral to their community organizing efforts. Through the collective work of all of the activists, these community events build social solidarity within this group of community workers, as well as attract new members. Also central to the success of these events is securing contributions of food, prizes, and needed goods from individuals and companies outside the Wentworth development. The activist Marcella Bryant described these organizing efforts:

Everybody [activists] goes together to pull off the event which is once a year, usually at the end of July or the first part of August. . . . We also have a Halloween party for the kids and a Christmas party. The parties are put on mostly by the LAC and the [Central] Area Council; and some people give us donations for different things. Especially for our Fun Fest we write letters for donations. People donate food and stuff, like . . . RC [soft drink company] gives us like a discount. And our LAC president plays a big part in getting things for our Fun Fest, and mostly like for the parties: Halloween, Christmas, and a Back-to-School party. Those are three events we have every year.

There is a minimal amount of financial support from the CHA; the success of these events is dependent on fund-raising efforts to solicit financial and material donations from community contacts outside Wentworth. For example, at the Back-to-School party, activists give out donated paper, folders, pencils, and other school supplies to the youth and their families who attend. Many Wentworth residents, because of their poverty, find it difficult to purchase these items for their children who are returning to school each fall. Thus, this "party" serves both practical and celebratory functions.

The dedicated cadre of workers who produce these events use organizing skills that they have developed over the years, first as community othermothers, then through participation in the regular orchestration of these events. Planning these events also requires that the organizers create and utilize bridging social capital, both in their fund-raising efforts and in the invitations sent to people who live outside the community. Over the course of years, the Wentworth event organizers have developed social ties to small and large businesses and nonprofits and have learned

---

[13] Durkheim discussed "collective representations" in his *The Elementary Forms of the Religious Life* (1954, pp. 376–388).

who are the best sources for supplies according to cost, reliability, and location. These contacts are important in order to secure the needed supplies, but this "gift giving" also can further support the community-building and bridging goals of women-centered organizing. In their community study *Yankee City*, Warner, Low, Lunt, & Stole (1963) stressed the integrative role of fund-raising in a community, building sociability among the event planners and between activists and the suppliers of funds and good:

The exchange of services and money, usually in the pleasant context of entertainment, constitutes one of the great contributions of the associations to the social unity of the community, for it knits diverse groups together. (p. 141)

We have attended some of these community events, as do a wide range of technical assistants, government, nonprofit, and local institutional representatives whom Wentworth activists have worked with over the years. By responding to requests to donate soft drinks, or a few dozen eggs to dye for the Easter Egg Hunt, we became participants, rather than just observers, and strengthened our social bonds with the Wentworth activists.

The complexity of assembling an event – "the rigors of successful party giving" – is evident only to those involved. The work involved remains largely invisible; hence often it is taken for granted. In fact, it is a contradiction that one measure of a community event's success is that it appears to be a spontaneous or effortless happening. Monica Ramsey, the daughter of Mrs. Evelyn Ramsey, takes her own children to the community parties and celebrations that she attended as a child. She related that it is now expected that in Wentworth Gardens the LAC will organize holiday and Back-to-School parties:

[T]hey [LAC] do a lot of things for people that they [residents] just don't . . . they see it, but refuse to acknowledge it. . . . Like, they have . . . all [the] holiday parties. Valentine's parties, Back-to-School parties. . . . And like now it's just kind of accepted that happens.

Although numerous Wentworth activists contribute to planning these events, typically a few are key; yet, even their essential individual contributions may be hidden, evident to only those involved. The residents who have participated in the craft of community party giving at Wentworth Gardens especially recognize the contribution of Mrs. Lottie Weathersby. Marcella Carter, who had worked with Mrs. Weathersby in the production of the Fun Fests, recalled that she was a key bridge person, "the one who had all the contacts. All I did was like take her [Mrs. Weathersby], drive her around and pick up all the stuff." As an LAC officer, a vice-president for two 4-year terms, Mrs. Weathersby has been actively engaged in the youth events at Wentworth Gardens, but she is best known for her organizing skills in the orchestration of community award events.

Mrs. Weathersby's first award banquet was on Valentine's Day weekend in 1979, an event she organized with her close friend Viola Henry, a former Wentworth resident activist along with several other residents. Mrs. Weathersby explained the purpose of this banquet, held in the field house:

[W]e was gonna do it as a surprise to Mrs. Amey and Mrs. Driver because they were so dedicated and worked so hard for so many years and did so much.

Even though the award banquet was a worthy cause, there were no available monies to stage the event. Moreover, the activists were hesitant to charge guests to attend because of the residents' low incomes. Using "creative financing," Mrs. Weathersby and Mrs. Henry approached the on-site CHA manager and secured very modest CHA funds, approximately $300 earmarked for community projects in the development.[14] Also, much of the food was prepared by volunteer residents. As mentioned in the previous chapter, communal cooking is essential in the community household. It also is a key "building block" in the construction of sociability (Daniels, 1988, p. 118) in women-centered organizing. Seventeen years after this event, Mrs. Weathersby could still describe the banquet menu:

We had fried chicken. We had string beans and corn, potato salad.... We had a vegetable tray.... We had the works. We had roast beef, cause we went up here to the Docs [local grocery store] and bought roast beef... and all of that.... We got some donations from some people.

As part of event planning, Mrs. Weathersby and other banquet organizers used their contacts with individuals, organizations, and businesses outside the Wentworth development to secure donations of food and party accessories. They also used their social connections to draw representatives from the CHA, the Central Area Council (CAC), and other Chicago government agencies to the banquet. Mrs. Weathersby:

There was a lot of people there that night... because we had invited people that they [Mrs. Amey and Mrs. Driver] didn't even know was coming.... Ricky Williams from CAP, Mrs. Randolph, Ms. Russell was the [Wentworth] manager, Mr. Herman Johnson, Mr. Dillonham, they was all out of CAC.... We just had... all of the old-timers people [residents] were there... all of those people here at night.

Lottie Weathersby contributed other special skills to the event, especially in creating a party atmosphere. She understands the background work that is necessary to create this ambience. She self-reflected, "I've always had a

[14] Each CHA unit is allocated a small amount of money ($0.75 per unit in 1979 and $1.50 per unit by 1996) for an area community project. At Wentworth, in 1979, that amounted to about $300.00.

big head about doing things." Mrs. Weathersby was clear that she wanted to set a special tone for the event, finding creative ways, for instance, in how she, Viola Henry, and other resident volunteers transformed the gymnasium in the field house into a celebratory space:

We bought tablecloths and had tablecloths for everybody. . . . It was beautiful. . . . I had jazz records. I had Duke Ellington and Jimmy Weatherspoon. . . . We bought certificates; we bought plaques.

Mrs. Weathersby's rewards for this function were the satisfaction of surprising Mrs. Amey and Mrs. Driver and the recognition she gave them and other award recipients. Yet she and Mrs. Henry incurred personal monetary costs for this function: "A lot of the money we spent out of our own pockets . . . me and Viola spent out of our pockets."

Mrs. Weathersby, along with other activists, continued this tradition annually for several years, but at later award banquets, attendees were coaxed and cajoled into purchasing tickets. The monies gained helped to defer the costs of the banquets not covered by donations and to decrease the difficult work of food preparation for the large number of people. Mrs. Weathersby:

After that we went on with banquets like every year. We went to Robert's 600 Room [restaurant on the South Side of Chicago] for two years and we paid like $3,000 for our banquets there because it was outside the community and we didn't have all of this cooking and all of this stuff to do. We did the decorating.

In the summer and fall of 1996, Mrs. Weathersby worked with an event planning team, once again to organize a surprise tribute dinner for Mrs. Hallie Amey.[15] The Tribute Dinner held in November 1996 accomplished its intended goal – to honor Mrs. Amey for her decades of community service – but this event contributed much more. In the transformed hotel banquet room, the Wentworth Gardens community was visually expanded into a collective representation to include all of those individuals and representatives of organizations and public agencies who had in some way contributed to and benefitted from their affiliation with Wentworth Gardens activists, in this instance, especially, Hallie Amey. Mrs. Weathersby and her "team" had effectively drawn together residents and resident alumnae, community organizers, service providers,

---

[15] Throughout the summer and into the fall of 1996, Mrs. Weathersby worked with her event planning team – several residents, a CHA employee with ties to Wentworth, and one of the authors, Susan Stall – to attend to the myriad details of careful event planning. Most meetings were informal ones in the LAC office, but one was held at Mrs. Weathersby's apartment for a home-cooked breakfast, and another at the hotel for a "food-testing lunch." All of these meetings were conducted in a sociable context to generate esprit among the planning team and deepen our commitment to the organizing work. But it was Mrs. Weathersby's ongoing persistence and encouragement that kept us working on our individual assignments, as well as selling banquet tickets to all we knew who had been touched by Mrs. Amey.

individuals from universities and granting agencies, and city and state employees, skillfully crossing barriers of race, class, gender, and age. Through her tenacious efforts and her organizational skills, she constructed hospitality to create the aura of sociability necessary to reaffirm their commitment, not only to Mrs. Amey, but to the Wentworth Gardens community. Equally remarkable, Lottie Weathersby organized this event without wealth or family or corporate connections, instead tapping into and strengthening her social and bridging bonds, a group of conscientious residents and professionals with whom she had long-term relationships.

Women like Mrs. Weathersby elevate hospitality to more than party giving. They develop a style of sociability that becomes an expression of self. According to Daniels (1985), "In a world where no formal title [or salary] can be offered to the successful, pride in a distinctive style of hospitality may have to suffice." (p. 368)

Mrs. Weathersby receives recognition for her skills only from those individuals and activists who have worked closely with her on these events; yet, her event planning work is invaluable. Mrs. Weathersby has ignited Wentworth residents' community spirit and participation, encouraging others to become involved in building a cohesive social fabric. She has a vision of what the community can accomplish and the ability to communicate that vision to others. Because of the strength of her vision and her abilities as a women-centered organizer, Mrs. Weathersby has been able to capture the interest and commitment of other Wentworth residents and individuals, groups, and organizations outside the development who have in some way contributed to and benefitted from their affiliation with Wentworth Gardens activists.

Although Mrs. Weathersby's work – the time and commitment – is remarkable, the work does take its toll. Lottie Weathersby, as are the majority of the older-generation Wentworth organizers, is at risk and often does suffer the consequences of activist burnout. Also, the knowledge of these demands makes it difficult for Wentworth activists to withdraw or to retire from the work. African-American community workers become "part of an ongoing system of activities which is the community's response to the routine problems it faces" (Gilkes, 1980, pp. 219–220). Gilkes (1980) quotes the words of one woman activist as a poignant representation of the great number and range of problems that African-American women community workers must contend with, and the increasingly complex politics that surround their solutions: she felt as if she were "holding back the ocean with a broom."

ACTIVIST BURNOUT

In Hill Collins's (1991) analysis of black motherhood, she underlines the importance of recognizing "the very real costs of mothering to

African-American women" (116). The community othermothers in Wentworth Gardens shoulder tremendous responsibilities in their own households, and once they become active in the expanded private sphere, they
realize how much work there is to be done.

From our observations, and in our interviews with Wentworth activists, it was obvious that frustration, overload, and burnout accompany
women-centered organizing. The reasons are both personal and political
and often are interrelated. Some of these reasons are that the community's
demands for their skills and energies may be greater than their abilities
and resources to handle the demands (Gilkes, 1980); that there are ongoing
frustrations of working with inactive residents who complain but do
not volunteer; and that there are myriad problems of working with
the inefficiencies and, at times, incompetencies of the CHA and HUD
bureaucracies.

We have observed meetings at which activists are visibly fatigued. Mary
Rias, cooking for a resident's funeral, still stopped in on a meeting; yet,
she could barely keep her eyes open. At times, resident activists explicitly
state that they are worn out. Mrs. Amey often falls asleep in a chair, taking
advantage of the opportunity to catch a quick nap if her attention at a
meeting is not immediately needed. This is especially true after there has
been a big push to stage a community event or an overload of meetings,
or when they are contending with a personal crisis (e.g., family illness or
death) – in addition to their everyday workload.

Beatrice Harris, for instance, often complains about being tired or exhausted. A few days after the late summer annual Back-to-School party,
and after she had taken Wentworth youth on a field trip on Labor Day, she
had dark circles under her eyes and a weary expression. After expressing
her satisfaction with the party's "success," Mrs. Harris complained about
her aches and pains, specifically pains in her side, back, and stomach. She
confided that she is sometimes hospitalized in the early fall because of
exhaustion due to her increased LAC responsibilities during the summer
months with extended youth programs and the summer food program. At
one point during our fieldwork, Mrs. Harris was so overworked that other
activists insisted she take a week of rest at home, carefully protecting her
privacy.

It is not surprising that it is the older activists (age 50 or above) who are
more likely to experience sheer exhaustion. Dorothy McMiller shared:

I'm tired. . . . I used to be involved in a lot of things. But . . . age kind of slows you
down.

At times, off-site meetings can even offer a respite from the never ending
demands. For instance, in the midst of the added organizing for a CHA-
sponsored event, Evelyn Ramsey discussed her annoyance that an all-day

work trip was canceled. Her doctor advised that she needed rest. The trip offered the opportunity for her to get away from the LAC office, even for one day.

All of the key activists are involved in at least one other organizing activity. Lottie Weathersby, as an example, works both in the LAC and as a key event planner. To manage potential burnout, she, as do other resident activists, needs to take a short break from the rigors of the role of community organizer periodically. In June 1996, Mrs. Weathersby, before she had geared up to orchestrate Mrs. Amey's Award Dinner, discussed her decision to step back from her active LAC role:

I'm not working for nobody this year. I'm tired. I'm sitting here now [LAC office] and my back is in so much pain 'til I can't hardly sit on this chair, cause I got arthritis. The doctor said I got arthritis all over my spine. . . . I don't hardly go out too much in winter. You know, when you see me I'm bundled up in a lot of stuff. This knee right now is bothering me a lot. So I'm probably gonna have knee surgery.

Burnout is exacerbated by the activists' impatience with those Wentworth residents who will not volunteer in the community. Residents may be limited in their ability to volunteer for a number of reasons: economic constraints; their need to work long hours at paid employment; lack of skills; lack of time; child-care or family responsibilities; fear, particularly in tenant security work; feelings they have nothing to offer; despair; or problems with addiction. Although resident activists recognize these constraints, they do at times express frustration with those who do not participate but desire or take advantage of the services and programs that activists organize; for example, Maggie Mahone complained:

If we just had more people concerned about it [drug problem] maybe it wouldn't be as bad. But a lot of people just sit and see it happen and don't try to do anything or say anything.

The older generation of Wentworth activists are well aware of the costs of burnout and, more generally, the need to expand their ranks. The challenge remains: to pass the baton to younger-generation activists.

THE NEXT GENERATION OF WENTWORTH'S LEADERSHIP

The older-generation activists such as Hallie Amey, Beatrice Harris, and Maggie Mahone have worked tirelessly for many decades and are cognizant of the need to develop the next generation of Wentworth leaders. To cultivate the potential of younger Wentworth women, they serve as activist mothers (Naples, 1992), actively recruiting and mentoring younger women to participate in community organizing. Day to day, the children and "fictive kin" of Wentworth activists witness firsthand their own mothers' and community othermothers' social ties and networking skills to support the work of the community household and to effect change in their community. Some, including Monica Ramsey and Gloria Smith, have become activists as well.[16]

Monica Ramsey was 4 years old when she moved into Wentworth in 1975 with her mother, Evelyn Ramsey, and her sister. Now, in her late 20s, she has raised her three young children in her own Wentworth Gardens apartment. As others did, she invoked familial terminology when she described her life in the development: "Everybody is like family." According to Monica, all of her best friends live in Wentworth. And her mother is close and available. Monica explains that she is a member of the community household:

I just feel comfortable here. . . . And it's so small, you will know if somebody else moves in. . . . I just feel comfortable around them [other residents]. They always lookin' out for me.

As one of the younger resident activists, Monica has been involved in community work since she was a small child through Mrs. Evelyn Ramsey's activist mothering. Monica Ramsey explains how she began working in the community:

I became involved by hangin' with her [her mother] . . . workin' in the store. I'd help in the store with her down there.

Monica has worked in the grocery store since age 6 and is still a mainstay volunteer, working on Mondays and Fridays. She more or less grew up in the LAC office, but in her late teens she became actively involved in the workings of the LAC. She began by attending LAC meetings, then served as the chair of the Tenant Relations committee until she was elected treasurer of the LAC in December 1995. Monica explains her motivation for her participation: "I like to help people." She sees her age as an advantage:

By me being younger, I can deal with the younger generation a little better. . . . They need somebody younger. . . . They always for some reason bring their problems to me.

---

[16] Other children of resident activists also have become activists. Francine Mahone, Maggie Mahone's daughter, is active in the community. In the late 1990s both she and her mother were serving as elected members of the Local School Advisory Council at Abbott Elementary School, Francine as president. Francine also was active in the Wentworth Gardens LAC. She continues to be active in Wentworth Gardens, even though she no longer lives there. Currently she serves on the board that organizes the yearly Wentworth Gardens resident reunion. Held for the last 15 years, it attracts former residents who lived in Wentworth as far back as 1955. Vickie Harris, daughter of Beatrice Harris, also is active in the LAC.

Monica and her mother admit that although they may not always see eye to eye because they are so much alike, Monica still has respect for her mother. She is especially aware that her current activism is related to, if not completely modeled on, her mother's:

I had a problem ... really communicatin' with other people. I communicate with people I know but I never know how to just strike up a conversation or just blend in a conversation with strangers ... 'cause I don't know 'em. But my mother, she always starts, so, I blend in and start talkin'. . . . Cause there was a time I wouldn't have been able to do this [interview].

As her mother is, Monica is involved in several activist efforts. Besides her work with the grocery store and the LAC, Monica is involved in Women for Economic Security, the local Park Council, the Youth Council, and the on-site children's food program.

One of Monica's close friends, Gloria Smith, says that she's been involved with activities in the development since she was 3. She started volunteering in the grocery store when she was only 8 years old. Although she started working with Mrs. Amey, it was Mrs. Ramsey whom she described as the person she could call on for help. Gloria's mother was busy working outside the home, and her father could not serve as her mother – "[He wasn't the same thing as talkin' to somebody that's like a mother." – She explained that Mrs. Ramsey was her othermother:

Mrs. Ramsey, she's always there for me, since I was a kid, she basically raised me. She's always been there.

As Monica Ramsey has, Gloria has good memories of her childhood in Wentworth Gardens. She remembers swimming in the pool, going on field trips, attending dances at the field house, and "skating and zoos and parks and stuff." Gloria described growing up surrounded by volunteerism: "It was a part of everything." And she said of her close friends who live in Wentworth Gardens, "[W]e do for each other," and added, "Anybody basically in this yard [Wentworth courtyard], I can ask and they'll do it." Gloria now lives in her own apartment with her three children. She described herself as someone who "was always helping people." In addition to working in the store, she has worked when needed in the laundromat and has volunteered with the LAC for years. In December 1995 she was elected to the LAC Board.

Nancy Naples (1998b) both points to the importance of early childhood socialization and social networks in constructing the motivation for community work. Both Monica and Gloria were socialized by strong organizers who are active members of a community household and who hold distinct positions as community caretakers in Wentworth Gardens. Both have been drawn into the community household by women-centered organizers who have developed an understanding of community needs that demand an organized response. These newer activists, like the more mature women who inspired them, are motivated by an ethic of care that directs their activism.

CONCLUSIONS

For Wentworth activists the "community is both a living space and a work site" (Pardo, 1998, p. 275). The women-centered organizing of LAC activists is an attempt to compensate for the inadequate quality and quantity of public services in the development. Their gender, race, and social class – experienced both as the obstacles these present and the strengths the activists have – shape the goals, strategies, and often the outcome of LAC organizing efforts (see also Naples, 1998a; Robnett, 1996). Mrs. Evelyn Ramsey makes up for the lack of response to a sick resident's call for a taxi or an ambulance by providing a makeshift chauffeur service, expanding her official workday hours to accommodate resident needs. Mrs. Beatrice Harris tries to compensate for the loss of sustained governmental funds for youth programming by scrambling harder to find programs and funding through her bridging relationships with, for instance, the CHA or Chicago Area Project. Mrs. Maggie Mahone, "Miss FBI," actively engages in personal surveillance of the development while she helps to create and support crime prevention programs. Mrs. Lottie Weathersby acts as an event planner to create communitywide celebrations and to give public recognition to those whose community work might otherwise be unnoticed.

Wentworth activists work behind the scenes, contributing specialized, valuable resources: time and commitment, unique skills and strategies, and ties to residents within the community and to people and organizations outside the development (see also Barnett, 1995). The services and programs these women have created through their women-centered organizing provide special activities for children, a safer community, and tributes for resident volunteers, but they also construct bonding and bridging social capital, at times recruiting new activists and drawing together the larger community. For the activists, the free spaces, like the LAC, offer arenas outside the family where they can develop a "growing sense that they [have] the right to work – first in behalf of others, then in behalf of themselves" (Evans & Boyte, 1981, p. 61).

Wentworth activists who work at the LAC serve as liaisons between the expanded private sphere of the community household and the public sphere with such actors as the CHA and other public agencies, public institutions, and nonprofit organizations. Private sphere concerns and objectives guide the types of resources they seek and the types of programs and services they support. To expand their capabilities to reach their goals, they utilize their bridging relationships to find needed social services and financial resources. Wentworth activists' work to create bridging social capital requires entrepreneurial spirit and skills. In fact, it can be argued that the complicated work of meeting the needs of the community is an occupation.

Gilkes (1988) in her research on the community work of African-American women describes how in doing "motherwork" or community caretaking, women harness their paid work to support their community activism as well as their motherwork.[17] Through their work in the LAC, Wentworth activists elaborate upon the community household, their extended community networks, and their collective domestic skills, formalizing othermothering through youth programs, community norms through tenant security, and kinship work through social events. Their organizing work challenges definitions of labor and the divisions between paid and unpaid work that are traditionally used to discuss women's work (Naples, 1992). It also challenges the fragmentation of social life that "falsely separate, paid work from social reproduction, activism from mothering, and family from community" (Naples, 1992, p. 459).

On the basis of their studies of community organizing of women of color, Gilkes (1980, 1988) and Pardo (1998) argue that we need to give due recognition to women's unpaid, or underpaid, community work. This work is essential because women, in compensating for the lack of adequate public services (e.g., youth recreation services, schools, police), are organizing their communities to provide "the conditions necessary for life" (Pardo, 1998, p. 275). Like that of the African-American women in the community studied by Gilkes, the occupation of the key women organizers at Wentworth Gardens – women like Mrs. Evelyn Ramsey, Mrs. Beatrice Harris, Mrs. Maggie Mahone, and Mrs. Lottie Weathersby – could best be described as "community person" (Gilkes, 1980, p. 219).

Throughout both this chapter and the previous one, the name of one woman organizer has repeatedly surfaced: Mrs. Hallie Amey. In 1988, Mrs. Evelyn Ramsey was instructed to write about a person who inspired her for an office training class. While other trainees wrote about movie stars, Mrs. Ramsey chose to write a paper entitled "The Life of Hallie Amey, A Community Worker." She concluded her essay this way:

Hallie has been a pillow of support to me and many of the residents of Wentworth Gardens. She is still working as a volunteer community worker. Hallie Amey is truly a super worker and super mother in her neighborhood.

[17] In her study of the community work of black women, Gilkes (1980) used an occupational analysis, rather than a social movement analysis, because she felt it better provided "a key to understanding the potential stress and strain which exists within Black communities as they deal with the routine problems of oppression." See Barnett (1995) for a social movement analysis of this organizing work.

In the next chapter, we examine the leadership traits of community organizers, such as Mrs. Hallie Amey. We explain how close attention to the craft
of organizing relationships that are rooted in the community household
and forming bridging relationships with individuals and organizations
outside Wentworth results in the development of an often unrecognized,
distinctive form of leadership.

6

Women-Centered Leadership

A Case Study

> I would like to reflect on, to say to you, and to the young people who are here,
> when you start hearing in school and reading about our African-American
> heroines who have been our civic leaders politically, and our organizers, and
> our Fannie Lou Hamers and our Harriet Tubmans, I want you to remem-
> ber Mrs. Amey; Mrs. Hallie Amey, who worked in Wentworth Gardens to
> make sure there were grocery stores and laundromats, because there were a
> need to have them. There was a need to make sure there were recreational
> facilities available for young people who were living in Wentworth Gardens.
> And there was a need to make sure that everyone was aware of changes
> too, that were happening in public housing. Today, Mrs. Amey, this is your
> day.... Tonight is our way of saying thank you to a heroine... our way of
> giving you your roses while you can smell them.
>
>   Sandra Harris, CHA Staff, Tribute Dinner for Hallie Amey, November 8,
>   1996

Feminist researchers have observed that women, especially African-
American women, exercise leadership at the grassroots in ways that are
differ from conventional notions of leadership (Barnett, 1993, 1995; Payne,
1989, 1990; Robnett, 1996, 1997; Sacks, 1988a). They argue, as does, Bernice
McNair Barnett (1993), that conventional conceptions of leadership need
to be reconsidered:

> I contend that we need to rethink the traditional notion of leadership, for organizing
> is one important leadership role.... The organizing activities of [the civil rights
> leader Ella] Baker and other Black women, especially working-class women at the
> grass-roots level, should be considered as valid leadership roles. (p. 176)

In the traditional view, leaders are elevated above the people they lead;
they become the person people look up to and follow. Formal leaders have
titled positions and are often recognized outside their hierarchical organization by the public or the state. They are the "public spokespersons"
of the people they represent. They speak publicly for their constituents

and provide press statements. These leaders are responsible for the decisions in regard to organizational tactics, goals, and strategies, and they may engage in confrontational negotiations for the people they lead (Gardner, 1995; Robnett, 1997, p. 18; Sacks, 1988a).

On the other hand, women-centered leadership, as in women-centered organizing, begins within the expanded private sphere. The leadership role that women frequently play in neighborhood organizing efforts stems from and builds upon their traditional roles and concerns in these neighborhoods (Haywoode, 1991, p. 171). Operating at the local level, behind the scenes, this leadership is often invisible to those outside the immediate community. Rather than focusing on or elevating individual leaders, women-centered leaders seek to model and develop "group centered" leadership (Payne, 1989) – leadership that "embraces the participation of many as opposed to creating competition over the elevation of only a few" (Education Center for Community Organization, 1989, p. 16).

Operating in relatively nonhierarchical settings and structures at the local level, women-centered leaders act in organizational free spaces (Evans & Boyte, 1986). Rather than the legitimacy of the state, their legitimacy rests with and is closely bound to the wishes and desires of those they interact with on a daily basis. Using a much more interactive or collaborative style, these women-centered leaders are important to the development of the emotional aspects of commitment and provide the day-to-day lessons on empowerment.

We first draw our conceptualization of women-centered leadership from Karen Brodkin Sacks (1988a). In her study of a hospital union organizing drive, Sacks used the term *centerwomen* to describe a particular type of leadership.[1] According to Sacks, centerwomen are rooted in the social networks within which they organize. They are leaders who engage with people one on one, enlisting their skills, ensuring that obligations are fulfilled. Centerwomen both develop and express group consensus around shared values and issues. They organize within the "collective and dynamic" process of creating involvement and connectedness with others (Sacks, 1988b, p. 77).

Complementary to Sacks's arguments, but in a distinct manner, Belinda Robnett (1996, 1997) in her "womanist/black feminist" study of the civil rights movement distinguished between predominantly female "bridge leaders" and the more recognized, formal, often charismatic male civil rights movement leaders. Robnett contends that a strong grassroots tier of leadership is necessary for "micromobilization" – grassroots-based

[1] Sacks (1988a) used the gendered concept of *centerwomen* because, in her investigation of union organizing, black women overwhelmingly assumed this role. However, she also used the terms *centerpeople* and *centerpersons* to recognize that it is possible for men to play this role. In our own research, as in Sacks's study, the centerpeople at Wentworth were all women; hence we chose to use the term *centerwomen*.

mobilization activities – utilizing recruitment tactics that build on an "intimate involvement with the community" (1996, p. 1681). Robnett's bridge leaders, as do the centerwomen described by Sacks, motivate people to be involved in organizing efforts because of the trust they have established through their local interpersonal ties. Utilizing organizing tactics that are aimed at "the development of identity, collective consciousness, and solidarity within community organizing efforts" (1996, p. 1667), these leaders cross the boundaries between the personal lives of potential activists and the organizing needs and activities of the community. Augmenting the work of Sacks, and expanding our conceptualization of women-centered leadership, Robnett (1996, 1997) underlined the importance of this "intermediate layer of leadership," recognizing individuals who cross the boundaries between public organizations (or movements) and the private sphere of grassroots activists and potential activists. Bridge leaders make connections that cannot be made by more formal organizational leaders, who contend primarily with the organization's "credibility, image, and relationship to the state" (Robnett, 1997, p. 23). Women, in particular, have legitimacy to engage in social bridging because of "their prescribed status as community bridges" (Robnett, 1997, p. 30), for example, first to schools and churches, and then to other organizations that can provide services for the community.

In our conceptualization of women-centered leaders, these women exhibit both the strengths and the organizing challenges of centerwomen and of bridge leaders. As Sacks (1988a), Robnett (1996, 1997), and Barnett (1995) have, we are broadening the traditional conception of leadership, which limits "both women's actual opportunities and their recognition as 'leaders'" (Barnett, 1995, p. 204).[2] Expanding dominant gender-biased assumptions about leaders as formal spokespersons, accomplished orators, and elevated decision makers, we attempt to include a more multidimensional view of leadership (Sacks, 1988a).

Both publicly recognized "formal leaders" and women-centered leaders are necessary for social change (Robnett, 1997).[3] Formal leaders, because of their organizationally acknowledged leadership role, make decisions with an eye to optimizing the political and legal outcomes of their organization. Women-centered leaders, although they may occupy a more formal position at the local level, are in most cases, because of gender discrimination, excluded from formal leadership and decision making at the higher organizational and institutional levels. In a perverse way, this sexism actually provides them with the resources and the freedom to make connections that cannot be made by formal, institutional leaders.

---

[2] Sacks (1988a) argues that traditional notions of leadership are not only gender-biased but also racially biased and class-biased.

[3] We have adapted Robnett's (1997) discussion in which she contrasts the "bridge leader" with the more traditional "formal leader."

In Wentworth Gardens, there are women who, because of their intimate knowledge of the needs of the community and their involvement with individuals within and outside their neighborhood boundaries, exercise women-centered leadership. They act both as centerwomen in local social bonding networks and as effective social bridges to key individuals and organizational resources outside the development. Women such as Evelyn Ramsey, Beatrice Harris, Maggie Mahone, Lottie Weathersby, and countless others, each in her own distinct manner, inspire resident involvement, create connectedness among activists through celebrations and parties and attract governmental and organizational support. But in all of our observations of community organizing at Wentworth, either Hallie Amey was present, or her name was raised in interviews as the leader who is most central to mobilizing and sustaining local activist efforts. In her key role as an othermother in Wentworth's community household and as an essential "super worker" in women-centered organizing, Mrs. Amey is integral to the cultivation of social relations and solidarity among resident activists at Wentworth Gardens. She also is a key person who bridges with professionals and technical assistants outside the development. If "organizing is one important leadership role" (Barnett, 1993, p. 176), the vitality of Hallie Amey's leadership is validated by the numerous activists she has recruited for organizing efforts, the strength of the relationships she has cultivated, and the loyalty and respect she has garnered from those who have worked with her.

We begin this chapter with a brief examination of Hallie Amey's life before she moved into Wentworth Gardens and her earliest organizing efforts. We examine the challenges she confronted and the choices she made that laid the groundwork for the development of her women-centered leadership style. We then analyze examples of the leadership she has exercised in her organizing work. First we examine Mrs. Amey's leadership as a centerwoman, to learn how bonding social capital is created and sustained, in particular how potential constituents are persuaded to become involved in day-to-day community work and organizing and how their involvement is nourished. We then examine Mrs. Amey's capabilities and work as a bridge leader, to understand how social bridging capital is cultivated, especially how outside constituencies are attracted to working with and providing resources to support Wentworth's community work and organizing efforts. We conclude by analyzing how in reconceptualizing leadership, we must also expand our understanding of power.

THE ROOTS OF HALLIE AMEY'S LEADERSHIP

It was difficult to get Mrs. Amey to sit down and talk about herself. She is not a person to engage in self-promotion; rather, she preferred to talk about the needs of the Wentworth development, resident activists' most current efforts, and ways we might assist in these efforts. The clothing Mrs. Amey wears similarly communicates her focus on Wentworth's organizing efforts. Other than at formal events and celebrations, she most often dresses in one of the T-shirts and baseball caps emblematic of a Wentworth activist effort, for instance, the Wentworth Gardens Security Patrol, or the first anniversary of Wentworth Gardens' Resident Management Corporation (RMC).

Much probing was needed in order to learn any details about Mrs. Amey's life before her activism in Wentworth Gardens. What is evident in the details she did provide is that, like that of the other-older-generation resident activists, her life was shaped by the legacy of slavery. Yet, Hallie Amey recalls a "very good childhood," when she worked alongside her "mother," a distant relative. This woman proved to be a key role model for the development of Hallie's strong work ethic and, later, her sense of responsibility to work on behalf of her community (also see Sacks, 1988a).

Hallie Amey was born in 1922, the middle child of five, but reared as an only child in a small Mississippi town. Because of the severe illness of her birth mother, when she was about 4 or 5, Hallie was "adopted" by a relative. She described her othermother as a hard worker who held several jobs: sharecropping on the farm and working in her own business ventures as a seamstress and hair dresser:

My mother was a very active person, a very smart woman, and a very busy woman. She sewed. . . . She could make dresses, just make anything. . . . She cooked, and . . . pressed hair . . . what you'd call then . . . a hair dresser because she had to take training for that. . . . She did a lot of things.

To assist her mother, Hallie, now an only child, worked picking cotton, feeding the livestock, and gathering eggs. She explained that she worked hard, often with her mother, in an attempt to lighten her mother's workload:

I learned at a very early age, I didn't want to see her work. . . . So I went right along with her. She went to the garden, I went to the garden. If she picked cotton, I picked cotton.

The church was central in Hallie Amey's family life: "We went [to church] on Sunday. We went Sunday night; you went Wednesday night." It was her mother's volunteer church activities that set a particularly salient example: "She [her mother] was always on some kind of [church] committee." Her mother also volunteered in Hallie school: "She would come to the school, and . . . volunteer there too. . . . [She was] very active."

Hallie Amey completed elementary school, graduated from the local racially segregated 3-year high school, and then traveled outside her small town to complete her fourth year of high school. Because of limited work opportunities, she left home to become part of the northern black migration in the 1940s. Moving to the South Side of Chicago to live with her grandmother, Hallie then took advantage of the opportunity, not available to her in the South, to take classes at a community college in the evening while working at a local printing company during the day.

When she was in her 20s, Hallie Amey began to assume a caretaking role within her extended family – a pattern of caretaking that remains central in her life today. When her uncle became ill, she moved to Detroit to care for him for 2 years. After her uncle's death, she moved back to Chicago, once again to her grandmother's home. She now worked evenings at Illinois Bell so that she could tend to her ill grandmother during the day. In fact, while working at Illinois Bell, Hallie Amey had the opportunity to be promoted from a cashier to an operator but turned down the promotion because it required her to work days, thus conflicting with her caretaking role.

After Hallie Amey married, she continued to work outside the home until the birth of her first daughter in 1949. In 1951, she and her husband and two daughters moved from their three-room apartment with a shared bath into Wentworth Gardens. Getting their two-bedroom walk-up apartment with its own bathroom was, according to Mrs. Amey, like "moving into our own home." Her memories of Wentworth Gardens' better past and its close community bonds echo those of other older resident activists (see chapter 3):

Everything was beautiful then. That's when they had rules and regulations that, you know, that had to be followed. . . . And I remember the janitor; he was real nice. . . . And we had nice neighbors then. 'Cause in the walk-ups I remember . . . we were on the second floor and the folk up over us was real nice. And the . . . folk on the first floor was real nice. . . . You know, helped each other . . . if you needed to go to the store . . . to watch your kids. . . . And do you know we still kind of keep in touch.

In 1958, when Hallie Amey was 36, and now a busy mother of four daughters, the youngest 4 months old, her husband unexpectedly died of a heart attack. When recounting her story, four decades later, Mrs. Amey did not dwell on this loss but instead quickly moved on to describe her first "involvement" in the community.

In conceptualizing the centerwomen model of leadership, Sacks (1988a) discovered that women who were the centers of social networks in organizing efforts had first learned that role in their family. They described a particularly close relationship in their childhood with someone who was the family center – a mother, grandmother, or aunt. For Hallie Amey, the relative who became her othermother in her early childhood served as this model for her and instilled in her the ethic of care that Hallie extended first to her "mother," then to her uncle and grandmother, then to her daughters, and soon after, to the larger community.

MRS. AMEY'S EARLY COMMUNITY ACTIVISM

As did many residents at Wentworth Gardens, Mrs. Amey explained that her first community volunteer work was initiated and motivated by her children's attendance at the local school, Abbott Elementary School. It was her neighbor who persuaded her to join the Parent Teachers Association (PTA). Mrs. Amey:

My neighbor next door was the PTA president.... [She] insisted that I come to school with her.... And that started me off with the PTA.... Yeah, started attending PTA meetings. And from there ... we sold taffy apples ... to ... have different programs to get money to – like ... when the children graduate ... we gave them a luncheon. And we had to have funds for all of that stuff.... I didn't really go into the classroom, but I was always in the school.

Because of Mrs. Amey's reliability and effective organizing skills, Abbott's principal offered her paid employment as the school–community representative.[4] In line with what would become a common pattern in Mrs. Amey's future public life, she was reluctant to take a paid organizing position, rejecting it because her children were so young. This did not stop her work in the school, which continued for decades. Mrs. Amey is modest in her appraisal of her activities at Abbott School; a former Abbott principal was not. At Mrs. Amey's Tribute Dinner in 1996, this retired principal referred to their time together serving on the more recently instituted Local Advisory Council: in particular, Mrs. Amey's willingness to take action far beyond what one might expect. He described Mrs. Amey as "truly a warrior":

encouraging and instrumental with the children of Abbott School. There was a time when no one else would go under the viaduct with me to get the gang bangers out. She did.

It did not take Mrs. Amey long to expand her activist efforts beyond the neighborhood school to the larger community, for she was soon in the middle of a CHA-initiated developmentwide organizing effort. In the early 1960s, CHA's Community and Tenant Relation Aid (CNTRA) had begun to send tenant aides to organize the developments. Mrs. Amey described how she became aware of the effort when she was coaxed, once again, by a another neighbor to attend an organizing meeting:

I wasn't plannin' to go to the meeting. Another neighbor came back. "You're goin' to the meetin'." "Nope, I'm not goin'." "Well, why aren't you goin'?" "I just don't feel like it, I ain't goin'." She said, "Miss Amey, put your shoes on and come on here, let's get up to the seventh block and see what they talkin' about. And that's how that began.... I got myself into it. Up over my head!

[4] As Gilkes (1980) observed, volunteers such as Hallie Amey, who demonstrate effective organizing skills, are sought out both by members in their own community and by organizations and institutions that work with community members.

Mrs. Amey explained that she and other residents worked with a tenant aide to organize Wentworth block by block.

What happened, they organized four blocks there.... Block 1, Block 5, Block 2, and Block 7.... [T]hey went around knocking on doors and passing out flyers to get people to the meetings.... When we got these four blocks together... we were really functioning.... [T]hat was the beginning of my work in here.

After this successful organizing effort, the residents decided to elect officers for a developmentwide Resident Council. At the time, there was some divisiveness and competition among the organized blocks. Mrs. Amey remembers a hotly contested race for Resident Council president in which she was opposed by another Block Club president. According to Amey, her opponent was an "argumentative" women who pitted her block against the other blocks in the development:

This lady, we knew she would not make a president.... She felt that... nobody... in the community was good as the folk in [her] Block 5.

Although Mrs. Amey was elected as the first president of Wentworth's Resident Council, the conflict did not end. As a women-centered leader committed to collaboration, Mrs. Amey now felt obliged to mediate the conflict, which came to a head at a council-sponsored Christmas party for the Wentworth children. Block 5 refused to contribute to the larger effort. Mrs. Amey recalled:

[Block 5] wanted to give a party, but just for that particular group.... Over there by themselves.... And I think it's the first time I felt like cryin'. I really did; I got so upset. They had ... much more [food] than anybody else. They was way over there, under a tree and just had a beautiful table, all kinds [of food].... And I said, "Well now, what we're gonna have to do: From each table, I want everybody to contribute somethin' for the [youngsters] ... like cookies or somethin' from the table." And do you know, they [Block 5] wasn't gonna to contribute anything? Neither was they willing to get over and help clean up.... It was some hard hearted people... not willin' to contribute anything; not willing to help.

Unlike the Block 5 residents, whose actions were divisive and self-serving, Mrs. Amey, by appealing to the residents' shared concerns about feeding the children, avoided direct confrontation and struggled to build social cohesion and a sense of common purpose among all the participating Wentworth residents.

In the midst of the Resident Council's organizing effort, Mrs. Amey was approached by CHA's community and tenant relation aid to work as a paid tenant representative. Once again she had to be pressured to take a salaried position – she did not need the money and her children were still young – but this time she put the needs of the community over her own reluctance and accepted. Mrs. Amey explained:

I really wasn't ready to go to work. Really wasn't ready to go.... It wasn't bad pay... I really didn't take it for the money.... [I] had my husband's pension. And, we had lived comfortable.... But I did take it.... The reason I took the position was to represent Wentworth... 'Cause I didn't feel, like after they kind of laid it out to me, I said, "Nobody is gonna do that... for my community. 'Cause... they're not that concerned."

As a CHA community representative for Wentworth, Mrs. Amey reported to the CHA management office, at that time housed in the Stateway Gardens high-rise development about 2 miles from Wentworth across the Dan Ryan Expressway. She worked in the position for about $2^1/_2$ years learning about various CHA and Chicago Park District programs and resources, then bringing them to Wentworth. She provided an example of the practical result of this social bridging work:

For instance now, like with Park District, they came up [with]... summer jobs for youth. And they needed a coordinator, [a] Youth Coordinator, and I knew just the young man.... Like I say, I got just the man over in my community.... I got just the person in my community.

Mrs. Amey's community activism has greatly expanded since the early 1970s. She has demonstrated women-centered leadership in the creation and maintenance of all subsequent Wentworth resident organizations – an active Local Advisory Council, Wentworth Gardens Residents United for Survival, and the Wentworth Gardens Resident Management Corporation, and resident programs and services: the laundromat and the convenience store. Mrs. Amey has been behind all of these community efforts, pushing, cajoling, and when necessary dragging new activists into community work.

CULTIVATING AND MOBILIZING THE SOCIAL BONDS OF THE COMMUNITY HOUSEHOLD

Listening to the voices and stories of the residents and professionals who have lived and/or worked with Mrs. Amey, some for over 40 years; recalling our numerous observations of her at meetings and events; or simply walking with her through the development provides a richer understanding of the qualities and traits she gives to her women-centered leadership – ethic of care and a caring mind-set, altruistic motivations, and charisma. Also illustrative are the means she uses to lead – group-centered leadership, recruitment and development of new activists, sustaining of involvement, building a vision and consensus around this vision, and cultivating and mobilizing social bridges with people, organizations, and institutions outside Wentworth.

Familistic Values—the Ethic of Care

As in women-centered organizing, the metaphors of family – the community household and homeplace – are essential to understanding the nurturance and caretaking that are so central to women-centered leadership. Familistic symbols and attachments can provide a basis for individual empowerment and shared social networks (Sacks, 1988a). The family idiom proves to be key to the success of centerwomen's leadership efforts.[5]

Hallie Amey operates as a "mother figure" or a community othermother to many of the children or former youth of Wentworth and is a central part of the extended kinship network of the community household. In her essay describing Mrs. Amey's community work, Evelyn Ramsey described her as a "super mother in her neighborhood." This theme was evident in the affection and the words that were extended to her at the Tribute Dinner organized for her in 1996. Marcella Bryant announced that Mrs. Amey is one of her "two mothers" (Lottie Weathersby was her othermother). A former resident, Doris Jackson, described how, as a child in 1971, she was welcomed into the Amey household by one of Mrs. Amey's daughters, "like a little stray cat, and the entire family embraced me." Twenty-five years later, now a principal of an elementary school, Ms. Jackson expressed her appreciation "for being loved as she was and is." Sandra Harris, the daughter of Beatrice Harris, explained that she loves Mrs. Amey as a close relative:

[Mrs. Amey is] like a grandmother, because she's trained my mother well. She's walking in her footsteps and I'm really proud to know that my mother chose such a lovely lady to pattern her life after.

Mrs. Amey herself used familial terms at this event when she addressed those who were recognizing her that evening:

I have four daughters . . . but I have many more daughters. They are all around this room: Sheila Radford-Hill, Mrs. Weathersby, Mrs. Harris. I can't name them all, there's too many. . . . I don't have sons in my house, but I got them all on my arm, and I love every one of them.

A Caring Mind-Set. At the core of women-centered leadership, as of women-centered organizing, is a strong ethic of care. If we define *caring* as the way we help others to grow, then women-centered leaders, whenever possible, try to support the growth and development of each member of

---

[5] Sacks (1988b) observed that the women hospital employees whom she studied "shared a family idiom: they celebrated family and life-cycle events and often referred to themselves as 'like family'" (p. 80). Sacks (1988a) extended this observation further: "Familistic symbols and values seem to be the antithesis of the confrontational or the radical, even when they are used to challenge the established order. Part of their strength lies in their multiple meanings and their ability to bridge racial, gender, and occupational divisions" (p. 127).

the community. In their book *Values-Based Leadership*, Susan Kuczmarski and Thomas Kuczmarski (1995) argue that a "caring mindset is essential for 'doing caring'" (p. 158). This mind-set includes

asking people personal questions that convey genuine interest, helping someone address a problem or issue with concrete action steps. . . . A caring attitude conveys a desire to give to others, be considerate of others, and convey genuine empathy and interest in others. (p. 158)

Also, to cultivate or create a caring community, this mind-set must underscore all communications and actions; it must be conveyed to all individuals, not just a select few.

Every person who has contact with Mrs. Amey is struck with her warmth and attentivenes, and is made to feel valued and respected. The Chicago Area Project's executive director, David Whittaker, remarked that Mrs. Amey "is full of love for . . . all of the people she works with and she meets." We have personally experienced Mrs. Amey's emotional warmth and witnessed how she draws people in by her genuine expressions of care and concern. Her attention and affection for Wentworth residents also were evident in all of our observations of her informal social interactions. Whenever we walked with Mrs. Amey through the development or visited one of its facilities, she cordially greeted whomever she passed. Everyone knew her and returned her greeting. Whether before meetings started, or after they concluded, Mrs. Amey was always speaking with other activists or guests with kind words that express concern about the individual's and their family's well-being.

Again, according to Kuczmarski and Kuczmarski (1995), "Caring orders other values around itself, and allows the individual to be 'in place' in the world" (pp. 157–158). Mrs. Amey's expressed care and affection for Wentworth residents have been inspirational for many of those whose life she directly touches, in particular to spur themselves and/or their family members to make changes in their own life and to take positive actions in their community. One young man at her tribute dinner, the son of a Wentworth Garden activist, described his own mother as "part of her [Mrs. Amey's] army to keep Wentworth safe." He shared how Mrs. Amey's "welcome arms . . . embraced him and his entire family," giving his "family the courage to move forward in life and to be a great part of Wentworth Gardens . . . and become better people in life."

When the resident activist Marcella Bryant was asked about how she became involved in community work, she explained that Mrs. Amey's personal concern at her loss of her mother inspired her to get "out the door," into school, and eventually into paid community work:

I have to thank Mrs. Amey for me being in the position I am in today. She came to me and knocked on my door, exactly the same year that I lost my mother. From then on I have soared through her efforts and her help. . . . I have three children I have raised. I managed to come out the door and get a degree in social service. I have also managed to come out the door and was employed by the Chicago Area Project as the first VISTA volunteer in Wentworth Gardens – employed with CHA as a building manager in senior housing. Now [I] work in family housing, manager of Wentworth Gardens. . . . All of this would not have been possible without Mrs. Amey knocking on my door and bringing me out of the depression after the loss of my mother, ten years ago.

A former resident, Vincent Walkins, is testimony to the fact that members of Wentworth's community household do not surrender their "member-ship" when they move from the development but are able to carry the strength of the lessons learned there to their new work and community settings. He also recalled the ongoing encouragement he received from Mrs. Amey while growing up in Wentworth Gardens:

Mrs. Amey has always been an inspiration to me; being the oldest of four kids [and my] mother was a single parent. Mrs. Amey always asked me, "Boy, what are you doing?" Every time she saw me, she always asked, you know, she al-ways called; and that's what we need in today's life with these children the way things are going . . . someone always there saying, "How's life treating you today?" Mrs. Amey always cared. . . . I remember when I was 17, I was working with the CETA program in the summer time. I was the youngest for the Johnson Product Company working at that particular time, but Mrs. Amey was still pushing me. Every time I talked to her, she had something for me.

Vincent Walkins, as a successful "alumnus" of Wentworth Gardens, was proud to publically share at Mrs. Amey's Tribute Dinner that he had served in the Marine Corps for 4 years, is a college graduate, works as a police dispatcher, and is pursuing a postgraduate degree in aviation management.

As is evident in the lives of people like Marcella Bryant and Vincent Watkins, Mrs. Amey, unlike a conventional leader, is not elevated above those with whom she works; rather, she is accessible to all and plays a cen-tral role in the everyday work of community kinship. She knows about and works closely with other residents, for instance, arranging birthday cele-brations, taking care of the ill and elderly, visiting the hospital, and arrang-ing and attending funerals. The resident activists can rely on Mrs. Amey, confident that she will assist in any way possible. Her caring mind-set is reflected in the words of Mrs. Mae Frances Jones:

Mrs. Amey's nice. . . . 'Cause she just thinks there's good in everybody. . . . She is a good hearted person. And [if] she can do you a favor, I believe she tries. So that's why I say that she's about the only one – the one I'd put my money on.

Altruistic Motivations. It is not surprising that women-centered leaders, who exhibit an ethic of care and a caring mindset, are also guided by altruistic motivations. Women-centered leaders do not expect, nor do they typically garner, public recognition or lucrative positions as a result of their leadership. Often working behind the scenes (Sacks, 1988a), they are motivated by altruism grounded in empathy and concern for others and a sense of duty to their community, not by traditional notions of power, fame, or fortune. One CHA employee, Gloria Seabrook, explained the impetus for Mrs. Amey's community leadership this way: "She's doing what she thinks she's supposed to do.... You know that anytime she does anything, it's for the people. She's not going to take anything for herself."[6] Similarly, a Chicago youth organizational administrator described Mrs. Amey as someone who works not for monetary reasons, but "from the heart and spirit and the soul."

We can hear the same altruistic motivations in Mrs. Amey's own words, when she spoke at an off-site CHA tenant-initiated resident workshop in the winter of 1988.[7] As a workshop presenter, she was reflecting on some of the reasons why she continues to live at Wentworth and to work for the betterment of the Wentworth community, reasons or motivations that remain important to her today:

I'm a senior citizen, and it's by my choice that I'm still in CHA; 'cuz I could live almost anywhere now. I am retired and I have enough [money] to live in a moderate [priced] place if I'd want to; but I choose to live there [Wentworth]. I feel like I have something to give to the community, and that's what I'm about. I do not plan to leave there at present . . . I feel like I can be kind of a guide 'cuz many of them – my council [LAC] workers who came along with me at the very beginning – are people who have moved out or some passed on. . . . But I feel that it is good for those who can still be there and carry on a dedicated work in the interests of the community. Because we can help the younger ones to come on, cuz public housing . . . gives a lot of people a nice place to live to raise a family. This is why I'm still working, because I feel like I owe this to the community. I have the experience, I have the time, and I have the dedication.

Charisma to Motivate Others

Charisma is most often thought of in terms of the extraordinary personal attributes of a particular individual or leader.[8] If we instead define charisma

---

[6] In her public recognition of Mrs. Amey at her Tribute Dinner, Gloria Seabrook remarked: "Tonight when I walked up to Mrs. Amey, and I said, 'Mrs. Amey, congratulations,' she said 'Isn't this something, can you believe all these people here? What is this about?' I said, 'Well, you deserve this, Mrs. Amey.' She said, 'Deserve what? I ain't done nothing but what I was supposed to do.' And that describes Mrs. Amey."

[7] This was a CHA Residents Taking Action (CHARTA) workshop led by Sheila Radford-Hill and Hallie Amey.

[8] The sociologist Max Weber contrasts the personal qualities of charismatic leadership with leadership based on social standing (e.g., doctor) or legal authority (e.g., judge) (Weber, 1947).

FIGURE 4. Upper left: Hallie Amey on the left and a resident in Wentworth's resident-operated on-site laundromat (photographer: Diana Solis). Upper right: Mrs. Amey with two youth in Wentworth's resident-operated on-site convenience store (photographer: Jack Naughton). Center right: Mrs. Amey at her surprise celebration (photographer: Susan Stall). Lower left: Mrs. Amey in the hallway in front of the entrance to the grocery store and the LAC office (photographer: Angela Kelly). Lower right: Mrs. Amey in the reception area of the former resident RMC office. A photo of Dorothy Driver, past LAC president, is on the wall behind her (photographer: Roberta M. Feldman).

in relational versus individualistic terms, then *charisma* is "the effect one individual has on a group of other individuals. Without the effect, there is no charisma" (Ellis, 1986, p. 6). Within a relational context, the purpose of charisma is not the bending of another's behavior to your will, "but a conversion of individual values and beliefs" (Ellis, 1986, p. 8).

The recognition of charisma draws attention to the emotional aspects of leadership – securing the commitment that is essential to organizing efforts (Robnett, 1997).

Mrs. Amey's charisma is manifested in and through her organizing work, particularly in her ability to inspire and motivate others. In her daily interactions, she has a positive and optimistic demeanor that makes even the most difficult challenges appear possible. Rather than a domineering demeanor, Mrs. Amey's charisma is grounded in her actions as a strong "mother" figure; her constant expression of care and nurturance motivate people into action. For instance, Susan Donald was drawn into organizing the Wentworth RMC, in part, by Mrs. Amey's charisma: "I love her personality. I love her attitude. She's so outgoing and cheerful."

Mrs. Amey's ability to inspire the participation of others and her stated intention to serve as "kind of a guide" in the Wentworth community are directly related to the next important characteristic of women-centered leadership – group-centered leadership.

Group-Centered Leadership

The civil rights leader Ella Jo Baker, who throughout her life modeled group-centered leadership stated, "Strong people don't need strong leaders" (Cantarow & O'Malley, 1980, p. 53). In fact, at one point Ms. Baker astutely observed, "I have always thought what is needed is the development of people who are interested not in being leaders as much as in developing leadership among other people" (Baker, 1973, p. 352). Ella Baker recognized that it is not organizational structures that motivate individuals to become activists; rather, each person must be persuaded to become involved. Activists engaged in this work are aware that the development of leadership is a process, nurtured within a dynamic, collaborative environment. This conversion process requires "individualized and location-specific methods of recruitment" (Robnett, 1997, p. 17). Taking the leadership initiative to secure new recruits for organizing efforts means talking to people in the community, usually face to face; enlisting them in some type of initial organizing task; and sticking with them to make sure that they follow through and stay involved.

The Recruitment and Development of New Activists. Women-centered leaders operate within the developmental tradition of leadership (Belenky, Bond, & Weinstock, 1997). Their leadership is informed by their "personal contact with community residents and conversations about the challenges in their lives" (Gittell, Ortega-Bustameufe, & Steffy, 1999, p. 44). According to Mary Belenky, Lynne Bond, and Jacqueline Weinstock (1997), in the practice of "developmental leadership" one is always asking herself questions, such as the following, when approaching a potential new activist:

Who is this person? Where is she now and where is she trying to go? What are the strengths she can build on? What kinds of experiences and challenges would support her development? How can we help her achieve her goals? (p. 263)

But at the same time, questions and concerns that address the broader needs of the community are also key when considering new recruits, questions such as

What are the problems facing this family (or this community, this movement, or this project)? What is it that we need now? What are your dreams for this community? How can we work together to see that these dreams are realized? What kind of contribution would you like to make? Are you ready to join this particular committee and help direct this project? (Belenky et al., 1997, p. 263)

Hallie Amey draws people into organizing the same way she was initially drawn in, through personal relationships – with her neighbors and friends. All but two of the resident activists we interviewed were initially approached and recruited by Mrs. Amey. Beatrice Harris, who has worked alongside Mrs. Amey for over 30 years, explained how Mrs. Amey recruited her:

When I moved here I met Mrs. Amey and she said, "You're new here." And I said, "Sort of, I've been here about 2 years." And she said, "Do you like it here?" And I said, "Oh, I love it!" She said, "Well, you know we have meetings and things; don't you want to come out to some of the meetings and find out what's going on in the community?" I said, "Yes, I would love to." And she told me when the meeting was and she told me to come. And so I came to the meeting and I said, "Okay." Then I told her that I'd like to know when the next meetings is 'cause I want to come; because you hear about what's going on in the community; and how you can find things for your kids to do; and how you can get involved yourself; and all these kinds of things. And that's what I wanted to hear, so I was coming to the meetings.

In Beatrice Harris's account of her initial meeting with Hallie Amey, we find details about how Mrs. Amey attracts new recruits to maintain the volunteer labor necessary for existing and new community programs and services. Mrs. Amey established a dialogue with Mrs. Harris built upon shared concerns for family and community. She began with exploratory talking and listening, "gently" pressuring her to join the organizing effort. Later, once Mrs. Harris began to attend community meetings, Mrs. Amey provided her with different options for further participation, in her case, encouraging her to become actively involved in the on-site, resident-operated laundromat; later, the grocery store; and then work with Wentworth's youth.

Working out of the group-centered leadership tradition, Mrs. Amey, especially in more recent years, has explicitly sought to recruit and cultivate young women activists such as Marcella Bryant, Susan Donald, Geraldine Scott, and Faye Perteet. Mrs. Amey believes that all residents have the capacity to be organizers and leaders. As with Mrs. Harris, she first engages the younger-generation recruits through exploratory listening and talking. Then, through her own persuasiveness and actions, she inspires them to get involved. Once they are recruited, she mentors the young women, working beside them while they learn the organizing process. Instead of moving people and directing events, she leads by teaching (Payne, 1989), attempting to balance the development of people with the development of the community (Belenky et al., 1997). She provides day-to-day role modeling (Robnett, 1997) and encouragement. At times she assists the new recruit to deal with personal troubles – in Marcella Bryant's case, the loss of her mother; in others a sense of inadequacy or low-self esteem – in order to involve them in sustained organizing efforts.

Susan Donald was one of the newer residents whom Mrs. Amey attracted. She served first as an RMC board member, later as the RMC office manager, and now as the executive director of the RMC. Susan grew up in Chicago on the West Side and South Side and moved to Wentworth when she had two small children. When she was in her mid-30s, and her one surviving child became a teenager, she decided to become involved in the RMC. While initially attracted by both Mrs. Amey's industry and her charisma, she also was motivated by a sense of duty to assist Mrs. Amey to improve the development. Susan reflected:

When I got involved with the RMC, I went to a meetin' one day. . . . And Miss Amey started talkin'. . . . She had been working . . . all these years. You seen her runnin' around trying to do this; trying to get that started; trying to get this; trying to get that. . . . She was askin' for help. You know, she said, "We need help. Come on out and help us." And, she touched me. And I said, "I'm gonna get up, and I'm gonna go out there and I'm helpin'."

Geraldine Scott, also a younger Wentworth activist, was similarly enlisted by Mrs. Amey, but for a different effort – to work on the development of resident management for Wentworth. For Geraldine, stories and sightings of Mrs. Amey preceded an actual meeting with her:

Basically, you know, I just started meeting people [neighbors] and, you know, they would tell me that, "Mrs. Amey, she just came and knocked on my door and got me and told me to come around here." And you know, I'd see Mrs. Amey, and other people talking about Mrs. Amey and stuff . . . and I knew she had been around here a long time; and she had been actively organizin' and doing a lot of things.

Not unexpectedly, Geraldine did get her own personal visit from Mrs. Amey:

Mrs. Amey came to my house and knocked on my door and got me. I told her she reminded me of my mother.... I told Mrs. Amey, "You twist arms better than anyone I know." And she got me out of the house ... and she say, "You'd better get on around here and act like you part of [the community]...." So I did, and that's why I'm here now.

As indicated in Geraldine's account, Mrs. Amey, while still gracious, can be forceful when she is determined to engage a new activist recruit.

Practiced in the skills of developmental leadership, Mrs. Amey recognizes that people need to feel valued and respected. She identifies, cultivates, and utilizes new recruits' strengths and particular skills, to build their confidence and self-esteem as well as to meet the needs of an organizing effort or project, as is apparent also in Faye Perteet's recruitment account:

When I moved here the first person that approached me was Miss Amey. She was telling me, you know, the things that they do around here and everything; and they try to better the place, try to better the lives of people that live here. I'm like, "Well, O.K." She said, "Well, you can come to one of the meetings [with me] and ... know for yourself...." After that, I came to the meetings.... So I volunteered for about a year [until she was hired as an RMC secretary].... [S]ince I'm the only one that actually ... was here that knew about computers and everything, and can type, I mostly worked on the computers; putting ... the minutes in the computer and typing up whatever else they had, you know.

Sustaining Involvement. Mrs. Amey is persistent and persuasive, always watching for opportunities not only to attract new recruits, but once they have been recruited, to keep them active in ongoing organizing efforts. Beatrice Harris explained these skills well:

And she's [Mrs. Amey] always pulling you; she's pushing you; and she's calling you, "We've got to do this!" She makes sure you don't forget what you have to do. Early in the morning she's on the phone, "Mrs. Harris, what time you coming out?" That was to say, "You gonna do it without me having to ask, or you giving me an excuse."

Mrs. Harris is not the only activist to be "pushed" and "pulled" by Mrs. Amey. Another activist explained: "Mrs. Amey is forceful, very quiet ... but man, when she demands you to do something, you do it." Again, in our observations, Mrs. Amey is constantly cajoling people to come to meetings and/or to participate in a particular organizing activity. For instance, immediately before every meeting we attended, Mrs. Amey was on the phone reminding those not present to come to the meeting. If there was adequate time, she might personally visit people in their homes, "requesting" their attendance. According to Gloria Seabrook, a CHA employee who has worked with the Wentworth community since 1990, Mrs. Amey is "the motivator" and "the drive" in the community. In a humorous aside, Mrs. Seabrook noted:

[T]hey [Wentworth activists] can all get together in a minute. All I have to do is call and say, "Miss Amey, I want the [RMC] Board there in a minute." And in a minute they're there. . . . I mean, that's the honest to God truth.

As a skilled women-centered leader, Hallie Amey, to sustain activists' long-term commitment, assesses the fit between an individual's skills and the community's needs. Whether informally or formally, she creates or cultivates specific roles and the associated responsibilities for each of the activists and works with other activists to create the organizational roles and structures to support these roles. Eventually, as new recruits' skills and self-confidence support their ongoing role, Mrs. Amey withdraws into the background. For instance, to show respect for Mrs. Janie Dumas's strong spiritual values and to encourage her active participation in ongoing organizing efforts, Mrs. Amey assured that Mrs. Dumas always gave the opening and/or closing prayer at meetings and events. When Wentworth Gardens Residents United for Survival was established, Mrs. Amey encouraged her to assume the chair of the newly established Spiritual Development Committee. The result is a division of labor among Wentworth activists that reflects both individuals' interests and specific issues in the community. One woman organizer might specialize in youth work, another in security issues, a third in event planning. Although the focus of their organizing work may vary, their shared efforts are united in meeting the needs of an evolving community.

Mrs. Amey, when necessary, does serve as a spokesperson for Wentworth activists. She is an eloquent speaker, as aptly noted by Susan Donald: "I love to hear her speak." Yet, in all of our observations, Mrs. Amey has assured that other activists, whenever possible, share this spokesperson role. She actively encourages and creates opportunities for them to speak at meetings and at public presentations. Mrs. Amey generally speaks first or last; however, she always asks, and if necessary rehearses, other activists to speak as well. Faye Perteet described how she was gradually pushed into public speaking by Mrs. Amey:

[Mrs. Amey would] volunteer me to head a, what you call that [a meeting chair], you know how you go into meetings and you get up and introduce people. And I'm like, "I'm not use to this." 'Cause I never actually got up in the public, in a place where a lot of people is and talked. I'm like, "Uh uh Miss Amey . . . everybody might laugh at me at the way I talk," or whatever, you know. So she was like, "Oh, you'll be all right. You'll have a piece of paper in front of you." I'm like, "O.K., I'll try to do this."

Building a Vision/Building Consensus. Mrs. Amey leads with a vision of Wentworth's better future. As noted by Beatrice. Harris, "She is the type of person who can bring a lot of good ideas to the community." Again, Mrs. Amey's vision, however, is not an individual construction, but rather one she has developed with other Wentworth activists and wider community supporters. She is a consensus builder. We repeatedly observed Mrs. Amey at meetings when she encouraged people to speak about their needs, concerns, and hopes while she patiently listened. These were not formal, visioning sessions, but rather dialogues, as Mrs. Amey attempted to assure that anyone who wanted to speak was given time and respect. We also observed her using informal "gossiping" (see chapter 4) to build consensus.

Wentworth resident activists, however, do not always agree about the community's needs and the strategies to address them. Conflicts have arisen. Mrs. Amey's mediation skills have been essential in defusing these conflicts. For instance, Susan Donald explained that the respect Mrs. Amey has earned has proved essential to mediate these potential conflicts:

And everybody love her and respect her. And when you dealin' with a person that everyone respect . . . because a lot of us make decisions, I suppose, based on relationships . . . one person is not gonna do nothin' that would cause conflict because we don't want her [Mrs. Amey] involved in the conflict. So we have to treat each other in a civil manner. . . . I think it's because of her that a lot of us kept our cool.

There have been occasions when Mrs. Amey has initiated directions and made decisions that have not been built through consensus. When time demanded, for instance, when decisions needed to be made quickly, Mrs. Amey had the unspoken respect and authority to decide for the group; or when the scale of the initiative was broader than any previously undertaken, for example, resident management of the development (see chapter 10), Mrs. Amey had to build resident confidence to undertake this challenging task.

Mrs. Amey's group-centered leadership, her ability to work with and through others, is well described by a former CHA manager, Sandra Harris:

[A]bove all, she [Mrs. Amey] has been a role model, because she has walked quietly . . . with a very, very big stick. You don't hear Ms. Amey yelling and hollering . . . about anything, because she is very patient, she's humble, and most of all she knows how to get things done through people. . . . She has shown that it takes community and people working together to make things happen.

BUILDING SOCIAL BRIDGES TO ACCESS RESOURCES

Recall that Robert Putnam (2000) distinguished two forms of social capital – bonding social capital and bridging social capital. Whereas bonding social capital looks inward and tends "to reinforce exclusive identities and homogenous groups," bridging social capital is "outward looking and encompass[es] people across diverse social cleavages" (p. 22). Leadership in creating and participating in bridging networks is necessary for establishing links to outside resources, and ultimately, for taking these needed resources back to Wentworth.

In her keynote speech at Mrs. Amey's Tribute Dinner, one CHA employee, Sandra Harris, clearly recognized Hallie Amey's leadership ability "to build bridges" with people and organizations outside the Wentworth development:

Leaders succeed through the efforts of their people. This room reflects that she [Mrs. Amey] has worked with community agencies, with church members, with CHA employees. . . . She has invested her life in people and in resources. . . . Leaders build bridges. I think that through her collaboration and her investment and time with agencies . . . and civic leaders, she has been able, with other residents, to make sure that Wentworth Gardens community has actually prospered and grown.

The words of Sandra Harris were confirmed within our own interviews and observations.

Throughout her years as a community leader, Mrs. Amey has created and cultivated bridging social capital with a variety of organizations, including the neighborhood elementary school, local nonprofit organizations, universities, and corporate foundations. We have observed multiple instances in which Mrs. Amey has drawn on personal contacts she has made with representatives of these organizations and institutions.[9] We also were repeatedly recruited by Mrs. Amey, who called upon each of us to assist when she believed we had something to contribute to Wentworth's organizing efforts. Upon first meeting us, she easily established rapport and unassumingly identified our expertise. Soon thereafter, each of us received a phone call from Mrs. Amey asking one of us whether we could assist with needed resources or information or knew of someone else who might be of help. Her work with two youth service organizations – Beatrice Caffrey and the Chicago Area Project – is particularly illustrative of her capabilities to engage in social bridging for the Wentworth community.

Bridging to Community Organizations

In his book *Making Democracy Work Better*, Richard Couto (1999) extends Putnam's (1993, 2000) definition of social capital to include the social

---

[9] Hallie Amey and other Wentworth resident leaders have worked with universities and university centers – such as the Nathalie P. Voorhees Neighborhood Center and the City Design Center at the University of Illinois; the Lindeman Center, formerly at Northern Illinois University; and the Illinois Institute of Technology – and with nonprofits, such as Women for Economic Security; and with churches, such as the Progressive Baptist Church.

172   *Everyday Resistance in the Expanded Private Sphere*

and public provision of economic goods and human services, including "housing, education, cultural expression, environmental quality, children's services" (p. 5). Focusing on Appalachia, he describes numerous
community-based "mediating structures," in which local leaders, supported by nonprofits, foundations, and government agencies, through
advocacy are "increasing the amounts of and improving the forms of
social capital – public goods and moral resources by which we produce and reproduce ourselves in community" (p. 4). Like Wentworth's
Local Advisory Council (see chapter 5), both Beatrice Caffrey and the
Chicago Area Project have been essential community-based mediating structures. These two nonprofit organizations have invested in the
Wentworth community through resource provision and, equally importantly, through their social and moral investment in local leadership to increase the social capital – in this case, youth services – at
Wentworth Gardens. The success of their organizational missions, has
been dependent on their strong social bridging relationships with local leaders and grassroots organizers in the communities in which they
work.

Beatrice Caffrey was founded in the 1940s with a focus on juvenile
delinquency prevention.[10] In the 1950s, the organization sent outreach
workers to low-income communities to develop organized satellites or
"committees." Wentworth Gardens became one of these committees. Over
the years, selected resident activist leaders, including first, Hallie Amey,
and then, Beatrice Harris, worked on Wentworth's Beatrice Caffrey committee. Mrs. Amey recognized and explained the strategic importance
of their work in securing this social bridging relationship with Beatrice
Caffrey for the benefit of Wentworth youth:

[W]e was forever pushin' to get somethin' for our community, cuz there were little
resources here. And so, Beatrice Caffrey, for a long time, was our source. You know
they would take people on trips, and they . . . had . . . classes . . . over here.

In exchange for a "a functionin' committee" residents activists accessed
needed resources for youth in their community.[11]

As a result of their involvement in Beatrice Caffrey, Wentworth resident activists indirectly became a part of the larger, better known Chicago
Area Project (CAP) (see chapter 5) when Beatrice Caffrey became an

[10] Beatrice Caffrey was a probation officer who volunteered to work with youth services.
Originally the organization named for her targeted predelinquent girls in after-school
programs; later it became a coed program for all youth at risk.
[11] Another indirect benefit was that resident Beatrice Caffrey committee members received
free tickets to major social functions that brought all the Beatrice Caffrey Committees
together as a reward. Mrs. Amey explained that she and other committee members, not
only enjoyed these events, but through their participation they learned how to effectively
organize larger events in their own community.

affiliate of CAP in the 1960s. Sheila Radford-Hill, a former employee of CAP, described this unusual organization this way:

Chicago Area Project is a very interesting place. It has the grassroots kind of aspect to it; but is also has an academic and a charitable side to it . . . a long University of Chicago history. . . . It's this eclectic mix of elitism and grassroots. . . . They've always had an empowerment focus . . . because . . . they felt, and correctly so, that only communities can deal with the problem of . . . juvenile delinquency. I mean, it's very difficult to solve that problem.

Founded in the 1930s, the Chicago Area Project hired local residents to organize their neighborhoods around youth activities, in particular to work to solve juvenile delinquency problems.[12] As noted by Sheila Radford-Hill, CAP is unique because, from its inception, it has sought to develop community residents' leadership potential and to assist the newly formed community groups to achieve local autonomy. Historically, CAP sought resident applicants who had a "thorough knowledge" of neighborhood residents and organizations as well as a "natural capacity for working with adults and youth" (Hallman, 1984, p. 113). These residents were trained and supervised by sociologists on staff but were given "'considerable latitude' when they organized the neighborhoods" (Hallman, 1984, p. 114).

In the 1970s, Hallie Amey's grassroots leadership was recognized by CAP. While volunteering as one of the Wentworth Beatrice Caffrey committee representatives, she was approached by CAP to become a community service worker. Mrs. Amey:

They don't just employ you just as an employee. They want folk who are already working [in the community]. And it's [the salary's] a stipend, in other words, for what you already doing.

At first, Mrs. Amey explained, she was reluctant to become a paid CAP employee, "because I had retired already, and I really just didn't want to get involved; "but the CAP representative persisted, according to Mrs. Amey, refusing to, "take no for an answer." Mrs. Amey finally agreed; eventually Mrs. Beatrice Harris took over her position.

The leadership to sustain Wentworth's continued partnership with the Chicago Area Project has been crucial for Wentworth resident activists' organizing efforts, particularly in CAP's attention to youth programing and community organizing assistance. Not only has CAP been strategic in its identification and employment of community-based leaders, such

---

[12] The Chicago Area Project was a "social experiment" designed by Clifford Shaw to address the problem of juvenile delinquency. He believed that "even in areas with high delinquency and seemingly immendable disorder, there exists 'a core of organized communal life centering mainly in religious, economic, and political activities'" (Korbrin quoted in Hallman, 1984, 113). According to Shaw, delinquency was an adaptive response by youth who had no other means to achieve social status.

as Mrs. Amey and Mrs. Harris, but its community outreach workers also are sensitive in their attempts to develop a real partnership versus a more traditional social service helping approach with these low-income community leaders (see Lappe & Du Bois, 1994).[13] In fact, it was in her board position at CAP that Mrs. Amey further deepened her social bridging relationship with Sheila Radford-Hill, whom she had first met at the Abbott School.[14] Sheila distinctly remembered working with Wentworth, because Mrs. Amey was clear in voicing her desire for a closer, more direct working relationship with CAP.[15]

Skillfully, Mrs. Amey leveraged her bridging social capital developed as a CAP board member and former CAP youth worker (Briggs, 1998).[16] She wanted to alter and strengthen Wentworth's relationship with CAP to increase the resources for Wentworth. Her goal was to have the community receive youth programming monies directly from CAP, rather than indirectly through their Beatrice Caffrey committee. David Whittaker, then the current executive director of CAP, reminisced about how Mrs. Amey

---

[13] In *The Quickening of America*, Frances Moore Lappe and Paul Martin Du Bois (1994) provide case studies of human service organizations that are less interested in program delivery than in discovering and building clients' capacities. Rather than a "service view" of the human services, in the "living democracy view" professionals operate not as expert problem solvers but "as facilitators to help people discover their own power" (p. 162). The Chicago Area Project's sensitivity in this regard is evident in the reflections of one CAP African-American male outreach worker who had been at Wentworth 1 to 2 days a week for 7 years: "I'm usually the advisory consultant. Instead of trying to put myself in the position of trying to initiate things, I let the residents initiate it and work as advisory consultant, and I go on and give them advice, resources, training schools. We do everything we can . . . black history education and all kinds of stuff."

[14] Sheila Radford-Hill met Mrs. Amey when she was working for another nonprofit, Designs for Change, on school-based organizing at Abbott Elementary School in the early 1980s.

[15] Sheila Radford-Hill explained why Mrs. Amey and the Wentworth activists wanted to alter their relationship with the Chicago Area Project: "[T]hey weren't happy with that status. . . . They liked Beatrice Caffrey. But they wanted a . . . more direct relationship with the Chicago Area Project. . . . Because when . . . resources were allocated . . . they didn't feel they were getting their fair share." An additional reason for altering their relationship with Beatrice Caffrey was the increased burden required to organize the social events that were once offered as a reward for volunteer work; in particular, residents were pressured to sell tickets and buy a table for these larger downtown affairs. Eventually the fund-raising became a burden as ticket prices rose each year. Community volunteers were told that they had to raise as much as a thousand dollars selling tickets for one event. It became more and more difficult to raise donations from the community, in spite of the youth resources they were receiving from Beatrice Caffrey.

[16] Xavier de Souza Briggs (1998) draws a distinction between two key dimensions of social capital – social support and social leverage. They can overlap, but the distinctions are important. Social capital includes social bonding and social bridging – social supports that allow individuals or communities to "get by." Social leverage is social capital that helps individuals or communities to "get ahead." It is accessing clout and influence that ultimately make socioeconomic mobility possible (pp. 178–9).

successfully pressured for this structural change and for continued CAP support of youth programming at Wentworth Gardens:

When I first met her, she was such an inspiration to me back in those days. I became Executive Director of CAP back in 1986, and [in] '87 . . . Mrs. Amey came to me and she said, "David, we gotta move. We're involved. We've got problems in this community that we've got to solve. We've got to work with these young boys and these young girls." I told her things take time, but she didn't hear that and she said, "And David, we got to hire our own staff people. We know who can do the job out there, we know what needs to be done. . . . And David, I want you to fund this organization. I want you to put our money out here and fund this organization." [I asked her], "Mrs. Amey, how long do you want to fund this?" And then she looked at me and said, "David, from now on." [I responded,] "Yes, Ma'am, so we'll be funding it from now on."

Taking advantage of the relationships she had cultivated with CAP staff, in particular, with Sheila Radford-Hill, Mrs. Amey and other Wentworth activists, with Sheila's assistance, eventually formed a nonprofit organization to organize against CHA's nonresponsiveness to Wentworth residents' needs. The relationship Mrs. Amey built with Sheila Radford-Hill would prove critical in the upcoming years. Mrs. Amey and other key activists called upon Sheila, in the White Sox battle and its aftermath and during the development of Wentworth's Resident Management Corporation, for essential assistance in these organizing challenges. Sheila Radford-Hill, at Amey's Tribute Dinner, with humor and affection, chided:

Mrs. Amey snatched me up and made me organize a whole bunch of stuff. . . . Some of the best organizing experience I have had is with this woman. I want to tell, most of you know, once this woman gets something in her head, it is just hard to get it out.

Bridging to Social Networks

In more recent years, Mrs. Amey's expertise and leadership skills in expanding social bridging capital have been repeatedly and effectively demonstrated. Two different occasions in two different locations are illustrative. The first was in the winter of 1989, when Mrs. Amey spoke to a large room of Illinois Institute of Technology University (IIT) students, faculty, and staff from CHA at an IIT-sponsored symposium. Although IIT is located directly east of Wentworth across the Dan Ryan, no formal relationship had previously been established.[17] This was the Wentworth

---

[17] One of the authors, Susan Stall, while a visiting lecturer at the Illinois Institute of Technology (IIT), organized this conference with IIT's Community Relations person, Leroy Kennedy. Stall and Kennedy organized the event to educate the IIT university community about their public housing "neighbors." The organizers were hoping to dispel stereotypes about people who live in the "projects" and establish a closer working relationship

Gardens residents' first public foray to this university campus. Perfectly at ease, Mrs. Amey, selecting to speak after the Wentworth residents Marcella Carter and Beatrice Harris, opened her remarks in a warm and booming voice saying, "Hi, neighbors!" Charming those in attendance, she continued do use the "neighbor" theme throughout her remarks, emphasizing the fact that Wentworth and IIT "share the same community." After a description of some of the history of Wentworth Gardens' activism, her concluding comments demonstrate both her graciousness and her bridge building skills:

I just want to let you know neighbor, I am very grateful and I welcome every opportunity like this to come and talk to you and let you know what we are doing. And some way we can join hands. And if you in any way can assist us, 'cuz we do need assistance, we will welcome that. And when you need us to come and help you with some thing, we will be right here. . . . [T]here's nothing like neighbors meeting neighbors. . . . It's time for us to get together and work together because we share the same community.

With that brief closing Mrs. Amey managed to establish a basis of reciprocity, clearly important in a working relationship versus an unequal helping arrangement (Lappe & DuBois, 1995).

In the second instance, in the fall of 1996, Mrs. Amey again demonstrated her skill at networking outside Wentworth, when she and other resident activists attended a Wieboldt Foundation Awards Reception held at an elegant downtown library.[18] Mrs. Amey gracefully interacted with the executive director of the Wieboldt Foundation and representatives from several other foundations. She made a point of chatting with the individuals she knew and meeting as many new people as possible. In one encounter, when she was introduced to one of the reception speakers and a board member of a major Chicago foundation, she added, "Now remember that name, Hallie Amey. You'll be hearing from me!" After this statement, she made certain to get his phone number.

CONCLUSIONS: UNRECOGNIZED LEADERSHIP / UNRECOGNIZED POWER

I am also humbled and honored by the experience of honoring a true warrior. An inspirational warrior in this area of community development. . . . She is such a powerful, powerful lady; a powerful leader. She is an outstanding organizer in the community, but she is so gracious. She is full of grace. She is full of love for the entire

---

between IIT and the residents of Wentworth Gardens, Dearborn Homes (directly north of IIT), and Section 8 certificate holders represented by Lakefront SRO Corporation.

[18] Wentworth had received funding for RMC support staff from Wieboldt (their first foundation award), although Wentworth activists were not winners of the Community Organizing award for which they had applied.

community and all the people she works with and she meets. . . . Mrs. Amey . . . you are an inspiration and role model for each and every one of us tonight. . . . We all love you.
(David Whittaker, executive director, Chicago Area Project, Amey Tribute Dinner, 1996)

In the tribute to Hallie Amey, when David Whittaker calls her a "true warrior," he is not speaking about a conquering hero, someone who subdues or rules others; instead he is referring to her as a liberator, someone who is "inspirational." In his description of Hallie Amey as "powerful," he notes her skills and successes as an outstanding organizer and leader, but also her "grace," a word not usually associated with traditional descriptions of leadership, or of power. If we recall that women-centered leaders operate from a different value system than one that equates power with domination over others, an ethic of care, then the importance of "graciousness"and even the mention of "love" make sense.

A recognition and analysis of women-centered leadership require us to expand our conceptualizations of not only leadership, but power as well (Stall, 1991; Stall & Stoecker, 1998). Women-centered leaders, embedded in an intricate structure of social relationships (Janeway, 1980), have power that is based on their community work, rather than positions in institutional hierarchies. They demonstrate "co-active power," the power to stimulate activity in others and to heighten vitality, willpower, and morale (Emmet, 1971). Exercising power as energy, strength, and effective interaction need not require the domination of others; rather, this form of power relies on collective motivation and participation. Unlike power that dominates or controls others, coactive power is transformative: That is, it supports people to attain a greater sense of self-reliance and independence, both traits essential for participation in grassroots activism (Collins, 1991).

Hallie Amey is gifted with many of the qualities that also are associated with a more traditional, formal leader: charisma, vision, ability to build consensus and mediate conflict, and the capacity to act as a spokesperson. But unlike the conventional leader, she does not express these traits through individual-centered leadership, using these traits to elevate herself; rather, she expresses them through a guided, group-centered process. Standing as an example of the power of women-centered leadership, Hallie Amey has established herself as a centerwoman skilled in the practice of developmental leadership, as an effective cultivator of bonding and bridging social capital in her community. An active participant and "othermother" in the community household, she shares its familistic values, especially a work ethic and responsibility to one's community. She draws upon the skills, strategies, and structure inherent in this expanded household to identify and work for shared goals and to act as a social force for change. In fact, Mrs. Amey mobilizes the social network of her community household in such a graceful manner that members go forward to take on struggles that will involve enormous time and effort, with few monetary and political resources. The effectiveness of these efforts, especially given the constraints, as seen by both Wentworth activists and outside supporters, is so impressive that Mrs. Amey is characterized as a "warrior" and "powerful leader." An inspiration to countless individuals, she has created and mobilized informal and more formal social relational networks, both within and outside the Wentworth community, to meet pressing needs in Wentworth Gardens, gaining the trust of residents and of community partners alike.

In her research to expose another tier of leadership in the civil rights movement, Belinda Robnett's (1996) analytical arguments have value for our own findings about leadership at Wentworth Gardens:

> The fact that African-American women, for the most part, did not share formal leadership titles should in no way obscure the fact that they were leaders. . . . Their social location as black, as women, and as economically marginalized was empowered in a context in which they were purveyors of political consciousness, in which they were able to lead relatively autonomously, and in which they were able to bring about group solidarity and social change. (p. 1689)

The roots of all resistance efforts lie in everyday social ties and networks and in the efforts to maintain and, when necessary, mobilize these networks. Women-centered leaders play the central role in "politicizing" social networks. They not only "hold these networks together as social forces," but translate the skills and values women learn first in their families and community into effective action (Sacks, 1988b, p. 80). In fact, these leaders embody and personify these skills, thus explaining why they are so effective in cultivating social and bridging networks and linking them to community organizing.

In the following chapter, we examine how the women-centered leadership and the women-centered organizing efforts of Hallie Amey and other key Wentworth residents have been essential in their struggles for their rights to and control over the spaces of Wentworth Gardens. In particular, we analyze how their empowering experiences to appropriate spaces to house programs and services have not only transformed the material setting of their housing development, but provided material evidence of their resistance and their legitimacy as agents of social change.

7

The Appropriation of Homeplace

Organizing for the Spatial Resources
to Sustain Everyday Life

> So I'm just saying this to tell you, there just comes a point and a time when there's a need for something, and a group of people gather and decide that they are going to do this for the benefit of their community – they can do it.
>
> Hallie Amey

The point and time were the 1960s, when, as we have described, public housing in the United States was beginning to witness the signs of governmental disinvestment. Daily life in Wentworth Gardens, as well as in other CHA housing, was beset with deteriorating physical facilities and services inadequate to meet the residents' needs. For Mrs. Hallie Amey, the point and time was when she and other women residents decided to challenge the closing of Wentworth Gardens' field house and the resultant dismantling of the youth recreation programs. It marked the Wentworth residents' first organized effort to improve the material conditions of their housing development.

APPROPRIATING THE FIELD HOUSE

When the development first opened, the on-site field house, or, as it was referred to in CHA documents, the "community building," was intended for use as an auditorium, for social gatherings, and for classes for preschool children conducted by the city's Board of Education (CHA, 1947). Called the Wentworth Neighborhood Center, these programs were established through the cooperative efforts of Wentworth's Resident Council and Grace Community Center (CPHT, 1949), a private social service agency providing recreational activities for all ages. The success of this collaboration was rooted in Wentworth activists' effective organizing to build bridging

This chapter elaborates upon material from Feldman and Stall (1994, pp. 167–199).

179

relationships with Grace Community Center. According to a CHA newsletter, the Neighborhood Center was a "pioneer venture" for public housing (CPHT, 1949).

In the early 1960s, however, CHA closed the facility. At that time, the field house had been used primarily for a youth recreation program, but also for community social events and Council meetings. Mrs. Amey explained:

[W]hen Wentworth was first opened they had an organized group in our field house. But over the years, you know how things just go – the organized group had gone, and they [on-site CHA management] were using the space for storage. And so there really was no organized recreation program for the youth at all!

The need for a facility and programs for youth recreation at Wentworth was particularly acute. The nearest park, Armour Square Park, just four blocks north of Wentworth (see chapter 8), has been "off limits" to Wentworth residents. The white community adjacent to the park have assured that African-American youths and adults alike will not use this recreational facility through acts of verbal hostility and physical violence. Although more frequent in the past, these acts of overt racism have not abated. The most recent racially motivated incident occurred in the late 1990s – a severe, disabling beating of a black child who ventured into the park, resulting in three young white men charged with hate crimes. The only other recreational facility is more than 2 $^1/_2$ miles away from the Wentworth development.

The Resident Council did not passively acquiesce to the field house closing; rather, with Mrs. Hallie Amey's leadership, a core of approximately 15 activists organized to reopen the field house and to reinstate the youth programming. Mrs. Amey recalled that it was, in fact, a local youth protest against the lack of community recreational programs that mobilized her and several other council members into action. Mrs. Amey described this precipitating event:

One day I looked out the window, I think we [the Resident Council] were giving a small fish fry or something, and there was a group of boys marching through the area with picket signs on them, picketing CHA. And I told the ladies, "They're picketing the wrong group. They [the boys] should be picketing us." I said, "If anything comes up in here for us, it's going to come through us."

The Wentworth activists' motivation to respond to this small youth protest was spurred by their prior actions and attachments as community othermothers in the Wentworth development and their women-centered concerns. Pressed into action by this small youth protest, the resident activists decided to pressure the CHA to reopen the field house, now used for storage, and operate a youth program in it. A member of the Resident Council recalled:

I remember that we used to have to write letters and petition, go over there [to the on-site management office] and petition . . . and present them [petitions] to

Miss McGraham [on-site manager] first. And they told us that this building wasn't built for children!

When continued appeals to CHA and on-site management failed to make CHA accountable, the residents approached the development manager to allow them to run a program in the facility. One of the Resident Council members explained that they "couldn't just come in here [the field house] and just say, and we'll use it for such and such." Rather, they had to request on-site management's permission to use the space, but management declined. According to Mrs. Amey, they deemed the residents unreliable and incapable:

[W]e went and talked to the manager, and at that time they specifically explained to us, "Over the years we [CHA management] have given this to groups and given that to groups, and they just rise and fall; nobody remains stable. So we are not going to do anything."

These residents' frustrations were palpable. Mrs. Amey continued:

This space [the field house] was [supposed to be] used for recreation and it had refrigerators and stoves in it! What little recreation material was there was locked in a closet, and they wouldn't even give us that.

Ignited by their ethic of care and concern that the youth have a recreation center and programs, the residents decided to act on their own, with their own material resources, to demonstrate their capacity to the CHA. As a united group, they continued to pressure the CHA manager; finally they secured an agreement to use one room in the field house.

Securing this space was only the first step; they now had to demonstrate their capabilities to utilize this space effectively. The activists applied the skills developed both in mothering and in othermothering to organize a preschool program called the Pied Piper. They brought materials and supplies from home or purchased them at their own cost. Mrs. Amey explained:

The only thing we had was a desire to start. . . . We didn't have anything. So what we did, we sat down and decided, what could we start with nothing. . . . [W]e decided we'd start a small preschool program because one would bring a ball and different little things that we had at home, and that's how we began. And we carried that program on for about two years.

This successful preschool program, accommodating 25–30 children, operated 5 days per week through the commitment and work of resident volunteers. Mrs. Amey:

And as the years went on, we kept this program going. And we knocked on doors to get other volunteers to come out and join us. And we ended up with about fifteen consistent, stable volunteers who didn't mind spending a couple of hours. See that's what it really takes – commitment.

Other members of the Resident Council, such as Mrs. Ella Fitzgerald, recalled, with considerable pride, the program's success:

And we had . . . a beautiful center out there. Beautiful center. Mrs. Amey ordered games and things for the center. . . . Kids and everything nice that they have. [There was] no fighting; no fighting! It was nice.

Another council member remembered the grade school teachers' comments commending the good preparation the children received at the preschool before entering elementary school. The preschool organizers had demonstrated that they had not only sufficient knowledge and skills, but strong social cohesion among the volunteers necessary first to create and then to operate a successful preschool program.

When the program was well established, the CHA officially granted the residents control of the field house. Ultimately, with technical assistance the Resident Council sought from the Illinois Institute of Technology and other outside institutions, the Chicago Park District was pressured to assume responsibility for youth recreation programs.

The struggles to reopen the field house were the first of several resident efforts to appropriate spaces in their development. When living conditions in both their development and their neighborhood continued to deteriorate, resident activists engaged in effective ongoing organizing campaigns and formed organizational vehicles, in part to gain the rights to and control over other Wentworth spaces. Without these material resources, there would have been no places to house on-site services and programs to meet Wentworth residents' unmet social reproduction needs. But these spaces serve more than instrumental functions: They stand as a material symbol that conveys the organizational presence and legitimacy of the Wentworth activists (see also Clark, 1994).

We begin this chapter with a brief overview of the space appropriation concept, which has been used in environment and behavior research to refer to individuals' and groups' authority, control, mastery, and/or power over a physical setting, to make it their own (see Korosec-Serfaty, 1976). We will examine the objectives and strategies residents have used, and the power relations that have constrained and enabled these ongoing everyday actions to appropriate and manage on-site facilities, including the following:

- In 1968, because there were no laundry facilities within walking distance, resident activists worked with the CHA to obtain space and funds to open a resident-operated laundromat. The laundromat is still operating today.
- In 1973, the residents secured and renovated space and raised the funds to open and operate a convenience store.

- In 1986, when the field house roof was in such poor repair that the scheduled children's summer food program was at risk of being cancelled, the resident activists organized to have the roof repaired.

In addition, one resident, Janie Dumas, gained the right to renovate and use a space for a spiritual development center open to Wentworth and Chicago's South Side residents, and residents for decades have

FIGURE 5. Upper left: Wentworth youth shooting hoops in the field house gymnasium (photographer: Jack Naughton). Upper right: Wentworth resident volunteer and customer in the resident-operated on-site convenience store (photographer: Jack Naughton). Center left: Mrs. Janie Dumas in her spiritual development center located in a Wentworth three-story walk-up basement (photographer: Roberta M. Feldman). Lower left: Residents converse in Wentworth's resident-operated on-site laundromat (photographer: Diana Solis); Lower right: Children in front of the community garden (photographer: Susan Stall).

appropriated spaces in the development to plant community gardens. One of these community gardens still thrives in a fenced plot of land shaded by two large trees on the south end of the development, serving both practical and community-building functions. Through the summer and fall the community gardener residents are rewarded with an array of flowers and vegetables, including tomatoes, collards, cabbage, bell peppers, carrots, lettuce, squash, string beans, onions, okra, and pinto beans. The gardening activity is an occasion for social contact and neighborly camaraderie. Also, the gardeners engage in informal surveillance over the immediate area and help to beautify a well-traversed community space.[1] Finally, although they do not have a permanent space, Wentworth activists have organized food programs for the infirm and elderly and for community events, using kitchen facilities in the LAC offices and their homes and barbeques on the Wentworth grounds.

In the descriptions of Wentworth activists' struggles to appropriate the physical settings of their housing development, we will see that they have not only been mediators in making real improvements in living conditions; they also have built upon their women-centered organizing and contributed to nurturing individual residents' positive self-concept and self-confidence, local leadership, and collective skills and resources for further social and political action. We will see how Wentworth Gardens activists' power to influence change lies, in part, in the empowering experiences of the everyday ongoing struggles to appropriate their homeplace. Through acts of space appropriation, Wentworth residents have transformed their marginalization to gain legitimacy as agents of change (see also Clark, 1994).

SPACE APPROPRIATION

Space appropriation is a concept that has been used to explain the ways in which individuals or groups transform the physical environment into a meaningful and useful place, one that the individuals or groups consider their own, and, in doing so, transform themselves (see Korosec-Serfaty, 1976). Inquiries about space appropriation typically have focused on either

---

[1] Janie Dumas, to augment her spiritual leadership in the community, requested space for a "spiritual development center" in the basement of her building, one of the walk-up apartments located opposite the basement store (see chapter 4). In July 1996, when we spoke to the community gardeners Geraldine Williams, Annie Stewart, and Mary Rias, they had been "working together" for over a decade. With two other women residents they garden yearly in the South Side location near the Resident Management offices. Originally there had been a garden in the northern part of Wentworth, but that closed in 1983 because of lack of resident involvement. Up through 1995, the CHA provided interested residents with the plants and took care of the watering for the community gardens. Mary Rias usually serves as "chair" of the garden, distributing the plants to the other resident gardeners.

the means or the ends of the process (see Korosec-Serfaty's edited volume, 1976). The means to appropriate a space are many. Individuals or groups may intentionally occupy the setting; possess, construct, modify, enhance, or care for a physical setting; mark a setting with identifying signs, symbols, or activities; and/or simply represent a setting in words or images. Similarly, the objectives of space appropriation may vary. For instance, an individual or group may appropriate space and give it particular characteristics to meet their needs and/or to communicate with others that they have possession of, or some social and/or legal claim to, the physical setting and therefore control who uses the space, and for what purposes. Thus appropriation of space not only provides a material resource necessary to meet needs for everyday life – a place they can call their own – but also is a potential source of both individual and collective empowerment (Feldman & Stall, 1994; Clark, 1993, 1994).

Appropriation of Homeplace

The place of the home holds a special status in researchers' conceptualizations of the processes of space appropriation (reviewed in Despres, 1989; Duncan, 1981; Hayden, 1984; Wright, 1981). Space appropriation researchers have considered homeplace as the most important place to satisfy and express appropriation "needs" (reviewed in Despres, 1989; also see Chombart de Lauwe, 1976; Cooper, 1974). Of all the physical settings that everyday environmental experience comprises, homeplace is deemed most important, if not universal: "Hearth, shelter, home or home base are intimate places to human beings everywhere" (Tuan, 1977, p. 147; also see Buttimer, 1980; Cooper, 1974; Csikszentmihalyi & Rochberg-Halton, 1981; Relph, 1976; Seamon, 1979). Not only is the appropriation of homeplace necessary to sustain everyday life: It is essential to experiences of psychological well-being and harmony with the world.

Space appropriation researchers generally agree that the primary site of space appropriation is the physical setting of the home, yet there is less agreement about its geographic referent: Is it the dwelling, the surrounding neighborhood, or some larger geographic area? Or all of these? One strategy that has been used is to question individuals about their designation of the places they call home to identify the "where" of homeplace. Empirical research has observed that when explicitly questioned, individuals indicated nested scales of the residential environment: special objects and the room(s) located within the dwelling, the physical structure of the dwelling and the area immediately surrounding it, the neighborhood, and, less frequently, the town, city, state, region, country, and structures within any of these geographic locales, and even the planet Earth (e.g. Giulliani, 1989; Hummon, 1992; Keller, 1968; Rapaport, 1981; Relph, 1976; Strauss, 1961; Taylor, Gottfredson, & Brower, 1985). Furthermore, researchers have observed that the saliency of these perceived nested referent scales of the geographic environs of home varies with the demographic characteristics of individuals, their needs and objectives, their residential history, and the properties of the physical environment (reviewed in Chawla, 1992; Fischer et al., 1977; Shumaker & Taylor, 1983; Keller, 1968).

Of particular importance to this study are the findings concerning an individual's social class. Among middle-class North Americans, the dwelling unit is central; however, for working-class and lower-income North Americans, the neighborhood environs are especially, if not considerably, more important in defining the region the inhabitants refer to as home[2] (Fried, 1963; Keller, 1968; Rappaport, 1981). Moreover, actions and experiences indicative of the appropriation of homeplace in working-class and lower-income communities extend well beyond the confines of the dwelling or apartment building into the neighborhood environs (Fried, 1963; Fried & Gleicher, 1970; Gans, 1962; Haywoode, 1991; Leavitt & Saegert, 1990; Suttles, 1968). For instance, socializing activities that generally remain within the boundaries of a middle-income household's dwelling, typically spill out onto the sidewalks of working-class and lower-income neighborhoods.

Wentworth Gardens residents' perceptions of the geographic extent of their home are like those of other low-income North Americans – the boundary is well beyond the walls of the dwelling and its immediate surroundings. According to all Wentworth resident activists, the entire housing development is their "home." It is particularly noteworthy, however, that with the exception of the black working-class neighbors who lived to their immediate north, Wentworth residents typically do not refer to the broader geographic neighborhood beyond their development as part of their homeplace. This is not surprising. The boundaries of the development are quite distinct – a limited-access highway, industry, and a major thoroughfare bordered by commercial facilities and vacant land. Also, Wentworth buildings are distinguished from the surrounding neighborhood by their early modernist architectural style. Moreover Wentworth Gardens residents are aware of the racist perceptions of public housing tenants and the discriminatory history of their white neighbors to the west and north of the original and current White Sox stadium. And as will become evident in this chapter, all of the residents' actions to appropriate spaces,

---

[2] The importance of the neighborhood for poor and working-class people may be explained, in part, by the smaller apartments they live in when compared with middle-class people. Because of limited mobility and the economic costs of recreational, athletic, and other, facilities, poor and working-class people also are more likely to form relationships based in their local area rather than nonspatial, interest-based relationships (Fried, 1963; Fried & Gleicher, 1970; Gans, 1962; Suttles, 1968).

with one exception, a community garden adjacent to the development, were focused on physical settings within the development – at least until, as we will see in the next chapter, their development was threatened with demolition.

Obstacles to Space Appropriation

Proshansky (1976), in his review of the literature on space appropriation, notes that the ends of space appropriation are not assured, nor necessarily long-lived. Space appropriation inquiries have been particularly concerned with uncovering especially the societal conditions that structure opportunities for, but also obstacles to, the rights to and control of space. Chombart de Lauwe (1976) and Grauman (1976) framed their work around the question "Is the appropriation of space by all possible?" They examined the economic, political, and legal obstacles, in particular, noting that in societies where land and development of built space are controlled by economic wealth and political power, appropriation of space by all is not possible.[3] Our research, however, contradicts these conclusions. As we will see, Wentworth activists have appropriated spaces even in the most oppressive circumstances; and that these acts of space appropriation, no matter how modest the space, are significant acts of resistance.

Other inquiries into the obstacles of space appropriation have expressed concern about how characteristics of the physical setting may contribute to the difficulty of appropriating space. For instance, inadequate amounts of spatial and material resources, poorly functioning space, or poorly maintained space can hinder appropriation processes.[4] Furthermore, current industrialized societies' modes of creating and relating to places also may be a hindrance. Places that are organized, codified, and institutionalized according to professional models privilege so-called expert knowledge and opinions over those of laypersons (see Korosec-Serfaty, 1976; also see Werner's edited issue of *Architecture & Behavior*, 1992). This professionalization and the resulting increasing impersonal means of designing, developing, and

---

[3] Drawing upon Marx's theory to answer this question, they cited capitalist modes of production as explaining inequalities in the power to appropriate nature. Graumann (1976) argued: "In the Marrxist view, appropriation, taken as self-actualization, is contingent upon the degree of alienation of man from the products of his work, from his fellow men, and from himself. The degree is said to be extremely high in capitalist society, where the monopolization of the means of production turns the products of labor into mere 'commodities', thus divorcing the subject of work from the objects which are not his."

[4] Also, the technological and social transformations of industrial society may hinder people's relative power or ability to appropriate space (Buttimer, 1980; Relph, 1976; Toffler, 1994, Tuan, 1977). The speed of change in the creation of new physical settings is increasing, leaving little time for individuals to gain familiarity with place.

giving recognition to the built environment have resulted in both sepa-
ration of production of spaces and space users, as well as increasingly
homogeneous physical settings that do not account for the variability in
people's spatial needs and aspirations.

As we have seen, Wentworth residents' rights to appropriate the spaces
of their development could not be taken for granted. Wentworth residents
lack the political and legal authority and economic resources to ensure
the ongoing availability, quality, and use of the physical settings of their
housing development to meet their everyday household and community
needs. Their struggles to reopen and maintain the field house for youth
programs are a telling example. To operate the youth programs the residents required CHA's permission to use the necessary physical facility
and material supplies. To gain these rights they had to organize to negotiate with and pressure CHA more assertively and to defy cultural stereotypes about their capabilities and legitimacy to control and manage this
facility.

In the United States, individuals who rent, rather than own, their houses
or apartments do not have the same rights to or power over their alter-
ation and use, making them dependent upon what Chombart de Lauwe
(1976) has called "social dominance." Low-income households are further constrained in their choice of the location, quality, and management
of their rental units (Clark, 1993). Moreover, it could be argued that in
the United States, public housing residents have the least legal rights to
or power over their dwellings when compared with renters in general.
Not only are they constrained by the location, quality, and management
of these developments, but they have no guarantee of its permanency.
Consider the ease and speed, at times with one day notice, with which
residents of two other CHA developments, Henry Horner Homes and
ABLA Homes, were evicted and their housing demolished. Consider, as
well, the additional occupancy standards now being applied by HUD to
public housing residents – for example, a household in which any member has been convicted of a felony may be evicted – when compared with
renters in the private market. In addition, public housing residents have
neither control over the physical and economic decay of their surrounding neighborhood, nor the economic resources needed to revitalize their
communities.

At Wentworth Gardens, residents' community activism to improve daily
life has necessitated ongoing resistance, organizing efforts to exercise their
rights over and use of the material and spatial resources of their housing
development, resources that are controlled by the city and local housing
authority. It is to these struggles we now turn. We will elaborate upon both
the means and the ends of the appropriation of homeplace by examining
the history of the development, maintenance, and management of the on-
site laundromat, convenience store, and field house.

THE LAUNDROMAT

The Wentworth Gardens on-site laundromat is the resident activists' most long-lasting, tangible accomplishment. Founded in 1968 by the Resident Council, it has been successfully operated through volunteer labor for over three decades. It is the residents' space – used for both instrumental and social purposes – and the signs of space appropriation are visible throughout. The darkness of the basement is lightened by fresh paint, a full announcement board, birthday cards adorning the walls, and the activity of residents doing the ordinary domestic work of clothes washing. Visibly impressive are new washers purchased with monies earned through years of an efficiently organized operation.

For 3 years before the founding of the resident-run laundromat, Wentworth Gardens had no laundry facilities. The nearest retail laundromat was several blocks away through the "unsafe turf" of another low-income neighborhood. The travel distance was especially hard felt in winter, particularly for those residents with young children. An original laundromat volunteer recalled:

I remember when all that snow was, and I had to take all the clothes . . . across the bridge [over the Dan Ryan Expressway]. . . . So many peoples in here had little babies. And it was hard for 'em to get across the bridge to do their laundry.

When it was first constructed, Wentworth Gardens had laundry rooms located in one of the buildings in each of the development's seven blocks. Each laundry room was fitted with washers, wringers, and bins for hanging clothes out to dry. At first, use of the laundry machines was free of charge. However, as a result of the frequent breakdowns and necessary repairs, the residents were required to purchase keys to the laundry room at a cost of $6.00 every 6 months. Resident activists attributed these breakdowns to resident misuse of the machines – some residents were "overloadin' the . . . machine while it runnin'; too much suds." As a result, the machines might be working for only "a couple of days a week or so." They also explained this misuse by the lack of management oversight and an inadequate number of machines – one to two per block – for the number and size of the families in the development. An original laundromat volunteer described how cycles of misuse and breakdowns continued, and when the overhead to maintain these laundry rooms became too high, CHA, in 1965 discontinued the on-site service:

The machines, they [residents] kept tearin' 'em up, they [CHA] kept coming back, fixin'. . . . And then HUD said . . . CHA or HUD, one of the two, "We are not going to fix the laundromats no more. What we are going to do is close 'em up, and you all have to wash the best you could."

With the closing of the laundry facilities, again the Resident Council was presented with both an immediate need and an opportunity. Mrs. Dorothy

McMiller explained that the Resident Council chose to assume the responsibility to attend to this everyday need:

[W]e all kept saying we need a laundromat. Then that's when they [Resident Council] started to havin' the meetings and things, and trying to figure out . . . and that's how we got started.

The Resident Council, however, had neither the legal authority nor the economic and material resources to act on their own. The success of the resident activists in meeting these needs was due to their effective women-centered organizing.

The need for convenient laundry facilities was common to all CHA family developments. The washers and dryers had been dismantled at all sites, as at Wentworth, because of excessive maintenance costs due to vandalism and misuse (*CHAT*, 1969). A few years later, with funds from HUD targeted to "improve the quality of life in CHA apartments" (*Sun Times*, May 18, 1968, p. 1), CHA made a special financial appropriation of $570,000 to establish resident-managed laundromats in 22 developments[5] (*Chicago Tribune*, August 8, 1969, p. 1). The CHA objective was to supply a needed service while giving residents valuable business experience. The model for the CHA resident-managed laundromat program was adopted from a successful cooperative laundry initiated at the Chicago family high-rise development Robert Taylor Homes in October 1967 (*CHAT*, 1969). Taylor residents, under the leadership of Mothers on the Move against Slums (MOMS), an organization of suburban women and Taylor women residents, planned the venture with the assistance of the CHA.

The CHA resident-managed laundromat program supported the renovation of existing laundry rooms to accommodate coin-operated laundry equipment. The rehabilitated space would be leased to a building council, or to any other qualified or recognized group of residents who agreed to assume responsibility to operate the facility. All policy decisions would be made by tenant managers of each laundromat. Profits would be used by the sponsoring resident group to fund social, recreational, and community improvement activities. It was reported in CHA documents, that there were 32 resident-operated laundromats created under this particular CHA program (*CHAT*, 1970).

The Wentworth Resident Council became aware of the CHA-sponsored laundromat program through the on-site manager, with whom they had

---

[5] In addition to the remodeling of the laundry rooms, $27.5 million in funds from HUD was targeted to selected developments for construction of day care centers, community centers, security hardware and lighting, apartment modernization, grounds beautification, resident employment in grounds beautification, upgrading of playgrounds, and a study to evaluate CHA services and determine future needs (*Chicago Tribune*, August 8, 1969, p. 1).

an effective social bridging relationship:

The manager presented what was given to him. The federal government said that they would put in the installation if a resident . . . would take the responsibility of operatin' a laundromat. CHA would furnish the space. The federal [government] would furnish the installation, and the rest would be left up to a committee to be responsible for the laundromat. We had to discuss it in the Resident Council at that time. . . . And, [the manager] told us, you know, what all our options were. And so, he was quite, a really very nice manager, Mr. Barrett, Elton Barrett. [original laundromat volunteer]

The Resident Council had the legitimacy, as a result of prior organizing successes, to partner effectively with the CHA management to open an on-site laundromat. They had the necessary leadership to orchestrate this effort and the organizing capacity, because of the bonding social capital formed through the community household and prior women-centered organizing efforts, to pull in residents to operate this essential service voluntarily. Mrs. Amey, as the Resident Council president, and Mrs. Mae Taylor, with the help of other council members, worked with the on-site manager to implement the laundromat program at Wentworth. The task took persistent effort guided by these two leaders. Beatrice Harris, referring to Mrs. Amey, explained that "if there's anyone that can help take these ideas through, [she] can." Mrs. McMiller described Mrs. Taylor's input similarly: "[Y]ou know, Mae Taylor was one of those types that when . . . she get a idea, she just go for it."

The Resident Council incorporated the laundromat as a not-for-profit corporation with a Laundromat Service Committee to plan and manage the facility, again under Hallie Amey's inspirational guidance and Mae Taylor's leadership as president. In order to ensure their success, both women expanded their knowledge and business acumen by visiting other CHA resident-operated laundromats, in particular, both Dearborn Homes and Robert Taylor Homes because "they had nice operations." The bridging social capital developed with the resident leadership of these public housing complexes provided ongoing beneficial support. Mrs. Amey, for instance, recalled a woman by the name of Mae from Robert Taylor Homes: "She's the one that came over to us and used to help us out and give us ideas and things too."

The council chose a space for the laundromat in an unused basement of one of the three-story walk-up apartment buildings because it was in the "most central" location and the "largest" space available. Working in partnership with the activists, the on-site manager arranged to have the space renovated to accommodate 10 washing machines and 10 dryers leased with initial funds provided by the CHA. Mrs. Amey remembered how proud the council members were: "When we saw it – oh, it was so beautiful."

The Laundromat Service Committee decided to save all monies earned to purchase machines because of the difficulties they experienced leasing. The service was satisfactory at first, but with time it deteriorated. Mrs. Amey:

You know . . . we had this five year contract . . . and when those five years was up, they [service company] was supposed to replace the machines . . . that had gone bad. . . . And, they was refusin' to do what they was supposed to do. . . . They had gotten so bad, and they would not service them, and really we just about had it.

The monies earned in the initial years of laundromat operation were quite modest, approximately $400 to $500 per month; most of the money was needed to pay leasing costs. However, in the 5-year period of the lease, enough funds were saved to purchase new machines, which are now owned by the residents. This was a "proud time," said Mrs. Amey. Profits were and continue to be modest because the cost to do a wash has been kept lower than the retail cost to keep it affordable – "We keep it cheap!" said Mrs. Carter.

The new machines were kept in good working condition through the watchful supervision of the resident laundromat volunteers and the long-term bridging relationship they developed with a serviceman, Mr. Fuller. One of the young adults, who was volunteering in the laundromat, was apprenticed to Mr. Fuller for several years to assist in repairs, and therefore the residents were able to make some repairs themselves. Because of the competent management of residents, the next purchase of new machines was not necessary until 1989. Once again, the volunteers spoke with pride about the new washers and dryers purchased with the impressive sum of $20,850, saved from laundromat proceeds.

Laundromat volunteers are represented by the Laundromat Service Committee, which first operated within the Resident Council and subsequently the LAC. The committee, made up of laundromat volunteers, has met on a regular basis, typically once a month, to resolve problems. According to Marcella Carter these included "Different problems and stuff; what's going on, machine breakdowns, and how the people are acting." The committee also has been responsible for prioritizing requests for laundromat profits above machine maintenance, repair, and replacement costs, which have been returned to the community to help support their local organizing efforts. Regular recipients have included the Girl Scouts, senior citizen activities, yearly community festivals, and scholarship funds. Mrs. Carter:

There was a time when the laundromat gave out scholarships for kids. They still do. Like someone in the community might have two kids graduating from grammar school . . . dues to pay, luncheons, clothes, robe rental.

The volunteers' schedules were guided by the council's intention to provide convenient hours of operation. Mrs. Amey:

And, what we did . . . together. We sat down as a group . . . and just that we, we knew we wanted to open . . . seven days when we first opened. . . . We were trying to accommodate the people, and we were just so proud of it.

And for over three decades, this ongoing volunteer work of women residents has assured the laundromat's continued operation. Volunteers worked several 3-hour shifts per week in order to keep the facility open from 7:00 A.M. to 10:00 P.M. 6 days per week, and 7:00 A.M. to 1:00 P.M. on Fridays: women like Mrs. Mae Frances Jones, one of the original laundromat volunteers, who, for 17 years, has worked for up to 3 hours per day, 4 days per week; Mrs. Henrietta Shah, described as the "Rock of Gibraltar" because in addition to her own shifts of up to 4 days per week, she often relieved other operators as the need arose; and Mrs. Dorothy McMiller, who has worked in the laundromat since it opened:

I did so many hours. . . . God would help me. Mrs. Walker, you know . . . me and her used to work together. . . . And so, then after that . . . we had a lot of volunteers like Mrs. Anderson . . . Mrs Driver, myself, and Mrs. Russell. . . . It was a whole bunch of us, you know. We only had like three hours and we'd get off and somebody else would be comin' on.

Mrs. Amey has tirelessly assumed the full responsibility for staffing the laundromat. Exemplifying her women-centered leadership, every resident laundromat volunteer we spoke with named Mrs. Amey when asked who encouraged them to become involved and then stay involved in the laundromat. Participants in the focus group we conducted about early Wentworth organizing efforts laughed in agreement when one volunteer explained Amey's persistence in "bringing people out":

Now I'm workin' [in the laundromat] one day a week. . . . Then Mrs. Amey call me sometimes. . . . I wouldn't answer at first. I say until Mrs. Amey called me sometime like everyday. And she could sound so pitiful too. One day she called me. . . . "Ain't got nobody . . . goin' today. . . . " Well I said, "I ain't gonna be down there all day, Mrs. Amey." She just say, "For a little while," and then for that little while you'll got all day.

To sustain the large number of necessary volunteers, and relieve the older-generation volunteers of potential burnout, Mrs. Amey has "brought in" younger-generation women, as well, such as Desiree Davis.

Volunteers have received free use of the machines and, in more recent years, modest stipends, but these monies and privileges earned are not adequate to explain their motivation for volunteering, especially for those who have volunteered over the course of several years. For the volunteers, the laundromat itself is a critical site of the community household, where social cohesiveness is cultivated through ongoing socializing among volunteers and with other residents in the development. One resident, who had volunteered for nearly 20 years, described the laundromat as "our community." Mae Francis Jones has found the work with other residents "fun. There was excitement. And it was lovely." She particularly liked "[w]orkin' with the peoples, bein' with the peoples." Mrs. Mary Rias explained that she loved her laundromat work because "I like meeting people, and you know everybody in the community." Solidarity between resident volunteers has been enriched not only through their actual work in the laundromat, but also through rituals such as birthdays celebrated in the laundry room, "*right down here.*" Perhaps the high degree of social cohesion can best be demonstrated by Mrs. Lucille Burns, who, although she and her husband moved out of Wentworth years ago, returned three times a week to work in the laundromat.

Moreover, all of the residents we interviewed, who first implemented and then worked in the laundromat, explained that they have been motivated not only by Mrs. Amey, but also by a sense of duty and a concern for their community to provide this needed service:

I am very proud of it. It's because I don't even use it half of the time, but it's for the peoples, and peoples really appreciate havin' their laundromat. (Long-term laundromat operator)

As long-term volunteers, they have gained a sense of significance by being a part of a core group of operators who have shared in the facility's successes. Mrs. Carter explained that "not just any resident can work in the laundromat." The volunteers must first be trustworthy – it is a cash business – and demonstrate commitment to other community work before being entrusted with a laundromat operator position. Mrs. Carter explained:

See, you have to find the right people because the laundromat is not coin operated.... It is operated with a key.... It's volunteers [who] cut on the machine and the people pay. So you have to have a person who is trustworthy because all this money is in your hands.

Furthermore, the volunteers' work is appreciated by the community. Wentworth residents rely on these facilities, which are convenient and cost-efficient. One volunteer described that Wentworth residents "had a fit" when the laundromat had to close for a month for painting. This sense of significance can be conceptualized as one dimension of empowerment.

Through working at the laundromat, volunteers gain skills and self-confidence that empower them to become involved in subsequent community ventures. Bertha McKinney explained that, while working in the laundromat, she learned to manage her time efficiently. With her new time management skills and with the moral support of her fellow volunteers in the laundromat, Mrs. McKinney returned to school to complete her high school education at night. Then, in turn, with her GED, she was asked to manage the resident-operated community store. Mrs. McKinney:

But you know, if it's something you want to do, there's a way to do it. Things'll come together. So it wasn't as hard as people think it is if you want to do it.

Through its ongoing operations, the laundromat also has been an important site to support other women-centered organizing efforts at Wentworth. The laundromat was initiated and supported by the Resident Council, and later by the Local Advisory Council through its Service Committee, and in turn, has strengthened these resident representative groups and its legitimacy with developmentwide residents and local management. It has served as a primary site of recruitment for subsequent resident grassroots activist efforts. Marcella Carter explained:

Most of the people started out working in the laundromat – Mrs. Driver, Mrs. Harris, Mrs. Amey, Mrs. Showers. [Y]ou ease them into the laundromat, you work around them for awhile, and you find that you can trust them.

Challenges and Obstacles

Women-centered organizers always operate within the context of a particular power structure arrangement that can both make possible and hinder their efforts. In developing the laundromat, Wentworth activists were approached by the on-site CHA manager because of the skills they demonstrated in the reinstatement of the field house youth programs. The spatial and financial resources required from CHA to open the laudromat were much more easily secured from the on-site management than for the field house, yet Wentworth activists could not rely on ongoing CHA support to sustain the physical facility and its operations. Rather, the ongoing success of the laundromat has required constant resident vigilance and careful attention.

Laundromat volunteers shared several concerns about the limits and constraints on their effectiveness, which, at times, have resulted in frustration and discouragement. First of all, sustaining adequate volunteer coverage of the laundromat has become increasingly difficult. Mrs. Amey has struggled with "bringing in new recruits." Coverage for several of the less busy shifts has been reduced from two to one volunteer. The original laundromat hours have been shortened. And unlike in the past, the trustworthiness of the new recruits has become an issue. Mrs. Amey:

And it never dawned on any of us to go and be in charge of the laundromat and think in terms of doing anything but working and being responsible for the money and passing it on to where it's supposed to go. . . . [T]his is the way we have really operated. But we have come to a fork in the road, and we have to think different, you know, now . . . in bringing in new recruits.

Mrs. Amey explained that trustworthiness was not an issue when the laundromat was opened because all of the volunteers were members of the Resident Council and had already been working as trusted volunteers for their community:

Now, in the beginnin', it was just the original group [Resident Council]. And, as I explained to them and to myself as well, this is ours. If you take, you cheat from yourselves. And, uh, nobody got time to watch you. Everybody's busy. When you're down there, this laundromat is yours; you're responsible. And that's the key. And, and really, with the beginning group, it never, it never dawn on nobody to be concerned about [theft] . . . 'cause see, with us, it's been a struggle, a struggle for our basic needs. . . . And so, whoever you have must take responsibility.

Past expectations of trustworthiness, however, could no longer be met because the new recruits do not have the same volunteer history; nor do they have an understanding of the struggles Wentworth activists have engaged in to open and sustain the laundromat. New recruits have become all the more necessary, as volunteers move out, age, and/or experience burnout. Many of the laundromat volunteers also have worked to develop and sustain other service activities and programs for their community, all the more contributing to burnout. As Mrs. McMiller shared, "I'm tired. . . . I used to be involved in a lot of things. But, I kinda' age, kind of slow."

For those residents who have continued to volunteer in the laundromat, the day-to-day operations have become more difficult. Volunteers, such as Mrs. Mae Francis Jones, complain that resident norms of respectful behavior in the laundromat have become a problem:

I used to be proud of it . . . the laundromat. But now I'm about to get discouraged with it. . . . You have to be worried with the peoples; the people are not the same. And I got older, and so, you know, my nerves more now. . . . But, they [residents] come . . . and before they put them [clothes] in the machine . . . they put up an argument with you. You go through that argument. Then they put their clothes in the dryer. [They say,] "Oh, the dryer's not getting hot." [I answer,] " I'm not a mechanic darling, just put them, take them out. . . . Stuff like that.

Not only are the newer residents less considerate of the volunteers, they lack social bonds with the older-generation residents. The problem has become especially difficult now that children often are sent to do the wash instead of their mothers. Mrs. Jones:

The kids talkin' loud . . . and everything. Wouldn't do what you asked them to do; would talk back to you.

Finally, Wentworth laundromat volunteers have had to make do with less than functional basement space. Especially troubling are the periodic floods. Even with these obstacles, Wentworth activists have managed to keep the laundromat operational and attractive through ongoing negotiations with the CHA management, purchase of their own machines, much ingenuity, and their own volunteer labor.

At Wentworth, and in public housing developments across the country generally, adequate functional spaces for community services and programs were not provided in the original designs, nor typically was space for retail facilities to meet daily needs. The need for facilities to purchase food and products for everyday life is particularly acute. As in other low-income neighborhoods in cities nationwide, Wentworth's neighborhood, South Armour Square, is underserved by commercial establishments (see Retail Chicago Advisory Panel, undated).

WENTWORTH'S COMMUNITY STORE

With the experience of and confidence from developing and managing the on-site laundromat, the resident activists proceeded to their next major project – the Wentworth community store. The CHA-sponsored newsletter *CHAT* heralded the opening of the store in 1973 as a major accomplishment:

Doing It Themselves, Wentworth Residents Open Food Store
Wentworth Gardens residents prepared for the big event for 18 months. On September 19 the day arrived. Planned and operated entirely by Wentworth residents, the new Wentworth Community Store opened.

Wentworth residents and people from the area no longer must travel long distances for food and hard goods. Now they go to 3750 S. Wells St.

The Wentworth Community Store is open long hours – daily from 7 a.m. to 10 p.m. and Sundays from 7 a.m. to 1 p.m.

For now, the store sells only nonperishable goods, but soon before the end of the year it will also sell perishable foods such as meat, vegetables and dairy products.

The store, a nonprofit venture, is staffed by some 15 Wentworth volunteers, most of whom gained experience over the last two years procuring food through a food buying club. Most attended consumer education classes.

Profits will be used to restock the store, to provide student scholarships, and to sponsor children's activities such as recreation trips. An original 10-member programming committee helped organize the store in cooperation with the Wentworth resident advisory council. CHA provided assistance during the start-up period.

A seven-member board of directors is to be named by the LAC to manage financial activities of all businesses at Wentworth, including the store and a laundromat. The store manager is Mrs. Beatrice Harris. (*CHAT* 1973, pages not numbered)

Before the development of the store, Wentworth residents had no convenient place to shop for everyday necessities: "We don't have anything around here, and we need [a store] in here because we service a lot of need in here," stated Mardia Earving. Grocery shopping required a bus ride to a supermarket. There was a liquor store across Pershing Road that had some grocery items, but it was poorly stocked, and crossing the road was particularly unsafe for children because of the heavy truck traffic. Mrs. Mardia Earving, who was the Wentworth community store manager in the early 1990s, was well aware that the problem would not be solved without the Wentworth activists' intervention: "[T]here's a tremendous need in here, and if we don't do something to help ourselves, ain't nobody else gonna do it."

To meet Wentworth residents' everyday shopping needs, the activists decided to develop a volunteer-run on-site convenience store. Again motivated to act by a basic need and their ethic of care for the Wentworth community, they secured CHA on-site management's approval to occupy a location they had selected. To take advantage of foot traffic, they chose a central location – the basement space near the laundromat, in the walk-up building that housed the LAC office.

The 1973 *CHAT* article mentioned a 10-member programming committee that "got the store off the ground." But, once again, it was the dedication, trustworthiness, and resourcefulness of the activist store managers and volunteers – such as Mrs. Amey, Mrs. Harris, Mrs. Ramsey, Mrs. McKinney, Mrs. Earving, and Mrs. Carter – that explain its operation.

As in the laundromat, all but one of the store managers we spoke with, as well as their assistants, became involved in the store through their relationship with Mrs. Amey. Mrs. Ramsey explained how Mrs. Amey's particular leadership style worked in enticing her initial and then sustained involvement:

Didn't have very much in the store. Had a couple of loaves of bread on the, on the shelf, and a few pops. . . . And she said, "I got to run for a minute. Do you know anything about cash registers?" I said, "Yes." She said, "Stay here until I get back." So I stayed until Mrs. Amey came back, and she said, "Do you got a little more time to spare? 'Cause I need to go someplace else." And I said, "Okay." She went. And when I left, she said, "Can you come back tomorrow?" And she just started knockin' on the door and sayin', "Look I got this meetin' to go to. And I need somebody to go [to the store]. . . ." I guess Mrs. Amey is organized. She gets someone, if they willing to come out.

Mrs. Ramsey managed the store for several years until taking her paid position in the LAC. Her dedication to the ongoing operation of the store, however, was apparent when the store lost the volunteer manager because of illness. Now, holding a full-time job, Mrs. Ramsey stepped in and also managed the store for 6 months, including doing all the purchasing, as well as assisting Mrs. Amey in the bookkeeping.

All of the store managers have worked 6 days a week, Monday through Saturday, often from 8:00 A.M. to 8:00 P.M., taking on all of the on-site responsibilities for the management and maintenance of the facility and the daily operations of the store. Mrs. Mardia Earving's words amply describe the substantial efforts required. A mother of five, she moved into

Wentworth in 1979 and began her service at the store after a hiatus from other volunteer activities at Wentworth to care for her young children:

[O]nce everything got settled with them [children] and they started getting out of the house, I found I had more time on my hands, and I said that I was doing a lot of other things but it just wasn't challenging enough. So I came down here [store] one day. I hadn't been down here for three or four years, and it was really in bad condition. And I asked them if they wanted me to give them some time 'cause I had plenty of time. And they said. "Yeah." They was glad to. So I said, "Okay," and that's how I ended up coming back.

The job was challenging: the facility poorly maintained at that time and no funds for its repair. But Mrs. Earving recalled when she was a child "being around" the small grocery store that her father had owned in the South, and now as an adult she described herself as both "good with people" and "good with sales," important assets for running a grocery store. Doing much of the work herself, Mrs. Earving began by cleaning and repairing the deteriorating grocery store space:

The first thing, I had to clean in here. It was just horrible. It was embarrassing.... They [rats] use to crawl on up under here and it was so bad. I didn't know where to start first. I just did a little a day along with trying to do what little service I could do, also just a little a day. And some Sundays, I would come down here and work all day Sunday. And then I repainted a little, here and there 'cause it was so bad.... It took about a month just getting the garbage and stuff out of here. Then we had to clean and wash down everything.

After the space was thoroughly cleaned, Mrs. Earving needed to raise the funds for the supplies to renovate the basement space and repair or replace the equipment. The shelving was in place, but the two freezers needed repair. She fund-raised by preparing and selling food – hot dogs and chili dinners. She would prepare the dinners in her apartment kitchen, paying for the food costs out of her own pocket:

I'm telling you, you just don't know the things I did. I sold dinners to get it started because I didn't have any money.... I would go purchase the food. Sometimes I had to use my [food] stamps to buy the stuff, and then I'd cook the food the night before.... I would sit up at night and roll change [earned from selling the prepared food]. And I would hold it and hold it until it accumulated. Then I would take it and deposit it [for the store]. And that is how I would buy items like I bought the freezer. Then I would start another project to get the freezers fixed.... I had all three freezers fixed. Everything was broken. One was five [hundred dollars]; one was six hundred [dollars].... Then we needed a cash register terribly, so I started saving for that; you know selling stuff for that.... I just did one thing at a time.

The "change" Mrs. Earving raised would slowly accumulate, eventually to purchase a third used freezer, pay for the repair of the existing freezers, and purchase a cash register.

When we visited the store in December 1991, after Mrs. Earving had been managing it for approximately 2 years, it was well stocked and maintained. Brightly painted, well lit, and clean, the space was bordered on three of the walls and down the middle with shelving. The store contained basic household staples, such as milk, bread, baby food and diapers, laundry detergent, and canned goods. According to Mrs. Earving, "Just things that you might run out of right away; to tide you over 'till you get to the store." To keep the food and merchandise affordable, prices are kept low. This requires careful purchasing, mostly from wholesale distributors – "Wherever I know it's cheaper, that's where I go." Mrs. Ramsey explained that when she was the store manager,

usually I go to, uh, 76th and State . . . L&P Wholesale. I buy cases . . . at L&P it's like $52 to $55. One day I went to Jewel's [a retail grocery store]. I was gonna get, take the tax exempt letter, and get a case of tissue from Jewel. And it was $77 for a case of Scot's tissue!

The store managers have been responsible for all purchasing. Although some food products are delivered – milk, soda, and bread – many companies will not deliver to a public housing development. Mrs. Earving was clearly frustrated with the situation:

They won't come out in our area. They won't deliver. I had to go in the street where people were delivering to beg them, "Would you please come with me now and I'll show you where I am and it's not bad." Cheetos, I still haven't gotten. I've been trying for two and a half years to get them. These are the things I was up against. I'm still up against it. They won't deliver. Certain warehouses won't deliver to us. It's really hard.

Without the advantage of a truck, managers would make frequent buying trips in their own or a borrowed car, often two to three times a week, to keep the store stocked. Mrs. Ramsey explained that she had to take care not to overload her car on these trips.

Well, I don't break the springs and stuff in my car. That's why I go two or three times [a week]. . . . Like, if I'm gonna get stuff like bleach . . . bleach is heavy. So if I buy a case . . . the only thing [else] is I'm gonna buy is probably a little candy or something that day.

Mrs. Earving didn't have a car so she had to ask people to drive her:

I go and get everything. I have a driver. He's a friend. I met him and I explained my problem that I was having, because every week I was stuck trying to find someone to take me to the store. So now, he's my permanent friend. He takes me every week.

The store's financial management is also the responsibility of the store manager with Mrs. Amey's oversight. In addition to stocking the shelves, they had to keep records of inventory, purchases, and sales. Mrs. Amey collected both the cash earned and the records and delivered each, respectively, to the bank and to an accountant. The managers then used these monies and food stamps to pay for their purchases. The Service Committee had oversight responsibility for the store, in particular the way the profits would be used; however, all of the monies earned to date have had to be used to keep the store in operation, leaving no significant funds, as in the case of the laundromat, to redistribute to the community.

Challenges and Obstacles

The development, management, and daily operations of the store have proved to be much more difficult than those of the laundromat. The activists have not been able to bridge to organizations and businesses that are crucial to the successful orchestration of this venture. Unlike for the laundromat, the CHA did not renovate the basement space for the store or provide any start-up funds for initial food inventory, shelving, and equipment. Attempts at securing other funds through grants written to foundations were unsuccessful. The space had to be renovated and food and equipment purchased all through volunteers' personal resources and fund-raising efforts. Perhaps most importantly, the store is a more complicated business to manage and operate. Consumer demand for food and products must be continually assessed, food purchased, shelves stocked, inventory checked, and books kept. More cash changes hands in the store than in the laundromat, also increasing management responsibilities. As a result, the store has not sustained continuous operation since its founding. When it has functioned effectively, it is because one individual, such as Mrs. Earving, has taken on the leadership and primary responsibility for the maintenance of the facility and equipment, ongoing management, and operational tasks.

Although the Wentworth activists have persisted in working diligently to keep the store open 6 days a week, there have been long periods when it was either closed or stocked less adequately. According to all of the store managers, staffing is the key problem. Although there is a modest stipend, it does not always serve to attract staff. Mrs. Ramsey underlined this fact: "In the first place, we don't ... have enough reliable volunteers." In order to attract volunteers, Mrs. Amey raised the stipend to $10 a shift, even for a partial shift, provoking understandable resentment among the long-term volunteers who had earned $5 for a full day of work.

The commitment of the store managers, of both time and effort, has been so substantial that the burnout rate has been high. The extraordinary demands on the store managers explain some of the resulting interpersonal conflicts, for example, between Mrs. Amey and Mrs. Earving. Mrs. Ramsey explained that after several years of managing the store, Mrs. Earving refused to comply with Mrs. Amey's "encouragement" to continue in the position: "Mrs. Earving gets upset and throw her the keys and tell her to do it herself." However, with some time off to rest and reflect, Mrs. Earving recognized that Mrs. Amey was not taking advantage of her, but rather just trying to assure the ongoing viability of the store:

You know how busy Mrs. A. is; she's on the go all the time. I haven't had a moment in the two years and a half to just really sit down and talk to her. I understand that 'cause she's busy with so many things. . . . That's another reason I came back. I know her [Mrs. Amey's] heart was breaking. I know her and I know how she was feeling about this [store]. And that's why I was also willing to come back because I know how she feels about these things. She loves this laundromat and she loves this store. She does not want to see it close, and I respect her a great deal.

When the store loses a manager, Mrs. Amey, if she has the time, given all her other volunteer leadership responsibilities, keeps it open for a limited number of hours daily; at times, however, the store remained closed for months until a new manager could be found.

Because the store is a cash business, theft has always been a concern for the managers and their assistants, but they have used various strategies to cope. Mrs. McKinney stayed vigilant, especially watching for strangers: "And just like I'm in the store, where I learn faces . . . simply because you never know who gonna come in there on you." Mrs. Earving not only watched for strangers; she kept very little cash around the store:

With the situation with the drugs, you still have one or two that will try [to rob the store]. But I'm so alert and I know what's coming in. . . . I don't leave a lot of cash in here. I take it out at a certain time just for precaution. Because when I was working down here before, I was held up, but they didn't get the money. They only got the change that was in the old register that we had. So I know what's out here and what can happen.

Finally, Wentworth activists operated the store with less than adequate space and equipment. The basement store, like the laundromat, is prone to frequent flooding. Mrs. Ramsey:

When it comes a hard pourin' down the rain, and you just settin' there, and all of a sudden you . . . know, to get your purse and stuff, and get out.

The resulting damage has been even greater than in the laundromat because of the refrigeration equipment and perishables stocked in the store. Mrs. Ramsey asserted that a new space for the store is critical to ensure its viability:

We really need to come out of the basement. . . . There's no way to get, to make that flood-proof down there. You know what happened. The last time, you see that big [electric] cable. We were without lights for three days. Because the basement was flooded and the water got all the way up to the wires. Just knocked us out. . . . I see it came all the up and went in the bottom of the refrigerator. That's how high it was.

As in their other organizing efforts, activists experience aggravations and disappointments as they struggle to operate and staff the store and to keep the basement space usable and attractive. So why do these activists persevere? Describing her work as "a little small kind of struggle to do something for the community," Mrs. Earving shared how her altruistic motivations have been questioned by others in the development:

Some people will come in and say, "Why do you do this? Do you get paid?" I say, "No." They say, "You must be crazy." I say, "No, it isn't really about money." And when I explain it to them they think I'm nuts.

And even she herself pondered why she continued to work as hard as she did:

Sometimes I ask myself, "Why do I do it?" I say, "I'm through. I'm not coming back no more." But I still come back.

To those who are not engaged in and committed to grassroots organizing, the efforts expended to develop and manage the store may seem misplaced or excessive. The work of these women-centered organizers, however, can be understood in the context of their attachment to their community household and the broader Wentworth community and the everyday need for this facility.

Despite this apparently less successful organizing effort, especially when compared to the preschool and the laundromat, the store has not been a failure. Quite to the contrary, the store, when in operation, not only has provided a needed service; in appropriating and struggling to maintain the space for the store, Wentworth activists have contributed to the ongoing development of their individual and collective empowerment. Store volunteers explained, despite their frustrations, that they gained a sense of significance, legitimacy, and solidarity in developing and operating this facility. Mrs. Earving:

I've been doing this [managing the store] as many hours as I've been doing because that's the only way I was going to have this type of success . . . but I get a good enjoyment out of it and I sleep good. The harder I work, the better I sleep. [W]e get a little fee of five dollars [a day]. That helped a lot when the kids were here [in her home], but it's not about money now. It's really not about money. . . . I enjoy what I do.

As are other long-term volunteers, Mrs. Earving is clearly proud of the store's success. Mrs. McKinney affirmed the store's importance: "[T]his is real convenient for everybody." Residents rely on the store. And Mrs. Earving elaborated:

They [residents] get really upset if this door is closed.... I'm telling you. They think I'm supposed to be here. I can't get sick. I've been here like 2 years and 3 or 4 months, and I had that virus last year and I was off one day. And if I go somewhere to get something, they're like, "Where's she at? What time will she be back?" They be very angry.

In support of Mrs. Earving's comments, a customer also attested to the residents' attachment to the grocery store: "We love this store."

The store, like the laundromat, has been a site for building bonding social capital and expanding the community household at Wentworth. Working in the store strengthens the social cohesiveness among Wentworth activists and builds relationships with other residents. Mrs. McKinney:

But it's just like a big family here. [I know] just about everybody, and most all the children I know by names. Because they in and out of the store.... I'm in the store from, what, almost ten years now.... Know their apartment numbers too.... You gotta know the people where you live.... And the, I'm in the laundromat too. The ones that I don't meet in the store, I might meet in the laundromat.

Mrs. Earving also recognized the store's potential to encourage residents' participation in Wentworth's social life. In particular, when asked whether she was satisfied with the store after all of the improvements she accomplished, she said, "No. I want much more." In particular, Mrs. Earving wanted to expand the store to add an eating area where residents could gather and socialize.

I would like to have a lunch area. I've been sitting here thinking, you know, you have two or three little tables with the chairs, and coffee and some donuts in the store. [For lunch] you have a speciality of the day.... It will adds more to the community.... That would be really nice in our neighborhood, somewhere where they could get a cup of coffee 'cause we don't have any restaurants. We don't have anything over here.... I know it could be done.

Store volunteers have gained individual empowerment benefits, as well. Mrs. Carter and Mrs. Ramsey explicitly noted that the self-confidence, skills, and networking developed through their management of the store supported other personal life endeavors. Mrs. Ramsey asserted that her volunteer work was essential to her securing paid, full-time employment with CHA in the LAC office. She would not have been offered the position without the reputation she gained as a responsible, capable person; the skills she learned in operating the store; and the networks she developed:

That's, if I hadn't been hangin' with Mrs. Amey and settin' around here [store and LAC office], I . . . wouldn't never ended up with this good job. This is a good job.

Mrs. Carter similarly secured employment with the CHA as a result of the skills and networking she gained at the store:

I got a little experience. And I got a job out of it. By me being down there, I was in the right place at the right time when the job came through.

REVISITING THE WENTWORTH GARDENS FIELD HOUSE

In the late 1960s, even with Wentworth activists' success in getting the field house reopened and the youth programming restored, CHA's maintenance of this structure was far from assured. In fact, by the mid-1980s, the field house roof was in such disrepair that the scheduled children's summer food program housed in the facility was at risk. Mrs Amey described the situation:

The Park District was another sore eye. We had problems there: no service, no nothing. And we were coming up to the summer months by then, and the field house was in such a bad condition, so many leaks.... [T]he room that they usually use to serve the free food for the children was in such a bad condition, and the inspectors had been out and said it could not be used again unless something was done. CHA said there was no money and they couldn't do a thing about it.

Despite ongoing complaints to on-site CHA management, CHA had not attended to the required roof repairs. Politically constrained by their CHA affiliation, some activists within the LAC had formed an "Action Committee." They had begun to meet regularly in 1986 to attend to the ongoing deterioration of Wentworth's buildings and site maintenance and inadequate services. Leveraging their bridging social capital with staff from the Chicago Area Project (CAP), the activists asked CAP's organizer, Sheila Radford-Hill to advise and work with them on the pressing issue of the field house roof repair. Sheila, accepted, in part, because she had been searching for a way for these activists "to get their arms around" a particular issue and to work on it in a "systematic way."[6] The field house was such an issue.[7]

Sheila recognized that Wentworth activists needed to expand their women-centered organizing strategies to challenge CHA's nonresponsiveness

[6] In nearly all cases the technical assistants, including the coauthors, were addressed by their first names by the residents.
[7] When we wrote an earlier article (Feldman & Stall, 1994), we understood that the resident committee's organizing to repair the field house roof followed the news of the impending new stadium development. Since then we have learned that the residents had been working as a committee for months, rather than weeks, before they learned about the possible destruction of their neighborhood in December 1986.

both for the immediate present and the near future. She devised a strategic organizing plan:

[T]his called for ... a three-part approach. You had to have direct action. You had to have ... a real capability of creating a learning community; of bringing residents along, so that they knew what the problems were, and why they were getting screwed. ... And it wasn't enough to act on the knowledge of having been screwed. You have to know why, you know. And, and so they had to have some learning capacity. And the other thing that was necessary is they have to have a ... short-term strategy, and a longer-term strategy. They pretty much always functioned on ... social service stuff. ... This had to go beyond that ... this had to be more systematic.

According to Sheila, activists' short-term goal – to organize to get the field house roof repaired for the upcoming summer food program – "was a good place to start.... [I]t was probably doable ... with some organized resistance." Sheila understood that because the residents were now working on "issues that were more systemic in nature" they were going to meet a "more entrenched resistance." Over the long term she hoped to foster residents' actual control or influence, that is, their empowerment, through development of both a critical understanding of the larger societal issues that explained their deteriorated living conditions and more formal organizational structures.

Mrs. Amey described the specific "organized resistance" they would be up against:

Each development can make requests for CIP [Comprehensive Improvement Program] money, but their [Wentworth Gardens'] requests for interior and exterior repairs had been regularly rejected. So they [CHA] said there was no money.

The CHA's Comprehensive Improvement Program monies systematically were awarded to the larger family developments because they were considered in more dire need of repair and renovations. Therefore, the residents' immediate challenge was to access the CIP funds to get the roof repaired. Their longer-term goals were to form a nonprofit organization and to access resources to maintain a viable community.

Sheila and a group of about 15 Wentworth activists, "an expanded LAC group," began meeting about 2 hours weekly in the LAC office space, outside the regular LAC meetings. She was assisted in her work by a CAP intern, a professional social worker from South Africa.[8] This intern did

---

[8] Sheila Radford-Hill noted that this intern's effectiveness was explained by her intelligence – she was "extremely smart" – but she was also racially sensitive since as an Indian woman, she had wrestled with racial discrimination in her own country: "She had some experience in the trenches. ... [B]eing Indian from South Africa, I mean ... she understood class, caste and color in a way that Americans, never, they don't seem to understand. I mean, I guess if they allowed themselves to understand they'd ... commit suicide or something."

"the legwork," the research, to find out the available resources and the legal requirements to establish a nonprofit organization. Sheila recognized that Wentworth was "a very resource-poor community"; therefore, they needed to extend their bridging social capital further, "to import resources . . . trying to get . . . people with resources that were paid for by third parties . . . grant writers, and researchers, and . . . organizers, and all of that . . . to . . . import their expertise." Sheila contacted two university research centers – the Lindeman Center at Northern Illinois University and the Nathalie P. Voorhees Center at the University of Illinois at Chicago – for technical assistance.

Sheila and Bill Peterman, director of the Nathalie P. Voorhees Center, worked with the residents on the first strategy – teaching the initial steps of making a community needs assessment, first by systematically gathering information that could be used to pressure CHA. Sheila:

[W]e taught the residents that when you're approaching people for change, you have to have your information gathered in a systematic way; and, we made them do . . . not made them, but we encouraged them to survey the community. [Bill] Peterman helped them organize the needs assessment and then . . . enter the data . . . and that's when we found out what people were saying many of the problems were and what the priorities were. So you had a response pattern. How many people thought, you know, the tuckpointing was most important. How many people thought the steps were most important. How many people thought the kick plates were most important, you know, that sort of thing. . . . [T]hen with . . . Bill's help and . . . with my help, the residents also began to understand the course of the funding that they had been systematically denied, which was the CIP dollars.

Armed with this information, a core group of as many as eight women activists began to attend the public CHA Board of Commissioners meetings to pressure for the roof repair. Mrs. Amey:

We had a station wagon. . . . And we would make the commission meetings. We didn't miss a one! And we were like a broken record. I couldn't get to the mike fast enough. I'd be up there every month saying the same thing – telling them about the condition of the field house.

Sheila described how she would "coach" the residents before these public meetings, preparing them so they could effectively present their facts:

So, we sort of had it like clockwork. . . . And . . . they were able to play various roles. We always talked about, well, who's gonna be the spokesperson; who's gonna go first; who's gonna get the data; who's gonna summarize. . . . And . . . I would tell them, if I call you up at 3 am in the morning and ask you what you're supposed to do . . . after you find out that there's nothing wrong, there's no emergency, and after you vent your anger at being waken at 3 am, I expect you to tell me what your part is.

At one of the CHA board meetings, they strategically invited the CHA commissioner at the time, Brenda Gaines, to "tour" their development. Mrs. Amey:

She was new, and she accepted – just what I was expecting. And she did come, and we toured the place, potholes, and just showed her everything. And the main thing that we keyed in on was the field house and the fact that we were not going to be able to have a summer food program.

When these Wentworth activists' efforts did not result in the needed funds, they tried another strategy. Sheila recalled:

[W]e ultimately went downtown and ... went to Gwen Jordan's [HUD regional director's] office and HUD and did a presentation for her senior staff.

This time, their prior organizing paid off. According to Sheila, the residents were well received by the HUD officials. In fact, she feels that "people were somewhat flabbergasted ... by the residents" because they had done their homework and were so well prepared; plus they made such "polished" presentations. Sheila described their division of labor at meetings such as these:

Mrs. Amey was the person who would sort of do the introduction 'cause she's so ... gentile and gracious ... so this disarmed people. Then, we hit 'em high and hit 'em low. So I think that was the sort of strategy.... [For example,] ... when we made the presentation ... to Brenda Gaines.... I don't remember everyone but I know Miss Driver, and Miss Ramsey ... [and] we had Miss Nolan ... and we'd have Miss Dumas ... you know, close with prayer.

After the residents' meeting with HUD, repair monies were located and allocated and the field house roof was not simply repaired, but replaced! Mrs. Amey:

[T]he Regional Supervisor met with us, and what they did [is] what they usually do. CIP money that was scattered around, they gathered it up. We didn't care where it came from; they had done that to us so often ... It was through that effort that we were able to have a summer food program. It was through that effort that we were able to get a roof.... And so, they not only re-roofed the CHA building and part of the Park District – they roofed the whole thing!

This victory was essential to building an organization that, according to Radford-Hill, now had the "vision and strength to organize" (Cagan & deMause, 1998, p. 129) and to represent their community's interests publicly. In order to replace the field house roof Wentworth activists began to broaden their women-centered organizing strategies to include confrontational organizing tactics. They now transgressed the boundary between their homeplace and the public realm in order to negotiate with and apply pressure to the powerful CHA board and commissioner, and the HUD regional director and staff. Leveraging and strengthening their bridging relationship with an outside community organizer, the women activists established new bridging social capital with several technical assistants and engaged in "direct actions" to press for the field house roof repair. Sheila, in the tradition of conventional community organizing, understood the importance of this victory. In order to build an organization, it is necessary to have cumulative victories – beginning with a winnable issue (Alinsky, 1971). The field house was a winnable issue, serving as a tangible symbol of Wentworth's Action Committee's growing effectiveness, as a recruitment tactic, and ultimately as a means to generate "energy" to build to the bigger, more complex struggles. Mrs. Amey shared this conviction: "We decided that we really needed something . . . to win that we could get some attention."

CONCLUSIONS: THE POWER OF SPACE APPROPRIATION

Wentworth women residents' struggles to appropriate homeplace – to reopen and then later repair the field house for youth activities, and to develop and operate the laundromat and store – are what we call "modest victories," "small, fragmented but positive changes in their lives" (Feldman & Stall, 1990, p. 114). We adapted the notion of modest victories from Celene Krauss's (1983) concept of "modest struggles," "small, fragmented, and sometimes contradictory efforts by people to change their lives" (p. 54). In conceptualizing Wentworth residents' grassroots organizing, we have found that modest struggles are not enough; rather, some modest victories are necessary to engender self-esteem and confidence for further action. Although they are small, modest victories are not insignificant. Through these modest victories, Wentworth residents have been "confronting institutions" and have come "to a better understanding of the power relations that affect their lives and of their own abilities – together with others – to have some influence on them" (Ackelsberg, 1988, p. 304). These small, subtle successful acts of everyday resistance impart, according to Woliver (1996), a sense of dignity and worth, despite "oppressed peoples'" marginal status in society and efforts to discredit them. Woliver adds that the acts "help keep alive and nurture reform ideas during periods of resignation and acquiescence. Resignation, though, it is important to remember, is not equivalent to consent" (p. 143). Rather, these modest struggles and modest victories "set the stage" for further acts of everyday resistance:

Small-scale acts of quiet resistance or simple demands for reform thus are not simply a coopted alternative to transformative politics. Rather, they often provide rehearsals of opposition that prepare the way for bolder challenges in more propitious moments. (McCann, 1994, p. 307, cited in Woliver, 1996, p. 143)

Wentworth activists recognize that their modest victories are tenuous, requiring constant vigilance and attention. Although they have managed to command some of the spatial and material resources controlled by CHA and have gained the right to run programs in these facilities, they understand that they are not guaranteed their ongoing use nor their viability. They remain at the mercy of CHA and on-site management. Moreover, the services they provide through both the laundromat and store would not be viable in the private market.

The tenuousness of their modest victories, however, does not undermine their benefits. In appropriating the spaces for these services and programs, residents defied CHA's definitions of who they were – unreliable and incapable – and what their rights were to develop, use, and manage the material and spatial resources of their housing development. These modest victories of space appropriation are particularly powerful because of their material nature and the constancy of their physical presence. Resident activists' actions were in response to real threats to the social reproduction of their community and resulted in real physical improvements in living conditions.

Wentworth activists' organizing to replace the field house and ensure that there would be a summer food program within it illustrates the synergistic relationship among space appropriation processes, grassroots organizing, and resistance. In moving outside the boundaries of their development and in utilizing confrontational organizing strategies, the activists were "transgressing" the expected site and their mode of organizing. They were violating established paternalistic and racist social norms that "define and normalize allowable political roles, discourses, and actions" for low-income, black women (Mele, 2000, p. 63). This transgression began to shape their identities as public political actors; the places the residents appropriated stand as visible, material signs of their growing political effectiveness and legitimacy – critical resources to support additional, and more formidable organizing challenges.

And indeed, as we shall explore in the next chapter, the Wentworth activists, shortly after their field house roof victory, were faced with their greatest community organizing challenge to date – a major battle to resist the possible destruction of their development and of the South Armour Square community.

PART IV

TRANSGRESSIVE RESISTANCE IN THE PUBLIC SPHERE

8

The White Sox "Battle"

Protest and Betrayal

[I]t was decided and approved that we would choose the name – Wentworth Garden Residents United for Survival – because we felt at that point that's what we really would be. Because here were the White Sox right up on us threatening to take our home, and here's CHA doing nothing for us in here. It was the only name that really fit what we were about to be about!

Mrs. Hallie Amey

It was the threat to the physical survival of Wentworth Gardens and its surrounding neighborhood posed by the proposed the new Chicago White Sox stadium that brought Wentworth residents into the political arena to engage in battle to protect their homes. A newspaper article showing the plans for the new Comiskey Park, which required the demolition of part of the Wentworth Gardens development, was their impetus to take action. According to Mrs. Amey:

[A]long around that time, around the end of 1986, then came out a newspaper with a map with the White Sox's listing taking up to 38th Street, and so that was it! That's what made everybody's hair stand up on end.

The activists agreed that they had no choice but to fight the proposed stadium. Not only was their home threatened by an irresponsible CHA, but their development and surrounding neighborhood now faced destruction. They were outraged by their lack of opportunities to participate in the stadium planning process. They were further inflamed by the racial injustice of the siting of the stadium in their neighborhood, especially when they learned that the stadium could have been located instead in an available nearby site in a predominantly white neighborhood – a location that would not have required demolition of neighborhood housing.

Shortly after the White Sox announcement, the resident-initiated on-site action committee, which had secured the field house roof replacement, officially incorporated as a nonprofit. They selected a name they felt was now appropriate: Wentworth Gardens Residents United for Survival (Wentworth United). In response to this direct threat to their community, again aided in their efforts by the local community organizer Sheila Radford-Hill, Wentworth United formed a coalition with neighboring homeowners, residents of the T. E. Brown Apartments (a subsidized senior housing development), and renters from the surrounding neighborhood. First called Save Our Homes (SOH), it later became the South Armour Square Neighborhood Coalition (SASNC) that led the struggle to stop the stadium construction.

To resist the threat of the demolition of their homeplaces and its inherent racial injustice, Wentworth activists, first through SOH then through SASNC, would again transgress the expected site and mode of their organizing efforts. In this chapter we draw on the community organizing literature to interpret the shift in their tactics to include confrontational, "Alinsky-style" organizing to engage in a heated public sphere battle. Wentworth activists extended their range of actions and experiences into the surrounding neighborhood and acted independently of the CHA to challenge the powerful actors supporting the proposed stadium – the White Sox Corporation, the Illinois Sports Facility Authority, and the City of Chicago.

This chapter begins by introducing the context of the White Sox battle: the physical, social, economic, and political history of the South Armour Square neighborhood and the stadium power brokers. Next, we describe the confrontational model of community organizing and early organizing efforts that facilitated the formation of the SACNC. Finally, we concentrate on the White Sox stadium proposal and approval process and the political challenges that the Wentworth Gardens resident activists, now part of the SASNC, confronted.

ARMOUR SQUARE

Armour Square is located about 2 miles south of the center of Chicago. A "polyethnic strip of urban land" (*Chicago Fact Book Consortium*, 1995), the community area is "twenty-one blocks long and only four or five blocks wide." It is bounded by Bridgeport on the west, the Dan Ryan Expressway on the east, 18th Street and the South Branch of the Chicago River on the north, and Pershing Road on the south (Holt & Pacyga, 1979, p. 103).

Historically, Armour Square has been and continues to be divided by race and ethnicity. As reported in *Chicago: An Historical Guide to the Neighborhoods*, it is "a community in name only" (1995, p. 107). In reality it is a set of three enclaves: white residents – Italians, Croatians, and Latinos – consider their community bounded by 35th Street on the south and 26th Street on the north (Sebastian, 1980); the numerically strongest ethnic group in the area, the Chinese-Americans live to the north of 26th Street; the

African-American population lives primarily south of 35th Street. Despite the diversity of the population groups in the area, they share two characteristics: First, 49% of neighborhood adults have not earned high school diplomas, and 59% of this group have only an elementary education or less, a low educational attainment compared to figures for the surrounding neighborhoods and the city as a whole. Associated with this low educational level is low income: In 1989, the median household income in Armour Square was $13,516, while in greater Chicago it was $25,525 (Department of Planning and Development, 1992).[1] In part, the low income of Armour Square residents may be explained by the disproportionate number of subsidized housing units located in the community.[2]

South Armour Square

The name *South Armour Square* is not an official designation, but rather one used by local residents, the media, and some political actors to designate the small black neighborhood located at the southern end of Armour Square. Historically a working-class district, it was originally settled by Irish, German, and Swedish laborers. After the first wave of black migration from the South, South Armour Square began to attract black families because of the availability of inexpensive housing in close proximity to the rapidly developing industrial areas on Chicago's South Side and the overcrowded conditions of the Black Belt immediately adjacent to the east (*Chicago Fact Book Consortium*, 1995, p. 120). Whereas in 1930 only 10% of South Armour's population was black, by 1950 blacks were 96.9% of the total population, and by 1980, 2,300 individuals lived in South Armour, all but 7 of whom were black (*Chicago Fact Book Consortium*, 1995; U.S. Census).

In addition to residential, industrial, and commercial uses, South Armour Square has been the site of several baseball parks. The Chicago

[1] In predominantly white Bridgeport, the educational attainment and incomes were significantly higher. In 1989, 58% of Bridgeport adults had a high school diploma or higher and the mean household income was $25,301 (Department of Planning and Development, 1992).

[2] Of the 19 Chicago neighborhoods that contain 80% of the city's subsidized housing units, Armour Square ranked 18th of the 19, with some 1,216 units until an additional 116 subsidized senior units at T. E. Brown were built. Wentworth Gardens was the first public housing built in Armour Square, but in the 1940s, these 422 units added less than 40% of the new units opened in Armour Square – the other 60% were created through the conversion of old apartments into smaller units. In 1952, the CHA, in city–state-financed construction, opened Archer Courts, 147 units in two seven-story buildings that occupied a little more than 4 acres at 23rd and Princeton, just west of Chinatown. Archer Courts, as has Wentworth Gardens, has been occupied almost exclusively by African-American residents since opening. In 1963, the CHA opened Raymond Hilliard Homes on 7 acres east of Chinatown, and in 1965, the 198-unit Armour Square Apartments for the elderly, two 13-story apartment buildings on $3^1/_2$ acres of land (Holt & Pacyga, 1979, p. 107).

White Sox professional baseball team played in an open field – interestingly, later the site for Wentworth Gardens – as early as 1900. In 1910, when the White Sox built their first baseball stadium, Comiskey Park, on a directly adjacent site, the American Giants, a Negro League team, took over the field (Ranney et al., 1997). In 1957, the construction of the Dan Ryan Expressway, a massive urban renewal project, resulted in the destruction of a large number of African-American homes and businesses and sealed off the South Armour Square community, in particular from its black neighbors to the east. This 10-lane north–south federally funded highway, originally to be located several blocks to the east of its current location, effectively eliminated the pressure and opportunity for further expansion of the black population north (beyond Comiskey Park) and west (beyond the railroad tracks) into Bridgeport (Laramore et al., 1989; Euchner, 1993). The shift in highway location and the redrawing of district boundaries also resulted in the black residents' political isolation. They became a minority in federal, state, and local electoral districts, and their ability to form political coalitions was hampered. For example, at the local level, the African-American residents of South Armour have had little political leverage because they are within the political jurisdiction of the white-controlled 11th Ward, where whites outnumber blacks by a three-to-one margin (Laramore et al., 1994; Euchner, 1993). Local politicians do not need the black population's support to win elections. Not surprisingly, all elected ward officials are white, as are all members of the 11th Ward Democratic Party Organization, which has a reputation for excluding blacks. South Armour residents as a result of this political racial polarization have received poorer city services than their white neighbors (e.g. "garbage pickup, police protection, traffic control, open space and park facilities," and maintenance of publicly subsidized housing) (Ranney, et al., 1997, p. 48).

Blacks who ventured north and west into "North" Armour Square and Bridgeport frequently have been verbally and physically assaulted. The attempts by a few black families to move into these areas have similarly been resisted (Euchner, 1993). Black residents' shopping is restricted to the small stores along 31st Street and Cermak Road and Wentworth Avenue in Chinatown (*Chicago Fact Book Consortium*, 1995). The Wentworth activist Mrs. Marcella Carter recounted the racial discrimination that she has experienced:

During the period that I have lived in Wentworth Gardens, I have been very aware of the racism of many of the White residents that live north of 35th Street and to the west in Bridgeport. I have been personally subjected to humiliating racial slurs and threats by White people from time to time when I have sought to shop on 31st Street or on Halsted Street. In addition, I know that generally, Black people, if they do shop in these areas, should leave them before dark at the risk of either being verbally or physically assaulted if they stay in the areas. In particular, on at least one occasion, myself and my son were humiliated by White youth who made racial slurs to us when we remained in the shopping area at the Jewel Food Store at 30th Street and Halsted after dark.

Mrs. Carter explained that racially motivated attacks, however, are not restricted to white areas:

From time to time while I have lived in South Armour Square, White people driving their automobiles have entered South Armour Square on Princeton Avenue and have driven up and down the street shattering the windows of vehicles that have been parked in the street by residents of South Armour Square, and have caused other harm. (Carter, affidavit, 1994)

The "focal point" of the Armour Square community, the 10-acre Armour Square Park for which it is named, has always been off limits for black residents who live just two blocks south of it. This park, directly north of Comiskey Park and south of Bridgeport, has a large, newly modernized field house; a baseball field; three softball diamonds; a swimming pool; three tennis courts; and two racquetball courts. The Armour Square Park's facilities stand in stark contrast to the small, two-room Wentworth Gardens field house facility and inadequate sports amenities that are supposed to meet the recreational needs of the 422 resident families. Mrs. Amey attested to these inequities:

Since its beginning, the facilities operated by the Chicago Park District in Wentworth Gardens have been totally inadequate.... [T]he land outside of the community center was not kept up, the asphalt was broken and cracked, [and] it was dangerous for children to use it, and many children were hurt while trying to play games or other activities there. The building used by the Park District for its programs was never intended for use as a recreational center. It essentially was a community building to be used by residents of Wentworth Gardens as a meeting place. It is totally inadequate for recreational activities. A meeting room has been set aside as a gymnasium. The room is too small to be used as a basketball court, the ceiling is too low, and there is no other equipment there. Only small children can realistically use the facility for basketball; it cannot be used effectively by older children because of its inadequate size. (Amey, affidavit, November 30, 1994)

The well maintained and spacious Armour Square Park is the white residents' "territory," controlled through de facto segregation and racial violence, which required police action on several occasions (Laramore et al., 1994; Euchner 1993). The nearly fatal beating of Leonard Clark by four Bridgeport young men in the park in 1997 made national headlines. Wentworth resident activists confirmed this pattern of violent racial discrimination with their personal experiences. According to Mrs. Amey:

There has always been a hostile attitude, and it was just understood that we [black residents] could, [but] we don't visit that park [Armour Square Park] . . . because there have been incidents, serious incidents with people going back and forth through Bridgeport, and we have just never been welcome there.

For instance, Mrs. Marcella Carter recalled a hostile incident toward her son and his friends at Armour Park in the 1980s:

[H]im and some of his friends went over to North Armour to play basketball. . . . Must have been around '85, '86. . . . [They were chased off the court by local youth]. So they ended up running back from over there. He, in the process, he fell and knocked his arm. . . . He had to have surgery on his . . . wrist. . . . His bone was cracked in his wrist.

The racial violence and discrimination experienced by the residents of South Armour neighborhood and the related physical, social, economic, and physical problems of the neighborhood have been largely ignored by politicians and private sector investors. The uncertainty of reinvestment in the neighborhood to solve its most severe problems is captured by Holt and Pacyga (1979) in the closing comments describing Armour Square in *Chicago: An Historical Guide to the Neighborhoods*:

No single policy will suffice to deal with the problems that remain in Armour Square: the disparities within the community area are too great. . . . The public housing already constructed in the southern half of the neighborhood has not provided sufficient stimulus for further improvement there and most of the dwelling units are old and badly worn. . . . Because Armour Square is a set of enclaves, its future is tied both to continued private investment and to public policies on demolition, renewal, and public housing. That future would also be affected by the development of a new sports complex for Chicago which is presently under consideration. (p. 107)

The White Sox "power brokers" did indeed intend to impact on the future of the South Armour Square Neighborhood, with no consideration for its residents.

THE POWER BROKERS

The battle over South Armour Square appears to be a textbook example of the effects of the unequal distribution and use of power in American cities. (Charles Euchner, *Playing the Field*, 1993, p. 133)

In Chicago, there are two Major League baseball teams: the Chicago Cubs, located on the North Side, and the Chicago White Sox, located in Armour Square on the near South Side of the city. As in other major U.S. cities that have a sports franchise, these teams are part of the cultural and geographic identity of Chicago's metro-area residents, many of whom identify themselves as either loyal "Cubs fans" or "White Sox fans." Both teams have a long history in Chicago, and in 1986, both were still located in two of the oldest and most architecturally "classic" stadiums in the United States. Comiskey Park, home of the White Sox since 1910, was the oldest facility in the Major Leagues. Although they had been complaining for decades, in the mid-1980s, the White Sox owners became particularly vocal about their need for a new ballpark, blaming the structurally unsound 75-year-old stadium and the change in the racial and economic status of the neighborhood to low-income blacks for their inability to attract white suburban fans, especially because of fear of crime (Euchner, 1993).

Professional baseball franchises, such as the White Sox, wield considerable power in their home localities because they have virtual monopolies. Owners of these franchises use their control of a scarce commodity to seek economic and political concessions from the municipality and state when seeking to build up-to-date sports stadiums. The typical ploy is to threaten to leave for another location in their negotiations with public officials, creating pressure by the prospect of losing professional sports entertainment. Because of the shortage of sports teams, other municipalities bid for the franchise, leading to the spiraling of stadium demands. The loss of a Major League Baseball franchise can pose an economic threat to its host municipality.[3] In addition, the owners of a sports franchise, such as the White Sox, occupy a unique position within the civic life of a U.S. city such as Chicago, drawing support from its civic leaders as well as the general population (Ranney et al., 1997). They are also unlikely to meet organized resistance because their demands do not directly negatively affect many power interests; stadium project opponents therefore encounter obstacles when attempting to develop opposing coalitions (Euchner, 1993).

In Chicago, the owners of the White Sox Corporation used their "monopoly power" to apply pressure to the first black mayor of Chicago, Harold Washington, to gain support and major economic concessions from the city and state to finance the stadium (Ranney et al., 1997). Initially the white Sox threatened to move to the white suburban community Addison, 35 miles outside Chicago in DuPage County, Illinois, a move favored by Governor James Thompson. In a 1986 referendum, however, Addison voters narrowly defeated this option (Euchner, 1993, p. 145). After the failed Addison referendum, White Sox representatives reopened negotiations with the city, threatening to leave Chicago, and possibly the state of Illinois, if they did not receive a public subsidy to build a new stadium near the original Comiskey Park (Euchner, 1993). Mayor Washington was under pressure to respond to White Sox demands because he was facing reelection and his opponents were planning to use the loss of a major league baseball team as an indicator of his inability to run the city.

Without any public hearings, the Illinois Sports Facility Act was passed on December 5, 1986, the last day of the legislative session (Euchner, 1993).

---

[3] The indirect economic value of a sports franchise was underlined and expanded upon in an editorial in the *Chicago Tribune* in 1986: "The value of a professional sports team to an urban area is difficult to measure in dollars and cents. The jobs and tax revenue generated may not look impressive in hard figures. But add in what the presence of the team contributes to the overall attraction of living in the area and visiting it, and it becomes immense" (as quoted in Bukowski, 1992, p. 4).

The Illinois Sports Facility Authority (ISFA) was established solely to provide financing and the land for the construction of the new Chicago White Sox professional baseball stadium. The legislation gave the authority bonding power to finance construction and committed a 2% hotel–motel tax to pay back the bond. In addition, the city provided $150 million in tax-exempt bonds to finance the stadium. The ISFA, a unique government entity without political or public accountability, would be governed by a board of Directors appointed by the Republican governor of Illinois and the Democratic mayor of Chicago. The legislation also gave the authority "quick take" powers of eminent domain to take control of private land by a specified date, leaving the negotiations to the owners for price and relocation costs for a later date (Ranney et al., 1997).

The political influence of the Armour Square and Bridgeport white neighborhoods in the "stadium deal" was apparent. The legislation ex-empted Armour Square Park, north of the stadium, from the quick take provision to save this social and recreational landmark for the surround-ing white neighborhoods.[4] The park site would not have displaced any residents and would have provided for more expeditious and economical stadium construction. It is noteworthy that even before the 1986 legislation was signed, key politicians had decided to build the stadium south of 35th Street adjacent to the existing Comiskey Park irrespective of the destruction of approximately one-third of the South Armour Square neighborhood.[5] Rather than involving community residents in the site selection process through public hearings or a referendum, the politically expedient choice of this site was made behind closed doors. The southern site was con-sidered more politically viable because the black South Armour residents were isolated and had no political support in their ward, in contrast to the powerful white voters of the northern site. Mrs. Carter, an officer of the SASNC, understood these racial dynamics:

[I]t was a racial thing, because we had proof that says it's better to go to the south because the Blacks have no political base but the Whites have. It's in

---

[4] The park's historical significance was recognized not only by Alderman Patrick Huels, but also by State Representative John Daley, and Senator Thomas Degnan. In addition, the architect of the park's field house, Walter Neutsch, was adamant that the park not be destroyed. He wrote a memo and utilized his political connections through his spouse, Senator Dawn Clarke Neutsch, to protect the site from stadium construction consideration (Euchner, 1993).

[5] The city was aware of the implications of siting the stadium in South Armour Square. This is evident in a July 10, 1987, memorandum from Robert Mier, the city's commissioner of economic development, to Mayor Harold Washington: "The Planning Department has finished preliminary studies of the area just to the south of Comiskey Park. There are 90 structures, mostly in good condition – with less than 10 vacant or abandoned structures. Five hundred people live within the community, many elderly, and crime is very low. It is an old, established community with strong bonds" (p. 2).

writing. . . . They could've went over in the park. They could've went north; there's a whole park over there in the back of White Sox Park. They could've built the park there but see they didn't want to inconvenience the Whites. (Carter, affidavit, November 30, 1994)

Rather than a public debate, a political struggle between Governor Thompson and Mayor Washington over control of ISFA appointments, construction contracts, and professional fees delayed implementation of the ISFA for 10 months (Euchner, 1993).[6]

During this time, Saint Petersburg, Florida, which had begun construction of a new $50 million domed stadium, began courting the White Sox. With this new bargaining leverage, the White Sox owners, arguing that the 1986 agreement was no longer valid, negotiated a new agreement providing an additional $30 million in subsidies from the State of Illinois. There were few public naysayers in the media, in spite of the fact that the state was so economically strapped that the Republican governor had called for a major tax increase in order to finance such basic services as education and health care (Euchner, 1993). Mayor Washington responded to the threatened loss of the White Sox by firmly supporting the stadium project and downplaying the stadium's impact on the residents of South Armour, even though this action directly contradicted his administration's position as an advocate for the interests of low-income and minority residents.

The residents of South Armour Square would face enormous challenges in their attempts to organize to halt construction of the proposed stadium. They were physically and politically isolated, with little support from their neighbors in surrounding communities and, on the whole, the general public. Their opponents were formidable. The White Sox Corporation had secured local and state government sanctions and financial backing through the ISFA legislation. The White Sox battle was a classic opportunity for an Alinsky-style organizing effort: a public sphere confrontation against the power elites.

THE CONFRONTATIONAL MODEL OF COMMUNITY ORGANIZING[7]

The very term *community organizing* is popularly associated with conflict and protest and is inextricably linked with Saul Alinsky. Through his

---

[6] Even after the state legislators satisfied the White Sox's demands, the team owners would not make a binding commitment to remain in Chicago. The franchise signed a "backup" agreement with Saint Petersburg in July 1988, keeping the option to move open (Euchner, 1993, p. 141).

[7] The descriptions of Alinsky organizing and the development of the confrontational model are directly adapted from an earlier article, "Community Organizing or Organizing Community? Gender and the Crafts of Empowerment" (Stall & Stoecker, 1998).

work and influence, the Alinsky style of organizing, which we refer to as the *confrontational model* of community organizing, has built powerful organizations and leaders who have secured low-income communities expanded city services, housing, and employment across the country and, in some instances, saved entire communities from destruction.[8] Whereas the women-centered model focuses on "organizing community," the Alinsky-style or confrontational model focuses on "community organizing" – engaging in public sphere battles between those who have power and those who need to win power. Although community problems may begin in the private sphere according to Alinsky these problems cannot not be solved within the private sphere, but rather through community representation in the public sphere (Reitzes & Reitzes, 1987).

The confrontational model and the women-centered model begin from different starting points: the rough and tumble world of aggressive public sphere confrontation and the relational world of private sphere personal and community development. Consequently, they have very different views of human nature and conflict, power and politics, leadership development, and the organizing process.

The confrontational model starts with the presumption that modern society is created through conflict, then compromise, between self-interested individuals operating in the competitive public sphere (Alinksy 1969, pp. 94–98; 1971, pp. 53–59) The organizer's task is to prepare citizens to engage in the necessary level of public conflict to be included in the compromise process (Reitzes & Reitzes, 1987). Alinsky treated the neighborhood as a public sphere arena, where small-scale conflicts against unscrupulous power holders could build militarylike victories and a sense of power (Reitzes & Reitzes, 1987, pp. 54, 65). To win the battle, "the rank and file and the smaller leaders of the organizations must be whipped up to a fighting pitch" (Alinsky, 1969, p. 151).

Alinsky was adamant that real power could not be given, but only taken. Modeled after predominantly male political and economic elites, this model holds that one is either advantaged or disadvantaged, either exploiting or exploited (Acker, 1990). Thus, poor communities can gain power only through organization, since "change comes from power, and power comes from organization" (Alinsky, 1971, p. 113). The organizing process is explicit and tactical in the confrontational model. "Organizers," paid professionals, are brought into the community (Bailey 1972; Reitzes & Reitzes 1987) to educate and move people to recognize their shared interests and to adopt a delegitimizing framework challenging the status quo (Ferree & Miller 1985; Gamson, Fireman, & Rytina, 1982). These

---

[8] The practice of the Alinsky style of organizing built such organizations as the Back of the Yards and TWO in Chicago, SECO in Baltimore, FIGHT in Rochester, MACO in Detroit, ACORN in Little Rock, ETCO in Toledo, and COPS in San Antonio, among others.

outside organizers provide the link that pulls private sphere indigenous leaders, and their communities, into public action. The organizer builds an organization from the community's preexisting formalized organizational base of churches, service organizations, clubs, and so forth. Outside organizers identify and train community leaders to occupy positions in the formal organization to extend their leadership beyond the community. These organizations typically have traditional decision-making structures that mirror the hierarchical public sphere structures they confront. The organizer's goal, rather than empowering community leaders, is to build an enduring formal organization that can continue to claim power and resources for the community in a competitive public sphere. Consequently, the organization needs to be public, large, and confrontational. In many cases, the organization also spawns community-based services, such as credit unions and day-cares centers, and may later engage in economic development initiatives.

The Alinsky-style organizing process has a defined protocol. It begins in identifying community "issues" through "door knocking"; those issues then become the means of recruitment to the organizing effort. The organization bills itself as the best, if not only, means of resolving those issues. The gathering of a great body of people at a "mass meeting" provides the context for framing issues and celebrating gains. Important to the process of building up to the mass meeting are cumulative victories, beginning with contesting an easily winnable issue, then securing a modest victory, and using the energy, skills, and commitments it generates to build to bigger issues. Multiple public activities such as the mass march, public rally, explicit confrontation, and celebrated wins are all part of the organizing repetoire to focus media attention on their issues and to develop a strong organization.

In practice, community activists who have relied on women-centered organizing eventually find they must transgress the expanded private sphere and confront powerful public sphere actors and entrenched interests in order to secure their communities. Governmental and corporate actors are simply too formidable to be tamed by women-centered organizing strategies. The confrontational model is more effective in dealing with an immediate threat perpetuated by an identifiable "enemy," and in organizing to challenge publicly the enemy to extract concessions. In fact, it was the possible loss of their homes that inspired the Wentworth activists to engage in and sustain a different type of organizing, one that was not completely unfamiliar.

Wentworth activists had engaged in modest direct public action protests, in particular the struggle to replace the field house roof. The activists worked with an outside organizer, Sheila Radford-Hill; defined an issue; carefully organized to overcome the opposition and negotiate with a powerful government opponent; and worked within a burgeoning organization, at that time a concerned resident action committee, to address their concerns more effectively.

The field house victory was essential to building a nonprofit organization that, according to Sheila, now had the vision and capabilities to represent the South Armour community's interests publicly. And the moment in their organizing history was right. The decades of community building and women-centered organizing work they had accomplished in the expanded private sphere and their Alinsky-style confrontational organizing to secure the field house roof had empowered them to take on this public sphere battle.

FORMATION OF THE SOUTH ARMOUR SQUARE COALITION

This is a close community of people who have spent their entire lifetimes living just a few blocks south of Comiskey Park. One day they decide that they want a new stadium and our community just isn't important anymore. (Susie Myers, South Armour homeowner, cited by Norris, June 10, 1997, sec. 2, p. 13)

Residents of the South Armour Square neighborhood were shocked to read about their possible displacement in an early December issue of the *Chicago Tribune* (Smith, December 7, 1986). According to the map in the news article, the proposed stadium boundaries included an area south of Comiskey Park, South Princeton Avenue from 35th to 38th Streets, and the area north of Comiskey Park to 33rd Street – most of Wentworth Gardens could be demolished. Also distressing was a statement by Chicago's mayor, Harold Washington, supporting the proposal: "A couple of hundred residents" will have to lose their homes. "Any displacement is unfortunate, but one must resort to it. A fair offer will be made for their property" (Smith, December 7, 1986, sec. 1, p. 1).

As anticipated, the surrounding neighborhood residents' responses to the White Sox announcement were divided along race and geographic lines. White Bridgeport residents were elated. Their neighborhood businesses would benefit from White Sox fan customers. A local tavern owner was quoted as saying, "It's great for the business, great for the neighborhood" (Johnson, December 4, 1986, sec. 1, p. 2).[9] In contrast, South Armour

[9] In what would become a common pattern in the upcoming months, news coverage predominantly focused on the South Armour homeowners' responses to the proposed stadium siting, and they were understandably upset. The Princeton Avenue resident Beulah Perrino stated: "It's just not necessary to move us out.... It's just too hard on folks." Another neighbor asserted, "My feelings about this are bitter. My parents have lived here 40 years and to uproot them now and expect them to move into a retirement home is heartless." Yet, some of the homeowners were supportive of the White Sox's remaining in Chicago, just not at the expense of their homes. Janice Bluitt, a resident on West 37th Street, explained, "I love progress, but when it costs us our neighborhood, I don't think it is fair." The news coverage noted that many homeowners were determined to stay put (Smith, *Chicago Tribune*, December 7, 1986, sec. 1, pp. 1, 4).

residents viewed the proposed stadium as a harbinger of the demise of their neighborhood. There were anger and concern that they were not part of the planning process.

To organize against the siting of the stadium, the residents of South Armour chose to build upon the neighborhood's preexisting very modest formalized organizational base, a block club on Princeton Avenue. They enlisted the assistance of the soon to be named Wentworth Residents United for Survival. The Wentworth activists' committee was better positioned than the homeowners to begin to fight the impending new stadium. Mrs. Amey explained how the neighborhood residents learned about their organizing efforts:

Some of the folk who live down there [in South Armour north of Wentworth] have relatives in here [Wentworth Gardens]. And they were telling them about the flyer. We sent out a very, very colorful flyer. We had a little man on it – a map and a wrecking ball...drawn on the paper [the flyer] and said, "Have you seen this?" And the man was pointing to the map about the White Sox Park and how far it [proposed stadium] was coming, and how much of Wentworth was going to be taken away.... Really the only organization they had down there was the Princeton Block Club ... And it was this block club that wanted to be invited to our [Wentworth United] meeting.

The saliency of the potential destruction of their community served to impel other residents from the South Armour community to join the battle, in large part through word of mouth. Mrs. Amey:

And after we got done there [meeting with the block club], some of the folk on Wells [Street] then got curious and said they had not been invited to a meeting. Some on Wentworth [Avenue] said, "What's going on, they never invited us?" And so by knowing some of them from the school they said, "Contact Mrs. Amey or contact Mrs. Harris or some of them down there at Wentworth." And that's how those others all came in.... Most of our time was hooked up after then trying to get this coalition together.

The Save Our Homes Coalition: Joining Neighbors

A coalition in the South Armour Square, which began as an informal group called the "Save Our Homes Neighborhood Coalition" (SOH) was formed by South Armour homeowners and renters; T. E. Brown seniors, residents of a subsidized high-rise building housing 120 elderly and disabled low-income people owned by the Progressive Baptist Church; and Wentworth Gardens residents. The major actors in the upcoming months, however, would be the homeowners and the Wentworth Gardens residents.[10]

---

[10] The T. E. Brown seniors were involved in coalition meetings when they were held at the senior complex. Because of difficulties in physical mobility, with a few exceptions, most of the seniors were unable to attend other meetings and hence were not as actively involved

Empirical research would predict that the homeowners, in particular in contrast to renters, have the greatest investment, both economically and psychologically, in their community, but it would not predict the strong commitment of the public housing residents. Wentworth activists have a profound place attachment to their development, but they were attached to the geographic area beyond the boundaries of Wentworth Gardens as well.

Unlike in most other Chicago neighborhoods with public housing developments, the lives of the Wentworth Gardens activists and homeowners were closely intertwined with South Armour Square. Over the prior 40 years there were shared attachments to the geographic locale and friendships among individuals and families that had been forged across homeowner – public housing economic and physical boundaries. Mrs. Amey:

I and other residents have always considered South Armour Square one community. . . . [O]ur community was from 39th to 35th. . . . [P]eople from the community, both the homeowners and Wentworth community, we all worked together from church and school. . . . [Wentworth residents] frequently visited with friends who resided in that area, took walks through the street into the north part of the community, visited stores. . . . [W]e communicated, visited elder people like myself and others . . . just keeping a friendship thing going . . . share little moments and things together. (affidavit, 1994)

Wentworth Gardens residents' and South Armour homeowners' children attended the same local elementary school and the same public high schools. They worshiped at the same local churches, including the local Progressive Baptist Church, which was located close to both the homeowners and Wentworth residents. As African-Americans in the highly segregated Armour Square and Bridgeport neighborhoods, the homeowners and the Wentworth residents frequented the same grocery stores and could meet together over a plate of ribs at a homeowner's restaurant below her apartment in her two-family residence. For instance, Dorothy and Eddie Laramore raised six children in Wentworth Gardens. Mrs. Laramore volunteered at Abbott Elementary School, where she later worked as a teacher's aide and was a member of the Progressive church congregation. Mrs. Laramore also remembered South Armour as a tight community:

All of them [in South Armour north of Wentworth] was my friends. . . . I mean, the addresses and all that wasn't important. We knew each other. Walk down the street, they were sitting on the porch. . . . You just knew them. You didn't know the address, but you knew where they lived and whatnot. . . . This was true where they knew my kids. They could talk to my kids. I knew their kids. My kids played with their kids. . . . My kids went to school together with their kids. . . . We

in the organizational effort. There were also some renters in the homes and two flats north of Wentworth who attended the coalition meetings.

were just that close, just like family. . . . That was the kind of community we had. (Laramore, deposition, December 10, 1991)

Yet, the history of Wentworth residents' and homeowners' socializing and their shared experience of racial oppression could not mitigate across the divide of their distinct economic and tenure statuses. Sheila Radford-Hill described the social ties, but also the structural divisions that existed between the two groups:

They had very close relationships over time. Marriages, divorces. . . . They really . . . grew up together, you know, so. They understand each other, you know. . . . [T]hey were getting along just fine, but . . . they did have different economic places in the social order. . . . And, I knew that it was gonna be hard to hold this thing together.

Coalitions formed across socioeconomic groups to confront a common issue are often fragile alliances, typically lasting only as long as the confrontation persists (Suttles, 1968). In fact, Howard Baum (1997), in his comparative study of two community organizations, found that identifying with a coalition creates a delicate bond:

A group must see something sufficiently the same among themselves to justify considering their aggregate as a community. Moreover, they must see something sufficiently special in the community – so idealize it – to feel it is worth identifying with and take its obligations as superior to mundane affairs. (p. 45)

On the basis of his research, Baum cautioned that the different groups in a coalition must recognize and be realistic about their similarities and differences to act effectively as a coalition on common issues. In an analogous way, Sheila Radford-Hill described her modest hope for the South Armour coalition: that she could "hold it together long enough to . . . get them a better deal."

The South Armour homeowners and the Wentworth United activists crossed real and perceived class differences to organize a political coalition to confront the common immediate threat posed to their neighborhood by the proposed White Sox stadium. Yet the groups had differences in organizational traditions and "interests in and impulses toward community action" (Baum, 1997, p. 8). The homeowners feared the loss of their social and physical place attachments, but they had limited inclinations for and experience in neighborhood-based grassroots participation. There had been some prior block club activity north of Wentworth Gardens, but as of December 1986, these block clubs were either dormant or dissolved. Also, as most other homeowners were, they were motivated by economic security, specifically, protection of their economic investment in their dwelling.

Wentworth United activists' willingness to participate in a coalition also stemmed from their fear of the destruction of their dwellings. Pragmatically, they were aware that even if Wentworth Gardens was saved, they would lose stores, services, and the spatial buffer zone between their neighborhood and the old stadium that they had depended on for their safety and security. Yet, unlike the homeowners, Wentworth activists had engaged in decades of neighborhood-based volunteerism motivated by their rich social attachments and their altruism. The White Sox battle would become another example of how Wentworth activists cared about one another and for their neighbors, including those in the coalition. Mrs. Amey described this ethic of care:

[Wentworth activists got involved] to try and save the homeowners. Now we were concerned about ourselves, but we were really concerned about them, because these were individual homeowners and many of them were old and had spent years establishing a home where they would have someplace to live in their old age. (Cagan & deMause, 1998, p. 129)

Sheila Radford-Hill noted the distinct differences between Wentworth activists' and homeowners' interests in and impulses toward community action from her earlier organizing efforts with Abbott school parents in South Armour.[11] She remembered working mostly with Wentworth Gardens because, as she explained, "They were the parents who were willing to make the waves":

[T]he Wentworth Gardens people had ... more of an organizing [background]. . . . They'd organized around issues in the past. They a little base of that kind of mentality.

In contrast, Sheila described the homeowners as "working class rising":

Individuals who are angry. But, will not become active unless they are faced with a direct, a direct threat to their own existence. . . . [T]he homeowners had more of a [attitude that] you can't beat City Hall. You can't fight City Hall kind of mentality. . . . [S]o I mostly worked with Wentworth.

Irrespective of their distinct class positions and/or their local organizing history, Wentworth residents and the homeowners did share a critical motivation for action: the violence and fears resulting from their surrounding white neighbors' racist assaults. For instance, Sharon Washington, who grew up in Wentworth Gardens from the time it opened in 1946 – "[I] was born, bred up in here" – became involved in SOH because of her psychological attachment to her childhood home, but also because of memories of discriminatory indignities by her white neighbors to the north and west.[12] Although she was no longer a resident of Wentworth Gardens, her work as

[11] Some of the Wentworth resident activists had also participated in a protest at Abbott Elementary School in the early 1980s. Sheila Radford-Hill in her work with Designs for Change, a nonprofit school reform organization, helped selected parents to organize to remove an incompetent teacher at the school.
[12] *Sharon Washington is* a pseudonym.

manager of the T. E. Brown Apartments from 1981 through 1993 and her on-going social bonds with old neighbors and friends made her involvement in SOH both a personal and a political issue:

I've been the product, and I continue to work with the community because it's home. . . . Went to Robert S. Abbott grammar school, went to Phillips [high school], went to kindergarten over in the [field house] of Wentworth Gardens years ago. . . . I decided that I would work with the organization . . . when, again the White Sox said they were going to destroy the neighborhood. That's the way I saw it be-cause I had lived here during the years when we could not go to Fuller Park [because of racial violence against blacks]. . . . It was the first real thing I could do to help.

Wentworth activists, as well as South Armour homeowners, were partic-ularly angered about the racial injustice their community was experiencing in the White Sox stadium decision making. Some felt betrayed by Mayor Washington, whom they had eagerly and loyally supported in 1984. A Princeton Avenue resident complained, "I think Mayor Washington is a good mayor, but I think the way he handled this situation stunk" (Kaplan, January 11, 1987, sec. 2. p. 3). Another resident criticized that the mayor was ignoring their concerns while supporting a white community's protest against another proposed ballpark renovation, specifically the Wrigley Field neighborhood's fight to block nighttime stadium lights: "Those peo-ple who live by Wrigley Field were told about the lights ahead of time, and they are fighting it. They didn't even give us a fighting chance"[13] (Kaplan, January 11, 1987, sec. 2, p. 3).

SOH's Strategies: Protests and Development Plans

SOH members were united in their demands, which included prevent-ing ballpark construction south of 35th Street, preserving and improving South Armour Square, and obtaining a fair share of stadium revenue for economic development of the neighborhood. To better press their demands SOH joined with Save Our Sox (SOS), an organization with a particular in-terest in the historic significance of the existing stadium. The connection be-tween the two groups was initiated by Sheila Radford-Hill to augment their political power. SOS, a predominantly white organization with a wider ge-ographic membership base, had a specific proposal – to remodel, rather than destroy, the 75-year-old Comiskey Park. If that should fail, SOH's back-up plan was an alternative site that would save their community's housing and stores; specifically, the stadium could be developed north of

---

[13] In spite of their "betrayal" by Mayor Harold Washington, it was our impression from our interviews with residents, and also Sheila Radford-Hill's observation, that the Wentworth residents continued to revere the mayor despite the fact that he was not supporting their interests. Sheila Radford-Hill reflected, "[T]hey loved, they all loved Harold."

35th Street on the large expanses of the existing Comiskey Park parking lots with the addition of Armour Square Park.[14]

Within a month after forming the SOH, South Armour Square activists began to plan their first public demonstration, a traditional Alinksy-style picket protest at the ISFA bill signing ceremony held, strategically, on Martin Luther King Day, January 19, 1987. The weekend prior, some of the SOH activists gathered in the kitchen of one homeowner, Lillian Brown; there they tore "up a bunch of cardboard soda-pop cartons and hand lettered some protest signs with Magic Markers" (McCarron, May 17, 1987, sec. 4, p. 1). While Mayor Harold Washington and Governor James Thompson signed the ISFA Bill at homeplate inside the old Comiske Park, SOH activists joined by SOS picketed silently outside. Called by one reporter "an amateurish demonstration," it was significant nonetheless. It was their first public confrontation effort, and the activists were able to "buttonhole some of the reporters and television crews on their way inside to cover the bill-signing" (McCarron, May 17, 1987, sec. 4, p. 1). The stadium demonstration resulted in a brief meeting with Mayor Washington approximately 1 month later. At that time, he only promised fair compensation for the homeowners, offering no other commitments until the ISFA legislation took effect on July 1, 1987.

SOH distributed a Community Survey with the intention of both identifying and involving residents in the South Armour community. The survey asked South Armour residents to indicate their tenure status (owners, renters, or senior or public housing residents) and either their support or nonsupport for the proposed location for the White Sox stadium. In addition, SOH instigated a Community Referendum in an attempt to solicit support for a "formal, chartered non-profit organization dedicated to serve the needs of the community," to assess what those needs were, and to expand their volunteer base.

In March 1987, the *Chicago Sun-Times* published a map that again showed the proposed location of the new stadium. According to this map, the new stadium and parking lots were "to cover the area between 35th and

[14] A Chicago architect, Philip Bess, was director of a research project for the Society for American Baseball Research, funded by the National Education Association, to explore alternatives to urban baseball stadium design. As part of this project, Bess designed a White Sox stadium for an alternative site. His plan located the new stadium immediately north of the existing stadium, using the original Comiskey Park site for a new city park. This stadium design resulted in a shift in the access to Armour Park from Bridgeport to South Armour Square, transforming park use from exclusively white to use by both blacks and whites. Bess's plan also included small-business development and integrated automobile and mass transit access (McCarron, July 26, 1987). Bess was supportive of groups like SOS and the SOH. He joined a lobbying trip to the state capital in June, 1988 and wrote a very pointed newspaper editorial exposing the class and race politics behind the South Armour relocation site decision (Bess, *Chicago Tribune*, August 8, 1988, sec. 1, p. 11). Neither the White Sox owners, the city, nor ISFA seriously considered Bess's alternative.

37th Streets and about half of Wentworth Gardens south of 37th" (Peterman, 2000, p. 99). A month later, Wentworth Gardens representatives of SOH and Wentworth United, Sheila Radford-Hill, and Bill Peterman, at that time the director of the Nathalie P. Voorhees Neighborhood Center at the University of Illinois at Chicago (UIC), spoke on a panel at a public housing conference at UIC about their immediate struggle.[15] An informal discussion after the panel resulted in a series of meetings between the coalition and the Voorhees Center to develop an alternative neighborhood plan. Within a few weeks, approximately 40 representatives from South Armour began the planning process by making lists of needed neighborhood improvements, including a general cleanup and, more specifically, on vacant lots and streets, a retail complex and a small neighborhood park. Bill Peterman and UIC planning students participated in two more planning meetings with South Armour residents that resulted in the development of a land use plan ratified by a voice vote. This plan became another tool in the coalition's struggle to save the neighborhood (Peterman, 2000).

The SOH coalition's work on neighborhood development planning did not slow their other organizing efforts and meetings with local, city, and state politicians. In early June 1987, SOH met with the neighborhood's alderman, Patrick Huels, and a representative from Mayor Harold Washington's office, Timothy Wright, in the Progressive Baptist Church to apply pressure for an alternative site for the stadium. According to Hallie Amey, this meeting, held 6 months after the passage of the ISFA Act, was the first time the group had received any attention from the local ward alderman. In this standing-room-only meeting neither the city's Representative Wright nor Alderman Huels offered a firm commitment to assist in altering the stadium plans. Rather, attempting to placate the South Armour residents, Tim Wright stated, "While the mayor wants to keep the Sox in Chicago, he wants to keep this community more than anything else." Alderman Huels was met with boos and jeers when he told the crowd that although he supported their struggle to save their homes, he could not support a plan to build the stadium at a different site. When pressed by South Armour residents to introduce an ordinance to protect the neighborhood from the stadium construction, he cautioned, "You are asking me questions that I have no authority over" (Norris, June 10, 1987, sec. 2, p. 13). Huels's insincerity was apparent when the press reported, a little over a month after his meeting with the SOH coalition, that Huels had reassured his constituents in North Armour Square that he would protect their interests, asserting that "Armour Square" [Park] should not be moved since the white ethnic neighborhood to the north liked it just where it was (McCarron, July 26, 1987). Governor Thompson similarly used this stalling

---

[15] This conference was "Women and Public Housing: Unclaimed Power" at the University of Illinois, Chicago (see preface).

tactic when, in mid-July 1987, SOH members protested outside the State of Illinois Center. Thompson addressed the group, stating that nothing would go forward until the ISFA held public hearings.

From December 1, 1986, through October 1987, Governor Thompson and Mayor Washington were at loggerheads about who would head the ISFA. This political delay in the implementation of the ISFA had both negative and positive repercussions for the opposition coalition. On the one hand, it was very difficult to plan effective offensive tactics since the legal authority in charge of stadium construction was not established; on the other hand, their deal making allowed SOH time to strategize and to lobby their political representatives and to become a stronger and more experienced organization.

Becoming a Formal Organization: The SASNC

On August 18, 1987, Save Our Homes orchestrated a mass meeting, a Community Forum at the Progressive Baptist Church. South Armour homeowners, Wentworth residents, and T. E. Brown residents were all represented on the agenda. Their purposes were to assess the status of the coalition and to plan further organizing strategies. Of particular importance at this forum was the discussion about formalizing the SOH's organizational structure. In addition, women-centered organizing concerns were represented in the discussion of one of the group's follow-up tasks – the planning of a "We Love Our Community Fest." This juxtaposition of these confrontatonal and women-centered organizing models would be evident in the actions that held the coalition together and in the concerns addressed in the upcoming 12 months. The coalition members were highly motivated and would engage in confrontational tactics to save their neighborhood, but they also consistently planned and participated in community-building events such as a holiday party, celebrations of family passages, and fund-raisers, such as "salad spreads."

In the fall of 1987, Save Our Homes was legally incorporated as a not-for-profit community development corporation[16] and was renamed the *South Armour Square Neighborhood Coalition* (SASNC). The SASNC, like SOH, was an all-volunteer organization. The SASNC had a 13-member board led by a president, George Marshall, the first vice president, Lillian Brown; and

[16] In their incorporation papers, the SASNC is named a community development corporation (CDC), but Ranney, Wright, & Zhang (1997) effectively argue that in reality, SASNC was a community-based citizen advocacy organization. Organized in a particular subarea in the city, "community-based organizations define their work in terms of definite geographic boundaries ... determined by the organizations based on how members conceive of their neighborhoods or community.... [T]he South Armour Square Neighborhood Coalition organized specifically to fight the relocation of a baseball stadium that threatened to destroy their neighborhood" (p. 17).

the second vice president, Susie Myers, all of whom were homeowners. Wentworth residents were prominent as other board officers and chairs of SASNC committees, including Marcella Carter as corresponding secretary and Hallie Amey as treasurer; Dorothy Laramore, as media chairperson, and her husband, Eddie Laramore, as parliamentarian, Rose Woods, as youth outreach; and Sharon Washington, former Wentworth resident and then manager of T. E. Brown, as recording secretary. The SASNC met bimonthly or weekly if necessary to respond actively to ever changing information, or the lack thereof, they were receiving. Organizational expenses were met by membership dues of $5.00, individual contributions from the membership and supporters, and fund-raising.

"Making a Ruckus"

Wentworth activists, now as members of SASNC, continued to oppose the siting of the new stadium actively. From the fall of 1987 through the summer of 1988, their organizing campaign would involve another demonstration at White Sox stadium; several meetings with local, state, and nationally elected public officials; development of position papers; testimony at public hearings; and, when necessary, confrontational encounters at city council meetings, for instance, at the ISFA and the Chicago Zoning Commission.[17] When the Illinois Sports Facility Authority at last held its inaugural session on December 14, 1987, in the state offices, the SASNC was in attendance. Thomas Reynolds, head of the ILSFA, promised to commission an engineering study early in 1988 to see whether Comiskey Park were structurally sound and could be rehabilitated. He drew cheers when he said, "[We are] going to do a legitimate good faith job of having the existing structure examined by structural engineers of unquestioned integrity." He added, "A lot of thought will be given to relocating those whose homes would be razed to make way for the new stadium if its shown that Comiskey Park is structurally unsound" (McCarron & Ziemba, December 15, 1987). Reynolds's disingenuousness, however, was apparent in an earlier news article in which he stated that he fully expected to find that the stadium would not be able to be rehabilitated (McCarron, January 29, 1987). A report from a commissioned engineering study was finally released in April 1988, with the finding that Comiskey Park was in "relatively good shape . . . and could be renovated for perhaps less money than it would take to build a new stadium" (Spielman, 1988, p. 8). This announcement provided the SASNC with new organizing ammunition (Peterman, 2000).

---

[17] These public officials included Alderman Patrick M. Huels, Alderman Timothy Evans, Acting Mayor Eugene Sawyer, Committeeman and State Senator John Daley, and national Illinois Congressman Charles Hayes.

Sheila Radford-Hill's role as an experienced community organizer was essential in strategizing and in orchestrating confrontational small- and large-scale direct actions against formidable political and corporate opponents. This included, according to Sheila:

demonstrating on Reinsdorf's [White Sox owner's] lawn, difficult to do with a bunch of senior citizens, but we did disrupt meetings. We had a press strategy. The idea was to make enough noise and be irritating enough that you could eventually blow the deal. (Cagan & deMause, 1998, p. 130)

Sheila also spent time educating the residents, recognizing that an organizer and organizing tactics should not go outside or beyond the experience of the people with whom they are working (Alinsky, 1971). She discussed and shared information on the nuts and bolts of running an effective meeting, doing constructive planning, developing SASNC position papers and legislative alerts, and presenting themselves and their grievances persuasively to elected officials and ISFA representatives.[18] The SASNC officer and activist Marcella Carter described Sheila's role:

Sheila said, "You always get prepared," and she helped us write the demands we wanted from the stadium, from the White Sox, and from the city and stuff....Then we began to go to the meetings and stuff. She found out when the meetings were and we began to go....Sheila knew how to do it....Sheila would come out and show us how to do different things [prepare for public meetings] that we had to do and how we had to go to the Sports Authority and protest.

Sheila agreed that she "was the lightning rod for the...strategic actions." She always attempted to alert SASNC activists to protest opportunities: "This is coming up, how can we turn this to our advantage." She recalled the time that SASNC board members went to Alderman's Patrick Huel's office: "We met over there and about...twelve of us wouldn't leave until he met with us." They pressured Alderman Huels to appear before the Zoning Board, where "we disrupted a few meetings....To make it look...you know, big and organized." On another occasion, when SASNC activists, including Wentworth residents, attended the Sports Authority meetings at the original Comiskey Park, Mrs. Carter recalled that Sheila suggested a particularly creative strategy (and one, in the spirit of Alinsky

---

[18] There were also educational opportunities outside the SASNC meetings and the South Armour neighborhood. In November 1987, more than 100 South Armour residents attended a day-long "neighborhood improvement" conference. Bill Peterman presented the neighborhood plan they had worked on previously. Wentworth Gardens residents were especially encouraged to attend an empowerment session on resident management development. Also, the board members of SASNC attended a session on leadership development (Peterman, 2000, p. 103).

[1971], that people would enjoy) to make their presence known:

There was one time when we went to the stadium, to the Sports Authority meeting, and we had little crickets [noisemakers]. And every time they said something we didn't like, we'd crick them . . . naturally, they threw us out

Sheila had prepared SASNC members to "make a ruckus" to get the opposition riled. The release of live chickens at another ISFA meeting caught the attention of authority appointees. On another occasion, to garner an emotional response, SASNC members wore purple or black armbands to indicate mourning for their homes and the neighborhood and put slogans and statements on placards stressing the neighborhood ties that would be destroyed if the stadium were built in South Armour Park.

Equally important to the success of confrontational organizing is gaining media attention. With Sheila's guidance, Mrs. Laramore described how she enticed the media to many of the coalition's meetings and protests, in part by attracting supportive individuals with media draw to these events:

[I] really kept [us in] the news, quite a bit. We was in the news for a lot of stuff. We had a lot of people helpin' us such as Danny Davis [then a black state legislator and now a national congressman] and all would come to our meetin's.

Frustrated by their inability to secure changes in the stadium siting, in December 1987, the SASNC voted, on the recommendation of Wentworth's Dorothy Laramore, to hire Mary Milano to provide legal counsel to their coalition. On January 19, 1988, 70 SASNC members, neighbors, and supporters attended a general neighborhood SASNC meeting at the Progressive Baptist Church for their first public meeting with Milano. They discussed strategies to block the stadium development and to support their goal to garner a revenue set aside for revitalizing the neighborhood.

At the same meeting, Sheila discussed the need to expand the coalition beyond the boundaries of South Armour Square. In response, coalition members activated their social bridging to SOS, inviting them to an SASNC meeting. SOS's citywide coalition and SASNC would jointly participate in several organizing efforts over the next few months. Mrs. Amey recalled:

We welcomed them and they welcomed us. Made our group a little bigger. And we all had the same goal. We were not fighting against progress and all of that. We was just fighting for the right to keep our homes for people. (Cagan & deMause, 1998, p. 129)[19]

---

[19] In another attempt to create potential allies, Sheila Radford-Hill suggested a February 1988 meeting in Armour Square Park with representatives from the SASNC, SOS, and the park superintendent and resident representatives from North Armour Park. She reassured the South Armour residents that this meeting could be beneficial, in particular for two purposes. First, it would make an impression on the city leaders, showing them blacks and whites working together. She also wanted to continue to "bridge to White people," especially to explain to the renters living north of the park that it was to their benefit to

For instance, in the spring of 1988, SASNC joined forces with SOS to strategize about a public confrontation during the upcoming baseball season.[20]
They targeted the Sox opening game on April 4. Their plan was to march
through the South Armour neighborhood, first holding hands at the symbolic corner of 35th Street and Shields Avenue, later culminating in a rally at
the Wentworth Gardens field house.[21] Building on their African-American
history and experience, SASNC activists enlisted the famous civil rights
slogan and protest song "We Shall Not Be Moved." Sheila reflected on
their direct protest action:

[W]e marched out of the development. I hired a photographer to take pictures of
us coming out of the development, and picking up residents' steam, and meeting
with Save Our Sox people at the [Sox] park.

The demonstration, as intended, captured media attention (see Sullivan,
Chicago Tribune, March 30, 1988, sec. 4, p. 1; Brotman, *Chicago Tribune*,
April 5, 1988, sec. 2, p. 1; Bratcher, *Chicago Defender, April 5*, 1988, sec. 1, p. 1).
SASNC president, George Marshall, used the occasion to target the ward
alderman, Patrick Huels, verbally for his failure to represent the South
Armour residents:

This neighborhood was set aside, was boxed in. We certainly haven't been getting
our representation that we should. We know for a fact, although this is the 11th

support the demands of SASNC: A new stadium could result in rising rents and the eventual displacement of the entire Armour Park area. She recalled that it was because of this
suggestion that she "really found out and began to understand the legacy of racism." The
SASNC activists voiced their hesitancy about venturing into Armour Park. One resident explained to Sheila that they all vividly remembered stories from a great-grandparent about
"the beating of Black people" who had moved into the community after the 1919 Chicago
race riots; "the hostility was historic" (see also Drake & Cayton, 1945). Given this history
of racial conflict, it is significant that white and black Armour Square residents did join
together in Armour Park on the evening of February 22. Yet, Sheila Radford-Hill remembered that although "people were outwardly cordial . . . it was very difficult to talk . . . the
air was just stifling." Nothing strategic resulted from this meeting. The white residents
were not willing to risk losing their park; nor did they want to lose the racial buffer zone
between them and their South Armour neighbors if a new site was chosen.

[20] SASNC activists met with members of SOS at a Bridgeport restaurant in late March for
a 3-hour dinner meeting "to iron out their plans" for their upcoming action at Comiskey
Park (Sullivan, *Chicago Tribune*, March 30, 1988, sec. 4, p. 3). This meeting was set up by
Sheila Radford-Hill and Mary O'Connell of SOS. Mary O'Connell remembered that when
she and Sheila Radford-Hill first walked into the restaurant, the SOS and SASNC groups
were sitting apart across a racial divide, and both she and Radford-Hill had to facilitate a
more integrated eating arrangement. In the end there were positive feelings expressed by
both groups about their organizing work together.

[21] SASNC and SOS were joined on April 4, 1988, by the Chicago–Gary Area Union of the
Homeless. A homeless-union board member explained why his group was supportive of
SASNC's efforts: "We are already homeless. . . . These people are scheduled to be put out
of their homes. We're here to let them know we support them" (Brotman, *Chicago Tribune*,
April 5, 1988, sec. 2, p. 1). In turn, some SASNC members visited the homeless union's tent
city after their rally in Wentworth Gardens.

Ward, Alderman Huels knows that we are not his constituents, so we've been looked over and forgotten about; and now they want to just push us out altogether. We don't want that to happen. (Bratcher, 1988, sec. 2, p. 18).

SASNC's Organizing Heats Up

The opening White Sox game protest in early April 1988 launched the SASNC's most intense period of organizing. The SASNC convened weekly, and more frequently when necessary. There were more meetings with Alderman Huels and State Representative John Daley and trips downtown to the ISFA and the Chicago City Council. They met regularly with their lawyer, Mary Milano. They also began to work with another attorney, Jim Chapman, originally invited by Sheila, who was highly respected in Chicago community organizing circles for his legal work on civil rights. They spoke with him about the possibility of filing a lawsuit and using other legal options to stop stadium construction.[22] By May 1988 the SASNC had established a Legal Defense Fund with the agreement that all future fund-raising monies would go into the fund.

In the 6-week period from mid-June 1988 through the end of July 1988, SASNC activists were working at a frantic pace. The SASNC gained more public visibility through the sale of buttons and the selective placement of collection cans throughout the South Armour Park neighborhood for their new Defense Fund account. The time expended by SASNC activists, a core group of about 15, was tremendous. Weekly evening board meetings would last from $1^1/_2$ up to 4 hours; longer meetings were necessary to strategize for upcoming direct actions. For example, in a single week in June 1988, in their attempts to "maintain a constant pressure upon the opposition" (Alinsky, 1971, 129), the SASNC activists' work was nonstop. Their regular board meeting on Monday, June 20, lasted over 3 hours and included careful planning for the week's events. The next evening, June 21, a SASNC Neighborhood Community meeting was held at the Progressive Baptist Church to rally broader support for their effort. At this meeting activists publicly affirmed their shared commitment to their community. The following day, Wednesday, June 22, SASNC representatives attended a City Council meeting in the morning and met with Acting Mayor Eugene Sawyer in the afternoon, asking for access, control of resources, and equity.[23] They exited council chambers singing a civil rights hymn and met with the press immediately after. Early the following morning, Thursday, June 23, the coalition activists departed for a prearranged lobbying trip to Springfield in southern Illinois ($3^1/_2$ hours from Chicago), their third

[22] Sheila Radford-Hill had recommended Jim Chapman as their lawyer when the SASNC first formed, but the organization had decided to hire Mary Milano.

[23] Mayor Harold Washington died suddenly in November 1987, shortly after he was elected to a second term in office. After Washington's death, a black alderman, Eugene Sawyer, was installed as the acting mayor.

trip to the state capital. They met with legislators, particularly members of the Black Caucus, urging them to oppose the pending bill supporting stadium construction in South Armour Square. Sheila explained their motivation:

It was to talk primarily to the Black Caucus . . . but we billed it as talking to anybody who wanted to talk to us. And we . . . sort of took over the . . . press room of the Capital. And we had . . . invited all the legislators.

Organizing momentum was intense as the legislative session drew to a close, and whereas the SASNC needed only two cars to transport activists for their first lobbying trip, by this last trip to Springfield they required a bus for all the SASNC members who attended.

Legislative Defeat

Despite $1^1/_2$ years of intense organizing, meetings, and protests, first as Save Our Homes, and then as the South Armour Square Neighborhood Coalition, on June 30, 1988, the $150 million White Sox Stadium bill was passed. SASNC members felt betrayed by the legislators, especially the members of the Black Caucus. According to the Wentworth Gardens resident Marcella Carter, the caucus had "promised" coalition members that they would not pass the bill:

The Black Caucus didn't do anything. They said they weren't going to vote [for it], but they did.

The White Sox's threat to leave for Saint Petersburg, Florida, was the final impetus for the legislature to pass the Sox stadium bill. The Illinois House, in a last-minute wheeling and dealing session, passed the measure by 5 votes (60 yes, 55 no) at 12:03 A.M., 3 minutes past the constitutionally mandated adjournment time. They did not follow the requirement for a three-fifths majority, or 71 favorable votes, if past adjournment time. Reporters described this postmidnight vote as "an animated display of political arm-twisting" by Governor James Thompson and House Speaker Michael Madigan, a Chicago Democrat (Kass & Egler, July 1, 1988 sec. 1, p. 1). Mrs. Carter called it a "trick." Even more damning to the SASNC's organizing effort was the June 30, 1988, amendment to the ISFA Act. In the initial legislation, the ISFA was specifically directed to hold public hearings to determine the stadium site. After a request by the ISFA, the White Sox, and the City of Chicago, the legislature amended the ISFA Act, without debate, to eliminate the authority's requirement to hold public hearings with published notice for selecting a site.

After this defeat, Sheila Radford-Hill explained that the SASNC continued "trying to get in as many people's faces as possible. . . . [I]t kept [us] from thinking about being sold out." In a final effort to gain city political support, SASNC representatives attended Chicago City Council meetings and met with city government officals. Mrs. Carter remembered:

[O]nce we found out that they [Illinois legislature] had voted, we started going downtown to city council meetings; and we went to our alderman [Huels], and we asked him and he said there was nothing he could do. It was a done deal.

In early July, after the legislative session, Acting Mayor Sawyer met with a "hostile crowd" at the Wentworth Gardens field house. Sawyer defended his support of the stadium construction in South Armour Square, noting the economic benefit to the community and stating that more than $30 million would be available for relocation costs. Additionally, there would be construction jobs and employment for residents in the new ballpark (Kass, *Chicago Tribune*, July 7, 1988, 1988, sec. 2, p. 1).

As late as the first part of July 1988, SASNC homeowners and public housing residents remained unified. They were still in agreement in their pursuit of a lawsuit, securing SASNC office space, and presenting a united front to the ISFA. In fact, when initially approaching the SASNC, the ISFA executive director, Peter Bynoe, had been rejected by the coalitions' board in his attempts to meet with only selected SASNC representatives. But a crack in the SASNC united front was exposed when Bynoe made his first relocation proposal to the SASNC on July 7, 1988. Bynoe clearly threatened the SASNC with the loss of relocation funds if they filed a lawsuit. After his presentation, several of the homeowners, including SASNC President George Marshall, became nervous about pursuing the lawsuit strategy. Within the next 3 weeks this crack in the coalition would expand to become a huge break in early August, when three SASNC officers presented an ISFA Relocation Package to their membership.

THE SASNC SPLIT: "THE BETRAYAL"

It was a thirteen member [SASNC] board, and ten people was there, only three of us missing. And everybody looked at it [ISFA Relocation Package] and said, "This is too much [material]. We can't read this; we need some time. Let's vote that we take thirty days to read this before we agree.... [O]nly three people voted to pass the thing, and the others voted for us to wait thirty days.... So George [Marshall, president of the SASNC] said, "No, this is the deal; it's all over. It's the deal and I'm going over here [Abbott School] 'cause I'm supposed to meet the people" [ISFA representatives]. We [Wentworth SASNC board members] didn't even know nothing about no meeting was at the school.

We crossed the street to Abbott School and there was all the Sports Facility Authority people over there. People from downtown were there; all the big shots and the alderman, all of them was there.... George Marshall, Susan Myers, and Lillian Brown was sittin' around the table.... I told Miss Laramore, "[Y]ou stand right behind George Marshall and make sure he don't sign nothin'." ... And then finally George went to sign something, and I said, "What's he signing?"

and Tim Wright . . . said, "Oh, he ain't signing nothing." And I said, "He is signing something." . . . So then after he had done signed it, that's when we found out, because the reporters, television was there. They were saying that the deal had been signed between the South Armour Square Coalition and the Sports Facility Authority, and we will have our new stadium. (Mrs. Marcella Carter)

On the summer evening of August 3, 1988, there was a "showdown" at Abbott Elementary School. Three to four hundred people, including representatives from the local media, were crammed into the school auditorium. George Marshall, Lillian Brown, and Susan Myers, the three homeowners and SASNC officers who had been selected to represent the SASNC in negotiations with the ISFA, signed a generous Relocation Package agreement. Wentworth residents were stunned by what was transpiring. They had been aware of the scheduled public meeting but had believed that it was for information sharing, not signing of a relocation agreement. The ISFA was strategic in pressuring, if not intimidating, the homeowners and renters to take advantage of their offer with undue haste. The room had been set up to facilitate the distribution of information about the individual contracts between homeowners and renters and the ISFA. Mrs. Carter remembered:

They had packages for the renters. They had separate packages for the homeowners. . . .they had everything. They said, "If you a renter get over here, if you're a homeowner get over here."

According to the dissenting SASNC Coalition Board members, the agreement signed by the homeowners was never ratified because it had not been properly approved by the full SASNC Board. Mrs. Laramore protested, "[W]e were sold out!" Wentworth resident activists had not been informed that the three homeowners had spoken for the SASNC and affirmed their support for the package agreement; nor were they given adequate time to respond to the more than 2 inches of documents that George Marshall presented to the SASNC board earlier that evening at their scheduled SASNC board meeting. Moreover, Marshall did indeed violate the SASNC by-laws by signing the contract without full SASNC board approval, thus paving the way for the construction of the new stadium. The result was a split between the homeowners, on the one side, and the elderly residents of the T. E. Brown Apartments and the public housing residents, on the other. The SASNC vice president and homeowner Susie Myers was clear about where her interests lay:

I worked all my life and struggled all my life to keep a roof over my head and pay that mortgage. I've got friends here that I may have lost. But I tell you, it's my money at stake. My life at stake. And I'm going to protect myself and take this deal. (Kass, *Chicago Tribune*, August 6, 1988, sec. 1, p. 5).

Ironically, the news media that the SASNC had courted over the proceeding 2 years were there in force to record the victory of the homeowners. And for one night Marcella Carter was a media star. Later, she reflected on that evening:

The [television] news was there, this truck was there with the screen on it, so I said, "Well, I'll be damned!" And I walks out and they grabbed me 'cause I was cursing and stuff. And I got to get on the news, and I said that it [the vote] was ten to three. I said that three people said they accept the deal and ten said no. I said, "How you going to overrule the majority?" I said, "It's not right."

In the *Chicago Tribune* Marcella Carter was quoted:

There's 300 of us here from Wentworth [out of 400], and we're angry because we aren't getting nothing. (Kass & Luft, *Chicago Tribune*, August 4, 1988, sec. 2, p. 8).

South Armour Square renters also were reported to be dissatisfied with the ISFA settlement:

[The deal] "is worse than slavery....We've been sold down the river, with no choice at all. It's either get out or get put out. (Kass & Luft, *Chicago Tribune*, August 4, 1988, sec. 2, p. 8).

Despite Mrs. Carter's and other Wentworth protestors' efforts to present their position to reporters, the media coverage did not accurately represent their role. In fact, rather than giving SASNC Wentworth activists credit for their nearly 2 years of committed organizing, they portrayed them as duped by others. The *Chicago Tribune* reported, "Residents of a nearby Chicago Housing Authority development, *who had been led by activists* [italics added] to believe they would receive benefits, walked away angry" (Kass & Luft, *Chicago Tribune*, August 4, 1988, sec. 2, p. 1).

Explaining the Betrayal

In retrospect this "betrayal" was set in motion weeks before the August 3 meetings. Once the ISFA funding package was passed by the legislature on June 30, 1988, the SASNC began to crumble. Taking advantage of their legislative success, the ISFA, ironically using an Alinsky model pressure tactic, began to split the SASNC by dealing only with the homeowners. Wentworth Gardens SASNC members' naivete caused their absence from these negotiations when they allowed themselves to be represented by three homeowner officers and "their" lawyer, Mary Milano. In hindsight, Mrs. Carter reflected on their "stupidity":

After they did all this downstate [passed the legislation], then the Sports Facility Authority said they wanted to talk to us to see what kind of deal we could come up with. When we found out they wanted to talk to us. . . . we had a president, and two vice presidents and all three of them were homeowners. We sit there like dummies, instead of sending one homeowner, one renter, and one Wentworth [resident]. We let all of them three presidents [one president and two vice-presidents] go down there [ISFA office].[24]

The impending SASNC split of the homeowners from the coalition was apparent at a SASNC meeting in late July 1988. Wentworth resident members and T. E. Brown members recommended that the SASNC approve moving forward and filing the class-action discrimination lawsuit against the stadium authority on the grounds that the stadium plan discriminated against blacks. Although they had been tentatively supportive up to that point, the homeowners rejected the proposal to pursue a lawsuit. They questioned the wisdom of continuing a confrontational stance when the legislature had already passed the stadium funding package.

Fear among homeowners had escalated. The homeowners, renters, and businesses had little time to strategize, threatened by ISFA's "quick take" power: The ISFA, homeowners, renters, and businesses had to enter into a contractual agreement with ISFA by October 15, 1988, or the ISFA had the authority to take title to the property and negotiate compensation later. In reality, however, the agreement did not have to be reached until a month later. According to one of the Wentworth residents:

The homeowners were told, "You have more to lose . . . and if you don't go along with us [ISFA] we will take your property and you get zapped." So the homeowners were scared. (Ranney et al., 1997, p. 74)

Wentworth activists' past women-centered organizing had not prepared them to suspect that the homeowners would pursue their own self-interest to the detriment of other members of the coalition; rather, their prior organizing experiences were built upon relationships of trust and reciprocity. The confrontational model, however, would predict otherwise. When the homeowners' self-interest was threatened, they acted to protect themselves. The ISFA knowingly took advantage of the self-interest of the homeowners to facilitate the split of the coalition.

---

[24] In a SASNC board meeting on July 11, 1988, President George Marshall insisted that he and the two SASNC vice-presidents represent the coalition in ISFA negotiations. The SASNC board meeting minutes reflect the tension in the room. There had been a motion on the floor to have three representatives, all homeowners, serve on the Displacement Committee. These would be the SASNC vice presidents, Lillian Brown and Susie Myers, but not George Marshall. Mr. Marshall opposed the motion and countered with a motion that included him on the committee. According to the July 11, 1989 SASNC minutes: "Mrs. Myers stood and requested we all stand and she began praying, because we had lost our way. After this much needed prayer, there was a motion made and seconded to have the President and two Vice-Presidents negotiate with the [Illinois Sports Facility] Authority. . . . Mrs. Brown motioned that no decision on coalition business should be made without the entire committee's approval on the motion. This was seconded by Mr. Laramore."

Although the Wentworth activists may have been naive, Sheila Radford-Hill was not. She attempted to stay abreast of the developments in the negotiations between the SASNC representatives and the ISFA but was treated with distrust, likely because they viewed her as an ally of the Wentworth residents.[25]

From their initial meeting in December 1986 through July 1988, South Armour homeowners, renters, and Wentworth residents were able to forge a common community identity, first through SOH, and then the SASNC. Whereas the homeowners always maintained an awareness of differences between them and their public housing neighbors to their south, Wentworth residents glossed over these differences and saw themselves as in an organizational partnership with the homeowners. So deep was their faith in the equality of their participation that they had no trouble with the fact that the three top officers in the SASNC were all homeowners.

In the reality of "dealmaking" with the ISFA it became apparent to the homeowners that this "ideal" of a united SASNC demanded too much. They recognized that they had more to gain by breaking their ties with the Wentworth Gardens and T. E. Brown residents and even with the renters who lived in their two flats. Mary Milano, now "their lawyer," convinced them that they should take the generous package offered by the ISFA rather than continue their former confrontational "them versus us" stance. At a certain point the homeowners perceived that there were more rewards in leaving the SASNC than in continuing to be a part of it. For them the coalition's purpose had been served.

The remaining SASNC members recognized the extent of the betrayal too late, but they also understood that it was not solely the homeowners' responsibility. They recognized that the homeowners had been isolated from the SASNC and clearly pressured by the ISFA to go "with the dollar

---

[25] Sheila Radford-Hill purposely stayed away from the SASNC Board meeting and the meeting at Abbott School on August 3 for two reasons: First, she had explained to the residents that her job was "to get 'em to the table" and then they would have to deal. "And I had explained many times . . . I was not there to stay. I wasn't trying to build a fiefdom. I wasn't trying to build a base for myself." Second, she was aware that the press was pushing "the troublemaker angle": "And . . . so I was very sensitive to that. . . . I really felt that . . . developing a, a scapegoat like myself, would have justified the deal." Mrs. Carter remembered the SASNC homeowners' growing antagonism against Sheila Radford-Hill: "Well, the first time they [SASNC officers] went down there [to meet with the ISFA], they came back with this great big book [contract draft]. Sheila went in there and they threw her out [of their meeting]. . . . [T]he homeowners had begun to turn against Sheila. They said that she didn't have a home to lose and that they did, and this and that. Then later that night or a couple of nights later, we had the [SASNC] meeting, and so they [SASNC officers] came. . . . Sheila had brought the big thing [draft contract materials] that they had, and one of the homeowners said, 'You might as well throw that in the garbage 'cause all of that has been changed; it's something different now.'"

instead of with the people." A Wentworth SASNC activist explained:

[The] White Sox involved had told them that, "You had the bigger to lose, so we need to negotiate with you. . . . If you don't go along with us, we will take your property, and you get zip." So therefore the homeowners got scared. . . . So in turn, instead of workin' with the entire community as . . . all of us had marched to do . . . [they] went with the dollar instead of with the people. So this is where we end up with this plight we have now.

The Wentworth residents also believed that they had also been "sold out" by the SASNC lawyer, Mary Milano.[26] And, in fact, the signed agreement was a "pseudo-transaction" because Mary Milano did not have the official backing of the coalition (Euchner, 1993, p. 155). Mrs. Laramore:

We had hired Mary Milano as our [SASNC] lawyer. . . . bless her sole heart. . . . [S]he went with them [the homeowners]. She was our lawyer. She didn't give us no notice, and no nothing, that she was leavin' us. And we was payin' her.

Attempts to Gain Concessions

Mrs. Amey, in August 1988, called George Marshall to schedule one final meeting of the homeowners, Wentworth United, and representatives from T. E. Brown. She hoped to pressure the homeowners to honor the demands of all of the SASNC membership. The only bargaining leverage she had left, however, was to appeal to the homeowners' former community social ties and allegiances, or their sense of altruism. Mrs. Carter described this meeting:

It was George Marshall, Lillian Brown, Miss Susie Myers . . . that came along with Mary Milano. They came down to the LAC office. We sit down and Mrs. Amey said, "Well, you all got your deal," to the homeowners, and she said, "We want something for Wentworth." She said, "I told you, do not go down there and come back from down there without something for Wentworth." George told her she better hurry up if she gonna get anything 'cause they about to close the thing out.

The Wentworth activists were hoping to gain some compensation from the ISFA, including the rehabilitation of Wentworth building exteriors, such

---

[26] Mary Milano had quite a different view on this. From her perspective, and her past work as a commercial real estate lawyer, she was proud of the deal she negotiated for the home-owners. She argued that she could not be expected to negotiate for the whole area. She viewed the homeowners alliance with other SASNC coalition members as only a strategic one. In the following quote her allegiance to the homeowners, versus the whole coalition, is clear: "I approached this project the way I approach a commercial real estate deal, which is my usual line of work. I tried to get the best deal possible for the people affected by the development. When I went in I thought our chances were remote. I think these people got the best condemnation deal in the history of the state. The thing to do was to get people involved with a collective mechanism [SASNC] until such time as the individual contracts were signed" (Euchner, 1993, p. 154).

as sandblasting, tuckpointing, new windows and doors, and painting. It is not a surprise that Mrs. Amey's plea to the leadership of the SASNC was ineffective against the bargaining power of the ISFA. The homeowners had already formalized their split from the SASNC by forming another group, the South Armour Development Company, immediately after the August 3 meeting. It was the South Armour Development Company that subsequently ratified an agreement with ISFA.[27] There was an additional $10 million added to the ISFA relocation budget because of the organizing efforts of the SASNC. Especially embittering for the remaining SASNC members was that the development company, now located in what was originally the new SASNC office, was an idea first conceived by Sheila Radford-Hill, months before, to benefit the whole coalition. According to Sheila, "Mary [Milano] took the South Armour Development strategy over."[28]

THE SASNC REGROUPS: MOVING FORWARD

It's the people who are still living there who are complaining. (Peter Bynoe, executive director, ISFA, Chicago Plan Commission meeting, December 8, 1988)

With no support from their former coalition partners, the remaining SASNC members pulled together and moved forward. Wentworth Gardens and T. E. Brown Apartments activists regrouped to identify and assess their options to continue their opposition to the White Sox stadium development in their community. During the fall of 1988, the remaining members of the SASNC attempted to stall construction and at the same time to obtain concessions to ameliorate the impending destruction of a large part of the South Armour neighborhood. They picketed at Comiskey Park, attended Planning Commission meetings, and sought to communicate directly with the Sports Facility Authority. Eventually, the SASNC arrranged two face-to-face meetings with the executive director, Peter Bynoe, but he

---

[27] In the homeowners' agreement with the ISFA they received the following provisions: The homeowners were provided with an office in the neighborhood. Several homeowners received jobs as relocation counselors to help the other residents decide on what option they wanted to take. Homeowners were offered (a) a cash settlement for their house amounting to appraised market value plus a $25,000 incentive payment; (b) relocation of their existing house to another site plus a $2,500 settlement; (c) a new house or two apartments paid for by ISFA that would cost the homeowner no more than his or her old mortgage payment; or (d) nothing at all if no mortgage existed. Renters in the private residences that were being torn down were offered a cash settlement of $4,500 and a moving allowance of $500 (Ranney, et al., 1997, p. 74).

[28] In the spring of 1988, Sheila Radford-Hill had suggested to Mary Milano and George Marshall that they should suggest that the ISFA fund the South Armour Square Development Corporation. The residents could work through this corporation and get paid for the settlement and the displacement negotiations.

would not agree to any concessions.[29] Marcella Carter:

[Peter Bynoe] came out and he talked and said he was going to see what he could do, and this and that. But he said he didn't have any money for Wentworth because he said, he ain't got no money to throw away. He said, "The place is going to be torn down anyway." Tim Wright [economic development commissioner] said, "If it had been left up to him he'd have took the whole thing."

During this period, the fall and early winter of 1988, the SASNC was making weekly trips down to the City Council meetings at City Hall each Tuesday to stall the stadium construction by obstructing the permit process. Guided by Sheila Radford-Hill and Bill Peterman, Mrs. Carter collected the necessary permit information. Mrs. Carter:

I went and researched at City Hall and I found out a whole lot of different things they [ISFA] had to have . . . and asked some questions. . . . Sheila and Dr. Peterman had showed us how to do it. . . . They had to have a permit to do the streets, a permit to do this, and a permit to do that. . . . Anyway, I got all the permits they had, and some of the permits they didn't have. . . . Then we went back to the City Council [chambers].

Mrs. Carter is referring to the Chicago's City Plan Commission[30] meeting held to approve plans for the new stadium on December 8, 1988. This public hearing was attended by approximately 30 South Armour Square residents who had traveled downtown together by bus. Sheila Radford-Hill; their new lawyer, Jim Chapman; and Sharon Washington testified in a session that was "often interrupted by emotional pleas of community opponents" who were voicing their fears about the adverse impacts of the stadium and its construction (Seigel, *Chicago Tribune*, December 9, 1988, sec. 3, p. 14). Prepared with Mrs. Carter's research, they noted the lack of several required permits and the current dangerous construction site conditions, including the failure to provide appropriate means of entrance and departure as alternates for the streets that were being closed and the lack of fencing around the demolition sites. Sharon Washington, speaking as the building manager for the 120 residents at T. E. Brown Apartments, argued that the elderly and disabled residents would have to keep their windows closed on hot days to protect themselves against construction noise and dust, but they could not afford air-conditioning costs. Abbott School's principal

---

[29] ISFA attempted to negotiate an offer of a 3-year low-interest loan to CHA for buildings and grounds maintenance and improvements at Wentworth Gardens, but no agreement with CHA could be reached.

[30] The Chicago City Plan Commission is a major actor in both the initiation and the review of Chicago's long-range urban development plans. "The Plan Commission reviews all major development projects in the city, as well as major zoning or land use changes. All of the Commissions's recommendations are reviewed by the City Council for final approval" (Ranney, et al., 1997, p. 18).

reiterated the same concerns about the elementary school children. Bynoe responded by promising to "help pay" for air-conditioning and possibly to relocate sick residents (Seigel, *Chicago Tribune*; December 9, 1988, sec. 3, p. 14).

Sheila Radford-Hill summed up the problem of identifying the impact of and appropriate concessions for the stadium construction, when, as she said, "We can't ask for redress without knowing what the [problems] are." The residents' concerns about the ISFA's lack of a comprehensive plan were supported by several of the Chicago City Plan Commission members and resulted in a direct response from the commission. Even though the ISFA's plan was not rejected, the ISFA was required to address community concerns before building permits would be issued. Elizabeth Hollander, city planning commissioner, was clear in her demands: "We've approved the development subject to the authority [ISFA] bringing us an operating plan to address all the questions that were raised" (e.g., possible construction and health hazards and quality of life issues). In response to the Chicago Plan Commission's concerns, Peter Bynoe promised to fund an environmental impact study to suggest solutions "to problems from construction noise and pollution, traffic congestion, and security as soon as possible" (Seigel, *Chicago Tribune*, December 9, 1988, sec. 3, p. 14). This was a small win for the SASNC, relished by SASNC activists, including Mrs. Marcella Carter:

Peter Bynoe, we had him, he was about to fall on his knees . . . . He was whining. . . . We had him . . . and they [Planning Commission] said, "Have you did this and have you did that?" "No, your honor, but I will do this and I will do that."

As a result of the SASNC's agitation and their continued pressure to negotiate benefits for nonhomeowners, ISFA agreed to air-condition half of Abbott Elementary School; compensate the T. E. Brown residents in the amount of $500.00 each to defray approximately one-third of their increased air-conditioning costs during the construction period; and close off the construction site (Ranney et al., 1997). The direct concessions for Wentworth Gardens residents were similarly modest, including the maintenance of roadways to assure residents access to 35th and 37th Streets, fencing with warning signs surrounding the construction site, an overnight security guard at the construction site, and the use of water sprinkling and temporary enclosures to limit dust and dirt during the 2 years of demolition (McCarron, *Chicago Tribune*, March 29, 1989).

Grieving the Loss of Home

The SASNC's organizing campaign culminated in a community mass meeting on January 17, 1989. A letter writing campaign had been organized to build support and garner representation from other community groups across the city. South Armour residents, former Save Our Sox baseball fans, and other people citywide were among the 300 to 400 in attendance. The remaining SASNC members, assisted by Sheila Radford-Hill; Patricia Wright, replacing Bill Peterman from the Voorhees Center; and other community organizers and technical assistants, staged a "funeral service" at the meeting, with a coffin as a prop, in the gym at Abbott Elementary School. Many Wentworth residents testified at the service, sharing their stories about growing up, raising families, and making friends over the years in the South Armour community. According to Baum (1997), staging a funeral was a particularly appropriate response, for when people face issues of community decline,

[they] feel like mourners, grieving the possible demise of both the community and that valued part of themselves they identify with it. They confront the possibilities that their community may simply die or that it may go on in ways that do not resemble the community they live in and love. (p. 50)

And indeed, Dorothy Laramore poignantly shared her personal sense of loss:

Sure, I was hurt, yes. We suffered because, I say I've suffered because . . . they have taken away our neighborhood. . . . That really hurt. I mean, you can't . . . understand how taking away something that's that much a part of your life . . . it hurts. (Deposition, December 10, 1991)

Pat Wright claimed that this mass meeting also brought closure to the organizing effort to stop stadium construction and marked a change in the SASNC's objectives, now to ameliorate the devastating effects of the new stadium on the South Armour community:

[T]hat really ended the organizing, the real strident organizing, where people hoped this would be turned around. And, a lot of people after that left. And then, it became just the people we know now that were primarily residents of Wentworth Gardens, meeting on . . . rebuilding the community.

Sheila Radford-Hill concurred with Pat that this event was a major turning point, mourning the demise of the original South Armour, but publicly witnessing a new phase of their organizing:

I knew it was the end of the neighborhood as we knew it. And that was bad. . . . And bitter . . . but . . . I didn't see it as . . . the end for the residents. Certainly, [I] knew that it was just a different phase in their struggle for empowerment.

A New Phase in Organizing: Seeking a Legal Remedy

For 2 years Wentworth activists, as part of the SASNC, had organized, lobbied, and attempted to negotiate to modify the siting of the new stadium. When they were unsuccessful, on February 9, 1989, the SASNC, now primarily representing residents of Wentworth Gardens and the T. E. Brown Apartments, and with their new lawyer, Jim Chapman, filed a federal lawsuit against the City of Chicago, the Sports Facility Authority, and the White Sox Corporation to stop the stadium construction. Forty-nine plaintiffs from the neighborhood charged that the planning and decision making for the stadium site violated the civil rights of the South Armour Square residents.

The court case argued that the decision to site the new Comiskey Park at the southern location was racially motivated (Ranney et al., 1997). The location of the new Comiskey Park, south of the old Comiskey Park, displaced more people than it would have if it had been located to the north, and all of the residents were black. Had a northern location been chosen, it would have displaced fewer people, and they would have been white. Another key point of the lawsuit was that public hearings on the relocation site of Comiskey Park that were required in the initial legislation creating the ISFA, although they were held in the White Sox's first choice for a site – the suburb of Addison – were never held in Chicago. Therefore, the residents of South Armour never had the opportunity to voice their opinion. In fact, recall that the Illinois legislature amended the ISFA legislation to remove this stipulation. In her lawsuit deposition, Mrs. Amey clearly stated her outrage at this injustice:

In a well established [white] community, nobody would come in and build a stadium without having hearings and let the community know what was going to happen and get that input. That was never done . . . there's not consideration. . . . That's just the point, they didn't come and say anything. You come and get ready to take a whole community away and you can't come in and talk to the people there no matter what color their skins are. They're all citizens of this city. This is America! (March 31, 1992)

THE DESTRUCTION OF SOUTH ARMOUR SQUARE: A FINAL ROUND OF ORGANIZING

Filing the lawsuit did not delay the stadium construction. By March 1989 all of the properties were vacated to make way for the bulldozers. The ISFA, however, did not follow through on its earlier agreement to protect the health and safety of the remaining residents. Residents of Wentworth Gardens and of T. E. Brown senior housing experienced many hardships during the demolition of the housing and businesses. Mrs. Amey elaborated on some of their concerns:

[W]hen the homes were being demolished, that did cause a whole lot of health problems for many people, because they had said that they were going to water it down as they went along, but they did not. . . . [I]t took a long time to even board up some of those empty houses after the home owners moved out. These things were serious problems.

Once again, the SASNC mobilized in order to obtain what had been promised and to orchestrate media attention to confront the neglect of the ISFA. Mrs. Amey remembered:

[W]e had to fight to get those folks to come and put up a barrier for those school kids, because you know how kids are, grammar school kids. The homes were vacant; we had to fight again, call and call to get houses boarded, vacant houses. You know how serious that is with school children in the area. All of these things, and even the senior citizens and handicapped building there.

Mrs. Marcella Carter:

We had to even call the newspapers 'cause the houses that weren't gone, the kids were up there playing and houses weren't boarded up and stuff. And one child that had went up there had fell down the steps.... We called Walter Jacobson [a well known local television investigative news reporter]... Mrs. Laramore was our media person so we had her to call... and he came out and did an interview on it. They came out and they boarded up the houses. Then right after that they started tearing them down.

The new White Sox stadium opened in spring 1991. Eighty private residences, including single-family homes and two flats containing 178 housing units, were lost. The destruction of 12 businesses meant the loss of more than 300 neighborhood jobs.[31] South Armour's population declined by 36% from 2, 292 persons in 1980 to 1,467 persons in 1990. The median income for South Armour households fell by 57%, because of the relocation of the working-class families and the cutbacks in social security and public aid during the 1980s (Ranney et al., 1997). The construction of the new Comiskey Park further isolated the remaining black community – the T. E. Brown Apartments, Abbott Elementary School, the Progressive Baptist Church, and Wentworth Gardens – from the white and Chinese communities in the surrounding neighborhoods. Long-term social ties with their former South Armour Square neighbors were destroyed. Mrs. Amey described this community disruption:

[O]ur whole community has been interrupted and disrupted and destroyed.... [W]hen we had a whole community we communicated, visited. And elder people like myself and others, we don't like a lot of things, but we do like, you know, visiting with our friends.... We've known each other over the years.... but now it's just different, because we just have Wentworth and the whole community [is] just interrupted.

---

[31] In their report to the United Nations on forces that impact on the effectiveness of community organizations, Ranney, Wright, and Zhang (1997) found that in South Armour: "One company that had been located in the area for 60 years and employed 70 persons moved out of the city. Seventy percent of the employees of the displaced businesses had lived in the surrounding neighborhood" (pp. 28–29).

FIGURE 6. Wentworth courtyard with two-story rowhouses in the left foreground and Progressive Baptist Church's Senior Housing behind, the Abbott Elementary School in the right foreground, and the new White Sox stadium, Comiskey Park – note the stadium lights – in the middle background (photographer: Susan Stall). Upper right hand corner: West side of the Wentworth Gardens development on Princeton Street with three-story walk-up apartments on the right and the White Sox stadium in the background on the left (photographer: Roberta A. Feldman).

The sense of safety and security experienced by residents in a community of known others also was lost. Mrs. Laramore:

But it wasn't that bad [before], because you could go down the street, the neighbors on the porches, and you wouldn't be afraid to walk down the street because everybody knew everybody and everybody lookin' out for everybody.... Stores was there; the service station was there; Tyler's Restaurant was there.... You could walk down the street. You could go out at night any time ... But now, you know, with nothin' there, you're afraid to walk down that way.

Mrs. Laramore's comments echo Jane Jacobs's (1961) notion of "eyes on the street," noting the importance of actively used sidewalks to support neighborly interaction and feelings of safety. In addition to the increased isolation of the South Armour community, troublesome, if not unsafe disruptions were caused by the White Sox games. For instance, an exploding scoreboard on top of the stadium wall emits fireworks each time a player hits a home run. This White Sox tradition rattles the elderly residents' apartments in T. E. Brown less than 200 feet away (Ranney, et al., 1996). Vehicular access to the surrounding homes also has been severely restricted on game days by the White Sox fans' use of local streets and the temporary conversion of regular two-way streets to a one-way traffic pattern. It took the direct organizing initiative of two Wentworth activists to turn this "personal inconvenience" into a public issue.

Alinsky tactics of direct confrontation were once again used to address the concerns of women-centered organizing on the day of the annual summer Fun Fest at Wentworth, when traffic exiting the White Sox stadium blocked Mrs. Carter and Mrs. Weathersby from entering their development to deliver food for the event. Mrs. Carter described how she openly defied the police who were directing traffic on the temporary one-way street:

[T]he police that was there.... He told me not to turn, but I turned anyway. And then, you know, I was like, stop, because these cars was comin' out. And, the guy said, "Miss, I told you not to turn." I said, "Look, I'm tryin' to get home. I got all this chicken in here, and it was hot. . . ." And a lady cop was in the middle of the street. And she asked the guy, "What's goin' on?" And he said, "She turned and she can't get through it." She said, "Give the B[itch] a ticket." And that pissed me off.

Mrs Weathersby, who is a formidable figure, would have made Saul Alinsky proud when she used a creative organizational tactic, staging a "showdown," further challenging the police authority. Mrs. Carter described her dramatic effort:

Weathersby jumped out the car and Weathersby started walkin' in front of me. And I'm ridin' behind, drivin' behind her. We're goin' through this traffic.... I got through.

Although she and Mrs. Weathersby succeeded in achieving their short-term goal, this incident and her treatment by the police infuriated Mrs. Carter:

The cops that . . . workin' out there was kinda . . . rough. They was rude; they was very rude . . . . And I was so mad . . . I sat down and wrote a[n] [editorial] letter.

After this incident, several residents, including Mrs. Laramore, Mrs. Weathersby, and Mrs. Carter, started a "police watch" to contest the conversion of Princeton Avenue into a one-way street on game days. Mrs. Laramore explained,

Remember me and Weathersby started standin' up there at the corner.

And Mrs. Carter added:

We did the traffic thing. . . . Every night, when the White Sox had a [game] . . . we would take turns standin' out there to make sure they didn't turn that street into a one way. We would write the officer's name down, and who was out there and everything. We had people [resident activists] linin' up there.

The residents' vigilance and multiple Alinsky-style organizing tactics – direct confrontation, letter writing, and resident monitoring of police traffic flows – did pay off. They garnered the attention of city officials. According to Mrs. Carter:

[S]ee, we was having so much problem gettin' in and out of here. Mayor Daley told him [Alderman Patrick Huels] that he needed to do something about it; 'cause we had a big meetin' up there [at the field house] with Eugene Pincham [former African-American mayoral candidate], and we had a lot of people came up there to the center. . . . [Former] Mayor Sawyer was here. . . . [A]ll of them came out to that meetin'. . . . We invited a lot of people.

As a result of this meeting, Alderman Huels formed the FACT Committee, Friends against Comiskey Traffic, and ultimately solved the problem. In addition, Mrs. Carter was proud to relate that they received a police apology for their rudeness:

I forget that little policeman that was in charge of them. He explained to us, 'cause he came up here and we had a meetin'. . . . And he said that those policemans was off duty [when they were directing baseball game traffic] and that it was overtime for them and stuff. And that he wouldn't tolerate 'em talkin' to us like that.

The residents involved in this protest effort recounted these stories with pride and seemed to enjoy cultivating a reputation as people to be reckoned with. Mrs. Laramore explained how their image as activists lived on months after the police monitoring efforts had ceased.

I was comin' over here once. . . . I was walkin' down the street towards the subway and I saw one of the police say, "Oh you're comin' to raise hell again?" He remembered me from the previous year. He thought, we was out there . . . one more time."

CONCLUSIONS

The Wentworth Gardens residents fought the destruction of the their neighborhood, but they lost. Yet, given the strength of their adversaries, and their lack of political and economic support, it is amazing that the activists accomplished as much as they did – a generous relocation package for the displaced residents and some concessions for the remaining residents during the period of stadium construction.

When the White Sox, the city and state politicians, and the Illinois Sports Facility Authority aligned to build a new Sox stadium in South Armour Park, it was difficult even to get the ear, let alone alter the plan, of these powerful opponents. By extending their women-centered organizing to include Alinsky-style confrontational protest strategies, several Wentworth activists went into, in their word, "battle." First, as part of Save Our Homes, and then in the South Armour Square Neighborhood Coalition, they worked closely with the organizer Sheila Radford-Hill, seeking pressure points at which to orchestrate their antistadium battles (Euchner, 1993). Their tactics were numerous: negotiating and lobbying through formal channels such as the alderman's or mayor's office; working with Save Our Sox to save the original stadium; approaching the Zoning Board and the Chicago Plan Commission to create delays so that the project might be moved or canceled; issuing flyers, petitions, and public statements; and staging protests to expand their support base, apply pressure on their opponents, and get their message out to the public. But they were not able to shift the balance of power, for at every level of their battle they faced at best, resistance, and at worst, betrayal.

As part of the SASNC they were never able to follow Alinsky's tactical admonishment, "Pick the target, freeze it, personalize it, and polarize it" (1971, p. 130). The activists were continually operating from a defensive rather than an offensive position.[32] They learned about the potential destruction of their neighborhood in a newspaper article and were never given the public hearings legally required in the legislation that created the ISFA. The Illinois Sports Facility Authority was a natural target, but the authority's implementation was delayed for almost a year because of political wrangling, hence it was not an easy target to "freeze." Attempts to "personalize" their targets were also difficult. The SASNC activists were fighting in a black political quagmire. Mayor Harold Washington agreed to the deal that sealed the fate of their homeowning neighbors before he died in 1987, and Acting Mayor Eugene Sawyer did nothing to challenge this agreement. The African-American ISFA appointee Peter Bynoe never pretended to be an advocate of South Armour. The legislative Black Caucus made promises to oppose the ISFA but proved to be unreliable allies. And, finally, the Wentworth Gardens residents were betrayed by the

---

[32] Alinsky (1971) understood why the organizer's task of picking one target was becoming increasingly difficult: "In these times of urbanization, complex metropolitan governments, the complexities of major interlocked corporations and the interlocking of political life between cities and metropolitan authorities, the problem that threatens to loom more and more is that of identifying the enemy. Obviously there is no point to tactics unless one has a target upon which to center the attacks. One big problem is a constant shifting of responsibility from one jurisdiction to another" (pp. 130–131).

very neighbors they had shared a community with for decades and fought side-by-side with for over 18 months. Emotionally, this was probably the most intense betrayal of all. The remaining SASNC members were particularly bitter because they believed a united SASNC had a chance to win the battle. As one member stated:

If people stay together, you're gonna win. I don't care what it is. . . . If you stayed together with it, we would have won.

It is true that the Wentworth resident activists' organizing effort in the White Sox battle is a tale of disappointments, defeats, and betrayals, but it is also a tale of courage. In publicly resisting formidable political, economic, and legal adversaries to defend their homes and their neighborhood, Wentworth resident activists empowered themselves to act in the future. They transgressed the boundaries of the Wentworth Gardens development and acted independently of the CHA in the public domain. In the process, they formalized their organizational structure, first in the formation of Wentworth Gardens Residents United for Survival, then in the creation of the South Armour Square Neighborhood Coalition. Wentworth resident activists increased their knowledge of the city and state political systems and their experience in a confrontational organizing model. They grew not only collectively, but individually. Residents, such as Marcella Carter, who became SASNC president after the coalition split, would now turn newly honed skills from protest to economic development. Finally, these women established new social, political, and technical networks that would become vital to their immediate and future plans. Sheila Radford-Hill voiced the potential she saw in these women activists:

There are tremendous opportunities if people can hang together. Involvement helps us to define our interests better. This whole process has helped the neighborhood to develop an identity and define a broad economic development program. It's an upside-down situation because we are turning losses into gains. (Euchner, 1993, p. 159).

The SASNC did not disband; rather, the remaining members, mostly Wentworth activists, regrouped and focused their efforts on the SASNC's earlier work with the UIC Voorhees Center: the development of an alternative neighborhood plan, especially a needed retail shopping center in the South Armour Square neighborhood. The reasons for their continued activism were to seek racial justice, meet their social reproduction needs, and affirm their attachments to their homeplace. Sharon Washington eloquently expresses why the remaining SASNC members would continue their transgressive resistance efforts:

I personally think it's important when it comes to generations, and, families that have lived in an area as for as long as we have, it's a community. And it's like cuttin' off an arm, you know, we have children. I have a history here, like I'm sayin', over

30, 40 years, and it's something that I have started tellin' my grandchildren about. And then they still come [back] because my mother still lives in the neighborhood, you know, and they look and see different things, but they can never imagine what was here when I was a child. So I think it's important, it's called roots.

If we just break up and disappear, we have nothing to tell our children that was ours, because we don't own land. Okay so this is it, this is as close as we're going to come to being landowners. And 'til we do the things that we're doin' now, and that's to sue, in order to get our piece of the rock. So, I think it is important that communities stick together. It's for protection, everybody is looking out for one another. It's been that way for years, and if the White Sox had not come in here, we would still have a vital community.

9

Linking Legal Action and Economic Development
Tensions and Strains

> I feel very strongly that in community struggles lawsuits can only be used
> as one arrow in your quiver.... I saw using the lawsuit as a leverage for
> development. We were too late to be a factor in saving the community as it
> was.... [T]he court suit has been able to make real the concrete work that
> needs to be done.
>
> Jim Chapman, legal counsel, SASNC

For the SASNC, as for many community organizations, a lawsuit is a strategy of last resort – and it was so in this case. The SASNC refocused the
demands of their 1989 lawsuit, first to seek reparations from the Illinois
Sports Authority, the White Sox, and the City of Chicago for the destruction of their neighborhood local businesses (see Zhang & Wright, 1992);
second, to implement an economic development plan for the rebuilding
of their neighborhood. Coalition members believed that, for justice to be
served, the redevelopment funds should come from the White Sox Corporation and the state and city governments. Supporting this opinion,
Mrs. Laramore, who had been a vital opponent of the White Sox relocation,
argued:

> I want money to come from the White Sox. That's where I want the money to come
> from. Because they the ones that destroyed what we had. And I think that they
> should be ... responsible for building back some of the things that we had.... Give
> us the money so we could start [re]building.

A successful lawsuit and plan would together provide a fulcrum for
leveraging concessions from the SASNC's powerful opponents and for
garnering additional economic and political resources for their plan.
The SASNC required a substantial economic award from the lawsuit –
$1.5 million alone was needed to construct the facilities to replace the
lost retail businesses.

Even before the development of the new stadium, the South Armour Square neighborhood had been underserved by commercial businesses.[1] The construction of the new Comiskey Park eliminated the few retail businesses that remained in the community: three large and eight small businesses, including two grocery stores, a gas station, a bar, and a restaurant. Subsequently, residents in the neighborhood have had to travel a minimum of approximately 2 miles to the nearest grocery store (Zhang & Wright, 1992). They must leave their neighborhood to purchase such basic grocery items as milk, bread, and child care products, or must pay inflated prices for a limited selection, and often lesser quality, of goods in the immediate area. This is quite a burden for the majority of the low-income residents, who are either senior citizens, persons with disabilities, or single mothers with children. Mrs. Mary Wright, a Wentworth resident for 31 years and a SASNC member, explained these difficulties:

[T]he White Sox ... they tore all the stores down. We don't have anything. . . . I have to go to 47th [Street] ... or 31st [Street] and Halsted [to shop].

Two-thirds of the residents now had to rely on public transportation, although the bus service is limited (Zhang & Wright, 1992).

The replacement of the commercial establishments and the creation of entrepreneurial opportunities and jobs for neighborhood residents would become the SASNC's first priority. To achieve this objective, Wentworth Gardens residents would now adopt another strategy – economic development – to continue their battle for racial justice and to sustain the viability of not only of their development, but now their neighborhood. For the residents, this means of transgressive resistance would require a tremendous shift in focus from the action orientation of confrontational organizing in the White Sox battle and the process orientation of prior women-centered organizing efforts, to the product orientation of economic development. To make this shift, the residents would need professional advocates to assist them. In this chapter we explore the complex and substantial resources required to develop the shopping center and the various strategies that the SASNC, with the assistance of committed professionals, used to attempt to garner these resources in the face of immense economic, political, organizational, and personnel constraints. Throughout this analysis we expose tensions that emerged between the SASNC members and the

---

[1] Since 1991, The City of Chicago has completed three major retail studies of the South Side of Chicago: "The Chicago South Side Neighborhood Commercial Plan," "Retailing in Chicago's South Side Neighborhoods," and "Retail Chicago: A Neighborhood Community Development Initiative." These studies demonstrate that the South Side of Chicago, including the South Armour Square neighborhood, are greatly underserved by retail establishments.

multiprofessional technical assistance team in the initial tasks necessary to produce an economic development plan, including: a market feasibility study, building of community support, building real estate development expertise, development of business plans and training, building and site design, and the ongoing struggles to garner funds for organizational survival.

The Professionals

Four professionals, enlisted through the SASNC activists' personal networks, played crucial roles in building the legal case and developing an economic development plan. Three had been active in the White Sox battle: Jim Chapman as legal counsel, Pat Wright, as a university planning and economic development analyst, and Sheila Radford-Hill, an organizer turned community developer, who assembled the real estate and business development team. One of the authors, Roberta Feldman, an architecture educator and activist, who had worked with Wentworth activists in the past, was the fourth. All agreed to continue to work with the SASNC because they believed the Wentworth residents had suffered a grave injustice. Jim Chapman explained that he knew of Bridgeport's reputation for racism and was ignited by the opportunity to challenge that racism:

Because, to me, I grew up in the '30s and '40s when Bridgeport was and is the symbolism of Chicago's deep-seated racism. . . . And when I grew up there were signs up there on the taverns, "Members Only," which was a way [to keep out blacks]. And then there were stories if a Black man walked in [to Bridgeport] he would get killed, and if a White man walked out of the neighborhood he would get killed. There were vicious stories emanating from my youth. . . . I thought [the Democratic regime's] unwillingness to challenge the racism which was inherent in Bridgeport was symbolic. It attracted me because I thought I had a feel for what was happening with them. . . . I felt I knew too much for me . . . to walk away from these people and my own beliefs and my own principles to let this go by unchallenged.

Pat Wright was inspired by the residents' resolve:

I found the residents to be really courageous to stand up and fight that whole [White Sox stadium] development. And against such great odds that I, I really felt compelled to stick with them on this. 'Cause I really, from the very beginning, I thought Mrs. Amey, and Marcella [Carter], and Sharon [Washington] really had a lot of guts and foresight to stand up to initially Mayor Washington and . . . [Mayor Eugene] Sawyer [the interim mayor of Chicago when Washington died]. . . . You had the public housing residents really standing up for their rights as a community; 'cause they really didn't have due process.

The professionals encouraged the SASNC to pursue alternative strategies to rebuild their community in addition to the lawsuit. Jim Chapman believed that a lawsuit can, at best, shift the balance of power or "change the site of the bargaining table," but it should be only "one arrow in your quiver." Jim hoped that an economic development strategy would reactivate the SASNC and inspire grassroots organizing efforts. He suggested to Pat Wright that she return to Wentworth to work actively with the coalition to develop and pursue the development strategy.[2] According to Pat:

Jim talked to me about the fact that he . . . thought it was very important to start having discussions with the South Armour residents and members about rebuilding the community.

Sheila Radford-Hill concurred that it made sense for Wentworth activists to engage in an economic development strategy, especially to prepare for the possible financial settlement from the lawsuit. In the meantime, to support the legal strategy, Jim Chapman needed technical data, including a report on neighborhood conditions before the construction of the stadium, information to support the need for a new retail center, and projected costs of a center. This information would also be useful in seeking alternative avenues for funding the economic development project.

The Challenges

Although the lawsuit was not a guaranteed "win", Jim Chapman was confident that groundwork was being laid for a well-supported and strong civil rights case:

It took me about 3 or 4 months to do all of the background work – to get the census tracts . . . about the racial divisions. . . . I worked like hell on that thing. . . . It was a huge undertaking. . . . I did investigate it. I talked to a lot of witnesses.

Even with a strong case, Jim was cognizant of the extended time frame of the legal process. With the discovery and depositions, legal delays, and appeals, lawsuit proceedings could continue for years. Jim explained, "It would go in waves . . . but there were cycles . . . there were periods that were very, very intense. "A major organizing challenge would be to keep the SASNC together as a viable community organization during the years of legal maneuverings. Jim was a strong proponent of using economic development as both a strategy to sustain the SASNC's solidarity over

---

[2] As early as 1988, during the organizing campaign for the White Sox battle, Pat Wright, at Jim Chapman's suggestion, had begun working with the SASNC on strategies the coalition might use to wrest control over the community's future economic development. Initially, Jim Chapman asked Pat Wright to prepare a report on alternative economic development options as well as a financial analysis of the White Sox stadium finances, in particular the public subsidies supporting the ballpark development.

the long haul and a means to gain control over the South Armour Square neighborhood's future viability.[3]

The idea of rebuilding the South Armour neighborhood initially fired the enthusiasm of the residents and provided immediate tasks and a revitalized organizational vision for the SASNC. Yet, engaging in economic development, even with the professionals' commitment and the residents' support, created its own risks and challenges. First, in the shift from the prior action orientation of the White Sox protests to the technical decision making of community development, the process would increasingly become expert-driven. Development is not only extraordinarily complicated, but tedious and time-consuming to learn (Stoecker, 1994). Second, as in the White Sox battle, the professionals and the residents were operating on an unbalanced political and economic "playing field." To make their justice claims public, grassroots organizing would need to be an integral part of garnering political support. Third, the exigencies of economic development would conflict with, or perhaps overshadow, the collaborative practices and values of the residents' ongoing women-centered organizing efforts. In fact, on the basis of his own research on two midwestern neighborhood community organizing groups' movement into community development, Stoecker (1995) cautioned that community development can undermine existing community organizing efforts.

GETTING STARTED

What were the requisites to initiate the first steps in the development of a shopping center? What was the scope of the necessary economic, material, and technical resources? What were the potential sources for these resources? What was required to gain access to these resources? These are only some of the issues that the technical assistants and SASNC activists faced in organizing efforts to launch the development planning for the shopping center.

Wentworth activists could not readily appropriate property for the shopping center. They could not, as they had in the past, rely on their bridging social capital with CHA management; nor was on-site space that was adequate to house the retail center available. No matter how tenuous their

---

[3] It is Jim Chapman's belief that "lawyers just can't be over here. The lawyers must be intimately involved in educating your clients as to what are the strengths and weaknesses of the law." In support of this belief, he tried to make the intricacies of the SASNC lawsuit understandable to the residents. He recalled a well attended meeting at Abbott Elementary School (50–100 people) in 1989 or 1990, in which he staged a mock trial: "[W]e put on witnesses as to why the White Sox and the defendants were wrong as an educational piece."

rights and control over the spaces in the development had been, acquiring and developing property through the operations of the real estate market posed a much more formidable challenge. The very modest monies that they had garnered from their personal resources and grants from the CHA and local foundations would hardly be adequate to purchase and develop the property.

The SASNC required substantial financial capital for professional services and construction costs, estimated at $1,500,000, plus additional funds for business development and training, and the community organizing necessary to implement the project. The SASNC could not depend solely on the lawsuit for all of the necessary monies to implement the economic development project; they also needed to seek development capital elsewhere. Securing funds through conventional means, such as from banks and venture capitalists, was not possible. From its inception the SASNC had operated with a meager budget. Attracting private investors would be difficult since they had no credit and the shopping center was unlikely to be highly profitable – in fact it was an economic risk. Instead, the SASNC in addition to settlement funds from the lawsuit, if successful, would need additional capital from government and foundation sources.

Securing the Initial Planning Funds

The initial planning for the shopping center included conducting a market feasibility study to demonstrate the market demand, identifying a site, and estimating costs for the construction of the shopping center. To begin these development tasks the SASNC required funds well beyond their personal resources. Several technical assistants were key in educating the residents about the availability of public funds and in helping them apply for and secure modest but crucial start-up monies. Jim Chapman identified a funding opportunity – a Community Development Block Grant (CDBG) from Chicago's Department of Planning and Development. Jim, Pat Wright, and their office staffs helped the SASNC with the CDBG application requirements. Pat, who was highly committed to resident involvement, explained that together she and Marcella Carter, the SASNC president, attended the CDBG hearing to obtain the application and listen to the detailed instructions, but it was Pat who wrote the grant, reviewing early drafts with the SASNC board members.

The SASNC's grant application, requesting $8,000 to conduct the market feasibility study, was submitted in June 1993. In January 1994, not only were they awarded the grant – it was for $16,000. The SASNC and the technical assistants were stunned by the doubling of the requested CDBG funds. It appears that Jim Chapman's connections with a deputy commissioner of planning favored the SASNC with additional funds for a part-time staff person for a limited period.

Upon receipt of the grant, however, there was evident tension when Marcella Carter and other SASNC activists expressed concern. They would be managing the grant on a day-to-day basis and were uneasy about the need to satisfy the grant reporting requisites. Pat Wright recalled:

> But frankly, Marcella and them didn't wanna take government money. They didn't want to do the paper work, which was extensive.... They had to do monthly reports. Once you get a city CDBG contract, you have to go all these meetings, 'cause then you become a delegate agency. Marcella really, nor Sharon really wanted to do all of that.

And indeed, the reporting for the grant proved to be a considerable burden for the SASNC volunteers, especially given its modest amount.

DEVELOPMENT PLANNING TASKS

The funds the SASNC received from the CDBG grant were not adequate to pay for the necessary professional expertise, nor to support a full-time staff person for the SASNC over the protracted planning period. Most of the technical assistance was contributed, as it was in the White Sox battle. Up to that time, Jim Chapman, Sheila Radford-Hill, and Pat Wright's services were pro bono. Toward the end of the initial development process, the Voorhees Center hired Sheila to complete the plan.

The multiprofessional team, with the participation of SASNC members whenever possible, produced the development plan. This plan was re-viewed at numerous SASNC meetings over the course of the next two years, from 1994 to 1996. The professionals devised and implemented the course of action including: assessing the market feasibility of the project; identifying and analyzing alternatives sites, selecting a preferred site and taking the first steps towards its purchase; creating schematic designs for the shopping center; estimating construction costs; and putting together a development team.

The Market Feasibility Study

A market feasibility study would support the lawsuit and attract economic resources for the shopping center development. With the CDBG grant in hand, the SASNC contracted with Pat Wright at the Nathalie P. Voorhees Center at the University of Illinois to conduct this study.[4] It was Pat's lead-ership and expertise that assured that three essential tasks were completed

---

[4] The SASNC contract with Nathalie P. Voorhees for the amount of $8,000 was very modest in comparison to the actual costs of the study.

throughout 1994: the first, identifying the SASNC's desired entrepreneurial opportunities; the second, a windshield survey of retail stores in the "trade area"; the third, a survey of the trade area residents to document their retail needs.

To accomplish the first task, Pat organized a series of workshops to discuss the SASNC members' entrepreneurial interests. Not unexpectedly, the Wentworth Gardens activists expressed interests in businesses that utilized their prior organizing skills and experiences in implementing and managing Wentworth's on-site facilities, specifically, a grocery store, laundromat/dry cleaner, and sit-down restaurant. The young male coalition members (in their late teens and 20s) wanted a video arcade. The feasibility of their objectives, however, would be assessed by Pat Wright and her research team in terms of the requisites of the marketplace: that is, through the market studies.

Marcella Carter, together with Pat and one of her research assistants, conducted a windshield survey of the competition in the trade area, documenting all of the businesses by type, location, and size. At the same time, Pat also worked closely with the SASNC to design a market survey to question area residents about their consumer expenditures and support for a locally developed commercial center. The technical aspects of the design and analysis of the market feasibility study were primarily the responsibility of the technical assistants, but the coalition members' social capital in the Wentworth complex proved crucial to the effectiveness of its outcome. The SASNC decided that they wanted to distribute the survey to every household in Wentworth Gardens, both as a way to collect the needed information and as a means of beginning to organize around the project. The survey would inform their neighbors about the proposed shopping center. Mrs. Amey, exercising her women-centered leadership skills, took on the responsibility of organizing the distribution of the surveys. She worked with the technical assistants to train Wentworth Gardens block captains to administer the survey form. One result of the resident activists' participation was a good response rate – 53% of all the Wentworth Gardens residents.[5] In addition, the SASNC's organizational capacity to mobilize around the effort was strengthened. Pat Wright reported:

> There was a lot of input.... [I]t was pretty much our core group [of activists], but there was ... probably ten or fifteen more. And then, Mrs. Amey at that time was bringing in new people.

Of the Wentworth residents who responded to the survey, 87% said they would shop at the locally developed retail center. The market survey found that there was a strong demand for a convenience grocery store and a

---

[5] The social methodologist Earl Babbie states that a survey "response rate of 50% is adequate for analysis and reporting" (2001, p. 256).

sit-down restaurant. The video arcade, however, would be dependent upon use from outside the trade area. The demand for the laundromat and dry cleaners was inadequate for financial viability. Many community residents indicated that they had washers and dryers in their apartments, and most neither used nor required dry cleaning services because of the expense.[6]

Tensions between Pat Wright and the coalition members arose over the market survey findings largely because of different goal orientations. The resident activists remained committed to meeting the social reproduction needs of their expanded household, whereas Pat, committed to meeting the requisites of a successful economic development project, stressed the economic viability of the project. Many of the coalition members were very disappointed about the lack of fit between the market study and the types of businesses they wanted to develop. They understood that their on-site laundromat, since its inception, had not made a significant profit, but it remained a needed facility for many Wentworth residents. Compromises had to be made.

The resident activists reluctantly agreed to eliminate the laundromat and dry cleaner, although desire for these two facilities was repeatedly expressed at subsequent SASNC meetings. Coalition members also expressed a preference for a food store with fairly extensive merchandise, but the market study indicated that there was too much competition for a store of this size. The grocery stored was scaled down to a more financially viable business. The young men who wanted to develop the video arcade were out-voted, not by the market study, but by other coalition members, who were concerned, as community othermothers, about rival gangs from other areas using the facility, and the ethics of having children spend their money on this form of recreation.

A facility for youth, however, stayed on the table. Resident activists acutely aware of the inadequacy of Wentworth's on-site field house, especially in comparison to the facilities at the Armour Square Park, had been attempting to secure a youth center in their neighborhood since the 1970s. The proposed retail development offered the first "real" possibility of satisfying their long-term need for an expanded youth facility. In an animated discussion, suggestions from the SASNC members were numerous. Mrs. Amey wanted a basketball court and skating rink; Sharon Washington, an old-fashioned soda-fountain with a jukebox and perhaps some video machines; Maggie Mahone, a gym; and one of the young adults, a tape and CD music store. Even when the technical assistants offered compelling arguments

---

[6] From her analysis of the competition and demand in the trade area, Pat Wright estimated the square footage of the grocery store, sit-down restaurant, and video arcade, and other rental spaces for the shopping center. (See Wright, 1995, for a complete report of the market study results.)

about the potential lack of economic feasibility and large amount of space that would be required, Wentworth activists remained adamant: "We want the center, the Youth Center!" (Marcella Carter). The coalition members prevailed. A large multipurpose room was included in the proposed shopping center to house both youth activities and rental space for community events even without firm evidence of financial viability from the market study.

Locating a Site and Gaining Site Control

From the very beginning of their efforts to develop the shopping center, SASNC activists were preoccupied with the location choice and acquisition. Other aspects of the initial planning were often highly technical and abstract; the choice of location was neither. Activists could visit the potential sites and understood the purchase requirements. The issue arose at virtually every SASNC meeting. Discussions often were heated, as members preferred different locations. Since the discussions led to no consensus and might have resulted in stalemate, Pat Wright organized a committee of core SASNC members to survey the neighborhood for potential locations. Once potential sites were identified, Pat researched their ownership and reported to the coalition.

   Ultimately, as in the case of the choice of businesses, economic feasibility prevailed in the choice of the preferred site. The property directly south of the Wentworth Gardens development on the southwest corner of Wentworth Avenue and Pershing Road presented an economically sound location for retail development. This site was desirable because of its prominence on a highly visible corner – the intersection of a major highway, the Dan Ryan Expressway, and a major east – west thoroughfare, Pershing Road. The three street frontages provided advertising potential and also relatively easy car access. Perhaps most importantly, the center would be accessible by public transportation (via bus and train lines) and was within walking distance of both Wentworth Gardens and the senior housing building. Jim Chapman was pleased with the selected site:

It seemed very logical to me. You put the development along 39th Street. That's kind of a wasteland over there.... And it was what they needed.... I thought is was a splendid idea. It faced the right way and was located in the right place. It didn't bother the White Sox over there [to the north]. It was what Wentworth needed. And you could have development on the other side.

   The majority of the 1.3-acre site was owned by the Catholic Archdiocese of Chicago.[7] It was hoped that the Chicago archdiocese's land would be

---

[7] The site was composed of six separate parcels totaling 1.13 acres, but the majority were vacant. One business, a liquor store, was located on the site immediately south of an

contributed, or at least could be purchased by the SASNC at a nominal sum. The Wentworth activists had established prior place attachments to this site. Before the church was demolished, Wentworth residents had attended the church, and some residents had occasionally utilized it as a meeting site. More recently, with the archdiocese's approval, several Wentworth Gardens activists had been using part of the abandoned church property as a community garden during the summer months.

The coalition did make some strides in procuring this property. Although Sheila Radford-Hill's initial discussion with a representative of the archdiocese did not lead anywhere, the social bridging bonds Mrs. Amey had built with selective archdiocese personnel, developed through her leadership role in the community garden, resulted in a breakthrough. It was both a disappointing and a productive day when Mrs. Amey, Sharon Washington, and two of the technical assistants arrived at the archdiocese office for an appointment, only to be informed by a secretary that their appointment was canceled. Luckily the secretary recognized Mrs. Amey from a past meeting about the community garden. Another appointment was made and kept, and some progress made. The archdiocese, according to Mrs. Amey, was "very positive" about donating the land, although the details needed to worked out.

Participatory Design Workshops

Shortly after the types of stores and their square footage requirements were identified and the preferred site was selected, Roberta Feldman was asked to contribute her architectural expertise to develop alternative designs and cost estimates for the shopping center. Together with Jack Naughton, an architect and faculty member at UIC, Roberta decided to use a participatory design process to expand the residents' collaborative opportunities. Roberta Feldman and Jack Naughton, as do other participatory design practitioners, believe that this design process can contribute to social justice by putting control of the design, management, and maintenance of the physical environment – all essential acts of space appropriation – in the hands of the public, and in particular people who typically are excluded from environmental decision making (e.g., the poor and women).[8] They also shared the belief that the intended user of a physical setting is the "world's greatest expert on his or her own situation" (Gibson, 1979, cited in Turner, 1977, p. 275). They draw on evidence of both material and

---

unpaved public right-of-way. Property could be assembled into a T shape with a total area of 47,930 square feet with the purchase of these two properties.

[8] *Participatory design* is a term that is used to cover multiple types of strategies to engage user participation in architecture and planning decisions as well as in building construction, management, and maintenance (Feldman & Westphal, 2000).

human gains from such participation including greater user satisfaction with the physical setting, social-well being, and empowerment (cf. Francis et al., 1987).

At the initial workshop with the SASNC in September 1994, Roberta and Jack presented the notion of participatory design to the SASNC.[9] The coalition members readily agreed, giving their recommendations for the first step: to use images of shopping centers as a means to discuss their preferences. At the next SASNC meeting in October 1994, Roberta and Jack showed slides, selected to represent a wide range of site plans and exterior appearances of shopping centers in Chicago, other U.S. cities, and some other countries. Nearly all were found unacceptable by those few coalition members who chose to be heard, especially Mr. Laramore. He found only one image acceptable, a familiar shopping center from a middle-income African-American community on Chicago's South Side. This was a retail development of large-scale stores fronted by a large parking lot. This center, which Mr. Laramore called "proper," fit his aspirations for the future of the neighborhood.[10] Images of shopping centers of similar scale to the preferred shopping center, but different in design, also were rejected by Mr. Laramore as "not like the way we live here." In contrast, his preference appeared to support his "place identity" – his conception of himself and his community as it relates to a type of place (Proshansky, 1978; Proshansky, Fabian, & Kaminoff, 1983).[11] Jack and Roberta were disappointed. They had hoped that the participants might have chosen more innovative models, but more importantly the scale of the preferred type of center required stores that were substantially larger in square footage than was economically feasible.

At the next participatory design workshop in November 1994, SASNC members were acquainted with the characteristics of the site and gave their input on site design. Jack Naughton was particularly concerned that the coalition members understood the full range of relevant technical

---

9 To lay the groundwork for the participatory workshops, several initial technical tasks were completed, including an examination of the zoning requirements and site analysis to assure that the intended facilities and parking could be accommodated. The property met these requirements.

10 Mr. Laramare and other coalition members also found the photographs of collective markets – a model that could accommodate entrepreneurial opportunities – "messy" "flea markets," where they believed inexpensive, used, and less desirable products are sold.

11 The theory of place identity was first discussed by Proshansky (1978) to extend the explanation of the development of self-identity to include experiences in the physical world. The theory proposes that one of the consequences of an individual's transactions with the multitude of physical settings that compose one's life is the development of relatively enduring conscious and unconscious ideas, feelings, values, and competencies that relate the personal and group identity of that individual to a type of place and provide dispositions for future engagement with the physical world.

information that would impact the design of the site plan. He devised several charts to illustrate this information, including the regulatory and functional requirements (e.g., site coverage, amount of parking, traffic patterns, parking patterns, surrounding land uses, building volumes). Second, three-dimensional kits of parts were used to give participants an opportunity to model the site organization, including locations of buildings, outdoor spaces, and parking.

The turnout for the participatory design workshop was large, with the field house room crowded with the core SASNC members, five other occasional participants, and the key technical assistants. The initial informational presentation did not elicit any input from the SASNC members, who sat silently for the entire first half-hour of the workshop. Sheila Radford-Hill felt that it was "too detailed." Hindsight indicated that it also was too technical. Coalition members became quite animated, however, during the modeling activity, moving the model pieces around the site and garnering comments from all the workshop participants. The modeling activity succeeded not only in eliciting SASNC participants' preferences, but also in evoking positive emotional responses. The technical assistants also appeared enthusiastic during this part of the workshop, offering their preferences as well.

With the information from the November 1994 workshop, Roberta and Jack developed and presented three representative schemes with cost estimates, soliciting feedback at the SASNC's next meeting. A preferred site plan – the plan that included the residents' multipurpose space for youth functions – still prevailed, despite Sheila Radford-Hill's warnings about the financial infeasibility of this alternative.

The modeling task and the resultant physical representation of the shopping center both accomplished the required technical tasks and supported the SASNC's community organizing efforts. It allowed for hands-on participation, engaging the interest of both the SASNC membership and the technical assistants in the project. In the words of one coalition member, "It makes it real." The participatory design workshops may have been particularly compelling because they represented a material expression of the SASNC's development objectives. Jim Chapman described his positive experience:

I really liked that. I liked it a lot.... [I]t was a realistic attempt to try to involve people.... I thought that was terrific. It was an honest attempt to have participation.

Furthermore, for Jim Chapman, the shopping center design, together with the market feasibility study, provided the supportive evidence he needed to make a strong case for a generous settlement. And after 5 years, in 1994, the legal negotiations were at a pivotal point – the motion for summary judgment. Jim explained:

We got that CDBG money right in the middle of [legal] negotiations. . . . [The judge] was bringing us into chambers. . . . Here was a plan and it was priced out. It only enhanced where theoretically I wanted to be. You change the bargaining table. . . . That was my goal. We got to the table. So strategically I was where I wanted to be.

Building Community Support

On the advice of the technical assistants, coalition activists organized several meetings from 1994 to spring 1996 to educate the community about the economic development effort and to build community support for the SASNC and its development goals. It was at these meetings that Wentworth activists again drew upon their social bonding capital in an attempt to involve a larger group of residents in the development process. Through these wider community meetings, attended by 20–100 people, the SASNC activists accomplished what they were most capable of contributing – "getting the people out."

The activists' organizing process, with its attention to relationship building, as always, was time-consuming, painstaking work. For instance, in June 1995, the leadership of the SASNC initiated a concerted effort to acquaint neighborhood residents with the proposed shopping center project and to enlist new participants. The field house meeting room at Wentworth Gardens was filled with 22 people, including the core leadership of the SASNC, several "new faces," and 3 technical assistants. The SASNC leadership had worked energetically to distribute meeting announcements widely to community residents. Marcella Carter was pleased, noting, "The flyer worked!" While waiting for the meeting to begin, Mrs. Carter and Mrs. Amey, as they had in the past, made last minute phone calls encouraging people to attend.

Sharon Washington reported on prior discussions about two proposed fund-raisers – a dance and basketball tournament. Funds were badly needed. The SASNC, operating out of the original RMC office, had built up a debt for their operating costs. The phone company, in particular, threatened to cancel their service.

Mrs. Carter introduced the "guests" – the technical assistants. Sharon Washington thanked everyone for attending, especially the new people, and moved on quickly to the meeting's objectives, evoking the community household metaphor:

We want to inform the community about what the SASNC is working on. [We are] trying to get the community interested in our *home*. . . . Speak to someone. Get them to come out. . . . We can't just build it [a shopping center]. . . . We want to know what you want. When we have a meeting and get out the flyers, tell someone and bring them out.

Sharon next reported on the SASNC's "mini shopping mall" project, first describing the property they were hoping to purchase. She expressed the hope that the owners of the largest parcel, the archidocese, would "give us the land" but noted that the SASNC would still need funds to build the center. Then she described the previously established business committees – the youth, laundry, grocery, and restaurant committees – that needed more volunteers. She explained the future work of the committees. Decisions had to be made concerning the ownership and management structure of center stores: "Do we want limited venture partnerships or have it all to ourselves?" More detailed market information would be required for funding applications and business plans:

We will want to see if it [the shopping center] is feasible, 'cause you can put anything on paper. . . . We will have people [technical assistants] to survey and someone from the committees [needs] to work with them.

And business plans also would be neeeded:

We need to do business plans. . . . How many people would patronize it [stores]? . . . How would we make money off of it?

Last, Sharon distributed sign-up sheets asking for additional volunteers. The lists were passed around, but few people volunteered other than those SASNC members who had previously signed up for the committees. Sharon added her encouragement:

Who's here now that will get on a committee? . . . Mrs. Amey, put your hand down! Does anyone here have experience or just want to learn something about a grocery store, restaurant, laundry? . . . You don't need to know how to run it.

Mrs. Carter reminded Sharon about the SASNC members who were not at the meeting but had volunteered in the past: "They'll still be on it." Sharon continued to press for new volunteers with some success: "Any of these young ladies [pointing to two new people] want to be on a committee?" She offered the volunteers her own and Mrs. Amey's telephone numbers. When the lists were completed, the four committees had three individuals each, including two new volunteers.

Sharon Washington then opened a discussion to brainstorm future fundraising strategies. Steve, one of the younger Wentworth residents present, posed the idea of a sports tournament and then "a talent show or gym show." Another resident suggested selling food. Sharon explained some of the steps involved in planning a successful fund-raiser and suggested an appropriate site – Abbott School.

The meeting ended, with an attempt to raise immediate funds with a request for personal donations. Nearly everyone in the room gave a modest donation – $1.00 was typical. Then, everyone stood and joined hands, while Sharon led the group in the Lord's Prayer, concluding with "It's been a long, long struggle, and I believe he [Jesus] is going to bless us."

Both activists and technical assistants were encouraged by this meeting. Mrs. Amey approached Roberta Feldman with a hug and stated: "Wasn't this meeting something. See those young ones – and them speaking up." She was thrilled that several young Wentworth men, such as Steve, in their late teens and early 20s, had attended and were actively involved during the meeting. Pat Wright also was animated after the meeting, enthusiastically observing, "I really want this [the shopping center development] to happen. I can taste it."

Orchestrating these SASNC meetings was a considerable organizing accomplishment. There were tensions, however, when coalition members were unable to translate their social capital – their "people energy" and "people power" – into the more specific technical tasks required for this economic development effort. At each meeting the same issues – small fund-raising initiatives, efforts to expand the SASNC membership, and efforts to recruit and encourage volunteers to join various working committees, such as the business committees – were raised, with little progress in their actual execution. Attempts by the professional team to expand resident responsibility by requesting assistance in grant writing, business planning, and other technical tasks also were, by and large, unheeded.

Building Real Estate Development Expertise

In spring 1995, Sheila Radford-Hill, who changed her role from community organizer to community development consultant, was hired to work for the Voorhees Center on the development plan. She was concerned that the SASNC members were being asked to participate and assist in economic development planning without adequate skills, in particular, an understanding of the technical information necessary to make critical choices about the shopping center development. An opportunity was presented to fill part of this need and, it was hoped, sustain resident interest. In the 1994 fall participatory design workshops, Craig Wilkins, an African-American architectural educator, was invited by Sheila to acquaint coalition members with real estate development and to elaborate on the schematic design of the shopping center.

During the summer of 1995, Craig offered to hold a series of nine 2-hour seminars to introduce the principles, phases, and participants in the land development process. To encourage interest, Sheila insisted that those individuals who wanted to play a role in the development project, and in particular to serve in a coordinating capacity, "must take the training [with Craig]":

We will then go through an application process of people who have the development training [to choose the coordinator], and the rest will make up the
[development] committee.

At the initial meeting, no questions were raised, seven SASNC members
signed up, and the training sessions were scheduled.

Unfortunately, unlike the participatory design workshops, the training
workshops were not viewed as successful by either the coalition participants, or Craig Wilkins. The seven SASNC activists attended regularly, yet
they did not complete the homework assignments or fully participate in the
seminar sessions. The amount of material Craig sought to introduce was
very ambitious, and the amount of time to learn this complex material was
very short. Perhaps, too, it was not the most appropriate time to introduce
this training; without the necessary funds or property, there was no sense
of urgency to learn about the technical aspects of the development process.

Craig's refinement of the shopping center design, however, was a
success. He resolved many of the disagreements and prior negotiations
between the desires of the coalition members and the technical requirements of the project. Formal innovation was achieved in Craig's proposal
through use of design elements derived from what he called "traditional
African architecture."

He created buildings with flat roofs, clad in modular masonry panels
with exposed beams, decorative tiles, and window openings reminiscent
of some vernacular architecture in Africa.[12] Activists' desires for en-
trepeneurial opportunities were accommodated by appropriately scaled
facilities in a "Community Economic Square" – several small retail facilities
clustered in one structure around a central interior court. In addition, the
resulting scheme included a grocery store, restaurant, and multiuse space
connected to the square. All of the core coalition members and technical
assistants were quite satisfied with his redesign of the center's building exterior, which combined practical considerations with cultural attachments.

NEXT STEPS

Each of the professionals was uniformly committed to keeping the SASNC
active and working toward the shopping center objective over the protracted period required to resolve the lawsuit, but all stressed different
immediate strategies. Sheila Radford-Hill emphasized the need to organize a development team and a completed plan to support the lawsuit, seek
funding, and provide the coalition with the necessary professional support

---

[12] Wilkins's design of the buildings' massing resembled the image and scale of the preferred
shopping center identified in the very first workshop.

FIGURE 7. Upper left: Wentworth's revitalized central courtyard (photographer: Susan Stall). Upper right: Kari Hunt's design for the SASNC's proposed shopping center on Pershing Road and Wentworth Avenue. Bottom: Participatory design workshop showing Wentworth residents creating a model of their design for the shopping center; coauthor Roberta Feldman, workshop facilitator, in upper left corner (photographer: Jack Naughton).

to move the project ahead. Pat Wright wanted to begin entrepreneurial training and business development with coalition members. As did Sheila, Jim Chapman pushed for the completed development plan because it would be very helpful to the lawsuit. He explained that "people often go to court saying they want to do development, but don't have clear plans."

Business Development and Training

Pat Wright consistently encouraged the SASNC to set up business development committees, but her repeated attempts to have them function effectively were unsuccessful. Despite the SASNC members' apparent lack of interest, Pat and her research assistants continued to schedule business committee meetings. Except for the Youth Committee, no business plans were developed or entrepreneurial training pursued.[13] According to Pat:

> People identified themselves with the different ventures, and some people were more attached to the laundromat, restaurant or grocery store. But, whenever we called a [committee] meeting, everybody came.... We never got to that point where we were supposed to do business [plans]... for all those different ventures.... We really never got to the business planning stage. And frankly, when we, I mean, after we did the market study, I was pushing... for them to start going to the Women's Self Employment Project downtown, and I was willing to raise money or even pay out of Voorhees for carfare.[14] And I thought it would be good for them... to do entrepreneurial training in a different setting, instead of it coming to them [at Wentworth].

Pat Wright was unable to expedite business development and training because, Sheila Radford-Hill and Theresa Prim, a business development consultant working on the plan, believed, her efforts were premature. Again, the lack of immediacy of this organizing goal may have been a key impediment to gaining coalition members' interest. Several other issues contributed as well: First, some Wentworth SASNC members experienced a time conflict, especially those who were heavily involved in resident management development (see chapter 10). Second, people who did not have previous for-profit business development experience, such as the coalition members, likely needed more direct guidance; as evidence, the one functioning business committee, the Youth Committee, was more successful because it was "kept going" by a male research assistant from the Voorhees Center.

Expanding the Development Team

In 1995–1996, Sheila Radford-Hill laid the groundwork for the South Armour project development team. In addition to Pat Wright, Teresa Prim and Carol Grant Hall, both business development consultants with the Women's Business Development Center, would work with South Armour neighborhood residents to develop and implement business plans. Also,

---

[13] Over the course of the year, from September 1995 to May 1996, Pat Wright's research assistant, Donna Cavatto, also tried to reactivate the business committees, in particular to support a SASNC business plan that was being developed by the Voorhees Center – "something that they can take to banks" (Donna Cavatto), as well as to pressure the archdiocese and the aldermen. As in the past, little progress was made. The residents' business committees existed on paper but did not function.

[14] The Women's Self Development Project is a Chicago nonprofit created to assist women in small business development ventures.

Melville Wormeley, a principal in a real estate development company, might partner with the coalition in that component of the project. [15]

Sheila kept coalition members abreast of the professional assistants' progress and, at SASNC meetings, asked for their input in developing the plan; however, their input was greatly constrained by technical issues and language. For instance, at a spring 1995 SASNC meeting, after the new development team was introduced to the coalition members present, the professionals' presentation ranged from attracting a "capital partner" and "tax incentives" for real estate developers, to determining how to "maintain an equity while still getting a window on capital" and other similarly technical issues. Roberta Feldman, who attended the meeting, had difficulty following and contributing to the discussion. It is not surprising that the SASNC members also did not raise questions or contribute to this exchange.

The Development Plan

At a September 1995 meeting, Sheila Radford-Hill presented the SASNC with the plan, prepared with the development team, for "their consideration" and "approval." Once again, the technical details were no more understandable than they had been in prior meetings. The attendance was low, but typical, with nearly all of the core SASNC activists and several of the technical assistants present. "Walking them through" the development proposal paragraph by paragraph, Sheila explained that the plan contained two components: real estate development and work force development. She recommended that the SASNC form a subsidiary corporation to handle the development aspects of the project, leaving SASNC to handle the work force development parts. She explained that the development subsidiary "shields assets and liabilities of the SASNC," but "it might make it easier to attract investors. The downside is more work." Sheila went on to describe the role of the SASNC:

> The SASNC will establish a joint venture with a leasing agent [to lease and manage the development]. It will operate as a turn-key. The role of the SASNC is to develop initiatives to maximize the impact. We want stores 'cause we lost stores, but [we also want] to train our people to work in these stores.

Sheila suggested possible sources for the business and entrepreneurial training and for securing of funds for this training.[16] In addition, she attempted to encourage optimism among the coalition members by

---

[15] Except Pat Wright, all of the development team members were African-American.

[16] Business and entrepreneurial training could be accomplished through partnership with groups such as Teresa Prim's Women's Business Development Center and the Retail Development Institute. Funds might come from HUD's STEP UP program.

enumerating the SASNC's organizational strengths to carry out the plan that were noted in the proposal: their strong leadership, stability, community and public sector support, contact with the business community, and effective partnerships with UIC and the Wentworth Gardens RMC.

Sheila concluded that the SASNC had several key decisions to make: "Do you wish to establish a parent corporation? Look for a joint venture partnership? You need to do it." She asked for the SASNC's support for the plan; she needed "to get back to the development team and say we are proceeding." She ended the meeting by describing several "strategic objectives" that the SASNC should pursue to strengthen their capacity to implement the plan. The first task she recommended for the coalition was to "raise equity from the community to show support" by holding community forums and requesting donations of $2.00 to $5.00 with "equity offers." Asked for clarification by a Voorhees research assistant, Sheila explained by providing an example: The SASNC could offer free grocery coop membership in return for the donation.[17] Second, she encouraged the SASNC again to approach the primary property owner of the site, the Archdiocese of Chicago, requesting a subsidy to assist in their purchase of the land. Third, coalition members should speak to the alderman of their ward, Patrick Huels, and Dorothy Tillman, the alderman of the neighboring district, who likely would be more supportive than Huels, to gain support for land acquisition and the necessary infrastructure improvements.

Throughout Sheila's presentation of the plan, no questions were raised; nor were any comments made by any of the coalition members, except Sharon Washington, who had several years of experience as a building manager:

I go along with a separate entity. We need to do that. We also need to deal with various organizations. They've got expertise. . . . We need to meet with them.

Sheila engendered animated discussion in only one instance, when she suggested the need to approach key individuals to request resources, a task the SASNC coalition members understood from past organizing efforts. She stressed that the SASNC, with all the work they accomplished on the development plan, needed to be prepared to make a presentation to the archdiocese, the aldermen, and the funders. This spurred a lively discussion about whether or not the ward aldermen, especially Alderman Patrick Huels, would be supportive. The coalition leadership was hesitant to approach Huels, since, as evident in the White Sox battle, Huels did not view the African-Americans in his ward as his constituency; nor had he been a "friend" in supporting their needs. They appeared more comfortable

---

[17] In the residents' market survey, 71% of the respondents indicated a willingness to participate in cooperative ownership. SASNC members also expressed an interest in cooperative ownership of the stores, especially the grocery store.

in approaching Alderman Tillman, in part because she is an African-American with an established commitment to her African-American constituents, but also because Jim Chapman was an acquaintance of hers; however, Sharon Washington, who volunteered that she knew Huels, offered to contact him.

The Struggle for Organizational and Financial Survival

The SASNC was in a "Catch-22." They required credibility as an organization to garner funding, but many of the indicators that funders use to evaluate credibility related to staff as well as space, and brochures or newsletters – whereas the lack of these elements was the very reason for the SASNC's funding requests. For instance, the SASNC was turned down by the Campaign for Human Development because the coalition had neither staff nor office space, yet the application was for $20,000 to support a full-time project coordinator.[18]

In an attempt to provide continuity of assistance in fund-raising to support the SASNC's immediate development objectives – staff, space, business committees, site procurement, and political support – Pat Wright asked Donna Cavatto, a Voorhees research assistant, to work with the coalition for the academic year, from September 1995 until May 1996. All of these objectives proved to be very difficult to accomplish.

Donna Cavatto's primary task was to assist the coalition to garner additional economic resources from the city government for the training and organizing components of the development project. Pat Wright identified the possibility of empowerment zone funds for business development. The preferred location for the shopping center site was originally suggested by Pat, in part, because it was located in an empowerment zone district, one of several sections of the city identified by the city government for financial development assistance. The empowerment zone proposal was prepared primarily by Donna, although she had made repeated requests for resident assistance at the SASNC meetings. Once again, however, the coalition members could play only a minimal role in the grant proposal preparation because of the highly technical requirements. The proposal, a request for $871,898 over a 3-year period, was submitted to the city by the SASNC in early January 1996 as a Commercial Area Program under the Economic Empowerment Initiative. The proposal drew upon Sheila Radford-Hill's development plan, requesting funds to maximize the economic impact of the shopping center development for South Armour Square residents and to spur neighborhoodwide residential and industrial development. Specifically, funds were sought to build community development

---

[18] The coordinator would assist in neighborhood-based commercial development and the promotion of leadership development and capacity building.

capacity through two programs: first, a Business Development Program to increase resident-owned businesses in the area[19]; second, a Workforce Preparation Program to assure jobs for neighborhood residents through entrepreneurial opportunities, cooperative ownership in a grocery store, and employment in the proposed retail facilities.[20] The empowerment zone funds also would be used to staff positions, including a project coordinator, a community organizer, and a commercial center manager.

Donna Cavatto prepared more modest grant proposals, in particular to fund a full-time staff person for the coalition. Pat Wright was keenly aware that the SASNC needed at least one paid staff position:

[T]he whole idea was for them to score on a grant of any [kind]. . . . I didn't care, just get a couple of thousand dollars together so they could hire a director, well, so that we would have someone to call and work with [the SASNC]. . . . I thought, to do this development we can't do this on all volunteer [basis].

Finally, in 1996, the SASNC was successful in securing two smaller grants from two local foundations, one from the Crossroads Foundation ($5,000), the other from the Peace Fund ($3,000), to hire a part-time staff person. The need for office space, however, was not resolved, but it was discussed, at Donna Cavatto's suggestion, with possibilities for spaces in Wentworth Gardens, including a room in either the old or new RMC office.

Donna also initiated scheduling a meeting with SASNC representatives and Alderman Dorothy Tillman to present the empowerment zone proposal. After 3 months of scheduling attempts, in February 1996, Donna was finally granted an appointment. She and two coalition leaders, Sharon Washington and Mrs. Amey, met with Alderman Tillman, but the meeting

[19] Consultants, Teresa Prim and Associates and Carol Grant Hall and Associates, and the Women's Business Development Center would assist neighborhood entrepreneurs to develop business plans, secure financing, develop marketing plans and pricing strategies, acquire product inventory, and realize sales. Technical assistance would be available to ensure successful business development on an individual basis to local residents. Funding would be used to hire a community coordinator responsible for networking and establishing working relationships with existing area business and development efforts.

[20] The Workforce Preparation Program would operate in conjunction with existing institutions offering job training and development programs to provide neighborhood residents with necessary skills to secure retail employment and ownership. The program would work with the Chicago Housing Authority and local community colleges and schools to provide direct training in retail sales, food service, customer service, maintenance, and security. Joint venture partners would assist SASNC to utilize Empowerment Zone employer tax incentives for hiring local residents trained through these programs. Empowerment Zone funds would be used to secure two job developers and experienced employment and training consultants to work with the SASNC to ensure preparation of local residents for future employment positions.

did not go well. At a SASNC meeting scheduled shortly after the meeting with Tillman, the leadership was clearly angry at the outcome. Sharon (shaking her head):

I have trouble with attitude. I was praying for fortitude and patience. . . . Tillman told us we were backwards; should have gone to her first to get support for the proposal.

From Tillman's vantage point, the coalition had violated political protocol by not approaching her earlier on in their economic development process. Furthermore, the SASNC did not have sufficient organizational credibility. Donna Cavatto commented:

One valid criticism she [Tillman] made was that South Armour [SASNC] needs brochures. Who is SASNC? Who's on the board?"

Marcella Carter reminded everyone that the SASNC had made a presentation to the City Council: "Didn't she remember us from city hall?" Sharon answered, "She said she did remember us, from coming . . . with Jim [Chapman]." Donna concluded, "She'll get back to us when the [review] committee is working on the empowerment zone application." Dorothy Tillman did not get back to the SASNC. The coalition had not organized further to apply pressure on her to support their proposal. Moreover, the coalition did not approach the alderman of their ward, Patrick Huels, because they did not expect his support, irrespective of any pressure they might exert.

Again, the SASNC was trapped in a "Catch-22" Both Alderman Tillman and Alderman Huels might have responded to Alinsky-style tactics, but the SASNC needed the help of a professional community organizer – the role Sheila Radford-Hill played in the White Sox battle – to help them orchestrate these confrontations. After spring 1996, however, Sheila Radford-Hill was no longer employed by the Voorhees Center, she had taken a position as an educational lobbyist with the State of Illinois in Springfield. The SASNC did not have the funds to hire another professional organizer.

Not surprisingly, both the SASNC members and the technical assistants were experiencing discouragement and burnout. The protracted time frame for the effort and the recurrent barriers to their achieving success were substantial. Except in receiving initial CDBG monies, and the two small grants, their inability to garner even small wins in the more modest, interim steps, such as securing the archdiocese property, was disheartening. Even more demoralizing, and ultimately truncating this multiyear organizing effort, would be the dismissal of the lawsuit and the loss of empowerment zone funding.

MAJOR SETBACKS

Over the course of 7 years, from 1989 to 1996, the opponents to the SASNC lawsuit had attempted to have the case dismissed. In the spring of 1996, they succeeded. The grounds for dismissal were particularly disheartening: The case did not have enough merit to go to trial. Moreover, the judge questioned the legal standing of South Armour Square residents even to bring the suit (Ranney et al., 1997). Not only was the lawsuit dismissed, but the conditions the judge established for an appeal would be prohibitively costly for the individual coalition plaintiffs: If, and only if, the plaintiffs waived their right to appeal his decision would the judge relieve them of their responsibility to pay for the defendants' legal fees and other costs in preparing the case, approximately $30,000, personally. Pat Wright was indignant about the injustice of the judge's decision:

[I]t really scared them [the SASNC] not to appeal. And I think that sets a very bad precedent for poor people, people without resources to fight a cause in court.... [T]he [lawyer for the] Illinois Sports Facility [Authority] was following through on this, saying that he disagreed with the judge, that he thought that they should pay. He was still pushing for them to pay the costs of the defense because, you know, they took it to court; so they lost, they should pay.... [T]here was twenty-eight plaintiffs named and they should each pay a $1,000. And so, they were pushing that very hard, and I think that's really dangerous.

Over the next few months there was an exchange of phone calls among the professionals and the SASNC core leadership about whether or not to appeal. Miscommunications and misunderstandings may have diminished the effectiveness of the response.[21] In support of the appeal, Jim Chapman recommended that two new plaintiffs, without assets, were needed to replace the original plaintiffs, especially the Laramores, who were now homeowners and could lose their house. Also, still cognizant of the need for a grassroots display of strength, he stressed the need to have a large enough number of SASNC members go to court for the appeal, at least 15, to attract press coverage. Mrs. Amey agreed to be one of the plaintiffs and appear in court.

On Friday, September 13, 1996, the day of the appeal hearing, the three core professionals, Jim Chapman, Sheila Radford-Hill, and Pat Wright, accompanied Mrs. Amey, Mrs. Mahone, and four young men in their 20s from the Wentworth Gardens Safety Patrol to the court hearing. This was

---

[21] Pat Wright and Sheila Radford-Hill both wanted to appeal. Marcella Carter made attempts to hold a SASNC meeting with Jim Chapman before the deadline for appeal, September 14, 1996, but could not reach him. Jim Chapman finally contacted Pat Wright stating he would like to appeal the decision. He expressed frustration because he believed that the SASNC members did not understand that they could appeal, although the White Sox Corporation and the City of Chicago could countersue.

clearly a much smaller resident representation than Jim had recommended
The request to appeal was denied.

Pat Wright was clearly upset. She ruminated about the lost opportunity
to create an organizing presence in the courtroom and reflected on what
she might have done to prepare better for the hearing:

I didn't really know the significance of Friday's court hearing.... We could have
brought a bus load of people.... [E]veryone should have been there because, for
one thing, it was the end.

Sheila was also distressed:

I was... really angered by the court decision.... I was angered by the judge's
tactic.... [T]he judge cited that we should... feel good because... [of what] the
city and the state had spent on the lawsuit... around 150 million dollars. So I'm
thinking, why should we feel good about that?

Predictably, Jim Chapman, who had invested countless pro bono hours and
tens of thousands of his own dollars in a lawsuit effort he truly believed
in, described the decision as "heartbreaking":[22]

I worked like hell on that thing.... It was a huge undertaking.... I talked to a lot
of witnesses.... And felt I had the basis of a good case.... We had all the racial
data – the history of Armour Park. Their [the Illinois Sports Facility Authority's]
failure to even consider going north. The lies that went on.... We had so much
[evidence].... But I knew the 7th Circuit [Federal Court] wouldn't change.... It
was a very conservative court.[23]

Jim felt somewhat culpable, since he did not push the appeal process
forward more forcibly, but he explained some of his reasoning:

It wasn't my finest hour in retrospect. I couldn't risk the Laramores [losing their
home if the appeal was lost]... I could have done more to appeal it, but I'm satisfied
that I went as far as I did.... I said, "Where am I going?"... If there ever was an
organizing momentum, by that time it had dissipated.... People are tired and are
trying to live their lives. You had the same people leading that group forever. The
same group.... [I] came to the conclusion... What are we fighting for?

The Wentworth activists were clearly frustrated, but they appeared to
be more resigned. Pat Wright recalled the conversation in the car after

---

[22] Jim Chapman had spent $50,000 to $60,000 in pursuing the court case, but he explained
that as a matter of principle he never accepted fees for community groups' legal work. He
did receive approximately $2,000 for investigative research costs related to the discovery
process. For example, SASNC paid him $750 to hire someone to test the sound volume
when the White Sox fireworks went off during home games.

[23] When the lawsuit was first filed in 1989, they went before Judge Rovner, whom Jim
Chapman described as "very fine and sympathetic." During the course of the next few
years, Judge Rovner was replaced by Judge Anderson, whom Jim described as "a very
conservative Reagan–Bush appointee."

the hearing and found one of the young men's comments particularly insightful:

I can't remember if it was Marvin or Bill. . . . The way he said, "Well it's the same old story, the rich against the poor." I mean, you know, just like cutting it right down to what it was all about.

Pat believed that the SASNC leadership were better able to deal with the loss of the lawsuit than she was, because they had more long-term experience with fighting injustices:

[I]n some ways they're used to it. I mean. . . . they're not upset because this is their life. . . . I mean, injustice and fighting, it is so much a part of their lives. . . . I'm sure, in their homes . . .[they are] feeling bad; but they're just so strong. . . . [T]his was just one more day that they fought and lost, and there'll be another day where they'll fight and lose.

Shortly after the appeals hearing, Pat Wright issued the following press release with the hope of encouraging media coverage:

Are Residents Being Silenced by Legal Chaos?
While efforts of westsiders to forge housing agreements near the United Center have won considerable attention, southsiders living in the South Armour neighborhood near the new Comiskey Park continue to struggle in their ongoing legal battle over the relocation of the old Comiskey Park and its impact on housing and local businesses – a battle that began in 1988. Just last week, Judge Wayne Anderson of the U.S. District Court denied a resident's request to appeal his spring decision that said the case did not have enough merit to go to trial. In the spring, Anderson had offered the residents a deal whereby they would waive their rights to appeal and would not have to pay the court costs of the defendants. The residents agreed with the decision, at first. On September 13, Hallie Amey, President of the Wentworth Garden Resident Management Corporation, appealed Anderson's spring decision; he denied her request, suggesting that some people have to suffer for the larger good and having the White Sox play in Chicago is part of the larger good. How convoluted is this case now? Residents currently seek to appeal the judge's decision that they can't appeal. "The judge is basically blackmailing public housing residents, threatening to hold them responsible for the White Sox's legal fees," says Pat Wright of the Center for Urban Economic Development at the University of Illinois. (Press release by Community Media Workshop, "Newstips," September 26, 1996, Columbia College, Chicago, p. 2)

The press release did not result in any media coverage of the appeal decision. It appears that the White Sox battle was old news.

Both Pat Wright and Sheila Radford-Hill continued to be committed to the economic strategy but disagreed whether or not the SASNC should continue to pursue the legal route.[24] It was apparent, too, after the appeal's

---

[24] Sheila Radford-Hill wanted to appeal the verdict, including creating a viable legal defense fund. Pat Wright disagreed for several reasons. She felt the idea of a legal defense fund

hearing, that Jim Chapman, who was getting ready to retire from his practice, was handing the case over to several younger attorneys. Pat was concerned.

I don't think South Armour residents can, you know, continue this fight on their own. It has to be picked up by the ACLU [American Civil Liberties Union] or some comparable defense fund that sees the importance of this case. And I think that's where it has to go at this point.

No individuals and no organization pursued a legal appeal.

Again, in September 1996, the SASNC experienced another significant blow to their efforts. They learned that their empowerment zone proposal was turned down. This loss was puzzling to the coalition, particularly to the professionals. Pat Wright was stunned: "I thought we were gonna get the money. [It] shocked me." Several months before the decision of the City Council, they had been informed by an "internal" source that their proposal received a top ranking from the review panel. At that time it was uncertain whether or not they would receive the full requested amount of $872,000, but Pat was led to believe that despite the proposal's weaknesses – the SASNC's lack of development experience and staff, in particular an executive director – the coalition would be granted $100,000 for initial costs. Subsequently, Wright found out from an "inside" informant that South Armour's ward alderman, Patrick Huels, blocked the approval of the SASNC's proposal.

What Next?

With two tremendous setbacks and only two small grants in hand, the SASNC was faced with the decision about whether or not to continue their efforts to develop a shopping center. Pat Wright, Sheila Radford-Hill, and Mrs. Amey still wanted to pursue the development project. Pat reflected on this decision-making process:

I have had a few conversations with Sheila about SASNC's future. Sheila and Mrs. Amey want to keep it alive to act as the development arm of Wentworth Gardens. I had suggested working everything through the Economic Committee of the RMC as another possibility.... We need to reformulate the empowerment zone proposal and resubmit in the next round.

Other leadership of the SASNC, Marcella Carter and Sharon Washington in particular, had a different opinion. Their views were much more in line with Jim Chapman's belief – that the SASNC's organizing momentum had

was "crazy." The SASNC had not been successful raising money in the past 8 years: "Why do think we're gonna do it now?" She believed that before new lawyers were hired, Jim Chapman should be repaid. Also, Pat was convinced that any SASNC funds "should go into rebuilding the community, not the appeal of the case."

been lost. Speaking for herself and Sharon, Mrs. Carter said that they were "sad" about the negative outcome of the lawsuit and the empowerment zone application, but they had lost all hope that the economic development project would go forward. Instead, they chose to abandon the effort, returning the $8,000 in foundation grant funds the SASNC had received months before. Marcella Carter:

It wasn't going anywhere. We never got an answer from the Archdiocese about the land. Sharon and I met with someone at the Archdiocese but couldn't get an answer. Sharon kept calling.... If you can't get the land, how can you gonna' get a grant [for development].

Increasingly, there were growing tensions among a few of the SASNC's key actors. Hallie Amey was upset that Marcella Carter and Sharon Washington had failed to consult the rest of the coalition members and the technical assistants before returning the funds. Mrs. Amey and Mrs. Carter's relationship had been strained by the SASNC struggle, and the effects had spilled over into other organizing efforts. They had been having disagreements for more than a year over job hiring and placements for the RMC office. Mrs. Carter recognized that Mrs. Amey wanted to pursue the development project through the RMC but disagreed, believing that there was no chance of real movement forward:

Mrs. Amey didn't want to let it go. People don't like to come to meetings and you get nothing done. It's a waste of time.

Mrs. Amey recognized that it was important that SASNC's internal dissension not extend outward and perhaps jeopardize their carefully nurtured social bridging capital with the professionals who had contributed considerable work to these resistance efforts. Exercising her women-centered leadership skills, Mrs. Amey personally called each of the key technical assistants. She apologized for the unilateral decision to end the development efforts and return funds and thanked them for their assistance. In addition, she reassured them that although the SASNC shopping center project was put on hold, it would, in the future, become an economic development project of the RMC.

CONCLUSIONS

What Was Won?

It would be easy to conclude that the legal battle and the strategies to develop the shopping center were a total loss. Not only did the SASNC not raise the funds necessary to begin to rebuild their neighborhood, but it is clear that the individual members were discouraged and frustrated, and, in the end, the internal solidarity of the SASNC coalition broke down. The losses, ultimately, had not been turned into a tangible gain. The SASNC lost their civil rights case and the right to appeal. Even working with a team of experienced professionals, the coalition was unable to garner the necessary, substantial resources to develop the shopping center. Without understating these large losses and their consequences – the lack of retail stores continues to be a substantial burden to the community – there were, however, some small gains for the SASNC as an organization, the Wentworth Gardens community, and its individual members.

The professional assistants noted that the SASNC core members did "hang together" for 8 years despite the formidable obstacles to success. Jim Chapman believed that the legal process "played a positive role in keeping the group together. We changed the site of negotiations to the courtroom" (quoted in Ranney et al., 1997, p. 75). Sheila Radford-Hill observed: "This whole process [of fighting the White Sox stadium] has helped the neighborhood to develop an identity and define a broad economic development program" (quoted in Euchner, 1993, p. 159). When asked what strengths the SASNC contributed, Pat Wright responded: "Tenacity.... Unbridling will.... Bull-headedness. Yeah. I mean, unrelenting spirit to keep going!"

To their credit, the SASNC leadership did experience moderate success, in particular, in their organizing efforts. They were able to garner and expand social bridging capital developed through prior organizing efforts. Both their social bonding and social bridging capital facilitated their successful organization of several community meetings that, if only temporarily, expanded the feelings of community ownership for the proposed development.

In addition, individual coalition members gained some benefits – specifically, the new leadership that was cultivated proved particularly useful for the development of Wentworth's RMC. Pat Wright:

I've seen new leadership like Tecora Butler, for one, who I've seen has grown through this process.... And I think if you look at the RMC Board, a lot of these women weren't on it initially ... and now are. So, there's been I think leadership development through this process.

Jim Chapman also proudly reflected on the way Wentworth women had "grown" as a result of the White Sox struggle. He spoke specifically about Marcella Carter, who was president of the SASNC during their economic development planning. Mentored by Sharon Washington, Mrs. Carter, who was at first "shy" and "uncomfortable speaking in public," now had "so much confidence. She handles herself so easily at public meetings."

Through the initial planning and design of the shopping center, the Wentworth SASNC members gained an elementary understanding of the real estate development process. Pat Wright attested, "I've certainly seen them change and become more understanding of issues." This knowledge became important to Wentworth activists' work toward resident management. The activists effectively administered the market research survey within the Wentworth Gardens community. Moreover, their participation in the development process did shape professional decision making about both the design and the facilities, especially the youth facility, in the proposed shopping center development.

Finally, within the Wentworth community, there was one tangible and prominent result of their legal strategy and their relationship with individuals like Jim Chapman – a major physical improvement to their development. The City of Chicago landscaped Wentworth's central courtyard area in the summer months of 1996. Jim Chapman is certain that this was a direct result of a petition presented and testimony given to the Chicago Park District Board. In the course of his fact finding for the lawsuit, Jim had discovered the tremendous inequities in recreational facility and grounds between the racially segregated Armour Park field house and the vastly inferior field house at Wentworth Gardens:

I presented a lengthy petition to the Park Board and brought about 15 people, including Hallie Amey and everybody. . . . That was a separate issue [from the lawsuit], but to me it was all part of the struggle. We presented it – a good documented petition. . . . I documented [the racism]. . . . It was like a lawyer's petition. . . . and then the testimony. . . . Hallie got up and said, "I know you'll do the right thing by us. . . . " She'd been on this issue since the 1970s. . . . Within minutes it seemed like – it was probably a few days – the world descended on this park [Wentworth's central courtyard] in direct response to what we'd said. It was the City. They had crews come from all over. It's how tight organizations respond. . . . In their own way they'll often respond to pressure. We may have been there twice to their Board hearing and got on their agenda. . . . Whatever happened it happened as a direct result [of the petition]. . . . It was very concrete. It is one of the few causes and effects I can point to.

Once a dilapidated and desolate area, Wentworth's central courtyard now had picnic areas, playground equipment, and basketball courts. Marcella Carter reflected on the contradictory nature of this material gain, wisely noting:

Isn't it really funny that, you know, how they [the City] just want to give us everything instead of just going and giving us the money and say we won the lawsuit. They don't want to say we won that lawsuit, do they?

For Mrs. Amey, this too was a bittersweet victory. She noted that the residents had no say in the types of improvements the development needed most; nor did they have a say in the design of the playground.

Why the SASNC Failed

The Wentworth women activists' attempt to enter the white, male-dominated world of economic development, sustained by political power, money, and control of property, ultimately was thwarted. Why did the SASNC fail in their efforts?

Certainly, the lack of political support, especially access to sympathetic elected officials who might have acted on the behalf of the SASNC in the larger political arena, was one of the most formidable impediments to the shopping center development When questioned about the SASNC's greatest obstacle, Pat Wright and Jim Chapman did not hesitate to respond. Pat:

[T]he political situation, frankly . . . the racism . . . that really destroyed their community to begin with because they were vulnerable and isolated. They could go in there . . . [and] tear stores down and without much outcry citywide.

Jim Chapman shared that the racism of the local "Democratic regime" was even worse than he had initially realized and agreed with Pat that the political obstacles were daunting:

I think there were forces at work that didn't want that [the shopping center] to be there. . . . I think there are forces at work that want Wentworth out of there. And so they're not going to make it easier for them to stay there.

The SASNC was unable to garner the political support that might have assisted them in raising the required public capital to replace the stores. Neither the professionals nor the coalition had sufficient bridging social capital that could be leveraged with politicians and public agency representatives who might influence the outcome of the lawsuit and empowerment zone grant. Sheila Radford-Hill, in retrospect, believes that expectations for political support were unrealistic, observing, "It [SASNC] just didn't have the [political] support, especially the necessary support of the mayor and alderman." As in the past, the ward alderman, Patrick Huels, did not support his African-American constituency in their empowerment zone application, and Alderman Dorothy Tillman, who questioned the organizational legitimacy of the SASNC, eventually secured development monies for her own 3rd Ward constituents.

The failure to win the lawsuit and the empowerment zone grant left the coalition without any other likely public funding options. Pat Wright believed that the activists could have accomplished the business and economic development plan had they only had the economic resources:

I think they have what it takes. . . . I mean they know what they want, they just need the money. I mean, resources for God's sake. . . . [T]hey would know how to spend that money . . . and, I'm sure begin to negotiate, to buy the land. . . . [I]t's not gonna be so easy, but they know what they want, they just don't have the resources to do it.

The SASNC's modest fund-raising successes obviously were insignificant compared with funds needed even to hire an ongoing full-time staff member to oversee the organizing effort for the project. Sharon Washington:

It's the fundraising that kills us – nothing we can see that makes enough money to be worth the work. . . . That's when we really started to get depressed.

The amount of economic resources required was too great, and the funding opportunities to realize the large costs of the shopping center project were too few. The SASNC was not in a position to benefit from other city programs that could have drawn public and private capital into their community because the South Armour Square neighborhood was not in a geographic area immediately slated for city revitalization efforts.[25]

The SASNC's organizational capabilities to orchestrate a major economic development initiative successfully were hampered by their lack of experience and legitimacy in this arena. The SASNC was not a community development corporation, with the advantages of professional staff and greater access to foundation and governmental funding resources to support development activities. Writing from his own firsthand experience with grassroots community development efforts, Randy Stoecker (1995) observed, "Doing development correctly . . . required massive attention to technical detail, which was hard with volunteer labor" (p. 18). Pat Wright also recognized similar difficulties with the SASNC's reliance on volunteers, rather than professional staff:

[M]ost of the other groups, if not all of the other groups I worked with are not volunteer organizations. They're community development corporations. They have professional staff. . . . I'm working with professional staff that have a community board. . . . And in this situation [with the SASNC], I'm working directly with the residents.

The professionals, as well as their research assistants, did the best they could to involve the coalition leadership in organizing themselves around the technical and political tasks, but they were largely unsuccessful. Although the SASNC had effective organizers in their membership, the technical requirements and language of the real estate development plan and empowerment zone proposal clearly exceeded the capabilities of the coalition's leadership. The development tasks that were accomplished were at the insistence of or, most often, through the work of the professional team. The technical assistants – not the activists – defined the business and development planning objectives. It was unclear whether or not the activists fully supported these objectives, because the activists did not make their

[25] The SASNC may have been premature in their objectives. In 15 years or so from the date of the loss of the lawsuit, when an area adjacent to Wentworth Gardens, Fuller Park, currently targeted by the city for economic and real estate development subsidies, is redeveloped, the city then may support a shopping center development in the area.

beliefs known. Although it is likely that they trusted the assistants to work on their behalf, they also were also highly dependent upon the goodwill and technical expertise of the professionals who were contributing much of their time.

The professionals often were forced, by the elaborate and time-sensitive requirements of the legal and the development process, to push ahead, with or without the residents. Again, Stoecker (1995) warned, when community organizations engage in community development they must "make complex decisions with dispatch, which inhibits community education and democratic debate" (p. 6). Both Jim Chapman and Pat Wright understood that they were, in Jim's words, "moving ahead of the SASNC," in particular in the preparation of a development plan, yet supported the effort anyway. Jim reflected on the whole White Sox organizing effort:

> Remember you are dealing with the exigencies of the moment. You're trying to develop something. . . . [Referring to the period after the SASNC homeowner – renter split] There was too much trying to be done in too short of a time in dealing with emergency situations. Boom, boom, boom! That's really part of a philosophy of the enemy. They can move quickly.

Additionally, particularly challenging for both the professionals and the coalition was the protracted time frame of the lawsuit. Jim Chapman:

> So when the lawsuit got to a certain point, then Pat [worked on the development plan]. . . . That type of organization, education and development . . . these problems took decades and centuries to make and we're not going to unwind them in this short time period. We're dealing with a well-oiled adversary. And it would have taken years.

Despite the technical assistants' best intentions, they could not give their full, continuous effort to the project; as a result, technical assistance was uneven over the several years of the development effort. Recall that one key adviser, Sheila Radford-Hill, changed her role from community organizer to economic development planner and then had to leave Chicago to take a job downstate. Most of the long-term technical assistants were volunteers, who also were engaged in other pressing professional demands on their time. Jim Chapman spoke about "the human toll," about feeling "empty and tired," since he was trying to keep a busy law practice going at the same time as he provided pro bono legal counsel for the SASNC. Some of the technical assistants, in particular the research assistants and those hired to work on the development team, understandably did not have a long-term commitment to the South Armour community.

For the coalition members, sustaining an organizing effort throughout the 7 years of the lawsuit was a daunting task. Whereas the technical assistants believed that working on the shopping center would engage SASNC activists and others in development activities, in reality, for most residents the shopping center remained an abstraction. The work of development "does not generate the level of interest and unity that organizing against a common enemy does" (Stoecker, 1994); also, it requires unlimited time and energy (Stoecker, 1994), is challenging, and can readily lead to frustration and burnout. Among the remaining SASNC core activists, the Laramores were no longer residents of Wentworth, and Sharon Washington held a full-time job at the adjacent T. E. Brown Senior Apartments. For the Wentworth activists, further involvement would have meant withdrawing effort from their other concurrent activist initiatives – the women-centered organizing efforts described previously – and the time-consuming work Wentworth activists were engaged in, concurrently, to become resident managers. Even before the SASNC's last two major losses, Mrs. Amey implied that such a commitment to sustained community organizing support for the development effort would be difficult to make without a surer outcome:

[We] will get the community organized if and when this [the lawsuit and empowerment zone grant] comes through. I know we can do it.

Mrs. Amey is suggesting that the organizing effort may not have been inadequate; rather, it was postponed.

Ultimately, the residents also needed to muster enough strength to place the lever on the legal fulcrum and push. Despite the professionals, all of whom had experience working with Alinsky-style organizers and had no scruples about yanking any lever they could find to attract public attention and political legitimacy, this did not happen. Alinsky-style confrontational organizing would have complemented and strengthened their negotiating position in the larger political and economic arenas in which they were operating. The archdiocese was a vulnerable target because of a history of donating church property to other social service and community organizations. Both Alderman Patrick Huels and Alderman Dorothy Tillman also operate in a political arena that responds to those constituents who appear to wield power. Jim Chapman had suggested that an Alinsky-style petition drive would show such power: "Any alderman pays attention to 1000 signatures." Moreover, incremental organizing challenges might have mustered more resident involvement and resulted in the type of visible win needed to sustain greater grassroots involvement in the extended development effort. Again, the lack of an available pro bono professional community organizer, as there was in the White Sox battle, hampered the coalition's attempts to extort concessions from the archdiocese and alderman.

In reality, the technical assistants as well as the SASNC activists were pragmatists, doing the best they could within a less than perfect political and economic structure and with less than optimal organizational capacities. They accepted the imperfect fit because it afforded an opportunity to address a bitter injustice and to provide needed stores and jobs for the South Armour Square neighborhood.

What Can We Learn?

Affordable, safe, and decent shelter has remained a central objective for public housing revitalization; now calls for economic opportunities also are being voiced. Along with good intentions, public housing residents require substantial professional and economic resources to engage in real estate and business development. As do all who do not have economic development experience, Wentworth activists needed ongoing professional assistance to guide them through the steps of creating a development plan and accessing sources of economic support to build and manage the development.

The importance of access to and effective use of technical assistance to implement economic development objectives in poor communities cannot be underestimated. For instance, Monti (1989) reported on community development projects at Cochran Gardens in Saint Louis, perhaps the most recognized economic development undertakings involving a public housing development, noting that a legal aid "ally" was central to the success of these ventures.[26] Operated by a Tenant Management Corporation (TMC) since the 1970s, Cochran Gardens activists, like those at Wentworth Gardens, had accomplished several on-site service initiatives to meet the everyday needs of their tenants, including a janitorial service, day care, and meals for the elderly and young. A legal aid lawyer who had assisted Cochran Gardens activists in their struggle for improved housing conditions and, ultimately, in the attainment of tenant management of their development, aided the TMC in parlaying their prior service projects into a maintenance company and a food catering service. This lawyer "ally" also was central to the TMC's most ambitious community development venture: a housing development project in the surrounding DeSoto–Carr neighborhood. He established a for-profit development company to build market-rate units in the neighborhood, returning some of the profits to the TMC. According to Monti: This lawyer–developer was "a great believer in sharing the profits as well as the risk in these projects with the local people who [had] made the neighborhood safe for his company's success" (p. 302). The housing development project also was successful because the highly regarded developer was able to acquire bank and investor financing, as well as city support in the amount of $4 million to subsidize the

---

[26] It is noteworthy that profits the TMC earned from these development activities were used to offset an inadequate management budget provided by the local housing authority. The limitations of these findings are also noteworthy; that is, these projects have failed to translate into jobs for the tenants (Monti, 1989). In addition, although several dozen residents could have been employed at both Cochran Gardens and Carr Square, another Saint Louis public housing site Monti (1989) studied, jobs often went to outsiders because residents are not qualified, and some of those residents who are qualified find higher-paying employment.

development costs and to make street and open space improvements in the area (i.e., park and tennis courts). Similarly, in the reported instances of economic development efforts at other public housing developments elsewhere in the United States, outside resources and technical assistance have been essential to the effectiveness of such initiatives (reviewed in Monti, 1989).[27]

The professionals assisting the SASNC in their development effort understood the activists' limited technical know-how. It was their intention, as Stoecker (1995) advocated, "to organize to guide development rather than to be developers. According to Pat Wright:

> We were proposing for them [SASNC] to do a very complex, major development. But, you know, we were always assuming that they would get a court settlement and we'd be able to hire the expertise. I mean, Sheila always used the car as the example. We're not asking them to . . . build a car; we're gonna give them the car to drive and they'll be in charge of driving it. . . . They just have to be in charge of the decision making and policies related to driving the car.

Perhaps even more damning, economic development is a well-intentioned idea but is difficult to implement "in the field" because of another Catch-22: Attempts at economic development serve to reify the class inequities in real estate and business development. They require expertise and monies poor communities do not have, especially communities headed by low-income minority women. In addition, as other researchers and our own findings document, women involved in community economic development face barriers that are more gender-specific. These obstacles can include the lack of freedom to ignore their domestic responsibilities, the unavailability of child care, and "feelings of powerlessness" – expressed concerns that they have limited experience and are not adequately trained. In the community development field there is a perception that women do not have the necessary skills, and therefore they are treated differently than men. Finally, women who work in female-led community development corporations report marginalization by financial institutions, politicians, funders, and even male-led development corporations (Gittell et al., 1999, pp. 116–117).

Despite the proliferation of community development corporations and their contributions to low-income communities, the emphasis on economic development may be misguided. Stoecker (1995) argues that the community economic development process challenges grassroots democracy,

---

[27] Clark (1993) also noted the importance of outside resources, including technical assistance, to the success of an assisted cooperative housing program in New York City. A city program funded squatters in abandoned buildings to form cooperative ownership organizations and rehabilitate and manage the buildings. Co-op leaders' abilities to garner and constructively use technical assistance and training programs contributed to the success of the co-op effort.

since "it requires money, expertise, and political power that is controlled by the few who set the conditions under which development can occur" (p. 17).[28] Ranney, Wright, and Zhang (1997) concur, describing how community economic development favors larger, more established private developers[29]:

[T]he complexity of decision making in the local development decision making process becomes a formidable obstacle to citizens with equity concerns. The aspect of the complexity that offers the greatest obstacle is the conjuncture between its formal institutional and its informal political aspect. The array of financing arrangements and local government jurisdictions means that different governments with different interests have stakes in specific local developments.... This offers a special advantage to development interests whose money, influence and know-how can break through the complexity. In essence there is a strong class bias built into the development process. (pp. xiii-xiv)

Wentworth women activists lost their battle because of the inherent class inequities in the economic development process, yet some urban theorists would argue they may have lost even more: The protracted time of their effort, the amount of funds required, and its legal and technical requirements might have negatively impacted their other organizing efforts (Stoecker, 1995; see also Stoecker, 1997). These arguments, however, are not informed by feminist theorists' recognition of the constancy of community-based women's attention to the social reproduction needs of everyday life and the empowerment and skill building that emanate from these activities (e.g., Bookman & Morgen, 1988; Haywoode, 1991). Grassroots activist efforts were never dismantled at Wentworth Gardens. As other low-income women of color, Wentworth resident activists did not allow the protracted real estate and business development initiative to overshadow or destroy their other essential, ongoing organizing efforts to sustain the viability of their housing development. In fact, their concurrent efforts to become resident managers of their public housing development may ultimately strengthen their abilities to engage in economic development, as resident management corporations have the best track record of economic development initiatives within public housing (Center for Community Change, 1994; Caprara & Alexander, 1989).

[28] The SASNC's lack of government financial support was particularly poignant when considering that a large portion of the White Sox Corporation's development capital was from state and city governments' subsidies.

[29] Ranney et al. (1997) further point out that the rise of community development corporations has been necessitated by both the class inequities apparent in U.S. governmental decision processes and the government's withdrawal from direct provision of social services for the poor (e.g., affordable housing). They suggest a more direct approach than economic development: requiring various governments, at the federal, state, and local levels, to become more democratic by generously financing vital local services.

10

Becoming Resident Managers

A Bureaucratic Quagmire

> Mr. Vince Lane [then director of CHA] came ... for a community meeting that
> we [Wentworth Gardens Residents United for Survival] had called together
> because of the problems we was having in our community.... Mr. Lane went
> to Miss Driver and said, "Miss Driver, I want you to go into RMC." And
> Miss Driver was our LAC President at the time, and she said, "No, I do
> not want to be bothered with no RMC...." After the meeting was over ...
> Miss Amey said, "Miss Harris, what can we do? Can we do it?" I said, "We
> can do it." I say, "Miss Driver, is it okay? She said, "If you all wanna' be
> bothered with it, go ahead." And so we went into our training. We started
> to going downtown to get [negotiate] our contract ... for the RMC. And we
> went to meetings.... We worked to nine, ten, eleven o'clock at night. But
> Miss Driver is right there with us. She did come. She said she would help us
> if that's what we wanted to do.... When we finished that contract, she sent
> it to Washington. The day she [Miss Driver] died was the day ... they [CHA]
> came over ... to tell us that we was accepted as a RMC.... That was sad, you
> know. Miss Driver had died and she never knew that we finished it; that we
> was accepted.... We thought we could manage ourselves better than CHA.
> Our objective was to make Wentworth a safe and decent place to live.
>
> Mrs. Beatrice Harris

In Chicago, in the 1980s, CHA and other prominent Illinois and Chicago political actors were promoting HUD's resident management program with
promises of financial and technical support. Seven CHA developments
decided to take advantage of the HUD program; Wentworth Gardens
was one.

Wentworth activists chose to apply for the HUD resident management
program as a means to resist government disinvestment in their homeplace.
They believed it was the only option they had to improve living conditions
and have some level of control over displacement from their development.[1]

---

[1] Of the activists we interviewed (23) and vocal participants at the RMC meetings we observed, 15 volunteered that they supported resident management of Wentworth because

Many of the Wentworth activists, such as Beatrice Harris, also believed they were in the best position to know what was needed, hence, would be the best managers. The Wentworth resident Juanita Brown explained this sentiment:

I feel that the RMC is gonna clean up things. Put us back on the road of recovery. See, Wentworth has become an ill house.... I would like to see the community back like it used to be ... or better, you know.... I feel like if we had some of the residents in, like managers ... they live here; they knows what goes on here.... Whereas if you don't live here, you don't know what's going on. As a matter of fact, you don't care what's going on.

Hallie Amey believed that they had nothing to lose – CHA on-site management at Wentworth had been downsized and was as inadequate as ever:

[W]e just got to take the chance. Because we feel, we can't do any worse. It has gotten to that stage. 'Cause in our management office now, we have two people [compared with six in the past]. A manager and one clerk. Now you know not very much can get done.

The Wentworth leadership claimed that they would not have sought resident management had the CHA properly managed their development. Gloria Seabrook, the training liaison to Wentworth from the CHA Department of Resident of Management and Opportunity, explained the dilemma as follows:

[T]here wasn't a good [CHA] manager. But if Wentworth could get a good [CHA] manager.... and kick down doors and get rid of these bad folks [noncompliant tenants].... And get some money to make these maintenance [repairs] ... they [Wentworth activists] would be happy.... You know, they really don't need this headache.... It's a big headache.... They don't care who runs it. They want to see it run [properly].

The resident leadership not only was concerned about proper management and improved living conditions; they believed Wentworth's very survival was dependent upon attaining resident management of their development. At a CHA conference organized for Chicago RMC offficers, Mrs. Amey emphasized their plight:

You're only two cents away from homelessness.... It's the only way you will save your housing, your communities. (Field notes, September 23, 1996)

it was the only means to improve the development. Of these 15 activists, 4 also believed that it was the only way to save Wentworth from eventual demolition; 2 of them believed that residents were in the best position to know what was needed for their development, hence would be the best managers; and 2 others argued that HUD was getting rid of their responsibility to manage public housing either by turning developments over to private management or by obliging residents to manage their own developments.

Other Wentworth activists agreed, for instance, Desiree Davis: "See how they [CHA] are tearing down other developments. We don't want them doing it to us." Wentworth activists' most trusted professional consultant, Sheila Radford-Hill, concurred.

When called upon by Mrs. Amey, Carol Deamer of the Lindeman Center, Northern Illinois University, provided technical assistance to incorporate the Wentworth Gardens Resident Management Corporation (RMC) and apply for the HUD program. In 1989, Wentworth Gardens RMC gained HUD's approval to participate in the public housing resident management program. They were granted $100,000 for resident training and technical assistance to create an RMC board and the required policies and procedures for resident management. Receiving this grant and fulfilling these requirements, however, did not assure that they would obtain a resident management contract with the local housing authority. To create a resident-managed development, activists would have to negotiate with bureaucrats in two powerful bureaucracies – CHA and HUD. Remarkably, Wentworth activists engaged in this protracted effort simultaneously with their struggles to stop the White Sox stadium construction and subsequently to develop the shopping center. Once again, Wentworth activists transgressed the boundaries of their homeplace to mobilize strategically and engage in intense negotiations with powerful public sphere actors to garner the rights and the assets needed to manage their development.

Although HUD provided the economic and material resources to pursue resident management status, they were not "free for the taking"; rather, the activists would have to work within the system to take advantage of the program. In particular, HUD required that the activists develop a bureaucratic organization with the attendant structures and procedures. As Stephanie Riger (1984) observed, bureaucratic organizations are impersonal, valuing efficiency of operations over the talents, needs, and growth of the members. Decision making is based on centralized power, a rational division of labor, and rigid rules and regulations, rather than a collective structure held together by close relationships and a sense of solidarity among participants, in which power is shared equally. Hierarchical organizational structures create inequalities of power that "can be dispiriting" (p. 105) or ultimately destructive for people seeking close personal ties and strengthening communal bonds. These bureaucratic organizational structures and processes do not value, and could possibly overwhelm, Wentworth activists' key organizational strengths – their collective practices and women-centered organizing efforts.

The Wentworth activists faced a dilemma. In order to become resident managers, they were required to comply with HUD-mandated regulations and work within a bureaucratic framework that would determine the RMC's organizational structure and practices. Yet, in order to sustain their collective practices and values – their community household, social reproduction activities, and ethic of care – Wentworth activists also would need to resist these bureaucratization processes. Daniel Monti (1989), in his evaluation of the implementation of an earlier HUD resident management program, recognized this conflict: "There is a tension built into an RMC. It must work like an efficient business even as it nurtures its communal roots" (p. 193) (see also Peterman, 1993; Saegert & Winkel, 1996; Clark, 1993).[2] He found that although no RMC he observed totally accomplished reconciling these tensions, those RMCs that failed were unsuccessful because:

> The primary strength and weakness of RMCs is that they are drawn simultaneously in two different directions. On the one hand, they are a communal group that works hard to keep its members behaving properly and together. On the other, they are a business organization overseeing a multimillion dollar real estate development. It is difficult enough to do one of these tasks well. (p. 193)

In this chapter we examine the tensions resulting from the forced compliance with CHA's and HUD's imposed bureaucratic structure and practices to become an RMC and the Wentworth activists' resistance to these requirements to sustain their collective practices and values. We will conclude first by examining the impact of these tensions on their organizational empowerment. We will end by introducing the theoretical conceptualization of transgressive resistance to interpret the activists' struggles to manage their development. To place Wentworth activists' efforts in a national context, we begin with an overview of resident management in U.S. public housing over the course of its brief history – from the earliest tenant management organizations that grew out of protracted grassroots struggles to the then-current government sponsored program that emphasized, at least rhetorically, resident empowerment.

RESIDENT MANAGEMENT IN ITS HISTORIC CONTEXT

Resident management, originally called *tenant management*, began in the 1960s in "what can be described as acts of desperation" (Peterman, 1993,

---

[2] Peterman (1993) described the difficult challenge of properly balancing community organizing and residents' managing of their public housing development: "They [RMCs] must have the support of the residents and work to build the social and economic character of the community. But at the same time they must collect rents, keep the grounds clean, and discipline misbehaving tenants. If these two roles are not properly balanced, RMCs can stumble and ultimately fail" (p. 164). Clark (1993), in her analysis of low-income-housing co-op members, also observed the necessary balance in responding to technical requirements of building management – "building managers, loan providers, lawyers, the courts, tax collectors and suppliers" (p. 137) – and responding to shared community values in making decisions about site and building improvements, resident policies, and everyday housing management. She found that the most successful housing cooperative maintained this balance.

p. 162).[3] Housing authorities across the United States were raising rents to pay for increases in operating costs, while public housing conditions were becoming increasingly deplorable (Meehan, 1979; The National Center for Neighborhood Enterprise, 1989). In protest, resident rent strikes in Boston and St. Louis forced local housing authorities to consider management alternatives. With considerable financial and technical assistance from the federal government, residents of Bromley-Health in Boston in 1971, and five St. Louis developments, the most well known, Cochran Gardens in 1976, assumed resident management of their housing[4] (Fuerst, 1988; Meehan, 1979; The National Center for Neighborhood Enterprise, 1989; Peterman, 1998).

The apparent, but unsubstantiated positive outcomes of St. Louis and Boston residents' struggles for tenant management provided the incentive for HUD to form a collaboration with the Ford Foundation to sponsor a National Tenant Management Demonstration Program (Meehan, 1974). With the conservative presidential 1973 moratorium on new construction of public housing, proponents argued that tenant management offered the promise of a lower-cost and better form of management (Meehan, 1979). In 1976, HUD committed to a 3 year demonstration program at 7 sites in 6 cities nationwide.

The Manpower Demonstration Research Corporation (1981), which assisted in both the demonstration program implementation and its evaluation, concluded that tenant management sites performed as well as, yet not significantly better than, conventionally managed sites, but tenant management was more costly – 13% to 62% higher – because of the additional financial costs for resident training, employment, and technical assistance.[5] There were other serious shortcomings, including tensions between the

[3] Resident management of public housing in the United States has had a short history. Unlike Europe, the United States has had little experience with alternatives to conventional local housing authority management (Monti, 1989).

[4] Resident leaders at Boston's Bromley-Heath development, experienced in organizing to improve social and health services at their development, called for a rent strike that lasted for years (Meehan, 1979; The National Center for Neighborhood Enterprise, 1989). Ultimately, the resident leaders proposed to take over their development's property management in 1969 and secured a contract in 1971 (Peterman, 1998, 1998). In Saint Louis, tenant management grew out of the settlement of the 1969 rent strikes and organized tenant protests that propelled the local housing authority to bankruptcy and reorganization. Over the next 5 years, with financial assistance from the Ford Foundation, tenants' organizations in five Saint Louis developments assumed management of their housing: Carr Square, Darst, Clinton Peabody, Webbe, and Cochran Gardens (Meehan, 1979; The National Center for Neighborhood Enterprise, 1989; Peterman, 1998).

[5] In 1983, the National Association of Housing and Redevelopment Officials (NAHRO) sponsored Robert Kolodny, an enthusiastic supporter of tenant management, to write a follow-up report on these four sites. Kolodny challenged the Manpower Demonstration Research Corporation's (MDRC's) findings about cost and feasibility. He pointed out that MDRC's calculations included modernization and operating expenses that he believed would have incurred without resident management (Chandler, 1991).

paid staff and unpaid volunteer board, nepotism and favoritism, political antagonism between on-site residents' organizations, and apathy of the general resident population. On the other hand, some benefits did result from these expenditures: resident employment, a sense of personal development among tenant managers, and increased general resident satisfaction. Ultimately, the Manpower Demonstration Research Corporation recommended against expansion of the program. By the mid-1980s, all but one development in the demonstration project reverted to housing authority management (Monti, 1989; Peterman, 1993).

Despite an apparent lack of long-term viability, resident management was championed in the 1980s by conservative policymakers and politicians. Resident management was being touted as a means to instill responsibility among public housing residents, while decreasing if not eliminating the federal government's involvement in public housing (Peterman, 1993, 1998). The National Center for Neighborhood Enterprise (NCNE), a politically conservative think tank became the principal proponent of resident management, equating it with resident empowerment. According to the NCNE,

Resident management is an empowerment process that places the responsibility for improving the quality of life in public housing properties into the hands of those who live there.... (NCNE, 1989, p. 1)

With a sizable grant from the Amoco Foundation, NCNE developed a resident management support program in 11 resident-managed public housing family sites. An independent evaluator of the program, Daniel Monti (1989), found that resident management corporations were not necessarily successful; rather, effectiveness was contingent upon, most importantly, good community organizing; strong leaders and an assertive board; adequate and continuing funding for operating subsidies, modernization, and technical assistance; and buildings and sites that were in good physical condition.

Irrespective of the short-lived successes of most of the demonstration projects, and the mixed findings from prior studies, the NCNE was instrumental in the passage of the resident management provision of the federal 1987 Housing and Community Development Act (Peterman, 1993, 1998). Formal procedures were set up to establish RMCs in public housing developments nationwide. A subsequent evaluation comparing RMCs with traditionally managed public housing developments again showed mixed findings and did not add any clarity to the costs and benefits (ICF Inc., 1992).

By end of 1992, growth of RMCs was modest: Three hundred resident groups were receiving some form of development and training assistance; of these, 27 had achieved some level of resident management responsibility (Peterman, 1998). Of the seven Chicago public housing family developments with RMCs in preparation, only one, LeClaire Courts, had achieved full resident management by the end of the 1980s.

WENTWORTH ACTIVISTS' ORGANIZATIONAL CAPACITY FOR RESIDENT MANAGEMENT DEVELOPMENT

Wentworth's activists were well positioned to take advantage of HUD's resident management program. Their homeplace, although physically deteriorating, was a stable community; because of both activists' years of community-building work, and the number of long-term residents. This was certainly Gloria Seabrook's impression when she first met with the Wentworth residents, as a CHA general manager, in 1990. Mrs. Seabrook shared:

I always liked Wentworth because it seemed that it could be made into an ideal community...into a place where everybody will wanna live. Everybody does wanna live there.... [I]t's a very stable community. It's probably one of the most stablest communities we [CHA] have, in terms of longevity for residents.

Wentworth's capacity for resident management development also was recognized by the then-director of CHA, Vincent Lane, who was aware of some of their accomplishments.[6] They had a respected history of effective organizing and leadership that they could mobilize and commit to the resident management effort. The CHA liason, Gloria Seabrook, agreed that resident management was a "natural" extension of Wentworth activists' other place-based efforts to improve their homeplace:

This Board is doing more than any other [CHA resident management] board. I mean [they operate] their own laundromat. They're running their own grocery store. They're out here knocking on doors, getting money. They're meeting with Armour Square.

Wentworth activists also had experience negotiating with bureaucrats and satisfying bureaucratic requirements. They had to fill out and submit complex and technical application forms to garner outside resources and to comply with often enigmatic and complicated reporting rules about how the resources were used. In taking advantage of CHA programs and services, Mrs. Harris and others met many bureaucratic requirements, for example, creating a system of report forms and letters of permission from parents for youth field trips.

The women residents had cultivated skills and competencies over decades of activism that, according to empowerment researchers, are

---

[6] The Wentworth activists' reputation preceded them. Both Wentworth resident representatives and Vincent Lane participated in the Women and Safe Shelter Conference at UIC in the spring of 1986 (see Preface). Mr. Lane had also witnessed their organizing capabilities when he attended a successful communitywide event that the Wentworth residents organized in fall 1988. Sponsored by the RAID pesticide corporation, this event, attended by both authors, was a true testament to the activists' abilities to take a minimal contribution of funds and food items and expand them to create a developmentwide community-building, celebratory occasion.

critical components of organizational empowerment: the ability to work
with those in power (e.g., on-site management, the local housing authority);
success in gaining a modicum of resources to meet their social reproduction
needs; experience in bottom-up pressure for participation in the political
decision-making processes and some understanding of the sociopolitical
environment they were confronting; a shared, common purpose to secure
their development and make it make a safe and decent place to live; and a
broadly, encompassing support system that both sustained a sense of community within Wentworth and attracted needed technical assistance from
outside Wentworth. (Feldman & Westphal, 2001; Maton & Salem, 1995;
Westphal, 1999; Zimmerman, 1995).

The activists were guided by strong, committed resident leaders. Hallie
Amey and Beatrice Harris were both important actors in seeking participation in the HUD resident management program; but it was Mrs. Amey
who was key in providing the guidance to mobilize around and sustain the
effort to gain full RMC status. In her work with the residents, Mrs. Seabrook
observed: "Miss Amey is the motivator. She is the drive in that community." She also gave recognition to the other activists' roles; in particular
Mrs. Harris's, through the LAC, as the liaison with CHA: "Now Miss
Harris is good . . . with different committees and bringing information
back," and "the other, active, long-term residents – they are our rocks."

Wentworth activists had long-standing social bridging relationships
with key technical assistants – most importantly Bill Peterman, director
of UIC's Nathalie P. Voorhees Center – that they could call upon to assist in preparing the proposal to HUD and later, for resident training. Bill
Peterman had first cultivated his relationship with residents during the
White Sox battle. He had both hands-on knowledge through his work
with the residents at LeClaire Courts in the development of their RMC and
an academic understanding through his comparative research on national
resident management models. In addition, Wentworth activists knew
several essential resident actors at other CHA developments that were pro-
gressing toward resident management under the same federal program –
even before Vince Lane's suggestion that they pursue resident management. Hallie Amey had established cordial working relationships with the
leaders at two of these developments, both of whom provided positive
examples and, over time, direct assistance. As Mrs. Amey explained:

Irene [Johnson, president of Le Claire Courts RMC] had come to assist with our first
initial training. . . . Alberta McCain [president of Dearborn Homes RMC] visited us
quite often and offered her help.

Gloria Seabrook, in her role as Wentworth's training liaison for CHA,
made it clear that she was there to work with the Wentworth residents throughout the entire resident management process. Employed by
CHA since 1971, she contributed nearly 25 years of knowledge of the
workings and politics of this bureaucracy to the resident management

development process. In the upcoming years, as their mediator with CHA, Mrs. Seabrook, a CHA spokesperson, would prove to be an invaluable source of long-term support and one of the activists' primary advocates with the CHA. Mrs. Amey appreciated Mrs. Seabrook's organizational knowledge, noting that Mrs. Seabrook's years with CHA allowed her to know CHA from the inside out.

Finally, Wentworth's RMC would have the support of a citywide Community Advisory Board. The task of the advisory board was to advise on and support the technical and organizing tasks of the RMC board throughout the resident management development process. This board included individuals with architectural, legal, security, economic development, and community organizing expertise.[7] Technical support was crucial since HUD's requirements to achieve official resident management status were daunting.

Irrespective of the Wentworth residents' strong organizational capacities, HUD's resident management program was less than ideal; the type and amount of resources HUD would supply and the federal agency's shifting conditions and requirements to become resident managers would at times both undermine and compromise the activists' efforts. Particularly challenging were the contested responsibilities of the LAC and RMC; conditional and inadequate financial and material support; unfamiliar and imposing bureaucratic requirements, including those related to organizational structure, management, and reporting; and political obstacles that delayed the process for years.

THE BURDENS OF BUREAUCRACY

To establish resident management, Wentworth resident activists had to overcome several bureaucratic obstacles: government-induced on-site resident organizational conflicts; limited financial and material resources, especially in light of HUD's restrictions on their use; and the challenge to establish the RMC's organizational structure and procedures to satisfy the government's bureaucratic requirements.

The First Hurdle: The LAC–RMC Conflict

At the onset, the federal resident management program was established without due recognition of the strengths and responsibilities of preexisting

---

[7] Mrs. Amey approached Susan Stall in 1989 and requested that she organize this advisory board. Roberta Feldman also served on the board. The board met irregularly, from 1990 to the present. Several of the board members and other Wentworth residents participated in an RMC retreat in fall 1997, organized by Susan Stall and facilitated by Sheila Radford-Hill. The advisory board's main contribution was to provide an expanded network of professional experts, including Alberta McCain, RMC president of Dearborn Homes, and volunteers (e.g., to serve as judges at RMC elections) for the Wentworth RMC resident board members.

on-site resident organizations and residents attachments and loyalties to these organizations. It is especially ironic because these ongoing organizations could have played an important role in developing resident management. Rather, HUD ignored the potential conflicts and power struggles that predictably would ensue between the new RMCs and extant resident organizations. In fact, at CHA developments, the RMC's and LAC's government-mandated responsibilities were so similar that the two organizations could not effectively delineate their respective distinctive roles. Wentworth activists noted that the CHA obviously had no organizational memory, since they had "done the same thing before." In the early 1970s CHA introduced the LAC, forcing the previously CHA-organized Resident Councils to disband.

From Sheila Radford-Hill's perspective, HUD and CHA "had systematically created the conflict... because they never... clarified the strategy and the relationship between the LAC and the RMC.... And they just let it alone, hoping it would go away." Sheila also confirmed our own observations that the pronouncements that eventually were issued by the federal and city housing authorities to attempt to clarify the distinction in organizational roles and responsibilities actually made conditions worse – they were confusing and open to competing interpretations. Sheila suggested that it was a classic case in which "[N]o one seemed to wanna exert any type of leadership. Everyone wanted to exert authority." Furthermore, in some of the public housing developments, the residents who pursued resident management were in fact adversaries of their on-site LACs. This was not the case at Wentworth. Although the LAC president, Dorothy Driver, was not eager to pursue resident management, rather than opposing it, she supported the resident management process. There was no struggle over status and power at Wentworth; instead there was conflict about overlapping responsibilities. Gloria Seabrook noted that it helped that at Wentworth both Hallie Amey and Beatrice Harris, who "jump back and forth" between the LAC and the RMC, were not focused "on position or power or anything"; rather, they had "their eyes on the prize." To Mrs. Seabrook these women represented an ideal model of how leadership should operate:

[I]f you stay focused... [on] the delivery of services to the residents and the representation of the community, that you say you represent, you don't get caught up in titles and names, and who's gonna call this shot and who's gonna call that shot.

Two leaders, no matter how committed to unity, however, could not alone resolve the mounting tensions exacerbated by HUD's and CHA's insensitive pronouncements. Equally distressing was the personal, emotional toll this conflict created for the residents who were participating in both organizations. Wentworth activists realized that they had to be proactive in order to preserve the viability of both organizations. One RMC board member, Juanita Brown, observed:

The only way that's we gonna get moving is we gonna have to come together.... 'Cause if you don't, we're sure gonna fall.

Mrs. Amey and Mrs. Harris asked Sheila Radford-Hill for mediation assistance. In 1994, Sheila conducted two workshops for LAC and RMC members, encouraging all participants to air their concerns. At the end of the second workshop, she asked the activists to choose among three solutions: "1. Divide up the tasks; 2. Disband one organization; or, 3. Go to court." The activists chose the first solution. Mrs. Brown was reassured: "I do believe we are on the right road now."

Although Wentworth had acted to resolve their on-site organizational differences, all of the Chicago sites developing RMCs were continuing to experience similar contested responsibilities with their LACs. In August 1996, CHA finally intervened, calling for a 2-day retreat of the RMC and LAC presidents to address the problem and to develop a Memorandum of Understanding. According to Mrs. Seabrook, representative activists from Wentworth Gardens were invited to speak at this retreat because of their success in achieving a working relationship between the two resident organizations. Before the retreat, Mrs. Seabrook explained what would take place:

You're going to have Wentworth tell their story. And tell the other groups and LAC's and RMC's how to make this work out... even the part about negotiating and having those meetings, and sitting down and trying to come to a consensus.... [W]orking together like this, helped to save the community.

Wentworth Gardens's prior organizing history and the residents' cohesive social bonds allowed their LAC and RMC to weather a storm. A continued LAC–RMC conflict minimally might have resulted in heightened tensions among the activists and maximally might have destroyed the effectiveness of one or both of the resident organizations. Over the upcoming years, the organizational leadership of the LAC and the RMC exerted a conscious effort, particularly at community events, to present a united LAC–RMC front.

The Second Hurdle: Restricted Government Financial and Material Support

Government resources are essential to effective resident management development. Daniel Monti (1989), in his evaluative comparisons of RMCs, observed that the success of resident management corporations was contingent not only upon the organizations' and residents' capacities, but upon adequate and continuing governmental resources, including funding and technical assistance.

Wentworth activists were dependent upon substantial financial and material resources from government sources to garner required technical assistance, personnel, office space, equipment, furnishings, and operating costs. HUD's $100,000 grant, however, as mandated, was used to hire a housing management consultant and to provide resident management training. These funds proved barely adequate, largely because of the protracted time frame of Wentworth's resident management development. CHA provided the necessary office space – first, the use of a four-bedroom townhouse, then, when this space proved inadequate, two townhouses were joined and renovated for office use. CHA also provided funds for basic office furniture and equipment. The amount of space was satisfactory, but the funds allocated for furniture and equipment were insufficient, especially in light of the government's requirements, including: computer hardware and programs to be used to satisfy HUD and CHA record keeping and reporting requirements, and a telephone system and furnishings to serve the needs of a fully staffed RMC office. Neither HUD nor CHA provided funds for office staff salaries, supplies, or operation costs.

Raising money for unmet staff and office operations remained an ongoing necessity and a daunting organizing challenge. Wentworth residents activated women-centered organizing strategies to raise several hundred dollars at a time, including donations from their own limited resources and fund-raising community events such as barbeques, talent shows, bake sales, and salad spreads. The RMC board also applied to local foundations, although the potential grant sources were very limited.[8] Over the course of resident management development and technical assistance in grant preparation, the RMC wrote applications for and received a total of $70,000 over an 8-year period from the Wieboldt Foundation[9] and $5,000 from the Crossroads Foundation. Although these funds were hardly adequate to sustain even one office staff person and basic operation costs for the 8 years, the RMC did not suspend their operations! When necessary, the RMC would operate with meager supplies, and, when funds for staff were temporarily exhausted, board members, typically Hallie Amey and others she could enlist, volunteered several hours a day at the RMC office.

---

[8] In our observations of RMC board meetings, fund-raising from foundations was repeatedly addressed by residents and technical assistants alike. Wentworth activists, in the past, had received funds from three foundations: the MacArthur Foundation, Crossroads, and Wieboldt, the first foundation to grant them funds. The technical assistants had been able to identify only four other possibilities: Allstate, Sears, Cole Taylor, and the New Prospect Foundations.

[9] The first grant awarded by the Wieboldt Foundation's executive director, Regina McGraw, was to Wentworth Gardens, and Regina admitted that she considered the relationship cultivated with the Wentworth residents over the years personally significant.

Wentworth activists had practical day-to-day experience in managing small-scale facilities at Wentworth, but they understandably had little acquaintance with the complicated technical requirements for resident management. Moreover, the scale and complexity of managing a 422-unit development would require additional technical skills. Wentworth activists were dependent upon the government and its representatives to teach these required management skills and to interpret the government's complex programmatic regulations.

A HUD-mandated housing management consultant, as anticipated, was key to developing Wentworth's RMC, but in attempting to comply with the mandate to hire the management consultant, Wentworth's RMC found themselves in a HUD-imposed Catch-22. They needed to determine the person's responsibilities and qualifications to hire the management consultant; yet, the consultant was the very person who was to assist them in establishing the mandated personnel policies.

To their credit, the RMC developed a job description, advertised the position, and ultimately hired a consultant, who proved to not be the best fit for their current needs. The board, utilizing their newly required wisdom about the desirable qualities and responsibilities of a housing management consultant, garnered from their first hiring experience, hired Curtis James from Chicago State's Inner City Center, an entrepreneurial assistance center on Chicago's South Side.[10]

The relationship the residents had established with Gloria Seabrook also proved to be essential. As the CHA representative, she provided and interpreted information that the residents and their management consultant needed to understand and navigate through the government requisites throughout resident management development. Furthermore, Mrs. Seabrook served as an advocate for the Wentworth RMC at the CHA and HUD regional offices. Mrs. Amey recognized Mrs. Seabrook's invaluable and ready support, commenting:

[S]he's straight and she's firm. She'll tell you the truth and would chew you out if you're wrong, and that's good. And would help you with anything. . . . [I]f we need to know somethin', then we, we call her, "Come on over here, we need to talk."

The Third Hurdle: Establishing Bureaucratic Structures and Procedures

The terms used to describe the HUD-mandated RMC's organizational structure and procedures are indicative of the sharp contrast between these

---

[10] Curtis James's responsibilities would include reviewing the management systems that had already been put in place, developing the other necessary systems, assessing and further implementing board development, providing training consultation, reviewing CHA contracts, and planning the transition to dual, then full management.

bureaucratic requirements and Wentworth activists' communal practices
and values: *policies and procedures, personnel and financial management systems, infrastructure and information management systems,* and *reporting requirements.* This hurdle would be particularly challenging.

Organizational Structure. All RMCs participating in HUD's resident management program were required to create a hierarchical organizational
structure, with specific policies and procedures, responsibilities, and accountability. At the top of the hierarchy is a board of directors and officers, elected by the development residents. The board is responsible for
planning and supervising resident management. Although HUD mandates that the board be unpaid, the responsibilities are extensive: policy
formulation, development of all business systems, and recruitment, hiring, and supervision of all paid personnel, including office manager and
staff; property manager, assistant manager, and staff; procurement spe-
cialist; maintenance, and other building and grounds managers, assistant
managers, and staff; social service staff; and professional consultants (e.g.,
legal, financial, and housing management). The board also is required to
establish committees to oversee specific tasks, such as those related to personnel, health and education, economic development, modernization, and
social services, as well as an advisory board of outside experts to contribute
additional technical knowledge and resources. Although the board is directed to delegate some responsibilities to committees, staff, and consultants, the board ultimately is responsible and accountable for the actions of
all of these entities and their highly technical, complex tasks (The National
Center for Neighborhood Enterprise, 1989).

The Wentworth RMC Board of Directors was democratically elected in
April 1995. Once established, Wentworth's RMC board began the work necessary to develop the government-required management plan, including
the RMC's objectives and the policies, procedures, and programs necessary
for achieving them. The goal, according to the government, is to establish
efficient and accountable management operations, including monitoring
and control over the flow of work. In addition, the management plan had to
include a financial monitoring and reporting system to meet government
specifications.

Given the striking tension between collective and bureaucratic organizations, it is not surprising that the Wentworth activists struggled as they
set up the RMC structure and management plan. It took the full 8 years to
implement the entire bureaucratic structure – all six levels![11] Throughout

[11] The final organization chart upon assumption of full management had six levels with each
lower level reporting to the next level above: (1) RMC board; (2) LAC board, advisory
board, and executive board; (3) executive director, attorney, accountant, office manager,
housing manager, purchase manager, and staff accountant; (4) a clerk who reports to the

the RMC development, individual board members verbally resisted by expressing their discomfort with hierarchical decision making practices. The activists wanted to include all RMC resident participants in decision making, not only the board members. They also preferred to use more collective processes in establishing policies and procedures. They were particularly uncomfortable with the indirect reporting structure, believing that it was more appropriate, as in the past, to intervene directly to solve a problem. Beatrice Harris:

Mrs. Seabrook...and different peoples over at...Tenant Program Development...[who] train us working with the staff, and letting us know that we [board] have to have a spokesman person that contacts the staff; and the staff have to have a contact person that's gonna work with the board. Because if I see someone out there doing something and they supposed to be working, I don't supposed to go up to them and say anything. I supposed to take it back to the board; and we get out the spokesman person to contact that person of the staff and ask them to come to the meeting, so we can go and solve it. (Field notes, May 11, 1998)

Despite their repeated exhortations, Gloria Seabrook kept insisting that the Wentworth RMC board follow the mandated hierarchical reporting procedures:

This is not a democratic process!...We are not voting. The board members are elected. They formulate the rules and regulations.

Yet, these exhortations could not prevent the resident activists from continuing to practice face-to-face resident problem solving in their everyday organizing efforts.

Significantly, although the board composition changed somewhat over time, Hallie Amey was elected president yearly throughout the RMC development process. Several other long-term women-centered activists, including Beatrice Harris, Mary Rias, Maggie Mahone, and Tecora Butler, also sustained their membership on the board throughout its 8-year development. Irrespective of the board structure, these activists did not abandon their concerns as othermothers; nor did they disengage from their community-building organizing objectives and activities; rather, they used their presence on the RMC board and their positions as chairs of RMC committees as springboards to focus the board's and committee's work, in addition to mandated activities, on their ongoing community-oriented work (e.g., youth issues and tenant security) as well.

Management Board Training. HUD required an RMC board of directors and prospective staff to take formal training courses through the guidance

staff accountant, and a maintenance supervisor who reports to the housing manager; (5) two clerks and two maintenance mechanics who report to the maintenance supervisor; (6) three maintenance staff who report to each of the two maintenance mechanics.

of the local housing authority, to prepare them for full management responsibilities. The Wentworth RMC board completed more than 1,000 hours of CHA "Windows of Opportunity" training workshops, classes, and retreats in the Chicago region and other areas of the United States.[12] The board was instructed in RMC management operations, community organization and development, management and supervision, real estate management, and business and real estate development. Board members reported on the demands of these training sessions. Marcella Carter expressed the sentiments of other trainees about the extremely hard work that was required:

It's an experience . . . we used to work, work, work, work, work! . . . We'd go to retreats [until] ten o'clock. We'd just comin' out of them things, you know, and gettin' right back up at seven o'clock in the morning and startin' again around nine. . . . I guess it was a lot of work to be done, so we had to do it, you know.

Board members were not paid while in training, but their expenses were covered. Attendance at the board trainings, however, was irregular for all but the core leadership, largely because of multiple commitments – family and work. Approximately half of the RMC board members attended each session.

CHA also required on-the-job training (OJT) for all prospective staff. Unlike the board, the OJT trainees were paid small stipends during training; however, they were so modest that one trainee, because of economic pressures, quit the training to take a better-paid job. There also was consternation about CHA's policy of mandatory OJT training irrespective of past experience. Two of the Wentworth residents, who were key prospective RMC employees as development manager and assistant development manager, had relevant management experience. They took a stand, supported by the RMC board, and refused to take the required OJT.[13] It took several years for the CHA finally to accept these women's prior "certification" as adequate.

We are unable to comment on the efficacy of the board and OJT training – we were not given permission to observe training sessions – but we did collect indirect evidence from observations and comments at RMC board meetings and the RMC group interviews. Most of the resident participants

[12] CHA staff and outside CHA management consultants provided the training, including lectures, case studies, role playing, observations of other RMC boards "in action," and visits by other RMC board members to Wentworth.

[13] Marcella Bryant had been chosen by the board as the development's manager. A resident of Wentworth, she was employed as a manager of a CHA senior building. Sandra Newman, also a resident of Wentworth and employed in a CHA management position, was slated for assistant development manager. Both Mrs. Bryant and Mrs. Newman objected to taking the required OJT. According to one of the Wentworth activists: "Marcella [Bryant] would have to quit her CHA job and settle for half the money" (Field notes, September 9, 1996).

found the experience useful, especially for learning the technical skills of resident management. Carole Robinson explained:

We [the RMC board] didn't know anything. I didn't know anything about the RMC.... I thought we could just do it, you know.

Mary Rias agreed:

They was teachin' us how to manage a project and teachin' us our do's and don'ts – what to say, what not to say – so we won't get sued and things like that.... They give us books.... What we say, they put it on the board and they type it up.... [They taught me] things I didn't know.... I don't know it all ... but I do know a lot of things [now].

Our observations of RMC board meetings noted that the material the residents were learning was highly complex. Gloria Seabrook concurred: "[T]his is pretty technical stuff." Several of the board members voiced understandable concerns about their ability to grasp this complicated information. Together, the board members and staff generally agreed, and appropriately so, that they would require professional assistance with the technical issues of property management to supervise and be accountable for the management staff properly.

In mid-February 1997, the federal government added further mandated RMC board training, especially for management supervision and operations. According to Gloria Seabrook:

Congress feels that the Boards are not trained because of problems at ... other developments. They fear that people don't know their responsibilities. *They don't mean to make this easy* [our emphasis]. (Field notes, February 18, 1997)

Mrs. Seabrook agreed that the Wentworth RMC board would benefit from more training:

[W]e've got to insure that the Board understands what should be going on, so that they won't get caught with ... in any kind of being taken advantage of.

Although the additional training created added burdens to the board members' time commitments and responsibilities, as well as delays in assuming management responsibilities, the board members complied with requirements. They did not want to find themselves in a situation that would compromise their ability to garner and sustain RMC status. The previous year Wentworth's RMC board had witnessed the dismantling of the first successful RMC in Chicago at LeClaire Courts. As reported in the *Chicago Sun-Times*:

The resident management corporation at LeClaire Courts, considered the "crown jewel" of tenant-run public housing, has been ousted by the Chicago Housing Authority amid allegations of misappropriation of funds, agency officials said Monday. (July 16, 1996, pp. 2, 49)

Wentworth RMC board members were outraged that the CHA did not notify LeClaire's RMC, particularly their friend the RMC board president, Irene Johnson, of their decision to assume control; rather, the CHA simply closed the RMC office by changing the locks on the doors. Apparently, one individual had misappropriated $40,000 from the management funds. Instead of dealing directly with that individual and assisting the RMC to ensure that this would not recur, the CHA immediately dissolved the RMC board and fired 26 corporate staffers. Mrs. Amey represented the feelings of all Wentworth's RMC board members when she reflected, "This is a very sad day" (Field notes, July 10, 1996). The Wentworth RMC board was inspired to take advantage of training opportunities to learn everything they could in order to prevent a similar occurrence at Wentworth.

During training, the board gained knowledge about what they "have to do," at the same time they were struggling with the government's bureaucratic requirements, in particular, the mandated personnel, financial, infrastructure, and information management systems.

Personnel Management System. The RMC board's initial personnel management task was the development of a personnel policy manual that established qualifications, responsibilities, and organizational structure; search and hiring procedures; and performance review procedures for all staff and consultants. These policies had to conform to government regulations and CHA contractual agreements such as Equal Employment Opportunity Commission (EEOC) compliance and CHA's collective bargaining agreement with unions. Susan Donald's description of the formal process the board had to use to select people stands in sharp contrast to Wentworth's leaders' personnel recruitment process that had been used successfully in the past:

Well, what they [RMC board] do is . . . like for any other job. They put out the flyers . . . then they [resident applicants] come in and they fill out applications, and then the board get together. They have a personnel committee . . . [made up of] members of the board. They have job descriptions for all the jobs. And then they . . . go over the applications and they choose who they feel is best for the job.

Because of the required technical procedures, the assistance of Curtis James, the executive director of the RMC, was essential; yet, even with his guidance, personnel planning and hiring were hampered, largely by CHA constraints. For instance, the board could not determine the final number of staff positions until they knew their final operating budget, but this information would not be forthcoming from CHA until the activists successfully achieved full management status. CHA's determination of hiring allotments was based on budget, not need or employment opportunities for residents. Moreover, CHA reviewed all of the board's hiring decisions, often asking the RMC board to reconsider. Despite these obstacles, the RMC board did have most of the staff in place over the course of the resident management development process, but toward the later part of this process, a change was required when the city resumed management responsibilities for the CHA from HUD. The newly reorganized CHA required Wentworth's RMC to rejustify all of its personnel proposals and required all of the staff they previously had hired to reapply.

The RMC board also was burdened by CHA's procedures for staff performance assessments (see also Riger, 1984). Curtis James described the required bureaucratic procedure:

The Board will look at the staff reports and look at their output, and that is how they will know whether the staff is doing a good job. They will analyze the reports using the CCS system.

A CHA consultant at a board meeting elaborated:

When you learn the CCS system, you will know the reasons behind everything. There is a big book [which she held up], and all of that information is in the book. If you look at their numbers, it will tell you whether those are good or bad numbers, and what to do about it. You will know if the numbers don't add up. The book explains how to monitor the staff and how to find errors. The board's responsibility is to monitor, and we do that through reports. One example: CHA evaluates managers. There is a process on a form, and you go down the list and ask how did they perform each task. You will need some help at first to get the hang of all this, but we are here to help you learn. (Field notes, December 8, 1997)

Mrs. Amey, responding to the board members' understandable confusion, reassured them:

Once a week the board will get everything together and meet with Curtis. That is why he is here. He is our consultant. He is going to help us. (Field notes, December 8, 1997)

These systematic procedures to monitor staff performance clearly were less direct and more burdensome than the more informal, but equally informative means resident activists had used before assuming resident management development status.

Within the constraints and complexities of the personnel management structure, the RMC board accomplished one of their key objectives: to use resident management development as an opportunity to expand employment for all Wentworth residents. There was no shortage of qualified resident applicants for most positions. All of the hires the board made, with the exception of professional consultants, were from this pool. The RMC board also took advantage of a CHA-sponsored entrepreneur landscape program to train Wentworth residents for eventual employment in landscape maintenance positions. Once again, CHA bureaucratic policies potentially blocked their intentions. The board had assumed that they would be able to hire the trainees directly out of the training program, but CHA required that landscape maintenance be contracted to a private company. Expectedly, the landscape trainees and board members became duly concerned. Mrs. Amey summed up the sentiment:

It's not fair. We must give them [trainees] something. Eventually; we must hire them.

Finally, after board members struggled with this issue for more than 2 years, raising it at numerous board meetings, Curtis James intervened by offering to assist the trainees to get around the CHA regulations by forming their own business.

Financial Management System. Financial management requirements were no more transparent than those for personnel management. The CHA's required fund allocation and financial monitoring and reporting systems were particularly difficult to comprehend. The board, understandably, was once again reliant on professional assistance, in this instance Gloria Seabrook, to explain the CHA's requirements. The complexities of the system are evident in Mrs. Seabrook's explanation of the payout of CHA funds to the RMC once they assumed full management responsibilities:

Each month, the RMC gets a subsidy from the CHA to pay them for managing the development. Now that goes to pay the bills – you can't keep it. You don't have an RMC corporate account now, but you have an account for the TOP grant [dual management funds from CHA]. When that money runs out, which will be pretty soon, you can use that account for the money that will be in your RMC corporate account. The RMC corporate account is where you deposit the monthly subsidy that you will get from the CHA.

One of the board members appropriately recognized, "But that money will be used for the payroll eventually, right?" Mrs. Seabrook responded, "Yes, the money will be transferred from one account to another. It [use of separate bank accounts] is a way to keep track of what you are doing." (Field notes, June 25, 1996)

The government's requirements for financial reporting not only were complex, but shifted over time. Initially resisting these formal procedures, especially since there were no guidelines from HUD, Wentworth activists successfully used their own, familiar system; managing their $100,000 HUD grant funds budget as they did the budget for the laundromat and store. They saved check stubs and calculated balances by hand or with a calculator. Susan Donald, attempting to meet the requirements for a formal system, later automated the accounting procedures by putting in considerable effort to learn a computer-based database program. When Curtis James was hired, he developed and implemented a formal financial record-keeping system that better fit the government's requirements. He also worked with the board to establish the multiple required bank accounts, payroll policies, a computer-based accounting system, and a filing system. Even with his assistance, the CHA was not satisfied and required a major change in the accounting system.

Infrastructure and Information Management Systems. The government required the RMC to establish building and site monitoring, maintenance, and "modernization" (rehabilitation) plans – but without providing the board with adequate information to tackle these tasks. For instance, at the request of CHA, Mrs. Harris explained, the board was asked to submit a "modernization wish list"; yet CHA, despite repeated requests, would not give the board information about building conditions, CHA plans for building and site rehabilitation, and the RMC's budget, if Wentworth achieved full management – all information crucial to make reasonable decisions. The CHA also left little room to negotiate budgetary items including those for maintenance and modernization. What information the board had was outdated and prepared by CHA.

In an attempt to grapple with CHA's lack of information and lacking confidence in the information CHA did provide, the board requested one of the authors, Roberta Feldman, to prepare an architecture and engineering report to guide the board's modernization request. The report, prepared pro bono by an architect and a mechanical engineer, found that Wentworth's buildings and grounds were in such disrepair that they posed a physical hazard.[14] Heating and plumbing systems were older than recommended by industry standards. The electrical system was inadequate to handle contemporary electric use. Outdoor stairs, walkways, and parking lots were in disrepair and hazardous, and outdoor lighting was nonfunctional and inadequate.

Just weeks before assuming full management responsibilities, the RMC still did not have information about vacancies, outstanding work orders, and building code violations – approximately 1,000 according to Mrs. Seabrook. Board members were justifiably concerned that the CHA full management contract would require that the RMC satisfy all work orders. One board member's astute observation was indicative of the inequity of this obligation: "They [CHA] want us to do what they won't do" (Field notes, February 18, 1997). Gloria Seabrook similarly was frustrated:

[We] needs CHA to document how many vacant units were rehabbed and how many are left for rehab. . . . I won't know anything until I see a report, and I am after them now to give me the report. I will have their report! Also, the code violations have still not been fixed, and when we take over the development those violations become ours – and our resident management agreement says that there would

---

[14] Feldman enlisted Michael Gelick, an architect and faculty member at the University of Illinois School of Architecture, and he in turn requested the assistance of Jacque Chatain, a mechanical engineer, to prepare the report with him.

be no hazardous violations left when the RMC takes over. So we don't want to take over until they fix the hazardous violations, which they have not done. The code violations will never all go away; it will never all be complete and perfect. If we waited for them to fix them all we'd be waiting forever, but at least the worst things should be dealt with. (Field notes, March 16, 1998)

The saliency of the poor building and site conditions troubled the RMC board throughout the resident management development period. These poor physical conditions often competed with, and at times overwhelmed, the board's other collectively determined and long-standing objectives – to increase social services in their community.[15] It is noteworthy that virtually none of the modernization needs identified by the board was satisfied during resident management development.[16]

The RMC board's concerns about the dire physical conditions of their buildings and grounds were warranted. In fact, they clearly understood what research has documented: The importance of the conditions of the housing stock in contributing to the success of resident management initiatives should not be underestimated. Monti (1989) observed that those public housing developments with better site and building conditions had more successful RMCs. Similarly, Leavitt and Saegert (1990) found that low-income New York City cooperatives with buildings in better physical condition were more likely to be successful.

A "Corporate" Office Environment. The new Wentworth RMC "Corporate Office" opened in March 1996. The original, smaller RMC office, dedicated in honor of Dorothy Driver, would now be used primarily for social service programs and for CHA on-site programs. Both Gloria Seabrook and Curtis James worked with the board to improve the efficiency of office practices and create what Curtis called "a proper business environment." The image portrayed by the RMC office was as important to Mrs. Seabrook and Curtis James as its functioning.

I think the corporate office, with the furnishings and the equipment . . . makes it look more professional.

---

[15] In a community organizing workshop requested by the RMC and facilitated by Sheila Radford-Hill, participants developed a plan to document what they believed were Wentworth's most pressing needs. Their first objective was a general goal – to move from dual to full management; other objectives focused primarily on social service objectives: to involve beat cops in resident patrols, encourage the participation of parents in youth programs, and provide an on-site GED program. Subsequently, when activists questioned Mrs. Seabrook about how, when they assumed full management, they might provide increased social services such as these, she responded that they first needed to stabilize the housing stock.

[16] Wentworth did receive very modest landscape improvements as a result of the Healthy and Safe Communities Initiative, apartment building exterior stairwells and doors were painted, and an undetermined number of apartments had some rehabilitation work.

The RMC corporate office, especially in contrast to the disorderly but animated LAC office, gives material evidence of the imposition of the government's bureaucratic requirements. There was no clutter and little trace, as there was in the LAC and old RMC office, of expanded private sphere activities; rather, the furnishings and materials on walls and surfaces pertained only to the business of the RMC. The outer office receptionist desk, for example, was carefully arranged with business accessories and other materials such as phone messages, memorandums and committee reports, and flyers announcing current RMC and CHA programs and services. There was a kitchen, but the CHA banned cooking in this office, although a refrigerator, small microwave, and automatic coffee pot were permitted. The conference room was furnished with a large new conference table and matching chairs. Occasionally, there were worksheets taped to the walls displaying the work of prior board and committee meetings. Unlike the rooms of the LAC and old RMC offices, where Wentworth residents felt free to utilize every inch of available space, on the recommendation of the consultants, the new RMC corporate office was restricted in its use to the RMC board and management staff, excluding all nonbusiness activities.

The RMC board and staff agreed to sustain the physical character of a corporate office to convey the legitimacy of their efforts. According to Susan Donald and other RMC staff and board members, "It is like an office should be." Yet the board resisted this bureaucratic requirement in their everyday use of the space. For instance, in a prominent position in the conference room, they proudly displayed a photographic mural of the core Wentworth activists engaged in the work of women-centered organizing.[17] Although cooking was not allowed in the office, residents brought food they prepared at home to share. Also, Mrs. Amey would not be spatially confined to her assigned upstairs office; rather, when not meeting in the conference room, she was observed by us in the reception area, either at the reception desk making a phone call or sitting with other residents in one of the chairs facing the front entry door to keep track of the "comings and goings" of the residents and visitors. As in the old RMC office, rather than delegating and supervising the RMC's business from the president's office, Mrs. Amey was at the center of the action, conducting business in her women-centered leadership style. Because the corporate RMC office could only be used for RMC business, and there was only one paid staff member, most of the rooms in the RMC office, with the exception of the reception area and conference room, were rarely used. Unfortunately, unlike the old RMC office and the LAC office, the corporate RMC office did not allow its empty rooms to be used to provide needed space for resident programs and services.

[17] This mural had been prepared by Feldman, Naughton, and Stall for a Chicago Peace Museum exhibit in 1994 and then donated to the residents.

HUD Reporting Requirements. Preparing reports to government agencies always proved burdensome. The one-person office staff, Susan Donald, could not meet the extensive demands. Mrs. Harris:

> HUD has a lot of the kind of [reporting requirements]... we had to do all that... a lot of it.... That's why we're trying to hire [a staff person] now. We need help with that. (Field notes, June 29, 1994)

In the meantime, Mrs. Harris explained, the responsibility fell upon Mrs. Amey, as president of the board, to fill the gaps:

> Mrs. Amey, she gets in there with the paperwork that have to go downtown.... Mrs. Amey can handle that paperwork.... The truth is, I know Mrs. Amey be down there [RMC office] at night and all the time with that paper.

Equally frustrating, HUD typically did not accept the report, sending it back for revisions, even when a CHA representative had assisted in its preparation. Without adequate specifications for report preparation, the RMC board and staff had to use trial and error until the report was accepted. Susan Donald:

> HUD said that the request that we had put out earlier... didn't meet all the requirements... so I had to revise it. Okay, because at first we had some people in CHA work on that [report] for us. But then this – [HUD stated] we're not done.... I don't know why [CHA] didn't have all the HUD requirements.... I gave [the draft report] to Miss Seabrook [to review].... And upon her approval... I submit it to... Richardson, [who] works with us, and he's in HUD [regional office]. And if he's approved of them, I submit [it to HUD] in Washington. (Field notes, June 29, 1994)

After this experience, Susan Donald decided to bypass several layers of bureaucracy by going directly to a staff person at the HUD regional office for assistance whenever she needed it.

COMMUNITY ORGANIZING CHALLENGES AND EFFORTS

All the while resident activists were working to comply with the government-imposed bureaucratic structure and processes to develop their RMC, they also continued, just as vigorously as in the past, their women-centered community organizing. Their goals were several: to sustain the solidarity among the resident activists, many of whom were involved in resident management development; to increase resident participation in Wentworth's RMC; to sustain the working relationship between the RMC and LAC; and, more generally, to continue to support community building and ongoing and new services and programs necessary to the social reproduction of their community. Achieving these goals proved challenging.

Because of RMCs' obligations to assume bureaucratic procedures and the hierarchical distribution of their work, especially in light of the shift from a primarily volunteer organization to include paid staff, interpersonal conflicts among the members may result (Riger, 1984). Also, as documented in research on other tenant management efforts (Manpower Demonstration Research Corporation, 1981), recruitment is difficult because of resident apathy and accusations of favoritism and nepotism by nonparticipating residents. Among the residents who do participate, sustaining their commitment to the effort also is challenging. Wentworth activists were continually confronting both the antagonism of other residents and their own frustration and burnout because of inadequate resources to meet goals and a protracted period for achieving objectives. Finally, the huge time commitment required to develop resident management not only contributed to the activists' frustration and burnout, but distracted from the also extensive time commitments necessary for community organizing. Ultimately, the activists prevailed, calling upon the social cohesion of their community household and their women-centered organizing strengths to overcome these obstacles.

Recruitment

The RMC board members understood that recruitment of new participants in Wentworth's resident management development effort was essential to the RMC's success. Mrs. Amey, in particular, made considerable efforts to draw in new board members – women such as Desiree Davis, Geraldine Scott, Barbara Andrews, Angie Johnson, Lucille Perry, Sandie Henley, Susan Donald, and Faye Perteet. To recruit these women, Mrs. Amey used the very same women-centered leadership strategies she had always used: repeated personal appeals; encouragement to take on tasks, even unfamiliar ones; and positive encouragement and support for their efforts.

Susan Donald was one of the newer and younger residents recruited by Mrs. Amey, first as a board member, later as the RMC office manager. She explained that she initially became involved in the RMC because of Amey's charisma: "I love her [Mrs. Amey's] personality. I love her attitude. She's so outgoing and cheerful." She also was drawn by a sense of duty to assist Mrs. Amey to improve the development. Susan Donald:

When I got involved with the RMC, I went to a meetin' one day.... And Miss Amey started talkin'....She had been working...all these years. You seen her runnin' around trying to do this; trying to get that started; trying to get this; trying to get that....She was askin' for help. You know, she said, "We need help. Come on out and help us." And, she touched me. And I said, "I'm gonna get up, and I'm gonna go out there and I'm helpin'."

Mrs. Amey sought to attract younger women, such as Susan Donald, not only to recruit new participants, but also because these women had needed skills, such as in office operations and basic computer programs. These younger-generation women were prepared to commit to regular work hours because of economic needs and aspirations, especially with the prospect of paid staff or OJT positions. In fact, of the newer activists who began as volunteer members of the board, three were hired for staff and OJT paid positions.[18] On the other hand, the older activists primarily remained in volunteer positions. Most of these older-generation activists felt burdened by the substantial increase in necessary volunteer work to create the RMC, especially given their commitments to other organizing efforts (e.g., SASNC and the laundromat) and, for many, child care – most were raising grandchildren.

The shift from the all-volunteer work to the RMC with some paid positions, and the coincidental intergenerational split, resulted in anticipated ongoing, interpersonal conflicts, especially among the older-generation activists and newer recruits. The reasons were several. First, the newer-generation activists, since they had only served a short time on the board, had little opportunity to form relationships of trust with the older-generation activists. Second, the RMC board, as a result of HUD regulations, were accountable for all RMC funds and operations and perceived it as their obligation to assure high-quality work by supervising the younger-generation staff; however, the younger-generation staff and OJTs, were more knowledgeable than the board members about the scope and details of RMC finance and management procedures. The staff, on the other hand, lacked direct access to resources and decision making. Moreover, although Mrs. Amey depended on the staff for the more technical tasks, she still relied on the older-generation activists when trust was paramount, especially when accounting for funds and supplies. Finally, a shortage of resources for staff and office supplies and the sheer amount of work further exacerbated the interpersonal, intergenerational conflicts. It was not possible, without additional volunteer assistance and funds, to operate the RMC office and supervise all of the personnel in a manner deemed appropriate by many of the board members; yet, these board members were unable to contribute any more of their time because of competing demands.

Riger (1984) recognized the essential role of conflict resolution to calm tensions resulting from an organizational shift from volunteer to paid positions. Mrs. Amey served in this role. She resisted relying on her authority as president of the RMC – which might not have been effective in this context – but rather utilized her woman-centered leadership skills to

[18] A RMC board member hired in an OJT or staff position was required, by government regulations, to resign from the board.

attempt to ease the intergenerational conflicts. Susan Donald described the importance of her personal efforts:

Everybody love her and respect her. . . . [A] lot of us make decisions, I suppose, based on relationships. . . . The rumors about people not wanting us [RMC] here – I think it went as smoothly as it did because of Miss Amey. . . . But I think with all the controversy going on, if Miss Amey was not here . . . I think I would have walked away from it. (Field notes, September 19, 1996).

When necessary, Mrs. Amey would take personal responsibility for many of the ensuing problems that arose and mediated by speaking with all of the people involved. Equally important, when work had to be done and staff and volunteer time was inadequate, as mentioned previously, Hallie Amey would do the work herself.

Involving the Wider Community

The RMC board and staff made a strong effort to engage the broader Wentworth community in the RMC development but were hampered by lack of economic resources and time. Mrs. Amey was keenly aware of the need for community organizing: "There's got to be somebody solid to do the community work" (Field notes May 17, 1996). A resident, Barbara Andrews, was hired part-time for approximately a year to organize the community in support of resident management. Unfortunately, the RMC did not have additional funding thereafter to maintain her community organizing position; the RMC fund-raising activities had to be directed to higher-priority needs, such as office staff and supplies. Without an organizer, the task became the responsibility of the board, whose time was already overcommitted.

Even with the limitations of time and economic resources, the board used multiple organizing strategies to encourage community participation. First, the RMC distributed newsletters describing the RMC's responsibilities and encouraging resident participation. Maggie Mahone understood the challenge of this work:

I guess really it's just getting people involved and really concerned about how they [Wentworth residents] live. . . . It seems like we've tried everything. . . . [W]e have material to give out and to read to them, and they look at it. And some might come back, and some just seem like they want to forget about it.

The RMC scheduled the required regular community meetings, announced by flyers distributed developmentwide, to keep their neighbors informed about the function of the RMC and the board's efforts. Most of these meetings, unfortunately, were sparsely attended.

One of the most insidious constraints to attracting resident participation was the residents' rightful lack of faith in the CHA. For example,

Mrs. Harris noted that many Wentworth residents believed that resident management was "doomed" to failure because of the lack of CHA support:

I think the other main thing is getting the residents motivated. . . . It's hard. . . . They [the residents] never did . . . believe that, that we gonna [get resident management]. We [activists] gonna prove them wrong. . . . They say they gonna tear it down anyway. . . . So we are trying to prove to them that we gonna have resident management.

Residents had experienced so many unfulfilled promises, according to Desiree Davis, that they had no trust in CHA: "I think that's why a lot of the residents are at this point too, because they've been promised so many things and they have not gotten anything" (Field notes, November 7, 1995).

Residents also expressed distrust of the RMC board and staff (see also Monti, 1989). They accused the board of nepotism: "the power bit; brought in daughters of her friends. . . . One hand washing the other" (Field notes, November 7, 1995). Many of the residents perceived that the RMC board was controlled by a clique who were promoting resident management for personal advantage. For instance, one person reported that residents were "disgusted. They're mad about it now; there's too much favoritism." Beatrice Harris rightfully blamed CHA for the residents' distrust of the RMC board and staff. According to Mrs. Harris, CHA did not properly inform residents about the role of resident managers; nor did they make it clear that the HUD resident management development funds were restricted to specific expenditures:

When we went into resident management they [CHA] put in the paper that Wentworth Gardens had $45,000 or $60,000 or somethin'. And when they [residents] read it, they all came to me, "What is you all gonna do with all that money y'all got? . . . We ain't got no money." I say . . . but they [residents] kept saying . . . "but they [RMC board] got all that money over there and they usin' it for themselves. You see, they ain't doin nothin' in these apartments." But what they didn't know was we could not use that [HUD grant] for no apartment, no way. It's only training money. . . . And so now, everybody lookin' at us like we a bunch of crooks. (Field notes, November 7, 1995)

Mrs. Amey and the RMC board may have inadvertently contributed to perceptions of nepotism by rewarding volunteer participation in the RMC with occasional modest benefits. For instance, Mrs. Amey had arranged to have 100 chairs donated through a Salvation Army program, Project Hero, and gave the chairs free to "[t]hose who work with us" (Field notes, January 23, 1997). At times, the benefits were more substantial, such as paid RMC positions. Although it is understandable that qualified board members would be given the opportunity to train for RMC office staff positions, such actions can be misconstrued as favoritism by uninvolved residents.

Board members became increasingly frustrated by the lack of resident involvement and the distrust of uninvolved residents. Beatrice Harris:

But you know what. As an officer on the board, I try to set a positive example . . . for all the residents who come to me with that line, [I am in it for personal advantage]. I'm for the community. I'm not in it for me. I don't get anything. You know, I work and I volunteer. . . . And they [believe] that we are getting paid . . . and that we are using the money for our benefit, not the residents' benefit. But I told 'em . . . "I'm just like you all. I don't even get a penny. I don't get nothin' for me." (Field notes, November 7, 1995)

Although frustrated by the insider–outsider conflict, RMC board members and staff did not cease their ongoing organizing work to encourage broader resident participation, for example, Susan Donald:

The younger people are sittin' here complainin', you know. And I tell them all the time, "Well if you think you don't like what's going on, and you think you don't want them [CHA] runnin' [the development] . . . we're gonna run it. If I was you, I'd come join us. You know, come get inside, come put a hand in the thing if you don't want them controlling your future."

Their most successful efforts to encourage broader resident involvement were hosting developmentwide celebratory events and socially bridging to take advantage of opportunities to improve residents' everyday lives. These RMC-sponsored events and improvements built goodwill for the RMC and communicated the board's legitimacy and effectiveness to act on behalf of the entire development. The yearly open houses, for instance, to celebrate the RMC's progress and attract new members, were well attended, often with hundreds of residents present, largely because the RMC board and staff' extended considerable effort to make them enticing and enjoyable events. Carole Robinson's description of an RMC open house gives some sense of the time and work commitment necessary to accomplish them:

October the 2nd, mmm mmm! We had barbecued hot dogs, potato chips. We had so much food out there. We had live entertainment. And the manager . . . came. And we took video tape. . . . It was really, really nice. We hung balloons, and all the children participated and helped clean up. . . . I was up there from eight to five. We fed almost five hundred! – which is huge! I mean we was cooking, we were moving. . . . I know a few [new resident participants] came out to help serve, and after then, you know . . . a few joined the [RMC] committees.

The HUD-sponsored Healthy and Safe Communities Initiative (HSCI), billed as a public housing community-building project, was another opportunity for Wentworth activists to broaden community support. In February 1996, CHA informed Wentworth Gardens that they were one of 10 public housing developments nationwide to participate in the

HSCI.[19] Although the activists' participation meant extra meetings and volunteer hours, HSCI provided an impetus for Wentworth activists to concretize their vision for Wentworth Gardens' future, in particular, in their words, to "beautify" the development and encourage residents to improve their lives. They sought to counter resident apathy and hopelessness through programs, including job training (Field notes, February 19, 1996). Wentworth activists also used these organizing events to cement the LAC–RMC partnership through this joint community effort. These goals are evident in Beatrice Harris's report about the HSCI to the RMC board:

[T]he 18th of May is going to be our big kick off [event]. . . . Organize our blocks, get *everybody* in the block out [for grounds cleanup and planting]. Best kept up block, from now on, it's up to us to keep it looking like that. That's what the Healthy Community is all about. Wentworth Gardens was chosen by HUD. Wentworth Gardens was a community, thank God! HUD looked at us and said, we can save it. We going for the gusto, we want HUD to fix up the inside too. This community been here since 1946, we need to clean up. *It's so important for us to get together* so we can ask for what we want. They're asking now, they might turn around and never come back. RMC and LAC will work together, remember, I came up here hollering and screaming about us getting together and fighting for our community [italics added]. (Field notes, April 8, 1996)

By far, the most visible outcome of HSCI was the May 18th community gardening event, a tangible sign of the ability of the LAC and the RMC to collaborate and affirm the legitimacy of their joint organizational leadership. There were newly planted sod, flowers, and shrubs. A much respected CHA landscaper who had worked at Wentworth in the past, Harry Belmont, not only participated in this landscaping improvement project, but later returned to assist the RMC and LAC in their ongoing grounds improvement efforts. Wentworth activists received assistance from CHA staff in developing a Youth Council, programs for seniors, and a drug rehabilitation program and in implementing the CHA's tenant patrol at their development. Furthermore, the activists expanded their bridging social capital, most importantly, through direct access to CHA staff and officials who attended HSCI meetings, and also through improved relationships with the Progressive Baptist Church and White Sox public relations representatives all of whom contributed to the May 18th event.[20]

---

[19] Hallie Amey and five Wentworth residents traveled with the director of CHA Resident Programs and two employees from this department to a HSCI conference in San Diego for training. Mrs. Amey reported that the San Diego training stressed "common sense." Part of this commonsense approach was a push for grassroots organizers to keep themselves "healthy" so that they could be more effective organizers (Field notes, February 26, 1996).

[20] There also were also disappointments. Although activists repeatedly attempted to hold CHA responsible for the development's dilapidated conditions and for promises made for modernization funds and social services and programs, CHA made no promises, instead utilizing empowerment language while turning the responsibility for the resolution of problems and issues back to the residents. Two of the key objectives they had articulated

Finally, the RMC board took advantage of significant community passages, such as Wentworth's 50th anniversary, to work closely and present a united front with the LAC. In June 1997, resident activists organized an all-day celebration that included a resident parade with over 100 participants, children's events such as a petting zoo and moon walk, picnic box lunches, and live entertainment.

The RMC board remained cognizant of the need to attract more residents to become involved in the RMC. Susan Donald described the strain this put on the RMC board and staff:

Well, right now, I would say the lack of involvement is the greatest obstacle. Because if you don't get more of our young people involved, how will we [RMC] survive? The people [long-term activists] are gettin' older, in their sixties. They're in their seventies; they're not gonna be here forever. Okay! . . . God forbid something happened to Miss Amey, or Miss Harris, all the women that have brung us this far; where would we go from there? Who's gonna stand up and take their places? . . . If you're not getting in there getting the knowledge, and something happen to one of those people, you're [RMC's] gonna fall. And they also need the people, like the younger people for the energy. These people don't have energy; they've been doing this for, what, fifty-five years? . . . They started in 1955, the [first] Resident Council started in '55; that's a long time ago. They're tired and they wearing out, you know.

Overcoming Burnout and Potential Demobilization

The time-consuming efforts required to comply with the bureaucratic requirements to develop resident management, their attempts to sustain their community organizing efforts, and the unduly long delays in achieving full RMC management, all took a toll on the activists. Whether older- or younger-generation, they all suffered burnout. Add the strain from the multiple roles they assumed and their burnout was exacerbated. Susan Donald observed that Mrs. Amey, not surprisingly, was particularly burdened:

Miss Amey is just all over, because you know, she's on the LAC Board as well. . . . She's just all over doing whatever she can . . . a lot of responsibilities. . . . Like I says, not enough time in the day for her.

A few RMC board members eventually resigned because of the strain of having too many other volunteer obligations, including long-term activists such as Dorothy McMiller:

"Yeah, she [Mrs. Amey] got me, but I made her take me off of there [RMC board]. . . . I made her take my name off there, because of, they would have [RMC board] meetin' at ten and one, every Monday. I'm down there [in the laundromat]. I'm missin' the

also did not materialize: There were no jobs for residents; nor had the CHA agreed to install a 5-foot wrought iron fence around Wentworth, a fence they had seen and admired at other CHA developments.

Board [meeting]. I'm missin' the whole show, you know. . . . I said, "Miss Amey, I cannot be in two places."

All of the activists made personal sacrifices to participate in the RMC, and these sacrifices affected the activists' other responsibilities. The RMC board member and LAC activist Carole Robinson remarked that she had not attended a recent RMC board training because she was, understandably, "so tired." She explained that she was still active in the LAC; worked for Abbott Elementary School each morning on truancy issues, often visiting students' homes; had custody of two of her grandchildren – one with severe asthma; and in addition, assisted her sister, who had Lou Gehrig's disease, traveling many miles each week to a western Chicago suburb. Faye Perteet, one of the newer RMC activists, similarly shared how her her new RMC position conflicted with her responsibilities as a mother:

Well, the sacrifices I'm thinking of, is my [not] being there for my teenage daughters. When I wasn't working, it was like, my kids was there and there wasn't no problems or anything. But when I started working, it's like, it started getting a problem . . . when I'm not around to watch them.

Woliver (1996) warned that burnout, resulting from bureaucratic requirements imposed on grassroots organizations, can result in "demobilization" (p. 144). Developing bureaucratic organizations deflects participants' energies from community organizing and diminishes their interpersonal commitments, thus weakening the power of the organization to achieve its goals. Monti (1989) similarly observed the inherent tension between the bureaucratic and technical requirements of property management and the residents' necessary responsibilities as community organizers:

People have just so much time and energy that they can give to something, and that includes an RMC. It appears that an experienced RMC cuts back on some of its more self-conscious attempts to organize people at the site as it wrestles with routine and not-so-routine management tasks. Yet this may create some serious problems for the RMC as it greets new residents and attempts to sponsor new ventures. (pp. 192–193)

Clark (1983) similarly raised cautions about the impact of the technical demands of co-op housing organizations on interpersonal relationships, particularly those based in sustaining daily life and the social and cultural life of a community, but she proposed that they need not be demobilizing. According to Clark, although conflicts are disruptive to social relationships, they do not necessarily debilitate the organization; rather, it is the breakdown of communication among participants that occurs when shared meanings and understandings are violated that can be demobilizing. It is not surprising that Monti (1989) proposed that conflict resolution skills are an essential component of successful RMCs; indeed, as previously reported, we observed that activist leaders like Mrs. Amey and Mrs. Harris put considerable efforts into facilitating conflict mediation and managed to keep demobilization at bay.

ACHIEVING DUAL-MANAGEMENT STATUS

Eight years after receiving the HUD resident management development grant, on February 28, 1997, Wentworth Gardens RMC signed a dual-management agreement with CHA. Remarkably, the residents had sustained their efforts throughout the undue government delays. Mrs. Amey spoke for all of the residents when she expressed her frustration: "You know we have just gone 'round in circles for so long. That's from '89 . . . what is this, '97? It's amazing!" The Wentworth activists could not expedite the process even with the pro bono legal help of a professor from the Marshall Law School who assisted them in contract negotiations and Gloria Seabrook's advocacy. The longer than typical delay is explained, in part, by HUD's takeover of the CHA because of its history of mismanagement. Mrs. Amey:

See, what has happened . . . they [HUD] changing [housing authority] management. We were right at the step into dual management. . . . Each time we get close, they go change something. . . . We nearly signed, we were at the door in '94. (Field notes, November 10, 1997)

Dual management is a transitional period in which an RMC continues training while assuming some resident management responsibilities. When Wentworth's RMC finally achieved dual-management status, they were given no choice in the contractual responsibilities. The CHA determined that the RMC would assume all responsibilities related to tenants. The CHA would maintain the responsibilities for building and site operations. Throughout dual management, however, the CHA would not be forthcoming with information needed by the RMC to carry out their contractual responsibilities, such as information on vacancies and renovation plans, pending work orders, leases, and accounts receivable. Even if the Wentworth RMC board had the information available to correct a problem, they had neither discretionary funds nor fiduciary powers over the modest funds they received, approximately $210,000, to intervene.

In their attempts to function effectively in their contracted dual-management role, the RMC became dependent upon CHA's representative, Gloria Seabrook, once again; however, Mrs. Seabrook too proved to have limited power to garner the necessary information and resources. For instance, she repeatedly asked CHA for information on Wentworth's vacancies:

What units are there? I mean, are they burnt up? Which ones need total reconstruction. . . . ? The vacant units have to turn over quickly. . . . [I] want a list of people [Wentworth residents] . . . who can house sit when a unit becomes suddenly vacant but [is] habitable. You [RMC] can have time to screen people to lease it out.

Mrs. Amey had suggested this same strategy years earlier when CHA onsite management had failed to inform the RMC of vacant units, which, as a result, were vandalized.[21] CHA's failure to fill the vacancies at Wentworth – the vacancy rate was higher than in the past – put the development at risk of demolition.[22] Mrs. Seabrook underlined this risk: "They may close you down!" (Field notes, June 9, 1997).

The RMC board's greatest frustration was that the CHA sustained virtually all of the real power for managing the development without meeting many of their management obligations. The best the board could do was to call the problems to the attention of the on-site CHA management, whose commitment to the development was in doubt. While resident management development was in process, CHA continually changed and reduced the number of on-site management personnel. Beatrice Harris believed that CHA was understaffing Wentworth because they were anticipating dual management and "don't much care anymore" (Field notes, July 14, 1997). Mrs. Amey concurred: "Going into full management – goin' into penny pinchin' time" (Field notes, November 10, 1997)

The predicament the Wentworth RMC board found themselves in was not unique. Bill Peterman (1998), in his study of dual management, also found:

Rather than empowering an RMC, the generally onerous site tasks cause the RMC to become a buffer between the authority and residents, and as such it becomes the target of resident displeasure when something goes wrong.[23] (p. 55)

[21] Mrs. Amey explained that when ABLA residents were displaced because their high-rise units were demolished, ABLA funds were used to repair Wentworth Gardens' vacant apartments for the ABLA residents. CHA, however, moved the ABLA residents into the apartments temporarily until Section 8 vouchers became available. The RMC was not notified when the ABLA residents moved out, and the vacant apartments, as anticipated by Mrs. Amey, were vandalized. Mrs. Amey stated that had the RMC been notified, the board would have had someone watch the apartments. Amey: "It's [vacant apartments] been open for so long, the units [approximately 15] have been vandalized." Amey noted, "If there was better communication, we could have gone a little further. We want to be involved" (Field notes, July 14, 1997).

[22] The federal government–mandated viability test required that those developments with more than 10% vacancy rates assess the cost of renovation with the cost of rental vouchers. If the former were greater, the development would be slated for demolition.

[23] From his findings Bill Peterman (1998) concluded: "Characteristically, authorities in shared management situations give only site-related powers to RMCs, such as responsibility for maintenance, security, and some clerical tasks. Major decisions about operating policies, redevelopment, and budget are retained by the housing authority. . . . Rather than taking control, the RMC in a shared management situation can find itself in the awkward position of acting as the authority's agent rather than as a representative of the residents" (p. 55).

Unfortunately, the Wentworth RMC were suffering the same fate: They became the buffer between the residents and CHA. In fact, Mrs. Harris had predicted that the Wentworth RMC would be held responsible for housing conditions irrespective of their influence over these conditions. When reviewing the draft dual-management contract with the rest of the RMC board, she repeated several times:

Remember, when we sign this, we become the CHA, and the residents *will turn to us* when things go wrong. They *will turn on us* when they don't get what they expect. They will not just be calling and writings letters, they'll be banging on your door demanding services. (Field notes, March 11, 1996)

And the residents did. When we observed the interaction of residents and the RMC, in particular at RMC open houses, residents directed angry comments to the RMC demanding better management services[24]:

"What is going on with management now?"
"Not much!"
"Who is managing, anyway?"
"What are they doing – nothing!" (Field notes, October 16, 1997)

Although the RMC had minimal power to affect CHA management, they were held responsible for CHA's poor management.

ACHIEVING FULL MANAGEMENT STATUS

Gaining full-resident management status, approximately $1^1/_2$ years later, did not prove any easier, but it took less time than dual management. During dual management, the RMC was evaluated on their performance in meeting bureaucratic and regulatory demands rather than their response to Wentworth tenants' management needs. Gloria Seabrook emphasized these CHA and HUD requirements:

For all your [work], you need to dot all your 'i's' and cross all your 't's'. . . . We need to be sure everything is in place. . . . It's going to get rocky (Field notes, March 10, 1997).

Wentworth activists worked up to the very last moment to fulfill all of the government requirements to assume full management, but many requirements were slow to resolve because of their technical nature. As a result, Curtis James was key to finalizing the required organizational,

---

[24] Residents also were concerned about the confidentiality of information they provide on their leases: "What about the confidentiality of the agreements between the tenants and the CHA? Now the resident managers will have access to this information!" (Field notes, February 11, 1998). Residents did not want their neighbors poking their noses into their "business" (Field notes, October 16, 1997)

legal, accounting, and payroll systems, and personnel and tenant regulation manuals. Even with his assistance, several important tasks, including filling some vacant RMC staff positions, were incomplete just 3 weeks before the effective transfer date for full management, largely because CHA's requirements kept changing and the final budget had yet to be determined.[25]

As a result of their experiences in dual management, the RMC leadership was now astute in voicing their concerns, particularly that the full management contract spell out the RMC's responsibilities, and especially their rights; however, the CHA would not negotiate terms. Unlike in their past contractual arrarangements with resident management corporations, CHA decided to forgo separately negotiated contracts; instead, they prepared a standardized contract to use with RMCs in the future. Mrs. Amey described their dilemma:

It just kept driftin' down, driftin' down.... [S]ee the old system, even in dual management, the attorney and the Board sat down and negotiated a contract. That has been erased.... I'm anxious to see what's going to happen then.... This present administration makes it very plain, very plain ... this is what you're gonna do. Take it or leave it.

Curtis James was similarly pragmatically resigned: "The CHA contract favors CHA, you all know this" (Field notes, April 13, 1998). The RMC board also well was aware that there would be no leeway in satisfying CHA's contractual conditions. According to Mrs. Harris, at a CHA board development workshop, board members were told: "They either do it and do it right the first time or they lose it. There would be no second chances." As we previously reported, the Chicago development, LeClaire Courts, lost their RMC management contract in July 1996. Less than 2 years later, on June 8, 1998, again to the consternation of Wentworth activists, one of the

---

[25] Several staff positions still had to be filled, either because the CHA was not satisfied with the RMC board's choice or because the recruits were still in training. Because the RMC board did not know the details of their final contract until the very last moment, the number of employees and their salaries remained unresolved. The RMC board was unable to secure competitive bids on the required employee health insurance without this information. The CHA required liability insurance for full management, but the RMC had no advance funds to pay for the insurance. Mrs. Seabrook, again, had to intervene to arrange for an "advance subsidy." Also, the computerized budget system Curtis James put in place did not correspond to the system required by HUD. Perhaps most frustrating, the board and professional assistants were aware that CHA requisites would change in the full resident management contract: Some of the business development tasks the RMC had accomplished would have to be revised. The corporate office staff requirements also would have to change. Corporate by-laws would have to be revised. Finally, the RMC board would have to initiate a new search for an accountant and lawyer despite their satisfaction with their current professional consultants.

first tenant-managed public housing developments in the nation, Cochran Gardens in Saint Louis, had its management contract ended abruptly, also over financial mismangement issues.

Wentworth RMC signed a full management contract with CHA on April 24, 1998, with an effective transfer date of June 1, 1998. The CHA remained the owner of Wentworth, whereas the RMC was a contractual agent to the CHA. The RMC would be monitored and audited by CHA to ensure that they followed all of CHA's and HUD's rules and regulations. The RMC board became legally accountable for all financial management and for building and site operations. The housing authority retained the responsibilities for rent collection and legal eviction processing, and they would provide extraordinary maintenance. Moreover, the CHA would be able to terminate its contract without redress or compensation.

The Wentwworth RMC had won no concessions in attempting to negotiate the contract. The board was particularly concerned about the poor condition of Wentworth's buildings and grounds. CHA had not attended to most of the work orders and code violations which now, by contractual agreement, would become the responsibility of the RMC. Perhaps most inequitably, the RMC would be contracted to respond to a work order within 6 days! Relying on their legal counsel, the best the RMC could do was include an addend letter in the contract stating the issues remained a problem.

At the last minute, the CHA determined that the Wentworth RMC contract would be for only 4 months rather than one year. They gave no reasons for this change other than that all CHA contracts with RMCs were on hold. CHA gave no guarantee that the Wentworth RMC would receive an annual contract after this period; rather, they would have to negotiate their contract on a month-to-month basis. With this disheartening news, the RMC board assumed complete property management responsibilities with a budget exceeding $3 million.

AN UNCERTAIN FUTURE

Over the 8-year course of resident management development, the federal government's support of resident management rapidly decreased. (See the Epilogue for an update of Wentworth's RMC status.) HUD programs shifted to favor public housing revitalization as mixed-income communities, Section 8 vouchers, and home ownership. As a result, the long-term future for Wentworth's RMC is uncertain. The RMC's leadership, and especially the younger women activists, are forthright about their lack of trust in CHA and HUD to give ongoing support not only to resident management, but to public housing and income support for the poor as well. The remarks of this younger-generation RMC board member clearly reflect this distrust:

To me . . . resident management was . . . somethin' that they [HUD] put together since a group of residents . . . asked to do this thing [RMC]. . . . And to me it looked like they wanted to say, well, "We gave them a chance to do it." But now . . . it's a lot of things happenin': a lot of trainin' that maybe they don't have yet; and you think about all the years the resident management has came to be. . . . You know, it's like it was planned for you to fail. . . . I don't believe they really want this to exist. . . . [T]hey tear down all these public housing buildings, and a lot of people are gonna end up in the streets or somewhere. They can say . . . "We gave them a chance to keep their houses. We provided training. We provided space. They just couldn't do it."

The Wentworth RMC leadership had good reason to doubt CHA's and HUD's commitment to resident management, and to public housing in general. Hallie Amey observed:

CHA has been looking to get rid of public housing for years. They're tearing down housing – Cabrini, Henry Horner. . . . Where will the residents go?

Mrs. Amey added that the new federal welfare bill would "make it worse" (Field notes, September 23, 1996).

If the Wentworth RMC board and staff had any doubt about CHA's and HUD's intentions, Gloria Seabrook did not dispel them; instead, she underlined the urgency of their attempts to make resident management work at Wentworth:

They are tearing down Stateway and Robert Taylor. Dearborn is already down. But no one is bothering about Wentworth, so we have a real opportunity here to fix the buildings, get them up to code, and possibly save the development. . . . HUD's budget is cut every year; and CHA would rather tear this place down, sell it to the White Sox for parking lots, and give you all Section 8. Look how many developments they have already torn down.

Mrs. Seabrook's solutions to the uncertainties confronting Wentworth's future lay within the framework now proposed by CHA and HUD:

We can't do anything without money, and the rents that you pay do not cover operating expenses; so we need people staying here that can afford to pay. Our dream equals money. Let's think out of the box. HUD will allow us to use mixed-income. You don't make money charging 30% [of someone's income]. What we have to do is make this a viable community. We must replace those people with people who want to live here and pay $400 for rent. (Field notes, November 10, 1997)

Wentworth board members, however, were not enthusiastic about this strategy. First, they did not want to force out residents who were good community members. Second, they could not believe the apartments were worth that much rent.

In the long run, looking beyond resident management, Mrs. Seabrook believed that Wentworth's only option was to take advantage of HUD's home ownership initiative and purchase the property:

The only way to be sure to keep it is to own it ourselves. Otherwise, the CHA could decide to tear this place down at any time. (Field notes, October 16, 1997)

Critics, however, criticize public housing home ownership efforts as "lemon socialism," an effort to get the government out of the public housing business and give deteriorating buildings to residents who cannot afford to maintain them (Peterman, 1994). They argue that if public housing residents had the financial means to purchase and maintain older public housing stock, they would not need to live in public housing.

Hallie Amey and other members of the RMC board were less certain about which future strategies they would need to employ to resist the wrecking ball and to save Wentworth Gardens, but they were sure that they would do whatever was needed to support the viability of their homeplace, irrespective of the changes in federal housing and welfare policies. Mrs. Amey, in reflecting on the decreasing federal support for low-income people, indicated her determination: "We will just have to put up a soup line, right out there [outside the RMC office]" (Field notes, September 23, 1996).

HAS RESIDENT MANAGEMENT DEVELOPMENT BEEN EMPOWERING?

The notion of resident management as a tool for empowering public housing residents seems to appeal to almost everyone. Images are invoked of "empowered" tenants, overcoming tremendous social and economic obstacles, taking control of and redirecting their developments from crime- and drug-ridden slums to safe and productive communities. It is a new version of the Horatio Alger story, with adult black women as Horatio. (Peterman, 1998, p. 47)

William Peterman (1998) observed that whereas most advocates of resident management, irrespective of their political leanings, claim that it is an empowering act, even though the means and ends they propose vary depending on their political leanings, he disagrees:

No matter which meaning of empowerment is invoked, resident management is neither the best nor necessarily even an appropriate means for achieving it. Because resident management by itself is not an empowering act, it should not be the sole or even the major focus of efforts to revitalize both the residents and the structures of public housing. (p. 47)

Cairncross, Clapman, and Goodlad (1994) are less conclusive in their analysis: "It all depends" (p. 2). They argue that public housing resident management and ownership, although not inherently empowering, do present opportunities for residents to achieve their own empowerment:

Strictly speaking, empowerment is not to be equated with owning or controlling or managing as such, but rather the gaining of the freedom to choose whether to own or not own, and control or not to control, to manage or not to manage. (p. 16)

Cairncross and associates' position is supported by the action research perspective: that is, you can support individual and collective empowerment, but you cannot endow someone or a group with power.[26] The minimal empirical evidence suggests that governmental support and resources are necessary for successful resident management, but this support and resources do not necessarily create conditions that support residents' empowering themselves (Cairncross et al., 1994; Meehan, 1979; Monti, 1989; National Center for Neighborhood Enterprise, 1989; Peterman, 1998).

At Wentworth, the government's resident management program did not empower the resident activists throughout resident management development and dual management; rather, it created countless obstacles to Wentworth's RMC's board and staff empowering themselves: inadequate informational, material, and economic resources; opaque and changing bureaucratic rules and procedures; and conditions that required reliance on CHA representatives. Moreover, Wentworth RMC's impressive social bridging to external support, including technical assistants, institutions, and funders, that had been so important to Wentworth activists' past successes (see also Monti, 1989; Saegert & Winkel, 1996), was insufficient to overcome all of these obstacles.[27] In addition, the buildings and grounds were in very poor condition – whereas good condition is a requisite of successful resident management – and the prospects for adequate, ongoing funding for operating subsidies and modernization were unknown.

Using Riger's (1993) qualification about the nature of real empowerment – to be empowered, an individual or group must have actual power – provides further evidence of the government's curtailment of Wentworth RMC's empowerment, especially during dual management,

[26] Gruber and Tricket (1987), for instance, point out that people who are in a position to grant individuals or groups power command power; hence the giving of power is always partial and conditional: "[T]here is a fundamental paradox in the idea of people empowering people because the very institutional structure that puts one group in a position to empower others also works to undermine the active empowerment" (p. 370).

[27] The support of professional assistance and the Ford Foundation, for instance, was essential to the successful, long-term resident management of one of the best known RMCs, Cochran Gardens in Saint Louis (Meehan, 1979; The National Center for Neighborhood Enterprise, 1989; Peterman, 1998).

when some level of control was expected. Wentworth's RMC's power over the contractual arrangements required for assuming full management also was minimal. They did not have the right to negotiate their contractual agreements with CHA on an equal basis, to choose the RMC's management responsibilities, to alter the agreement, or to redress and gain due compensation in the event the CHA defaulted on the terms of the agreement.[28]

It is our view, however, that the Wentworth Gardens activists did empower themselves during resident management development, in spite of the government's obstacles. Wentworth activists not only gained real power through full resident management status – no matter how constrained – they also kept at bay the destruction of their homeplace and community. If we use the government's measures of organizational capacity, the activists accrued greater political legitimacy through the development of Wentworth's RMC. Moreover, in the process of resident management training, individual members of the resident management board and staff learned the technical and bureaucratic organizational skills necessary for the challenges of managing their development.

Wentworth activists were not overwhelmed by the government's bureaucratic rules and procedures, or the unequal power they had to negotiate with the powerful HUD and CHA bureaucracies; instead, they contested the dominant ideologies of their identities as poor black women and transgressed the boundaries that separated them from the white male–dominated public domain of real estate management. Their overcoming intransigent government bureaucracies and requisites to achieve resident management of their development amply illustrates Wentworth activists' capacities for transgressive resistance; yet, Wentworth activists engaged in a more subversive form of defiance as well. In our participant observation research of this nearly decade-long resident management development process, we witnessed the activists' engaging in a complicated dance of compliance and resistance as CHA and HUD attempted to reshape the activists' collective identity, practices, and values to fit an impersonal, rigid, hierarchical bureaucratic structure.

Wentworth activists' efforts to resist and transgress the HUD-imposed organizational competition between their LAC and RMC, and their

---

[28] The resident management evaluation literature suggests that the relationship between the CHA and Wentworth RMC may not have been in their best interest. The Wentworth RMC found themselves in a close relationship to the CHA because they were supporting the RMC financially and with technical assistance. Although there is disagreement in the literature about the most appropriate RMC stance toward the housing authority, no research suggests a close relationship as best (Monti, 1989). Some evaluators have argued that a strongly antagonistic stance toward the housing authority is most successful, and a very close relationship is less successful (Monti, 1989), whereas Monti (1989) found that the most empowering relationship is exhibited when there is a degree of "creative tension."

ability to enlist the support of competent technical assistants and to maintain relationships with often embittered residents are testimony to their organizational strengths – the cohesiveness of their community household, their social capital, and the women-centered organizing that they sustained throughout the arduous resident development process. In fact, Wentworth's activists began this challenge as an empowered organization because of these assets. Susan Donald:

We talkin' about years of wisdom. We're not talkin' about just organizin' skills, but people skills. . . . [Y]ou need all of that, and they have all of that. You know, these are women that have watched these people grow up from birth. So they know them, they love 'em, they care about 'em. All they have to do is nurture 'em and teach 'em, and they will produce a powerful, powerful organization.

Wentworth activists' transgressive resistance reveals the complex and diverse means low-income women of color use to "mediate and respond to the interface between their own lived experiences and structures of domination and constraint" (Giroux, 1983a, p. 108). In his theory of resistance, Henry Giroux insists that individuals do not just submit to domination; rather, they struggle against it through various forms of oppositional attitudes and behaviors. Furthermore, these forms of resistance take on a "radical significance" when they stem from "moral and political indignation" (1983b, p. 289) – informed by a critical worldview, including an understanding of the relations of domination and resistance. Rather than being mechanistic role bearers of the governments' requisites, of the governments' domination and constraints, Wentworth activists resisted by not allowing their collective identities, practices, and values to be discredited.

Although appropriately cautious about what lay ahead, the core group of Wentworth activists remain optimistic that if they "stick together", work hard, and are persistent, they will accomplish their overarching goal: to manage their development effectively and in the process improve their material conditions and everyday life. Juanita Brown's words lucidly reflect this confidence:

I feel like as a whole, if Black peoples get together, baby we can do something. We can move mountains. If we pull in together, you see. But if we go one way, our separate ways, we're gonna fall; we can't do nothing. And I feel like working with this RMC, you know, with a bunch of us, sincere in working, we can do wonders with this place. Okay! Now that's the way I felt about it and that's what I was in there for: To give my time, not to waste my time, but to give my time, and give this place . . . something that I can be proud of; because we have to fight together, stick together, to make it a safe environment. And we can do that. . . . Believe it or not, womens, Black womens are some powerful peoples. Once we put it together, we're very powerful.

Wentworth RMC's ability to continue to empower themselves through full resident management will be dependent upon whether or not they gain and sustain actual ongoing power and the necessary resources to manage their development over the long haul. We cannot predict this long-term future. Wentworth activists have assumed full management at a difficult moment in public housing history, one of rapid devolution in federal funding and an emphasis on privatization. The very future of public housing is uncertain. Wentworth activists' efforts and those of public housing resident managers around the United States require and deserve a commitment of ongoing, long-term government support, support that, at present, is not forthcoming.

PART V

CONCLUSIONS

11

Resistance in Context

INTRODUCTION

INTRODUCTION

Mark of Success
Attitude is latitude.
The loser says, "Why?"
The winner says, "Why not?"
The loser says, "I don't know."
The winner says, "I'll find out."
The loser says, "It's too difficult."
The winner says, "I'll give it my best."
The loser says, "That will never work."
The winner says, "Let's give it a try."
The loser says, "It's too risky."
The winner says, "Let's take a chance."
The loser says, "This will have to do."
The winner says, "Let's make it better."
The loser says, "We hadn't planned for that."
The winner says, "Flexibility is our strong point."
The loser says, "It's not my job."
The winner says, "How can I help?"
The loser says, "Is it time to go yet?"
The winner says, "Time flies so quickly here."
The loser says, "We've never done it that way."
The winner says, "We are not bound by our past."
The loser says, "You don't understand."
The winner says, "Let me explain it this way."
The loser says, "I'm not cut out for this."
The winner says, "Now I can learn something new."
(Excerpt of poem by Maggie Mahone, Wentworth Gardens activist)

This excerpt from Maggie Mahone's poem, composed for Wentworth
Gardens' 50th anniversary celebration, June 28, 1997, speaks to the
courage, resilience, and persistence that have sustained Wentworth women

residents' activism for more than 40 years. Wentworth activists are extraordinary women who have struggled for the viability of their housing against seemingly insurmountable odds. These women are heroes, not only because of what they have accomplished but also because they continue to resist. They have had the courage and conviction to pursue the possibility – no matter how constrained – of a better future for themselves and their neighbors (see also hooks, 1990; Noble, 1990).

Although the term *heroism* has rarely been applied to characterize low-income African-American public housing women, Patricia O'Brien's (1995) used it to describe resident managers of another midwestern public housing development:

The dreams these women described reflected their hope for the future and the belief in their ability to make things happen in their lives. Almost all the women were actively working to make their dreams real. They were taking responsibility for creating their future even when there were no guarantees that it would be any better than their present or past. It is this characteristic, more than any other, that makes these women heroic. (p. 174)

Throughout our book, however, we have attempted not to romanticize these women's heroism. As Patricia Hill Collins (1991) has aptly advised, black women should neither be portrayed "solely as passive, unfortunate recipients of racial and sexual abuse" nor "solely as heroic figures who easily engage in resisting oppression on all fronts" (p. 237). Rather, black women's experiences can be best understood as "the ongoing interplay between Black women's oppression and Black women's activism" (p. 237).

The activists at Wentworth Gardens did not choose to become heroes. Their housing development, their homeplace, was becoming unlivable. They wanted, if they had the option, CHA to maintain and manage their development according to their memories of Wentworth's better past. Furthermore, the costs of their ongoing activism have been substantial – personal financial sacrifices, ill health, role conflicts experienced with making a living and taking care of their children, little time for leisure, interpersonal conflicts, and burnout. Yet, Wentworth activists have emerged as heroes because of their personal and collective strengths. They took a heroic stand not only to survive, but to sustain their dignity.

APPROPRIATING HOMEPLACE: AN ACT OF RESISTANCE

Whatever the shape and direction of black liberation struggle (civil rights reform or black power movement), domestic space has been a crucial site for organizing, for forming political solidarity. Homeplace has been a site of resistance. (hooks, 1990, p. 47)

Drawing on the legacy of the black liberation struggle, hooks (1990) reconceptualized homeplace as a site where African-Americans may obtain social validation of the existence of "domination" and its transformation into "resistance" to address the political issues that affect their daily lives. Wentworth activists have maintained this legacy. To take control of their housing development, whether the small-scale facilities and services they provided or the entire development, Wentworth women have had to defy conventional conceptions of their capabilities and institutional regulation of their rights to control these settings. In the spaces they have appropriated as their own, Wentworth women activists have obtained social validation of shared structural and institutional barriers to their access to safe and decent shelter and have acted to resist these obstacles. At Wentworth Gardens, the ongoing struggle to appropriate homeplace not only provides a site for resistance: *It is an act of resistance* (Feldman & Stall, 1994).

Our research reveals the nature of public housing women residents' resistance – its roots; its impetus; their specific actions; the individual and shared assets they effectively bring to these actions; the outside people, organizations, institutions, and other resources they creatively enlist to support these efforts; and why some of their organizing efforts have been more effective than others. Finally it explicates how these acts of resistance are implicated in Wentworth activists' ongoing empowerment to organize their neighbors to sustain the viability of their homeplace. Wentworth activists' acts of resistance to appropriate their homeplace and socially reproduce their community reveal not only the individual and collective nature of empowerment, but its material nature as well (see also Sadan & Churchman, 1993; Saegert & Winkel, 1996).

THE ROOTS OF RESISTANCE: CLASS, RACE, AND GENDER DYNAMICS

The roots of Wentworth women residents' resistance – the ways in which they have both comprehended and ultimately opposed the particular economic, political, and cultural inequities and injustices that circumscribe their everyday lives – are found through an understanding of their "situated activism": that is, the ways their experiences as activists have been shaped by "a particular localized interplay of unequal class, race, and gender relations" and the ways their identities as activists emerge through their engagement with the political culture (Mele, 2000, p. 81). This broader cultural, political, and economic environment structures the material context that affects "how activists define their relationship to specific struggles, what political actions might be effective, and what resources are available" (Naples, 1998b, pp. 332–333).

The broad forces of economic restructuring and political conservatism in the last decades of the 20th century created multiple crises in low-income communities. The deindustrialization of the U.S. economy resulted in lost jobs and sources for reemployment. The feminization of poverty, especially among minority women, exacerbated their inequality and struggles for survival. The 1996 welfare "reform" legislation made assistance to the poor temporary and cut monies to such supplemental programs as food stamps and child nutrition.[1] The operations of the real estate market diminished the availability of low-cost housing. Moreover, low-income communities' geographic and social isolation from mainstream society has greatly exacerbated these obstacles. Federally subsidized housing programs in the United States failed to provide adequate housing for the increasing numbers of poor families, and the public housing that did exist was impacted by the shift in public attitudes and the concomitant lack of government support of low-income, racial minority communities and women-headed households. Reflecting this broader national sociopolitical culture, agencies and institutions such as churches, schools, social service providers, and philanthropies and foundations have grown more tentative in their support of public housing and of its residents (Venkatesh, 2000, p. 205).

Although the Wentworth activists have not explicitly described their resistance in gender-, class-, or race-based terms, they recognize that their identity as low-income African-American mothers has greatly constrained their opportunities for safe and decent housing. The activists understand that the deterioration of their housing conditions is the result of larger structural and institutional factors, including CHA's and HUD's policy decisions and inadequate funding. Inspired by memories of a better past, the grounds for the activists' resistance was the immediate impact of Wentworth's marked physical deterioration, the lack of services and programs for youth, places for children to learn and play, spaces to wash clothes and purchase groceries, and the threat posed by actual material obstacles to their safety and security. As active members of the community household, Wentworth women came to share the recognition that any positive changes in their homeplace must come primarily from their own direct intervention. Remember Mrs. Hallie Amey's rallying cry: "If anything comes up in here for us, it's going to come through us."

CULTIVATING EMPOWERMENT THROUGH RESISTANCE

At Wentworth Gardens, the women residents acted to save their homeplace. These acts of resistance have expanded over time, in scale and

---

[1] In addition to the federal and local governments' decreasing support for public housing, welfare reform's impact on public housing residents had yet to be evaluated. A *HUD User* newsletter (April 1998, p. 1) noted that the Personal Responsibility and Work Opportunity Reconciliation Act in August 1996, which ended "welfare as we know it," provides only relatively short-term income assistance if the adults in the family participate in work-related activities. The implications for public housing authorities are dependent on the number of resident adults required under this act to seek employment and contribute to rent revenues. Substantial numbers of public housing residents have been required to move from welfare to work when they reach their time limits. The newsletter, however, did not report whether these residents remained in public housing or, when their incomes increased, sought housing elsewhere.

complexity, from their earliest modest victories to their ultimate actions to manage and save their entire development. Wentworth residents' actions were not mere adaptations to the conditions of poverty (see also Seagert, 1989; Venkatesh, 2000) – they were not merely "coping" or just "getting by." Rather, they have been empowering themselves through their ongoing acts of resistance. Wentworth activists creatively and strategically have organized themselves to strengthen their capacity for collective action. They have linked the concerns that grounded their everyday resistance to a wider network of people and resources to support their transgressive resistance efforts, including blocking government threats to raze their homeplace.

Wentworth activists' acts of resistance to save their homeplace well illustrate the developmental process of empowerment. Their individual and collective empowerment is cultivated through an ongoing accumulative process (Kieffer, 1984; Rappaport, 1987); that is, Wentworth activists' empowerment has been built up through repetitive cycles of actions and reflection that develop their skills and resources to work toward positive change. They were initially motivated to act by the dismantling of the field house and its youth recreational programs; by what Kieffer (1984, p. 18) called the "era of entry" marking the onset of the long-term and ongoing process of empowerment. Kieffer proposed that initial provocations that lead to empowerment are a result of an "immediate and physical violation of the sense of integrity" and a "personally experienced sense of outrage or confrontation" (p. 19). Indeed, a core group of residents were outraged by the immediate and negative material impact on Wentworth's youth.

Wentworth resident activists' everyday resistance continued on this small scale supported by the strong foundation of their community household and their personal and collective values and capabilities as black mothers and othermothers. Filling the gap between inadequate resources and services and community needs, they created youth programs, tenant security measures, and local fund-raising efforts. In appropriating the spaces for the preschool, day care program, laundromat, and grocery store, Wentworth activists supported pressing social reproduction needs now extended from their households to their community. For the preschool, the residents drew upon the resources they had on hand. For the laundromat, the activists garnered the material resources they required from a CHA program and bridged with other CHA developments for technical assistance and repair personnel they could trust. In contrast, in developing the grocery store, they had to obtain and maintain store equipment and stock totally through resident initiative and organization. In fact, rather than supportive partners, Wentworth store managers have had to contend with the prejudicial practices of vendors who refuse to deliver to a CHA development.

With each new act of everyday resistance the activists gained new skills, obtained new information, and increased their resources, demonstrating their growing strategic capacities as grassroots organizers. They increased their self-confidence, built upon and expanded their social bonding and social bridging capital, and augmented their leadership and management skills. What began as a loosely structured core of concerned residents in time became a respected group of organizers with attendant organizational structures and maintenance activities and with legitimacy with development residents, the CHA, and local nonprofit organizations. Finally, the activists' everyday resistance led to a more critical worldview, an awareness that their deteriorating local conditions were integrally related to larger economic and political structures and policies, opening the possibility for resistance beyond the boundaries of the expanded private sphere (see also Saegert & Winkel, 1996).

Ultimately, empowerment researchers agree that without positive outcomes, empowerment is only a potential outcome (reviewed in Kieffer, 1984; also see Kroecker, 1995; Morgan & Bookman, 1998; Rappaport, 1981; Riger, 1993). The resident programs and services, the actual power over the on-site facilities of their development, and the visible improvements in material conditions for everyday life indeed were integral to Wentworth activists' growing individual and collective empowerment (see also Clark, 1993; Sadan & Churchman, 1993; Saegert & Winkel, 1996). Although implementing and managing the programs they developed and the spaces they appropriated required hard daily work, the material evidence of their powers to effect change supported their stubborn determination to sustain their efforts.

By the 1980s, Wentworth activists' everyday resistance proved insufficient to keep up with the devastating impact of the federal government's disinvestment in public housing. Adding further to their challenges, the state and local governments decided to support the construction of the White Sox stadium in their stable lower-income African-American neighborhood. To resist the increased scale of the threats to their survival, Wentworth activists crossed the boundary from their immediate homeplace into the male-dominated and elite-controlled public sphere. Wentworth activists transgressed their roles as othermothers to engage in confrontational community organizing in the political battle with formidable corporate and political opponents, to file a civil rights lawsuit, to tackle the technical tasks of economic development, and to challenge governmental bureaucratic quagmires to become resident managers. In these acts of transgressive resistance, Wentworth activists made public, and later legal, claims for space, resources, and services to redress social, economic, and political injustices. They gained greater power over the near future of their development, and, for the present, have warded off CHA's wrecking ball.

Throughout Wentworth activists' cultivation of their empowerment, their efforts to build and sustain cohesive, interpersonal relationships have been critical. Without this socially cohesive community, resident activists would have been demobilized when the housing authority replaced the Resident Council with the LAC. When the activists formed a nonprofit organization outside the auspices of CHA, Wentworth Gardens United for Survival, the relationship between this organization and the LAC and CHA could have become antagonistic.[2] Similarly, the conflict between the LAC and RMC could easily have become disabling. Most currently, the residents sustained their RMC and resisted the bureaucratization of their everyday practices because of their strong interpersonal affection and respect for one another. These activist women have thwarted the perceived threats to the very existence of their development. Their continuous, hard work is illustrative of the transformative potential of poor women of color to create both the reality of their current resistance and their empowerment for future resistance to survive and thrive.

WHEN RESISTANCE IS NOT ENOUGH

Throughout this book, we have sought to recognize and explain the significance of the residents' resistance for transforming the material conditions of their daily lives and, in the process, empowering themselves for future actions. Although they are impressive, Wentworth activists' efforts cannot provide a model for ensuring viable housing.[3] Wentworth women activists are well aware of the limitations of their resistance efforts – they confront them daily. Their accomplishments alone cannot stem the ongoing increasing dilapidation of their buildings and grounds; cuts in social, educational, and health services; the ever-present drug and gang activity; and increasing unemployment and poverty (see also Powers, 1996; Williams & Kornblum, 1994). Wentworth activists' resistance is not a substitute for larger-scale political intervention, especially government commitment to provide ongoing adequate and appropriate economic and material resources to resolve the larger problems of the public housing crisis and of the low-income community.[4] No amount of everyday or transgressive resistance can

---

[2] One of the authors, working with the Near Westside Coalition, observed that at another CHA family development, ABLA, an alternative resident representative group did indeed have an antagonistic relationship with both the LAC and CHA.

[3] Sudhir Venkatesh (2001), based on his observations at Robert Taylor Homes – CHA's largest high-rise family development, argues similarly, noting that despite the tenants' "impressive efforts to cope and make life meaningful amid a dearth of resources . . . ultimately . . . the resilience they displayed could never provide a permanent basis to foster habitability" (pp. 274–275).

[4] In a related manner, Warren, Thompson, and Saegert (2001) note the risks of oversimplifying or exaggerating the benefits of social capital for stemming poverty (see also Briggs, 1998): "Social capital is not an alternative to providing greater financial resources and public services to poor communities. Rather it constitutes an essential means to increase such resources and to make more effective use of them" (p. 2). Xavier de Souza Briggs (1997,

substitute for the essential support of local and federal programs for decent, safe, and affordable housing; nor can it take the place of employment development and training, educational and leadership opportunities, and social programs and services that can assist public housing residents to overcome poverty.

Anne Power (1996), in her evaluative study of UK housing authorities' efforts to improve estate (public) housing viability, provided evidence that the most critical foundation of a sustainable public housing community is an appropriate level of assistance from the government. Multifaceted government support to upgrade physical conditions, improve management and use of resources, increase income, and provide social support "can transform an [public housing] estate from a situation bordering on chaos to relatively stable conditions" (p 1548). Most important to our argument, Power found that "residents can only succeed if their efforts are linked to the wider community and if they received sustained, consistent and sensitive [government] support" (p. 1554). Furthermore, although government-funded and nonprofit programs are imperative for the survival of low-income communities, they have the most far-reaching impacts when residents are involved in the decision making and take responsibility for or control over solutions to local housing issues.

In the United States, the government's past role in public housing residents' lives and their struggles for safe and decent shelter, however, has been contradictory. Wentworth women have been subjected to the gender, race, and class inequities inherent in public housing policies while benefitting from these policies as well. CHA and HUD have been implicated in the residents' actions both as a target of their grassroots organizing challenges and as a source of support for some of their efforts. Many of the residents' struggles were responses to the actions or inactions of CHA and/or HUD; yet, these agencies also provided resources for resident organizing to meet their everyday needs.

Today, the government's role remains contradictory. In the 1990s, the federal government shifted its housing policy to support resident self-sufficiency programs and redevelopment of public housing developments that the government deemed unviable. HUD's current HOPE VI redevelopment program emphasizes demolishing these distressed public developments and replacing them with economically mixed-income, lower-density "communities." In Chicago, as of 2003, the implementation of the HOPE VI

1998) similarly cautions against oversimplifying or exaggerating the benefits of enriched individual and collective social capital for community well-being, particularly when in the domain of urban politics: "Establishing patterns of trust and reciprocal obligation is crucial not because it eleminates important conflicts of political interest but because the former make it easier to reconcile the latter in creative and sustainable ways. Social capital is a vital resource for cities, neighborhoods, and individuals because of power and politics, and not in place of them" (1998, p. 178).

program will result in the demolition of all CHA high-rise family developments. Demolition of these purportedly unviable public housing developments began in the 1990s with the wrecking ball tearing down high-rise
buildings at Robert Taylor Homes, Lakefront Homes, Cabrini Green, and
Henry Horner Homes. CHA planned to meet the federal government's
demands, working in partnership with private developers, to rehabilitate
or replace most of these sites and priviatize most of the agency's functions.
The number of replacement units in the mixed-income developments are
30% less than the number of units razed. The result is a dramatic decrease in the number of public housing units for current public housing
residents.

Those residents who are moving into the new housing are likely to benefit from the greatly improved physical housing conditions and the end of
their isolation in segregated communities. The remaining "rent compliant"
public housing residents are being displaced, receiving rental vouchers for
housing in the private market.[5] These households could benefit from the
opportunities to choose their place of residence; however, every indication
is that, in Chicago, their choice is restricted to rentals in equally dilapidated
housing in racially segregated and isolated communities.[6]

It appears that public housing residents have a choice about the redevelopment of their communities – the HOPE VI program mandates resident
participation. Our observations indicate, however, that, in practice, participation generally is tokenism. The only residents who have had substantial
input into the redevelopment process have been forced to use the courts to
gain a voice in decision making. Chicago public housing residents are not
being asked how they would like to live: They are being told how to live.

Instead, the HOPE VI program, as other current government programs,
treats public housing residents as socially and morally deficient. It intends

[5] HUD and CHA have set conditions for residents to maintain and to renew their leases.
These conditions are subject to frequent revision. For instance, in 2002, the leaseholder had
to be up to date on rent payments, have every adult household member listed on the lease,
and have no household members who had a felony record. In addition, because of the
changes in the federal welfare policies every household member over 18 must be in school,
be in an education or employment training program, or have paid employment.

[6] An unpublished study that followed public housing residents who were forced to relocate
due to demolition and modernization was reported at the 3rd Annual Briefing of the Coalition to Protect Public Housing on April 10, 2003. The 3200 families receiving Section 8
vouchers as of the end of 2002 had relocated in areas of the Chicago metropolitan region
that were equally segregated and only slightly higher in income than the public housing
communities they had left. Only 34 families had found housing in the suburbs. The rest
of the families had relocated in the lowest-income African-American neighborhoods in
Chicago, also some of the lowest-income communities in the United States. In subsequent
moves, the prior public housing residents fared no better. They again relocated to equally
poor, racially segregated African-American communities. It was reported that the reasons
for this relocation pattern was racial and class discrimination in Chicago's housing market
and the lack of relocation assistance.

to "uplift the poor" through its transformation of public housing. Residents purportedly will benefit from the role models and mentoring of their working- and middle-class neighbors (Smith, 1999) and through a new town planning model intended to create socially cohesive communities. As did housing reform advocates of the past, today's public housing redevelopers assume that the low-income "culture of poverty" can be changed to a more acceptable middle-class culture by housing poor people among middle-class people and in middle-class housing archetypes. They have masked their paternalistic attitudes toward the poor by adopting a housing and neighborhood form that is particularly desirable in the dominant society.

Influenced by the New Urbanist perspective, a current town planning model, the HOPE VI redevelopment plans promise a return to a lost sociability and security of neighborhood life of the past by recreating the scale, site organization, and building forms of traditional small towns and urban neighborhoods. Although well intentioned, the New Urbanist model is misguided by a belief that a change in the built environment will cure urban problems. This simplistic notion of environmental determinism has been amply discredited by decades of environment and behavior research. The built environment does not determine people's behavior, social organization, or well-being. The New Urbanists' premise fails to recognize the complex interaction of social, economic, and political factors that impact on low-income people's lives and living conditions, as well as the role of human agency in the ways people use and the meanings they attribute to the built environment. The strengths of low-income communities and satisfactions residents gain from living in these neighborhoods remain opaque to outsiders' perceptions. Most critical to the observations of this case study, the vital communities public housing residents have created over decades – so necessary for their everyday survival – may be destroyed.

This is not to suggest that public housing cannot be better designed to support community building and to meet the needs and desires of its residents. Although we are critical of housing reform models that rely on environmental determinism for their rationale, we are not suggesting that the built environment plays no role in a community's social organization or residents' satisfaction with the place where they live. As we have documented at Wentworth, among the essential needs of low-income residents are access to and rights over adequate, appropriately designed spatial resources.

We are proposing that the failure to engage public housing residents in a meaningful manner in the redevelopment process is unjust and unwise. It is unjust because public housing residents have the right, as citizens, to participate in the decisions that will affect their homes and their lives. It is unwise because prior urban renewal programs teach us that if residents do not have a say, we will repeat the mistakes of the past. Furthermore, it is not enough to engage residents as disembodied individuals. Public housing residents live in community households and participate in vital community organizations. To ignore their collective voices and collective strengths truncates their power to have a say in their future.

The 40-year history of Wentworth women residents' activism flies in the face of conceptualizations of public housing residents as pathological or apathetic victims of despair and of their homes as places of chaos and misery; rather, it reveals the strength and resourcefulness of low-income people to challenge the social inequities and injustices that impact their daily lives. Through this case study, we have sought to support the grounds of community action and social change by making visible the intimate connections between public housing residents' everyday lives and their grassroots activism. We concur with Julian Rappaport (1981), who charts a course that gives clear precedence to examining and supporting bottom-up political efforts of people to gain control over their lives:

[A] social policy of empowerment] demands that we look to many diverse local settings where people are already handling their own problems in living, in order to learn more about how they do it. . . . [I]t demands that we find ways to take what we learn from these diverse settings and solutions and make it more public so as to help foster social policies and programs that make it more rather than less likely that others not now handling their own problems in living or shut out from current solutions, gain control over their lives. (Rappaport, 1981, p 15).

By attending to public housing residents' everyday and transgressive resistance, we reveal new understandings of politics and social change. We are suggesting alternative means for formulating housing plans and policies that are relevant to the experiences of low-income people of color and that include residents' meaningful participation. Necessary, effective governmental support of public housing viability must be grounded in local conditions and responsive to the voices of local activists who know the needs and priorities of their communities. With sufficient political, economic, and technical support, Wentworth activists have not only the valor and dignity to resist: They have the dedication, skills, and resourcefulness to succeed.

Our convictions are articulately expressed by Wentworth resident, Maggie Mahone, in these closing lines of her poem:

> The loser says, "It's impossible."
> The winner says, "Anything's possible."
> The loser says, "It isn't worth my time."
> The winner says, "Think of the possibilities."
> The loser says, "It's too expensive."
> The winner says, "It's worth the investment."

Epilogue

As we conclude our book, a strongly worded editorial in *The New York Times* entitled, "Facing Up to the Housing Crisis," argues for federal responsibility to provide decent affordable housing for poor and working-class people. Reporting findings from a bipartisan Congress-appointed Commission, the Millennial Housing Commission, the editorial asserts:

[T]he housing shortage facing the country today is nearly as severe as the one that spurred Congress to act just after World War II [in its passage of the Federal Housing Act of 1949].... In terms of the wealth they created and the communities they stabilized, the federal housing laws were among the most crucial initiatives of the 20th century. (*The New York Times*, July 5, 2002, Part A, p. 20)

The editorial recognizes that the current Republican administration is unenthusiastic about national support of affordable housing, but that there will be no solution to the housing crisis "unless the federal government gets back into the game".

Despite the affordable housing crisis nationwide, the number of public housing units continues to fall dramatically, as developments are demolished to make way for new, mixed income housing. The number of affordable housing units also is shrinking in Chicago, while the destruction of CHA public housing units continues – over 24,000 units are ultimately slated for demolition. In Chicago, advocacy groups and organizations focused on affordable housing issues: the Chicago Affordability Coalition, the Chicago Rehab Network, the Chicago Coalition for the Homeless, and in particular, the Coalition to Protect Public Housing, all monitor the actions of the local, state, and federal housing authorities to protect and increase the number of units and the integrity of affordable housing in Chicago region.

Wentworth Gardens, currently slated for modernization, has managed to avoid the wrecking ball. The date and the extent of this renovation have yet to be determined by CHA. Meanwhile, 21% (90) of Wentworth's units are vacant, a stark contrast to the 1990s when the percentage of Wentworth vacancies was less than 10%. Depending upon one's interpretation, this is either good news – CHA is leaving the apartments vacant because modernization is eminent – or it is indicative of CHA's plans to demolish most or all of the Wentworth Gardens development.

The Wentworth Gardens Resident Management Corporation (RMC) is still in business. However, within their first year of assuming full resident management, the CHA decided not to renew the residents' RMC contract because they deemed the Wentworth RMC "unprofessional." The RMC board utilized the legal advisor to the Chicago Association of RMC Corporations (CARMAC) – the representative organization for all CHA's RMCs – to contest CHA's decision. Obviously, the Wentworth RMC won; the CHA renewed their full resident management contract.

Hallie Amey continues to serve as the RMC Board President. In 2000, she was one of three CHA residents appointed to the citywide CHA Board of Commissioners. Mrs. Amey's two committee positions on this decision-making board – Finance and Audit, and Tenant Services – provide her, and thus the Wentworth activists, with the most current information about CHA planning and operating proposals. The Wentworth RMC employs fifteen full-time Wentworth residents: five in clerical and administrative assistance positions, seven as janitors, one maintenance supervisor, and two engineer trainees. Recently, the RMC was awarded a $100,000 HUD grant to create further resident employment opportunities. Wentworth's goal is to develop a resident-operated moving company, most immediately, to relocate the residents during the upcoming renovation. This grant has allowed the RMC to hire three younger residents to work on this and other economic development initiatives.

Wentworth residents remain concerned about security issues, although the crime rates are going down in CHA housing. The *Chicago Tribune* reported in June, 2001, that from 2000 to 2001, the rates of crime in Chicago's public housing complexes had declined at a greater than in the city as a whole, 18% in CHA versus 11% across Chicago (Ford, 2001). According to the CHA Chief Executive Officer, the decrease could be attributed to expanded community policing efforts within CHA developments. Yet, some Wentworth resident activists expressed frustration with the local 9th District police officers, who participate in the Chicago Community Policing (CAP) program, but remain in their patrol cars in lieu of walking or biking through the Wentworth community.

The resident-operated laundromat is operative from 7:00 a.m. to 4:00 p.m. five days a week, but is in dire need of new machines. The convenience store has been closed since 1997 because of the lack of a committed resident with adequate time to take on the difficult challenges of managing the store. The Spiritual Development Center is no longer open due to basement flooding. The community vegetable gardeners have retired. The landscaper employed by the Wentworth RMC has planted a manicured flower garden in its stead, although residents speak about the possibility of a resident garden on a small plot of land south of the development.

The effective LAC-RMC partnership at Wentworth has garnered physical improvements for the development including the residents' long sought after wrought iron fence. Installed in 1999, the fence encircles the Wentworth development providing a "residential feeling" they so desired, and a barrier to the White Sox baseball fans who had used Wentworth grounds as a pedestrian thoroughfare to Comiskey Park. The Chicago Park District has agreed to renovate Wentworth's field house. The Park District has budgeted one million dollars for these physical improvements. Planned for the fall, 2003, the residents have reactivated their local Park Advisory Council in order to contribute to the restoration plans and ensure their completion.

In 2001, the Chicago Boys and Girls Club closed their Wentworth location. Wentworth Gardens was one of the last four of Chicago's Boys and Girls Club extension centers to be closed. All four of the remaining centers were located in public housing. The closing of the centers was cited as "a good business decision" by the interim president of the organization, since there were inadequate funds to cover the expenses of the extension sites and "[m]any of these facilities are in very poor condition" (*Chicago Tribune*, June 22, 2001, Sec. 2, p. 5). The youth work of the activists in the LAC office has greatly expanded as a result of the loss of the Boys and Girls Club center as well as the downgrading of the field house from a "park" to a "playground" with its attendant cuts in Park District staff and programs in 1998.

Shortly after the Boys and Girls Club closure, the Local Advisory Council (LAC) moved into this now vacated and repainted two story, three bedroom townhouse apartment. Housed in the former LAC offices is a new initiative, "Reach One, Teach One," created by former Wentworth Gardens resident, Dr. June Bailey. This program offers training in computer literacy for youth and adult residents on donated computer equipment and serves as a site for after-school tutoring for Wentworth children. Also, as a result of a recommendation of the RMC's needs assessment, resident, Melinda Powell, directs "Mothers in Transition", a home daycare training and support center that opened in a centrally located ground level Wentworth apartment in 1999. Finally, multiple yearly celebrations still support and fuel the Wentworth Gardens community, the most recent being the RMC open house in June, 2002.

In a recent visit to Wentworth in early July, the activists's persistence and vitality was apparent. In the RMC office, Mrs. Amey was posted in "her chair" in the RMC reception area. There were rumblings about what needed to be done about youth overturning trash cans and the irritating presence of some young men loitering within the development. Administrative secretary, Bertha McKinney, wrestled with the aging xerox machine, while Mrs. Amey enlisted several RMC Board members and executive administrative assistant, Susan Donald, to join her in a meeting with plumbers to once again repair some of the deteriorating, leaking pipes. Later, as we chatted in front of Mrs. Maggie Mahone's apartment, she commented on her hopes for Wentworth's renovation, noting with both pride and resignation "Well, we're still here!"

APPENDIX A. *Timeline of Wentworth Gardens Resident Activists' Key Initiatives.*

Everyday Resistance

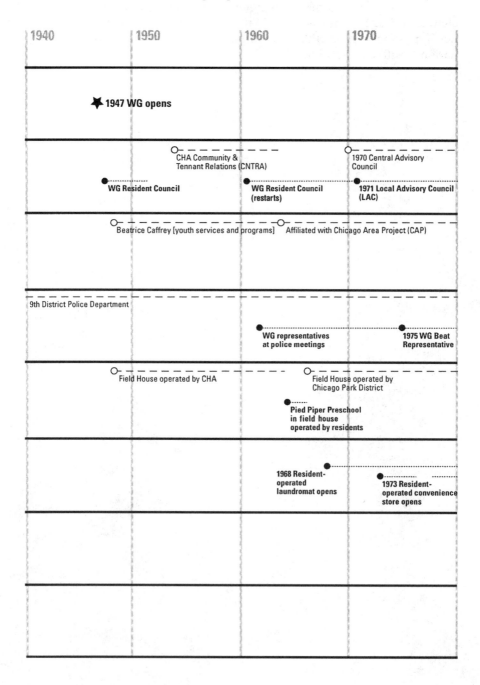

Everyday and Transgressive Resistance

1980	1990	2000	2010

1986 Resident Committee
1987 Incorporation of Wentworth Gardens
Residents United for Survival (WGRUS)

1996 WG Tenant Patrol

1998 Downgraded from park to playground

1987 WGRUS replaces Field House roof

December 1986 Proposed Comiskey   1997 Comiskey Park opens
Park stadium announced in media

January 1987–July 1988: Stage protests to stop stadium construction. September 1987: South Armour Square Neighborhood
Coalition (SASNC) incorporated.1989: File lawsuit.1994: Awarded CDBG funds. January 1996: Apply. April 1996: Denied
empowerment zone funds. 1996: Lawsuit dismissed.

CHA/HUD Resident Management Program

1989 WG RMC   **February 1997 Dual-management contract**
incorporated   **July 1998 Full-management contract**

APPENDIX B. *A Demographic Profile of the Resident Community Activists*
Interviewed, 1992–1998
Interview Total: 23

Cohort of Older Activists (15)

Name	Approximate Age in 1998	Length of Residence in WG in 1998
Hallie Amey	76	47 years
Juanita Brown	65	38
Tecora Butler	72	21
Marcella Carter	54	24
Janie Dumas	64	30
Mardia Earving	60	19
Ella Fitzgerald	79	36[a]
Beatrice Harris	60	32
Mae Francis Jones	71	23
Maggie Mahone	71	34
Dorothy McMiller	68	41
Evelyn Ramsey	60	23
Mary Rias	64	33
Carole Robinson	50	28
Lottie Weathersby	63	24

Cohort of Younger Resident Activists (8)

Name	Approximate Age in 1998	Length of Residence in WG in 1998
Barbara Andrews	28	4
Susan Donald	36	13
Desiree Davis	43	11
Geraldine Scott	46	8
Bertha McKinney	48	16
Lucille Perry	48	11
Faye Perteet	34	7
Monica Ramsey	27	22

	Older Residents		Younger Activists	
Level of Education	N	%	N	%
Less then high school	2	13	0	
Some high school	8	53	1	12.5
High school graduate[b]	3	20	5	62.5
Some college	2	13	2	25
TOTAL	15	99%	8	100%

[a] Moved out of WG in 1994
[b] Includes those who attained their high school completion through a GED Certificate Program.

References

Ackelsberg, M. (1988). Communities, resistance, and women's activism: Some implications for a democratic polity. In A. Bookman & S. Morgen (Eds.), *Women and the politics of empowerment* (pp. 297–313). Philadelphia: Temple University Press.

Acker, J. (1990). Hierarchies, jobs, bodies: A theory of gendered organizations. *Gender & Society, 4,* 139–158.

Advisory Council on the Chicago Housing Authority (1998, June). *The report of the Advisory Council on the Chicago Housing Authority: New strategies, new standards for new times in public housing.* Chicago: Chicago Housing Authority.

Allen, K. R., & Baber, K. M. (1992). Ethical and epitstemological tension in applying a postmodern perspective to feminist research. *Psychology of Women Quarterly, 16,* 1–15.

Alinsky, S. (1969). *Reveille for radicals.* New York: Vintage.

Alinsky, S. (1971). *Rules for radicals.* New York: Vintage.

Altman, I., & Churchman, A. (Eds.) (1994). *Women and the environment.* Human behavior and environment series. Vol. 13. New York: Plenum.

Altman, I., & Low, S. M. (Eds.) (1992). *Place attachment.* Human behavior and environment series. Vol. 12. New York: Plenum.

Altman, I., & Rogoff, B. (1987). World views in psychology: Trait, interactional, organismic, and transactional perspectives. In D. Stokols & I. Altman (Eds.), *Handbook of environmental psychology* (Vol. 1, pp. 1–40). New York: Wiley.

Amey, H. (March 31, 1992). Discovery deposition transcript. Dorothy Laramore et al., plaintiffs, vs. the Illinois Sports Facilities Authority, a municipal corporation, the city of Chicago, a municipal corporation, and the Chicago White Sox, Ltd., a limited partnership, defendants. United States District Court for the Northern District of Illinois Eastern Division, No. 89 C 1067.

Amey, H. (November 30, 1994). Affidavit. Dorothy Laramore et al., plaintiffs, vs. the Illinois Sports Facilities Authority, a municipal corporation, the city of Chicago, a municipal corporation, and the Chicago White Sox, Ltd., a limited partnership, defendants. United States District Court for the Northern District of Illinois Eastern Division, No. 89 C 1067.

Anderson, E. (1990). *Streetwise: Race, class, and change in an urban community.* Chicago: University of Chicago Press.

Atlas, J., & Dreier, P. (1994). Public housing: What went wrong? *Shelterforce*, September/October: 4–5, 27.

Babbie, E. (2001). *The practice of social research*. Belmont, CA: Wadsworth.

Bailey, R. Jr. (1972). *Radicals in urban politics: The Alinsky approach*. Chicago: University of Chicago Press.

Baker, E. (1973). Developing community leadership, In G. Lerner (Ed.), *Black women in white America* (pp. 345–352). New York: Vintage.

Barnett, B. M. (1993). Invisible southern Black women leaders in the civil rights movement: The triple constraints of gender, race, and class. *Gender & Society, 7*, 162–182.

Barnett, B. M. (1995). Black women's collectivist movement organizations: Their struggles during the "doldrums." In M. M. Ferree & P. Y. Martin (Eds.), *Feminist organizations: Harvest of the new women's movement*. Philadelphia: Temple University Press.

Baum, H.S. (1997). *The organization of hope: Communities planning themselves*. Albany: State University of New York Press.

Bauman, J. (1994). Public housing: The dreadful saga of a durable policy. *Journal of Planning Literature, 8*(44), 347–361.

Becker, H. S. (1966). Introduction. In C. F. Shaw (Ed.), *The jackroller: A delinquent boy's own story*. Chicago: University of Chicago Press.

Belenky, M. F., Bond. L. A., & Weinstock, J. S. (1997). *A tradition that has no name*. New York: Basic Books.

Bess, P. H. (August 8, 1988). What S. Armour Square needs is a latter-day Nathan, *Chicago Tribune*, Sec. 1, p. 11.

Birch, E. L. (1978). Woman-made housing: The case of early public housing policy. *Journal of the American Institute of Planners, 44*, 130–143.

Birch, E. L. (Ed.). (1985). *The unsheltered woman: Women and housing in the 80's*. New Brunswick, NJ: Center for Urban Policy Research.

Bookman, A., & Morgen, S. (Eds.). (1988). *Women and the politics of empowerment*. Philadelphia: Temple University Press.

Boulding, K. (1981). *A preface to grants economics: The economy of love and fear*. New York: Praeger.

Bourque, S. C., & Grossholtz, J. (1974). Politics an unnatural practice: Political science looks at female participation. *Politics and Society, 4*(2), 225–264.

Bowley, D., Jr. (1978). *The poorhouse: Subsidized housing in Chicago, 1895–1976*. Carbondale: Southern Illinois University Press.

Bratcher, J. (April 5, 1988). Residents take swing at stadium plans, *Chicago Defender*, Sec. 1, pp. 1, 18.

Bratt, R. G. (1989). *Rebuilding a low-income housing policy*. Philadelphia: Temple University Press.

Brenner, J., and Barbara Laslett. (1986). In U. Himmelstrand (Ed.), *Sociology from crisis to science? The social reproduction of organization and culture*, vol. 2 (pp. 116–131). London: Sage.

Briggs, X. D. S. (1997). Social capital and the cities: Advice to change agents, *National Civic Review, 86*(2), 111–117.

Briggs, X. D. S. (1998). Brown kids in white suburbs: Housing mobility and the many face of social capital. *Housing Policy Debate, 9*(1), 177–221.

Briet, M., Klandermans, B., & Kroon, F. (1987). How women become involved in the women's movement of the Netherlands. In M. F. Katzenstein & C. M. Mueller (Eds.), *The women's movements of the United States and Western Europe: Consciousness, political opportunity, and public policy*. Philadelphia: Temple University Press.

Brietbart, M. M., & Pader, E. J. (1995). Establishing ground: Representing gender and race in a mixed housing development. *Gender, Place and Culture*, 2(1), 5–20.

Brotman, B. (April 5, 1988). Protest groups make their pitches at White Sox opener, *Chicago Tribune*, Sec. 2, p. 1, 6.

Bukowski, D. (1992). *Baseball palace of the world*. Chicago: Lyceum Books.

Buttimer, A. (1980). Home, reach, and the sense of place. In A. Buttimer & D. Seamon (Eds.), *The human experience of space and place* (pp. 166–187). New York: St. Martin's Press.

Cagan, J., and deMause, N. (1998). *Field of schemes: How the great stadium swindle turns public money into private profit*. Monroe, ME: Common Courage Press.

Cairncross, L., Clapman, D., & Goodlad (1994, Summer). Tenant participation and tenant power in British council housing. *Public Administration*, pp. 177–200.

Cantarow, E. (1980). *Moving the mountain: Women working for social change*. New York: The Feminist Press.

Carter, M. (November 30, 1994). Affidavit. D. Laramore et al., plaintiffs, vs. the Illinois Sports Facilities Authority, a municipal corporation, the city of Chicago, a municipal corporation, and the Chicago White Sox, Ltd., a limited partnership, defendants. United States District Court for the Northern District of Illinois Eastern Division, No. 89 C 1067.

Castells, M. (1983). *The city and the grass roots*. Berkeley: University of California Press.

CHA Statistical Report 1948–1984 (1985). (Report published by the Chicago Housing Authority.)

Chandler, M. O. (1991). What have we learned from public housing resident management. *Journal of Planning Literature*, 6, 136–143.

CHAT (1948). V. 3 (Newsletter published by the Chicago Public Housing Authority.)

CHAT (1969). V. 10 (Newsletter published by the Chicago Public Housing Authority.)

CHAT (1970). V. 11 (Newsletter published by the Chicago Public Housing Authority.)

CHAT (1973). V. 14 (Newsletter published by the Chicago Public Housing Authority.)

Chawla, L. (1992). Childhood place attachments. In I. Altman & S. Low (Eds.), *Place attachment* (pp. 63–86). New York: Plenum.

Chicago Fact Book Consortium. (1995). *Local community fact book: Chicago metropolitan area 1990*. Chicago: Academy Chicago Publishers.

Chicago Housing Authority (1943, March 10). The Chicago Housing Authority: Manager and builder of low-rent communities. (Report issued by the Chicago Housing Authority.)

Chicago Housing Authority (1947). (Report to the Mayor.)

Chicago Housing Authority (1947, September 30). The Tenth Year of the Chicago Housing Authority. (Report issued by Chicago Housing Authority.)

Chicago Housing Authority (1950). The Livability of Low-Rent Public Housing: A Pilot Survey of Five CHA Projects.

Chicago Housing Authority (1985). CHA Statistical Report, 1948–1984.

Chicago Housing Authority (1997). Residential Satisfaction Summary:Year-End 1997. (Report issued by the Office of Management Analysis and Monitoring, Chicago Housing Authority.)

Chicago Housing Authority (1991). Department of Research and Program Development.

Chicago Tribune (1986). The Chicago wall. Special report compiling a 1986 series published in the *Chicago Tribune*.

Chicago Tribune (June 22, 2001). Sec. 2, p. 5.

Chombart de Lauwe, P. (1976). Appropriation of space and social change. In P. Korosec-Serfaty (Ed.), Appropriation of Space: *Proceedings of the Third International Architectural Psychology Conference* (pp. 23–30). Strasbourg, France: IAPS

Clark, D. (1973). The concept of community: A re-examination. *Sociological Review*, 21(3), 397–416.

Clark, H. (1993). Taking up space: Redefining political legitimacy in New York City. *Environment and Planning*, 26, 937–955.

Clark, H. (1994). Sites of resistance: Place, "race' and gender as sources of empowerment. In P. Jackson & J. Penrose (Eds.), *Constructions of race, place, and nation* (121–142). London: UCL Press.

Collins, P. H. (1991). *Black feminist thought: Knowledge, consciousness, and the politics of empowerment*. New York: Routledge.

Cooper, C. (1974). *The house a symbol of self* (Report No. 122). Berkeley: Institute of Urban and Regional Development.

Cooper Marcus, C., & Sarkissian, W. (1986). *Housing as if people mattered: Site design guidelines for medium-density family housing*. Berkeley and Los Angeles: University of California.

Cott, N. F. (1977). *The bonds of womanhood: "Woman's sphere" in New England, 1780–1835*. New Haven, CT: Yale University Press.

Couto, R. A. (1999). *Making democracy work better*. Chapel Hill: The University of North Carolina Press.

CPHT (1949). V. 11 (Newsletter published by the Chicago Public Housing Authority.)

CPMT (1948). V. 10 (Newsletter published by the Chicago Public Housing Authority.)

Crooks, R., and K. Baur (1999). *Our sexuality*. Pacific Grove, CA: Brooks/Cole Publishing Co.

Crozier, M., & Friedberg (1980). *Actors and systems: The politics of collective action*. Chicago: The University of Chicago Press.

Csikszentmihalyi, M., & Rochberg-Halton, E. (1981). *The meaning of things: Domestic symbols and the self*. Cambridge: Cambridge University Press.

Daniels, A. K. (1985). Good times and good works: The place of sociability in the work of women volunteers. *Social Problems*, 32(3), 363–374.

Daniels, A. K. (1987). Invisible work. *Social Problems*, 34(5), 403–415.

Daniels, A. K. (1988). *Invisible careers*. Chicago: The University of Chicago Press.

Davis, A. (1981). *Women, race and class*. New York: Random House.

Delamont, S. (1980). *The sociology of women*. London: George Allen and Unwin.

Dellios, H. (January 20, 1988). Sox stadium foes plan strategy, *Chicago Tribune*, Sec. 2, p. 3.

De Vault, M. L. (1991). *Feeding the family: The social organization of caring as gender work*. Chicago: University of Chicago Press.

Despres, C. (1989, August). *The meaning of home: Literature review and directions for future research and theoretical development*. (Paper presented at the International Housing Symposium. Gavle, Sweden.)

di Leonardo, M. (1987). Female world of cards and holidays: Women, families and the work of kinship, *Signs: Journal of Women in Culture and Society 12*(3), 440–453.

Drake, S., & Cayton, H. (1945). *Black metropolis*. New York: Harcourt Brace.

Dryfoos, J. G. (1998). *Safe passage*. New York: Oxford University Press.

Duncan, N. G. (1981). Home ownership and social theory. In J. S. Duncan (Ed.), *Housing and identity: Cross-cultural perspectives* (pp. 98–134). London: Croom Helm.

Durkheim, E. (1965). *Elementary forms of the religious life*. New York: Free Press.

Education Center for Community Organizing (ECCO). (1989). *Women on the advance: Highlights of a national conference on women and organizing*. Stony Point, NY: ECCO.

Ellis, R. J. (1986). *A theory of charismatic leadership in organizations*. Berkeley: Institute of Governmental Studies in Public Organization, University of California, Working Paper No. 86-2.

Emmett, D. (1971). The concept of power. In J. R. Champlin (Ed.), *Power* (pp. 78–103). New York: Atherton Press.

Epp, G. (1996). Emerging strategies for revitalizing public housing communities. *Housing Policy Debate, 7*(3), 563–588.

Euchner, C. C. (1993). *Playing the field: Why sports teams move and cities fight to keep them*. Baltimore: John Hopkins University Press.

Evans, S. M., & Boyte, H. C. (1981, Summer). Schools for social action: Radical uses of social space. *Democracy*, pp. 55–65.

Evans, S. M., & Boyte, H. C. (1986). *Free spaces: The sources of democratic change in America*. New York: Harper & Row.

Feldman, R. M. (1988). Psychological bonds with types of settlements. In H. Van Hoogdalem, N. L. Prak, T. J. M. Van Der Voordt, & H. B. R. Van Wagen (Eds.), *Looking Back to the Future: Proceedings of the Tenth International Association of People Environment Studies Conference* (Vol. 2, pp. 335–343). The Netherlands: Delft University Press.

Feldman, R. M. (1990). Settlement-identity: Psychological bonds with home places in a mobile society. *Environment and Behavior, 22*(2), 183–229.

Feldman, R. M. (1994). Society's salvation or demise: The meaning of the city/suburb distinction in contemporary U. S. metropolitan society. In M. Baldassare (Ed.), *Suburban communities* (229–251). Greenwich, CT: JAI.

Feldman, R. M. (1996). Constancy and change in attachments to type of settlements. *Environment and Behavior, 28*(4), 419–445.

Feldman, R. M., & Stall, S. (1989, June–July). Women in public housing: "There just comes a point. . . . " *The Neighborhood Works*, pp. 4–6.

Feldman, R. M., & Stall, S. (1990). Resident activism in public housing: A case study of women's invisible work of building community. In R. I. Selby, K. H. Anthony,

J. Choi, & B. Orland (Eds.), *Coming of age: The proceedings of the Environmental Design Research Association annual conference* (pp. 111–119). Urbana-Champaign, IL: IAPS

Feldman, R. M., & Stall, S. (1994). The politics of space appropriation: A case study of women's struggles for homeplace in Chicago public housing. In I. Altman & A. Churchman (Eds.), *Women and the environment* (pp. 167–199). Human Behavior and Environment Series, Vol. 13. New York: Plenum.

Feldman, R. M., & Westphal, L. M. (2001). An agenda for community design and planning: Participation and empowerment in practice. In R. Lawrence (Ed.), *Sustaining human settlements: A challenge for the new millenium* (pp. 106–139). Newcastle-Upon-Tyne, England: Urban International Press.

Ferree, M., and F. Miller. (1985). Mobilization and meaning: Toward an integration of social psychological and resource perspectives on social movements. *Sociological Inquiry, 55*, 38–61.

Fischer, G. S., Jackson, R. M., Steuve, C. A., Gerson, K., & Jones, L. M. (Eds.). (1977). *Networks and places: Social relations in the urban setting.* New York: Free Press.

Fischer, R. (1959). *Twenty years of public housing.* New York: Harper & Brothers.

Flanagan, R. M. (1997). The housing act of 1954: The sea change in national urban policy. *Urban Affairs Review, 33*(2), 265–286.

Focus (1985). Who lives in public housing? (Newsletter of the Joint Center for Political Studies, Washington, DC)

Ford, L. (June 19, 2001). CHA crime down most. *Chicago Tribune*, Sec. 3, pp. 1, 6.

Foucault, M. (1979). *Discipline and punish: The birth of the prison.* (A. Sheridan, Trans.). New York: Vintage.

Francis, M., Moore, R., Iacofano, D., Klein, S., & Paxson, L. (Eds.). (1987). Design and democracy. *Journal of Architectural and Planning Research, 4*(4), 273–359.

Franck, K. (1995). From courts to open spaces to streets; Changes in the site design of U.S. public housing. *Journal of Architectural and Planning Research, 12*, 186–220.

Franck, K. (1998). Imagining a way of know: Some reasons for teaching "architecture of utopia." *Utopian Studies, 9*(1), 120–141.

Fried, M. (1963). Grieving for a lost home. In L. Duhl (Ed.), *The urban condition* (pp. 151–171). New York: Basic Books.

Fried, M., & Gleicher, P. (1970). Some sources of residential satisfaction in an urban slum. In H. M. Proshansky, W. H. Ittelson, & L. G. Rivlin (Eds.), *Environmental psychology: Man and his physical setting* (pp. 333–346). New York: Holt, Rinehart & Winston.

Fried, M. (1963). Grieving for a lost home. In L. Duhl (Ed.), *The urban condition* (pp. 151–171). New York: Basic Books.

Fried, M., & Gleicher, P. (1970). Some sources of residential satisfaction in an urban slum. In H. M. Proshansky, W. H. Ittelson, & L. G. Rivlin (Eds.), *Environmental psychology: Man and his physical setting* (pp. 333–346). New York: Holt, Rinehart & Winston.

Fuerst, J. S. (June 1988). Tenant management in low-rent public housing. *Social Service Review*, pp. 337–345.

Gambetta, D. (1988). Can we trust? In D. Gambetta (Ed.), *Trust: Making and breaking cooperative relations.* Oxford: Blackwell.

Gamson, W. A., Fireman, B., & Rytina, S. (1982). *Encounters with unjust authority*. Homewood, IL: Dorsey.

Gans, H. J. (1962). *The urban villagers*. New York: The Free Press.

Garbarino, J., Kostenlny, K., & Durbrow, N. (1991). *No place to be a child: Growing up in a war zone*. Lexinton, MA: Lexington Books.

Gardner, H. (1995). *Leading Minds: An anatomy of leadership*. New York: Basic Books.

Garland, A. W. (Ed.) (1988). *Women activists: Challenging the abuse of power*. New York: The Feminist Press.

Garza, M. M. (April 22, 1999). *Chicago Tribune*, Sec. 2, p. 3.

Garza, M. M., & McRoberts, F. (1999, October 1). *Chicago Tribune*, Sec. 2, pp. 1, 4.

Gilkes, C. T. (1979). *Living and working in a world of trouble: The emergent career of the black women community workers*. Doctoral dissertation, Northeastern University.

Gilkes, C. T. (1980) Holding back the ocean with a broom: Black women and their community work. In L.R. Rodgers-Rose (Ed.), *The Black woman* (pp. 217–232). Beverly Hills: Sage.

Gilkes, C. T. (1985, Summer). Together and in harness: Women's traditions in the sanctified church. *Signs*, p. 679.

Gilkes, C. T. (1988). Building in many places: Multiple commitments and ideologies in Black women's community work. In A. Bookman & S. Morgen (Eds.), *Women and the politics of empowerment*. Philadelphia: Temple University Press.

Gilligan, C. (1977). In a different voice: Women's conceptions of self and morality. *Harvard Educational Review*, 47(4), 481–517.

Giroux, H. A. (1983a). *Theory & resistance in education*. London: Heinemann Educational Books.

Giroux, H. A. (1983b). Theories of reproduction and resistance in the new sociology of education, *Harvard Educational Review, 53*, 257–293.

Gittell, M. (1980). *Limits to citizen participation*. Newbury Park, CA: Sage.

Gittell, M., Ortega-Bustamante, I., & Steffy, T. (1999). *Women creating social capital and social change*. New York: Howard State Management and Policy Center, The City University of New York.

Gittell, R., and Vidal, A. (1998). *Community organizing: Building social capital as a development strategy*. Thousand Oaks, CA: Sage.

Giuliani, M. V. (1989). Attachment to place: Some reflections on residential environments. Paper presented at the International Housing Symposium, The Meaning and Use of Home and Neighborhood, Gavla, Sweden.

Giuliani, M. V. (1993). Place attachment in a development and cultural context. *Journal of Environmental Psychology, 13*(3): 267–274.

Giuliani, V., & Feldman, R. M. (1994). Review of I. Altman & S. M. Low (1992), *Place Attachment* (Human Behavior and Environment, Advances in Theory and Research, Vol. 12), New York: Plenum Press. *Journal of Environmental Psychology, 13*, 267–274.

Glaser, R. G., and Strauss, A. L. (1967). *The discovery of grounded theory: Strategies for qualitative research*. New York: Aldine.

Glenn, E. N., Chang, G., & Forcey, L. R. (Eds.). (1994). *Mothering: Ideology, experience, and agency*. New York: Routledge.

Gluckman, M. (1963). Gossip and scandal. *Current Anthropology, 4*(3), 308–315.

Graumann, C. F. (1976). The concept of appropriation *(aneignung)* and modes of appropriation of space. In P. Korosec-Serfaty (Ed.), *Appropriation of space: Proceedings of the Third International Architectural Psychology Conference* (pp. 113–123). Strasbourg, France: IAPS

Grimes, A. (1983). Women organize: Public housing tenants from support groups for survival, *The Neighborhood Works, 6* (11), pp. 1, 5–8.

Gruber, J., & Tricket, E. J. (1987). Can we empower others? The paradox of empowerment in the governing of an alternative public school. *American Journal of Community Psychology, 15* (3), 353–371.

Gutierrez, L. M., and Lewis, E. A. (1992). A feminist perspective on organizing with women of color. In F. G. Rivera & J. I Erlich (Eds.), *Community organizing in a diverse society.* Boston: Allyn & Bacon.

Hallman, H. W. (1984). *Neighborhoods: Their place in urban life.* Beverly Hills: Russell Sage.

Harding, S. (1981). What is the real material base of partriarchy and capital? In L. Sargent (Ed.), *Women and revolution: A discussion of the unhappy marriage of Marxism and feminism,* (pp. 135–163). Boston: South End Press.

Hartmann, H. L. (1981). The family as a the locus of gender, class, and political struggle: The example of housework. *Journal of Women in Culture and Society, 6*(3), 366–394.

Hartsock, N. C. M. (1979). Feminism, power, and change: A theoretical analysis. In B. Cummings & V. Schuck (Eds.), *Women organizing: An anthology* (pp. 2–24). Metuchen, NJ: The Scarecrow Press.

Hayden, D. (1984). *Redesigning the American dream: The future of housing, work, and family life.* New York: W. W. Norton.

Hayward, D. G. (1978). An overview of psychological concepts of home. In R. L. Brauer (Ed). *Priorities for environmental design research* (pp. 418–419). Washington, DC: EDRA.

Haywoode, T. (1991). *Working class feminism: Creating a politics of community, connection, and concern.* Ph.D. dissertation, The City University of New York.

Heilman, S. C. (1976). *Synagogue life: A study in symbolic interaction.* Chicago: University of Chicago Press.

Henderson, H. (May 29, 1998). There goes their neighborhood. *Reader,* Sec. 1, 27(34): pp. 1, 18, 20, 23, 24.

Henig, J. R. (1982). *Neighborhood mobilization: Redevelopment and response.* New Brunswick, NJ: Rutgers University Press.

Hirsch, A. (1983). *Making of the second ghetto: Race and housing in Chicago: 1940–1960.* Cambridge: Cambridge University Press.

Honchar, C. (January 12, 1971). CHA given ultimatum on federal funds, *Chicago Tribune.*

Holt, G.E., & Pacyga, D. (1979). *Chicago: An historical guide to the neighborhoods, the Loop and the South Side.* Chicago: The Chicago Historical Society.

hooks, b. (1990). *Yearning: Race, gender, and cultural politics.* Boston: South End Books.

Huberman A. M., & Miles, M. B. (1994). Data management and analysis methods. In K. D. Norman & Y. S. Lincoln (Eds.), *Handbook of qualitative research* (pp. 428–444). Thousand Oaks, CA: Sage.

HUD (October 1, 1999) *The widening gap: New findings on housing affordability in America*. Available at: hudsuernews@aspensys.com.

Hummon, D. M. (1992). Community attachment: Local sentiment and sense of place. In I. Altman & S. Low (Eds.), *Place attachment* (pp. 253–278). New York: Plenum.

ICF Inc. (1992), *Evaluation of resident management in public housing*. Report prepared for the Office of Policy Development and Research, U.S. Department of Housing and Urban Development, December.

Jackson, K. T. (1985). *Crabgrass frontier: The suburbanization of the United States*. New York: Oxford University Press.

Jacobs, J. (1961). *The death and life a great American cities*. New York: Vintage Press.

Johnson, S. (December 4, 1986). "Stadium plan has plenty of Sox appeal in Bridgeport," *Chicago Tribune*, Sec. 1, p. 2.

Jones, H. L. (December 9–22, 1993). Why Wentworth works. *South Street Journal*, p. 3, 11.

Kahn, D. (March 4, 1941) Pioneer in public housing, Elizabeth Wood blazes way for other women, *Christian Science Monitor*, p. 1.

Kaplan, T. (1982). Female consciousness and collective action: The case study of Barcelona, 1910–1918. *Signs: Journal of Women in Culture and Society*, 7(3), 545–566.

Kaplan, J. (January 11, 1987). White Sox's neighbors want mayor to go to bat for them, *Chicago Tribune*, Sec. 2, p. 3.

Kasarda, J. D., & Janowitz, M. (1974). Community attachment in mass society. *American Sociological Review, 39*, 328–339.

Kass, J. (July 7, 1988). "Sox stadium foes offered homes, jobs," *Chicago Tribune*, Sec. 2, pp. 1–2.

Kass, J. (August 6, 1988). Authority Oks deal for Sox neighbors, *Chicago Tribune*, Sec. 1, p. 5.

Kass, J., & Egler, D. (July 1, 1988). Bipartisan rally pushes deal through, *Chicago Tribune*, Sec. 1 pp. 1, 8.

Kass, J., & Luft, K. (August 4, 1988). Sox neighbors agree to stadium deal, *Chicago Tribune*, Sec. 2 pp. 1, 8.

Keller, S. (1968). *The urban neighborhood: A sociological perspective*. New York: Random House.

Keys, L. D. (1991). *The effects of resident empowerment in community planning for African-American underclass populations*. Doctoral dissertation, University of Illinois at Chicago.

Kieffer, C. H. (1984). Citizen empowerment: A developmental perspective. In J. Rappaport, C. Swift, & R. Hess (Eds.), *Studies in empowerment: Steps toward understanding action* (pp. 9–36). New York: Haworth.

Korosec-Serfaty, P. (Ed.). (1976). *Appropriation of Space: Proceedings of the Third International Architectural Psychology Conference*. Strasbourg, France: IAPS

Kotlowitz, A. (1991). *There are no children here: The story of growing up in the other America*. New York: Doubleday.

Krauss, C. (1983, Fall). The elusive process of citizen activism. *Social Policy*, pp. 50–55.

Kroeker, C. J. (1995). Individual, organizational, and societal empowerment: A study of the processes in a Nicaraguan agricultural cooperative. *American Journal of Community Psychology, 23*(5), 749–764.

Kuczmarski, S., & Kuczmarski, T. (1995). *Values-Based Leadership:* Englewood Cliffs, NJ: Prentice Hall.

Lappe, F. M., & Du Bois, P. M. (1994). *The quickening of America.* San Francisco: Jossey-Bass.

Laramore, D. et al. (1989). Plaintiffs legal complaint. D. Laramore et al., plaintiffs, vs. the Illinois Sports Facilities Authority, a municipal corporation, the city of Chicago, a municipal corporation, and the Chicago White Sox, Ltd., a limited partnership, defendants. United States District Court for the Northern District of Illinois Eastern Division, No. 89 C 1067.

Laramore, D. (December 10, 1991). Discovery deposition transcript. D. Laramore et al., plaintiffs, vs. the Illinois Sports Facilities Authority, a municipal corporation, the city of Chicago, a municipal corporation, and the Chicago White Sox, Ltd., a limited partnership, defendants. United States District Court for the Northern District of Illinois Eastern Division, No. 89 C 1067.

Laramore, D. et al. (1994a) Plaintiffs' memorandum in opposition to defendants' motion for summary judgment. D. Laramore et al., plaintiffs, vs. the Illinois Sports Facilities Authority, a municipal corporation, the city of Chicago, a municipal corporation, and the Chicago White Sox, Ltd., a limited partnership, defendants. United States District Court for the Northern District of Illinois Eastern Division, No. 89 C 1067.

Laramore, D. et al. (1994b). Plaintiffs' statement of additional facts which require denial of defendants' motion for summary judgment. D. Laramore et al., plaintiffs, vs. the Illinois Sports Facilities Authority, a municipal corporation, the city of Chicago, a municipal corporation, and the Chicago White Sox, Ltd., a limited partnership, defendants. United States District Court for the Northern District of Illinois Eastern Division, No. 89 C 1067.

Lawson, R., & Barton, S. E. (1980). Sex roles in social movements: A case study of the tenant movement in New York City. *Signs: A Journal of Women in Culture and Society, 6,* 230–247.

Leavitt, J. (1993). Women under fire: Public housing activism in Los Angeles. *Frontiers, 13*(2), 109–130.

Leavitt, J., & Saegert, S. (1984, Summer). Women and abandoned buildings: A feminist approach to housing. *Social Policy,* pp. 32–39.

Leavitt, J., & Saegert, S. (1990). *From abandonment to hope: The community-household in Harlem.* New York: Columbia University Press.

Liebow, E. (1967). *Tally's corner: A study of Negro streetcorner men.* Boston: Little, Brown & Co.

Listokin, D. (1990). Federal housing policy and preservation: Historical evolution, patterns, and implications. *Housing Policy Debate, 2*(2), 157–184.

Little, D. (1998, August 23). *Chicago Tribune.* Sec. 1, p. 1.

Low, S. M., & Altman, I. (1992). Place attachment: A conceptual inquiry. In *Place attachment.* Vol. 12. Human behavior and environment: Advances in theory and research (I. Altman & S. M. Low, Eds.) (pp. 1–12). New York: Plenum.

Luxton, M. (1980). *More than a labour of love: Three generations of women's work in the home*. Toronto: Women's Press.

Lynch, L. R. R. (June 23–July 6, 1988). Public housing hands in the balance. *Streetwise*, 6 (20), 1–3.

Manzo, L. C., & Wolfe, M. (1990). *The social production of built forms, environmental settings and person/environment relationships*. Paper presented at the International Association of People and Environment Studies, Ankara, Turkey.

Martin, A., & McRoberts, P. (December 8, 1998). *Chicago Tribune*, Sec. 1, p. 1, 10.

Maton, K. I., & Salem, D. A. (1995). Organizational characteristics of empowering community settings: A multiple case study approach. *American Journal of Community Psychology*, 23(5), 631–656.

McAdam, D. (1982). *Political process and the development of black insurgency, 1930–1970*. Chicago: University of Chicago Press.

McCarron, J. (May 17, 1987). City 'stadium wars' rage on 3 fronts, *Chicago Tribune*, Sec. 4, pp. 1, 5.

McCarron, J. (July 26, 1987). Expert offers his dream Sox stadium, *Chicago Tribune*, Sec. 2, pp 1–2.

McCarron, J. (November 29, 1987). Sox stadium boss gets the job done, *Chicago Tribune*, Sec. 2, pp. 1, 9.

McCarron J. (March 29, 1989). Subsidies urged in Sox area, *Chicago Tribune*, Sec. 2, p. 3.

McCarron, J., & Ziemba, S. (December 15, 1987). Comiskey to receive a 2nd look, *Chicago Tribune*.

McCarthy, D., & Saegert, S. (1979). Residential crowding and design. In J. R. Aiello & A. Baum (Eds.), *Residential crowding and design* (pp. 55–75). New York: Plenum Press.

McClain, J. (1979–80). Why two years? Access, security, and power: Women are still second-class citizens in the housing market. *Status of Women News*, 6(1), 15.

McCourt, K. (1977). *Working-class women and grass-roots politics*. Bloomington: Indiana University Press.

McKernan, J. (1991). *Curriculum action research*. New York: St. Martin's Press.

McRoberts, F. (June 20, 1997). Housing rally has date with history. *Chicago Tribune*, Metro Chicago: 1–2.

Meehan, E. (1979). *Quality of federal policymaking*. Columbia: University of Missouri Press.

Mele, C. (2000). Asserting the political self: Community activism among black women who relocate to the rural south. *The Sociological Quarterly*, 41(1), 63–84.

Metropolitan Planning Council (1986). Tenant management: The challenges and the possibilities. (Report issued by the MPC Task Force on the CHA, May).

Metropolitan Planning Council. (1986). Untapped potentials: The capacities, needs and views of Chicago's highrise public housing residents. (Report issued by MPC, September).

Metropolitan Planning Council. (1988). Our homes, our neighborhoods: The case for rehabilitating Chicago's public housing. (Report issued by the MPC, April).

Meyerson, M., and Banfield, E. (1955). *Politics, planning and the public interest*, Glencoe, IL: Free Press.

Mier, R. (July 10, 1987). Memorandum to Mayor Harold Washington: Stadium Authority Board/White Sox Park.

Mitchell, C. U., & LaGory, M. (2002). Social capital and mental distress in an impoverished community. *City & Community, 1*(2), 195–215.

Molyneux, M. (1985). Mobilization without emancipation: Women's interests, the state, and revolution in Nicaragua. *Feminist Studies, 11*, 227–254.

Monti, D. J. (1989). The organizational strengths and weaknesses of resident-managed public housing sites in the United States. *Journal of Urban Affairs, 11*(1), 39–52.

Moore, Jr., W. (1969). *The vertical ghetto: Everyday life in an urban project.* New York: Random House.

Morgen, S., & Bookman, A. (1988). Rethinking women and politics: An introductory essay. In A. Bookman & S. Morgen (Eds.), *Women and the Politics of Empowerment* (pp. 3–29). Philadelphia: Temple University Press.

National Council of Negro Women. (June 1975). *Women and housing: A report on sex discrimination in five American cities.* Commissioned by the U.S. Department of Housing and Urban Development, Office of the Assistant Secretary for Fair Housing and Equal Opportunity, U.S. Government Printing Office.

Naples, N. A. (1988). *Women against poverty: Community workers in anti-poverty programs, 1964–1984.* Doctoral dissertation, *City University of New York* (University Microfilms International, Ann Arbor, MI)

Naples, N. A. (1992). Activist mothering: Cross-generational continuity in the community work of women from low-income neighborhoods. *Gender & Society, 6*(3), 441–463.

Naples, N. A. (Ed.). (1998a). *Community activism and feminist politics: Organizing across race, class, and gender.* New York: Routledge.

Naples, N. A. (1998b). *Grassroots warriors.* New York: Routledge.

Nenno, M. K. (1996). *Ending the stalemate: Moving housing and urban development into the mainstream of America's future.* Lanham: University Press of America.

Norris, M. L. (June 10, 1987), Ald. Huels pledges to help Bridgeport in battle with Sox, *Chicago Tribune*, Sec. 2, p. 13.

North, D. C. (1990). *Institutions, institutional change and economic performance.* New York: Cambridge University Press.

Newman, O. (1972). *Defensible space.* New York: MacMillan.

O'Brien, P. (1995). From surviving to thriving: The complex experience of living in public housing, *AFFILIA, 10*(2), 155–178.

Ollman, B. (1971). *Alienation: Marx's conception of man in capitalist society.* Cambridge: Cambridge University Press.

On-Site Insight (1991). *Physical needs assessment and modernization cost estimates.* Final report on Wentworth Gardens, prepared for the Chicago Housing Authority, February 21.

Pardo, M. (1998). Creating community: Mexican-American women in eastside Los Angeles. In N. Naples (Ed.), *Community activism and feminist politics: Organizing across race, class, and gender* (pp. 275–300). New York: Routledge.

Payne, C. M. (1989). Ella Baker and models of social change. *Signs: Journal of women in Culture and Society 14*(4), 885–899.

Payne, C. M. (1990). Men led, but women organized: Movement participation of women in the Mississippi Delta. In V. L. Crawford, J. A. Rouse, & B. Woods (Eds.), *Women in the Civil Rights Movement: Trailblazers and Torchbearers, 1941–1965* (pp. 1–11). New York: Carlson.

Payne, C. M. (1995). *I've got the light of freedom*. Berkeley, University of California Press.

Pearce, D. (1978). The feminization of poverty: Women, work, and welfare. *Urban and Social Change Review, 11*: 28–36.

Pearce, D. (1983). The feminization of ghetto poverty. *Transaction: Social Science and Modern Society, 21*(1).

Perkins, D. D. (1995). Speaking truth to power: Empowerment ideology as social intervention and policy. *American Journal of Community Psychology, 23*(5), 765–794.

Perkins, D. D., Brown, B. B., & Taylor, R. B. (1996). The ecology of empowerment: Predicting participation in community organizations. *Journal of Social Issues, 52*(1), 83–110.

Petras, E. M., & Porpora, D. V. (August 1992). *Role, responsibility and reciprocity: Participatory research with grass roots and community organizations*. Paper presented at the American Sociological Association annual meeting. Pittsburgh.

Platt, J. (1984). *The meanings of case-study method in the inter-war period*. Paper presented at the American Sociological Association annual meeting. San Antonio, TX.

Perkins, D. D., & Zimmerman, M. A. (1995). Empowerment theory, research, and application. *American Journal of Community Psychology, 23*(5), 569–580.

Peterman, W. (1993). Resident management and other approaches to tenant control of public housing. In R., Allen & S. Hays (Eds.), *Ownership, control, and the future of housing policy* (pp. 161–175). Westport, CT: Greenwood Press.

Peterman, W. (1994). Resident Management: A good idea gone wrong? *Journal of Housing*, May/June, 10–15.

Peterman, W. (1998). The meaning of resident empowerment: Why just about everybody thinks it's a good idea and what it has to do with resident mangement. In Varady, D., Preiser, W. F., Varady, D. P., Preiser, W. E., & Russel, F. P. *New directions in urban public housing*. (pp. 47–60). Rutgers, NJ: Rutgers University, Center for Urban Policy Research.

Peterman, W. (2000). *Neighborhood planning and community-based development: The potential and limits of grassroots action*. Cities & planning series. Thousand Oaks: Sage.

Philpott, T. L. (1978). *The slum and the ghetto: Immigrants, blacks, and reformers in Chicago, 1880–1930*. Belmont, CA: Wadsworth.

Popkin, S. J., Gwiasda, V. E., Olson, L. M., Rosenbaum, D. P., & Buron, L. (2000). *The hidden war: Crime and the tragedy of public housing in Chicago*. New Brunswick, NJ: Rutgers University Press.

Power, A. (1996). Area-based poverty and resident empowerment. *Urban Studies, 33*(9), 1535–1564.

Proshansky, H. M. (1976). The appropriation and misappropriation of space. In P. Korosec-Serfaty (Ed.), *Appropriation of Space Proceedings of the Third International Architectural Psychology Conference* (pp. 31–69). Strasbourg, France: IAPS.

Proshansky, H. M. (1978). The city and self-identity. *Environment and Behavior, 10,* 147–170.

Proshansky, H. M., Fabian, A. K., & Kaminoff, R. (1983). Place-identity: Physical world socialization of the self. *Journal of Environmental Psychology, 3*(1), 57–83.

Putnam, R. D. (1993). *Making democracy work.* Princeton, NJ: Princeton University Press.

Putnam, R. D. (2000). *Bowling alone: The collapse and revival of American community.* New York: Simon & Schuster.

Pynoss, J. (1986). *Breaking the rules: Bureaucracy and reform in public housing.* New York: Plenum.

Radford-Hill, S. (2000). *Further to fly: Black women and the politics of empowerment.* Minneapolis: University of Minnesota Press.

Rainwater, L. (1966, January). Fear and the house-as-haven in the lower class. *American Institute of Planners Journal,* pp. 23–31.

Rainwater, L. (1970). *Behind the ghetto walls: Black family life in a federal slum.* Aldine de Gruyter.

Ranney, D. C., Wright, P. A., & Zhang, T. (November 1997). Citizens, local government and development of Chicago's Near South Side. Geneva: United Nations Research Institute for Social Development, Discussion Paper 90.

Rapaport, R. N. (1970). Three dielmmas in action research. *Human Relations, 23,* 499–513.

Rappaport, J. (1977). *Community psychology: Values, research, and action.* New York: Holt, Rinehart & Winston.

Rappaport, J. (1981). In praise of paradox: A social policy of empowerment over prevention. *American Journal of Community Psychology, 9*(1), 1–26.

Rappaport, J. (1986, August). *Terms of empowerment/exemplars of prevention: Toward a theory for community psychology.* An address delivered at the Annual Meeting of the American Psychological Association, Washington, DC.

Rappaport, J. (1987). Terms of empowerment/exemplars of prevention: Toward a theory of community psychology. *American Journal of Community Psychology, 15*(2), 121–148.

Reinharz, S. (1984). Women as competent community builders. In A. U. Rickel, M. Gerrard, & I. Iscoe (Eds.), *Social and psychological problems of women* (pp. 19–43). Washington, DC: Hemisphere.

Relph, E. (1976). *Place and placelessness.* London: Pion.

Reitzes, D. C. & Reitzes, D. C. (1987). *The Alinsky legacy: Alive and kicking.* Greenwich, CT: JAI.

Richards, C. (August 23, 1998). Mayor getting ready to bring CHA home. *Chicago Tribune,* Metro Chicago: 1–2.

Richards, C., & Martin, A. (April 22, 1999). CHA looms as next snarl for Daley. *Chicago Tribune,* Metro Chicago: 1, 5A.

Riger, S. (1984). Vehicles for empowerment: The case of feminist movement organizations. *Prevention in Human Services, 3,* 99–117.

Riger, S. (1993). What's wrong with empowerment. *American Journal of Community Psychology, 21*(3), 279–292.

Riger, S., & Lavrakas, P. J. (1981). Community ties: Patterns of attachment and social interaction in urban neighborhoods. *American Journal of Community Psychology, 9*(1), 55–66.

Robnett, B. (1996). African-American women in the civil rights movement, 1954–1965: Gender, leadership, and micromobilization. *American Journal of Sociology, 101*, 1661–1693.

Robnett, B. (1997). *How long? How long?* New York: Oxford University Press.

Rohe, W. M., & Burby, R. J. (1988). Fear of crime in public housing. *Environment and Behavior, 20*(6), 700–720.

Rodgers-Rose, L. F. (Ed.). (1980). *The black woman*. Beverly Hills: Sage Publications.

Rossi, P. (1955). *Why families move: A study in the social psychology of urban residential mobility*. New York: The Free Press.

Sacks, K. B. (1988a). *Caring by the hour: Women, work, and organizing at Duke Medical Center*. Chicago: University of Illinois Press.

Sacks, K. B. (1988b). Gender and grassroots leadership. In A. Bookman & S. Morgen (Eds.), *Women and the politics of empowerment* (pp. 77–94). Philadelphia: Temple University Press.

Sadan, E., & Churchman, A. (1993) Empowerment and professional practice. In R. Feldman, G. Hardie, & D. Saile (Eds.) *Power by design*. Proceedings of the 24th International Conference of the Environmental Design Research Association, Oklahoma City: EDRA, pp. 196–201.

Saegert, S. (1989). Unlikely leaders, extreme circumstances: Older black women building community households. *American Journal of Community Psychology, 17*(3), 295–316.

Saegert, S., & Clark, H. (1989). The meaning of home in low-income cooperative housing in New York City. (Paper published by Housing and Environments Research Group, Center for Human Environments, Environmental Psychology Program, Graduate School and University Center, City University of New York.)

Saegert, S., & Winkel, G. (1996). Paths to community empowerment: Organizing at home. *American Journal of Community Psychology, 24*(4), 517–550.

Schill, M. H. (1993). Distressed public housing: Where do we go from here? *The University of Chicago Law Review, 60*, 497–554.

Schumaker, S. A., & Taylor, R.B. (1983). Toward a clarification of people–place relationships: A model of attchement to place. In N. R. Feimer, & E. S. Geller (Eds.), *Environmental psychology: Directions and perspectives* (pp. 219–251). New York: Praeger.

Scobie, R. (1975). *Problem tenants in public housing: Who, where and why are they*. New York: Praeger.

Seamon, D. A. (1979). *A geography of the lifeworld*. New York: St. Martin's Press.

Sebastian, P. (July 27, 1980). "Solid" community around ballpark, *Chicago Tribune*.

Seigel, J. (December 9, 1988). "Commission Oks Sox stadium with a proviso for neighbors, *Chicago Tribune*, Sec. 3, p. 14.

Shanley, M. L., & Schuck, V. (December 1974). In search of political women. *Social Science Quarterly*, pp. 632–644.

Sidel, R. (1992). *Women and children last: The plight of poor women in affluent America*. New York: Penguin Books.

Siefer, N. (1973). *Absent from the majority: Working class women in America*. New York: National Project on Ethnic America of the American Jewish Committee.

Slayton, R. A. (June 1988). *Chicago's public housing crisis: Causes and solutions*. Report for the Chicago Urban League.

Small, S. A. (November 1995). Action-oriented research: Models and methods. *Journal of Marriage and the Family, 57*, 941–955.

Smith, W. (December 7, 1986), Comiskey neighbors have own game plan, *Chicago Tribune*, Sec. 1, pp. 1, 4.

Smith, J. L. (1999). Cleaning up public housing by sweeping out the poor. *Habitat International, 23*(1), 49–62.

Spain, D. (1995). Direct and default policies in the transformation of public housing. *Journal of Urban Affairs, 17*(4), 357–376.

Spielman, F. (December 11, 1987), "Mayor stirs Sox stadium issue with housing deal," *Chicago Sun Times*, p. 8.

Sprague, J. F. (1991). *More than housing: Lifeboats for women and children.* Boston: Butterworth.

Stack, C. (1974). *All our kin.* New York: Harper Colophon.

Stall, S. (1986). Women organizing to create safe shelter. *Neighborhood Works 9*(8), 10–13; 9(9), 10–12.

Stall, S. (1991). *"The women are just back of everything . . .": Power and politics revisited in small town America.* Ph.D. dissertation. Iowa State University.

Stall, S., & Stoecker, R. (1998). Community organizing or organizing community? Gender and the crafts of empowerment. *Gender & Society, 12*(6), 729–756.

Stoecker, R. (1989). *On the "N of 1" question: The need for case study research in sociology.* (Paper presented at the Midwest Sociological Society annual meeting, St. Louis.)

Stoecker, R. (1992). Who takes out the garbage? Social reproduction an social movement research. In (G. Miller & J. A. Holstein, Eds.), *Perspectives on social problems.* Greenwich, CT: JAI.

Stoecker, R. (1994). *Defending community: The struggle for alternative redevelopment in Cedar-Riverside.* Philadelphia: Temple University Press.

Stoecker, R. (1995). Community organizing and community development in Cedar-Riverside and East Toledo. *Journal of Community Practice, 2*, 1–23.

Stoecker, R. (1997). The CDC model of urban redevelopment: A critique and an alternative. *Journal of Urban Affairs, 19*(1), 1–22.

Stokols, D., & Altman, I. (1987). *Handbook of environmental psychology.* New York: Wiley.

Stokols, D., & Schumaker, S. A. (1982). The psychological context of residential mobility and well-being. *Journal of Social Issues, 83*, 149–171.

Strauss, A. (1961). *Images of the American city.* New York: The Free Press.

Sullivan, P. (March 30, 1988). Group out to rescue Comiskey, *Chicago Tribune*, Sec. 4, p. 3.

Susman, G. I., & Evered, R. D. (1978). An assessment of the scientific merits of action research. *Administrative Science Quarterly, 23*, 582–603.

Susser, I. (1982). *Norman Street.* New York: Oxford University Press.

Suttles, G. D. (1968). *The social order of the slum: Ethnicity and territory in the inner city.* Chicago: University of Chicago Press.

Taylor, R. B., Gottfredson, S. D., & Brower, S. (1985). Attachment to place: Discriminant validity and impact of disorder and diversity. *American Journal of Community Psychology, 13*, 525–542.

The National Center for Neighborhood Enterprise (1989). The grass is greener in public housing: From tenant to resident to homeowner. (A report on resident management of public housing prepared by The National Center for Neighborhood Enterprise, Washington, DC)

The New York Times (June 2, 1991). "Public housing tenants organizing for self-help."

The New York Times (July 5, 2002). Facing up to the housing crisis (editorial). Sec. A, p. 20.

Tilly, L. A., & Scott, J. W. (1978). *Women, work, and family.* New York: Holt, Rinehart & Winston.

Troester, R. R. (1984). Turbulence and tenderness: Mothers, daughters, and "other-mothers" in Paule Marshall's "Brown Girl," "Brownstones," *Sage: A Scholarly Journal on Black Women 1*(2), 13–16.

Tuan, Y. (1977). *Space and place: The perspective of experience.* Minneapolis: University of Minnesota Press.

Tuan, Y. (1980). Rootedness versus sense of place. *Landscape, 24,* 3–7.

Turner, J. F. C. (1977). *Housing by people: Towards autonomy in building environments.* New York: Pantheon Books.

Turner, J. F. C., & Fichter, R. (Eds.). (1972). *Freedom to build.* New York: Macmillan.

Van Ryzin, G. G. (1996). The impact of resident management on residents' satisfaction with public housing: A process analysis of quaisi-experimental data. *Evaluation Review, 20*(4), 485–506.

Vale, L. J. (1996). Destigmatizing public housing. In Crow, D. (Ed.), *Geography and identity: Living and exploring the geopolitics of identity.* Washington, DC: Maisonneuve Press.

Vale, L. J. (1997). Empathological places: Residents' ambivalence toward remaining in public housing. *Journal of Planning Education and Research, 16*(3), 159–175.

Vale, L. J. (2000). *From the Puritans to the projects: Public housing and public neighbors.* Cambridge, MA: Harvard University Press.

Varady, D. P., Preiser, W. E., & Russel, F. P. (1998). *New directions in urban public housing* (pp. 47–60). Rutgers, NJ: Rutgers University, Center for Urban Policy Research.

Venkatesh, S. A. (2000). *American project: The rise and fall of a modern ghetto.* Cambridge, MA: Harvard University Press.

von Hoffman, A. (1996). High ambitious: The past and future of Amerian low-income housing policy. *Housing Policy Debate, 7*(3), 423–446.

von Hoffman, A. (1998). The curse of durability: Why housing for the poor was built to last. *Journal of Housing and Community Development, 55*(5), 34–38.

Wacquant, L. J. A., & Wilson, W. J. (1989). The cost of racial and class exclusion in the inner city. *Annals of the American Academy of Political and Social Science, 501,* 32–39.

Warner, W. L., Low, J. O., Lunt, P. S., & Stole, L. (1963). *Yankee City.* New Haven, CT: Yale University Press.

Warren, R. L. (1972). *The community in America.* Chicago: Rand McNally.

Warren, M. R., Thompson, J. P., & Saegert, S. (2001). The role of social capital in combating poverty. In Saegert, S., Thompson, J. P., & Warren, M. R. (Eds.), *Social capital and poor communities* (pp. 1–28). (Ford Foundation series on asset building.) New York: Russell Sage Foundation.

Washburn, G., & Garza, M. (1999, May 28). *Chicago Tribune,* Sec. 1, p. 1.

Weber, M. (1947). *The theory of social and economic organization.* A. Henderson & T. Parsons (Trans.). New York: The Free Press.

Weisman, L. K. (1992). *Discrimination by design: A feminist critique of the man-made environment.* Urbana: University of Illinois Press.

Wekerle, G. R. (1980). Women in the urban environment. *Signs: A Journal of Women in Culture and Society* (Special Issue Supplement, Women and the American City), 5(3), 188–214.

Wekerle, G. R. (1996). Reframing urban sustainability: Women's movement organizing and the local state. In R. Keil, G. R. Wekerle, & D. V. J. Bell (Eds.), *Local places in the age of the global city* (pp. 137–145). Montreal: Black Rose Press.

Werner, K. (Ed.). (1992). Group appropriation of space. *Architecture and Behavior, 8*(1), 1–79.

West, G., & Blumberg, R. L. (Eds.). (1990). *Women and social protest.* New York: Oxford University Press.

Westphal, L. M. (1999). *Growing power? Social benefits from urban greening projects.* Ph.D. thesis, University of Illinois at Chicago.

Williams, T. M., & Kornblum, W. (1994). *The uptown kids: Struggle and hope in the projects.* New York: Putnam.

Wilson, W. J. (1987). *The truly disadvantaged: The inner city, the underclass, and public policy.* Chicago: University of Chicago Press.

Wilson, W. J. (1996). *When work disappears.* New York: Alfred A. Knopf.

Wittig, M. A. (1996). An introduction to social psychological perspectives on grassroots organizing. *Journal of Social Issues, 52*(1), 3–14.

Wolfe, M. (1990, July). *Whose culture? Whose space? Whose history? Learning from Lesbian bars.* Keynote address at the 11th Conference of the International Association for the Study of People and Their Surroundings (IAPS), Ankara, Turkey.

Woliver, L. R. (1996). Mobilizing and sustaining grassroots dissent. *Journal of Social Issues, 52* (1), 139–143.

Wright, G. (1981). *Building the dream: A social history of housing in America.* New York: Pantheon.

Wright, G., & Rabinow, P. (1982, March). Spatialization of power: Discussion of the work of Michel Foucault. *Skyline,* pp. 14–15.

Wright, P. (1988). *The South Armour Square strategy plan.* Report for the Nathalie P. Voorhees Center for Neighborhood and Community Improvement. Chicago: University of Illinois at Chicago.

Wright, P., Zalalem, Y., deGraaf, J., & Roman, L. (1997, May). The plan to voucher out public housing: An analysis of the Chicago experience and a case study of the proposal to redevelop the Cabrini-Green public housing area. Publication # V-155. Nathalie P. Voorhees Center for Neighborhood and Community Improvement, University of Illinois, Chicago.

Zhang, T. W., & Wright, P. (1992). *The impact of the construction of the new Comiskey Park on local residents.* Report for the Nathalie P. Voorhees Center for Neighborhood and Community Improvement. Chicago: University of Illinois at Chicago.

Zimmerman, M. A. (1995). Psychological empowerment: Issues and illustrations. *American Journal of Community Psychology, 23*(5), 581–600.

Index

Abbott Elementary School. *See* Robert S. Abbott Elementary School

activism: theory and methodology of, 12–16. *See also* community activism

activists, Wentworth Gardens: and burnout, 143–5, 196, 280, 325–7; demographics of, 16–20; as heroes, 342–3; homeplace attachment as motivation for, 66–8, 84–8; older and younger generations of, compared, xiii–xiv, 16–18; relations with technical assistants, 247, 248, 259–60, 263, 265–6, 268–9, 272, 302; younger generation of, 17, 145–8, 193, 319–20, 331–2. *See also* Amey, Hallie; Andrews, Barbara; Brown, Juanita; Bryant, Marcella; Burns, Lucille; Butler, Tecora; Carter, Marcella; Davis, Desiree; Donald, Susan; Driver, Dorothy; Dumas, Janie; Earving, Mardia; Fitzgerald, Ella; Harris, Beatrice; Harris, Sandra; Henry, Viola; Jackson, Doris; Jones, Mae Francis; Nolan, Edna; Laramore, Dorothy; Laramore, Eddie; Mahone, Maggie; Mahone, Francine; McCain, Alberta; McKinney, Bertha; McMiller, Dorothy; Perry, Lucille; Perteet, Faye; Powell, Melinda; Ramsey, Evelyn; Ramsey, Monica; Rias, Mary; Robinson, Carole; Scott, Gloria; Shah, Henrietta; Smith, Gloria; Stewart, Annie; Taylor, Mae; Washington, Sharon; Watkins, Vincent; Weathersby, Lottie; Williams, Geraldine; Woods, Rose

Alfred, Helen: and early housing reform movement, 26

Alinsky, Saul: and confrontational community organizing, 221. *See also* community organizing: Alinsky confrontational style

Altman, I.: on homeplace attachment, 67

Amey, Hallie, 176–8, 344, 352, 354; and activist burnout, 144, 325; attachment to Wentworth, 84, 86; biography, 154–6; as bridge leader, 154, 170–6; as caretaker, 156; as charismatic leader, 163–5; and convenience store, 198, 200–1, 202; on deteriorating conditions, 81; and dual management, 327, 328; early community activism, 157–9; and economic development plan, 259, 264, 267, 270, 271, 272, 279–80, 281, 285, 290; and field house repair campaign, 206, 208, 209; and food sharing, 105; and full management, 330, 333; as group-centered leader, 165–70; and LAC-RMC conflict, 305; and laundromat, 191–2, 193; as othermother, 97, 159–63; on racial discrimination in Armour Square

Amey, Hallie (*cont.*)
   neighborhood, 217; and resident
   management, pursuit of, 296, 302,
   307, 322, 332; and RMC board, 309,
   317, 318, 320–2; as SASNC officer,
   223; on stadium impact on
   community, 250; tribute banquets
   for, 141–3; and youth programs, 128
Anderson, Elijah: on limits of
   community household, 111
Andrews, Barbara: and resident
   management, 319, 321; on security
   concerns, 82
Armour Square neighborhood: profile
   of, 214–16; racism in, 180, 216–18,
   228. *See also* South Armour Square
   Neighborhood Coalition; White Sox
   stadium

Bailey, June: and "Reach One, Teach
   One," 354
Baker: Ella: on leadership, 165
Barnett, Bernice McNair: on
   leadership, 151
Barrett, Elton: and laundromat, 191
Bauer, Catherine: and early housing
   reform movement, 26, 28; critique of
   housing projects, 46
Baum, Howard S., 248
Beatrice Caffrey (youth service
   organization): and support of
   Wentworth activists, 171, 172–3,
   174–5
Belenky, Mary: on recruiting activists,
   165–7
Black Caucus, Illinois State Legislature,
   254; fails to support SASNC, 238
Black migration, 32, 34, 62, 63, 65
Block Watches: and security at
   Wentworth, 134
blockbusting: and racial segregation,
   33
Bond, Lynne: on recruiting activists,
   165–7
bonding social capital: limitations of,
   132; in women-centered organizing,
   159–70. *See also* community

household; community kinship
   work
Boulding, Kenneth: on gift giving and
   community, 106
Bowley, Jr., Devereaux: on Chicago
   public housing, 7
Boyte, Harry D.: on concept of free
   space, 123
bridging social capital, 285, 302–3; and
   contributions to special events, 141,
   142–3, 149; and field house repair
   campaign, 205–9; in women-centered
   organizing, 170–6. *See also* Amey,
   Hallie: as bridge leader
Brooks, Edward (U. S. Senator), 48
Brown, Juanita: and community
   kinship, 101; on deteriorating
   conditions at Wentworth, 78, 80; on
   empowerment, 336; moving to
   Wentworth Gardens, 73, 76; as
   othermother and church activist,
   98–9; on resident management, 305
Brown, Lillian: as SASNC officer, 222
Bryant, Marcella: on Amey as
   community organizer, 160, 161, 167;
   on community, 77; and special
   events organizing, 139; and youth
   programs, 127
Burby, R. J.: on security concerns, 83
Burns, Lucille: and laundromat, 194
Butler, Tecora: and community kinship,
   101; and gossip, 107; moving to
   Wentworth Gardens, 73, 74, 75; and
   RMC board, 309
Bynoe, Peter: as ISFA director, 245–7

Caincross, L.L: on resident
   management, 334
CAP. *See* Chicago Area Project
Carter, Marcella, 256; on Black Caucus,
   238, 254; and community kinship,
   101–2; and convenience store, 204,
   205; on deteriorating conditions,
   79–80; and economic development
   plan, 259, 264, 266, 270, 271, 272, 280,
   284, 285, 286; and events organizing,
   140; and laundromat, 192, 194, 195;

moving to Wentworth Gardens, 73; as othermother, 97; as SASNC officer, 223; on racial discrimination in Armour Square neighborhood, 216–17, 218; on racial injustice in White Sox stadium site selection, 220–1; on Radford-Hill as organizer, 234–5 and resident management, 310; on security concerns, 82; on stadium impact on community, 250; and stadium protests, 252–3

Catholic Archdiocese of Chicago: and economic development plan, 266

Cavatto, Donna: and economic development plan, 278–80

Chapman, James, 246; and economic development plan, 257, 259, 260, 263, 266, 269–70, 274, 281–2, 286, 290; as legal advisor to SASNC, 237

Chicago Area Project (CAP): and funding for youth programs, 126–30; and support of Wentworth activists, 171, 172–5

Chicago Beat Representative Program: and security at Wentworth, 134

Chicago, city government: City Plan Commission, 245–7; Department of Planning and Development, 262

Chicago city officials: Hollander, Elizabeth, 247; Huels, Patrick, 231, 236, 236–7; Sawyer, Eugene, 237; Tillman, Dorothy, 277–8; Washington, Harold, 219–21, 224, 230, 231

Chicago Housing Authority developments: ABLA, 60, 187; Cabrini Green, 60; Dearborn Homes, 191; Henry Homer, 60, 187; Ida B. Wells Homes, 31; LeClaire Courts, 311–12; Robert Taylor Homes, 7, 43, 190, 191

Chicago Housing Authority (CHA), 348; and Board of Commissioners, 353; and Central Advisory Council, 119; and Community and Tenant Relation Aid (CNTRA), 157; establishes Local Advisory Councils,

49 (*See also* Wentworth Gardens Local Advisory Council); and high-rises, 43–6, 349; lack of maintenance funds, 48, 50; mismanagement and corruption in, 50–1, 52, 131–2; and racial discrimination in site and tenant selection, 30–4, 40, 47–8; and tenant rules and regulations, 76; and urban renewal, 39–43; and Wentworth Gardens field house, 205–9; and Wentworth Gardens resident management, 296, 304, 305–7, 310, 312–15, 318, 321–2, 324

Chicago Housing Tenant Organization: and Local Advisory Councils, 119

Chicago Police Department: collaborates on security at Wentworth, 132, 133–6

Chicago politics. *See* Democratic Party Organization, 11th Ward

Chicago Tenant Bill of Rights, 64

Chombart de Lauwe, P.: on appropriation of space, 187, 188

City Design Center: as source of technical assistance, xviin2

Civil Rights Movement: as source of support for tenants, 47, 49

Clampan, D.: on resident management, 334

Clark, H.: and housing management, 326

Clark, Helene: on social networks in co-ops, 94

Clark, Leonard: assault on, in Armour Square Park, 217

class, social /economic: and biases in economic development, 294; and divisions within SASNC, 226–8; and inequity, 348; and resistance, 343–4

Coalition to Protect Public Housing: opposition of, to displacement of tenants, 59–60

Collins, Patricia Hill: on activist burnout, 143–4; on Black women activists, 8, 342; on othermothering, 96, 98

Comiskey Park. *See* White Sox Stadium
community activism: motivations for,
  72–8, 98–9, 147, 155, 162–3, 163–65,
  225–9; women's role in, 8–9; as
  place based, 9–12, 343; men's
  absence in, 18–19. *See also*
  activism; activists, Wentworth
  Gardens; community organizing;
  resistance
community gardens. *See* Wentworth
  Gardens resident initiatives:
  community gardens
community household, 112–14, 345;
  defined, 93–5; gossip as information
  sharing in, 106–17; gossip as norm
  setting in, 108–10; laundromat,
  contributions to, 193–4; limits of,
  110–12. *See also* community kinship
  work; food sharing: role of in
  community household; community
  othermothering
community kinship work: defined,
  99–100; and mutual aid, 100–3. *See
  also* community household: gossip as
  information sharing in; community
  household: gossip as norm setting
  in; food sharing: and community
  organizing
community organizing: defined,
  xiii–xiv; Alinsky confrontational
  style, 208, 214, 221–4, 250, 252–3, 254;
  bureaucratic requirements clash
  with values of, 261, 290, 293–4,
  297–8
community othermothering, 345;
  defined, 95–6; at Wentworth
  Gardens, 96–9; youth programs as
  extension of, 126–32. *See also* Amey,
  Hallie: as othermother
convenience store. *See under*
  Wentworth Gardens resident
  initiatives
Cooper, Clare Marcus: on opposition to
  public housing, 27
Couto, Richard: on importance of
  community support networks, 114;
  on social capital, 171–2

crime: gossip as deterrent to, 108; in
  housing developments, 50. *See also*
  security concerns
Crossroads Foundation: and economic
  development plan, 279
Cuomo, Andrew, 58

Daniels, Arlene Kaplan: on activists,
  143; on sociability work, 138–9
Davis, Desiree: attachment to
  Wentworth, 84, 85; on community
  life, 77; on deteriorating conditions,
  81; and gossip, 107; and laundromat,
  193; moves to Wentworth Gardens,
  71; and RMC board, 319; on security
  concerns, 83
Democratic Party Organization, 11th
  Ward: and political isolation of South
  Armour Square, 216
Donald, Susan: on Amey as
  community organizer, 167, 169, 170;
  attachment to Wentworth, 85; moves
  to Wentworth, 71; and resident
  management, 312, 314, 317, 318, 319,
  325, 336, 355
Driver, Dorothy, 124; tribute banquet
  for, 141–2; and resident management,
  304
Dumas, Janie: on Amey as community
  organizer, 169; attachment to
  Wentworth, 85, 88; on community,
  77; and food sharing, 104–5; moves
  to Wentworth Gardens, 69; and
  spiritual development center,
  183–4

Earving, Mardia: and convenience
  store, 197, 198–200, 201–2, 203–4; and
  food sale fund raising, 106
economic development plan,
  Wentworth Gardens, 257–9, 276–8,
  284–6, 292–4; and business
  development training, 272–5;
  community support for, 270–2;
  development team for, 259–60,
  275–6, 289, 290; empowerment zone
  proposal for, 278–80, 288; failure of,

due to political and economic inequity, 287–90; funding for, 262–3, 278–80, 289; lawsuit dismissal, 281–4; and leadership development, 286–7; and market feasibility study, 263–9; and participatory design workshops, 267–70; site location and control, 266–7, 291

economic development: potential conflict of, with community organizing, 255, 258, 261

empowerment, 333–7, 344–7

environmental determinism: as expressed in public housing developments, 46, 350

ethic of care, 95, 156, 160–3, 181. *See also* community othermothering; community kinship work

Evans, Sara M.: on concept of free space, 123

everyday resistance. *See* resistance

Feldman, Roberta: and deteriorating conditions at Wentworth Gardens, 78; and economic development plan participatory design workshops, 267, 268, 272, 276; on homeplace attachment, 66–7

field house. *See under* Wentworth Gardens resident initiatives

Fitzgerald, Ella: church involvement of, 98; and homeplace attachment, 88; moves to Wentworth Gardens, 76; on Pied Piper preschool program, 182

food sharing: role of in community household, 103–6, 141; and fund raising sales, 106

Foucault, Michel: on power relations, 10

Francis, M.: on participatory design, 81

Fried, Marc: on homeplace attachment, 85–6

Gaines, Brenda: and field house repair campaign, 208

Gans, Herbert: on homeplace attachment, 86

Gautreaux v. Chicago Housing Authority. See CHA: racial discrimination in site and tenant selection

gender and gender inequity, 348; and barriers to participation in community development, 293; and feminization of poverty, 18–20; impact of, on social activism, 118; and leadership, 153; and resistance, 343–4

Gilkes, Cheryl, 98; on community activists, 126, 143, 149

Giroux, Henry: on empowerment, 336

Gluckman, M.: on role of gossip in community, 106

gossip. *See under* community household

grassroots activism. *See* community activism

grassroots organizing. *See* community organizing

Grauman, C. F., 187

Hall, Carol Grant: and economic development plan, 275

Harris, Beatrice; on Amey as community organizer, 166, 168; and activist burnout, 144; and CAP, 173; and CHA, problems with, 322; on deteriorating conditions at Wentworth Gardens, 3, 79; and HCSI, 324; and laundromat, 191; on limits of community household, 111–12; and LAC, 148; moves to Wentworth Gardens, 70, 74, 76; and resident management, 295–6, 302, 305, 315, 329, 330; and RMC board, 309, 323, 324; and youth programs, 127–32

Harris, Sandra: on Amey as community organizer, 170, 171

Hayward, D. G., 100

Haywoode, Terry: on women as organizers, 123

Henderson, Harold: on Section 8 rental assistance, 56
Henley, Sandie: and RMC board, 319
Henry, Viola: and special events organizing, 141
Holt, G. E., on Armour Square problems, 218
homeplace attachment. *See* place attachment
hooks, bell: and homeplace appropriation, 342–3; on place-based activism, 9–10
housing advocacy groups, 352
Housing and Urban Development (HUD), U. S. Department of: bureaucratic requirements of, 308–18; and CHA, 51; and demolition of public housing, 6; Healthy and Safe Communities Initiative (HSCI), 323–4; and HOPE VI, 348–50; and LAC, 119; rental vouchers, 349; and resident management, 298–300, 304, 305–7, 308. *See also* public housing programs, federal
Huels, Patrick, 253; lack of support for Wentworth Gardens, 231, 236, 277–8, 280, 284, 288

Illinois Institute of Technology University (IIT): and Amey's use of bridging social capital, 175–6
Illinois Sports Facility Act. *See* White Sox stadium: Illinois Sports Facility Authority
IFSA. *See* White Sox stadium: Illinois Sports Facility Authority
Illinois state officials: Thompson, James, 219–21, 231–2; Madigan, Michael, 238. *See also* Black Caucus

Jackson, Doris: on Amey, 160
Jacobs, Jane: on community, 252
James, Curtis: and resident management, 307, 312, 314, 316, 330
Johnson, Angie: and RMC board, 319

Jones, Mae Frances; on Amey as community activist, 162; and laundromat, 193, 196; moves to Wentworth Gardens, 71; on security concerns, 81
Jordan, Gwen; and field house repair campaign, 208
Juneteenth Day demonstration, 59–60
juvenile delinquency. *See* youth programs

Kieffer, Charles H., 345
King, Martin Luther, Jr.: leads Chicago marches, 47
Krauss, Celene: on value of modest victories, 209
Kuczmarski, Susan and Thomas: on role of caring in activism, 161

LAC. *See* Wentworth Gardens Local Advisory Council
Lane, Vince: and resident management, 295, 301, 302; on Wentworth Gardens' past, 72
Laramore, Dorothy, 248; and economic development plan, 257 recommends Milano as SASNC attorney, 235; on South Armour community, 226–7; and SASNC, 223, 240; and stadium, 250, 252
Laramore, Eddie, 226; and economic development plan, 268; as SASNC officer, 223
laundromat. *See under* Wentworth Gardens resident initiatives
leadership: types of 151–3. *See also* women-centered leadership
Leavitt, Jacqueline, 93, 316; on community household, 93, 94–5; on public housing activists, 8
Lindeman Center: as source of technical assistance, 207
Local Advisory Council. *See* Wentworth Gardens Local Advisory Council
Low, S. M.: on homeplace attachment, 67

Mahone, Maggie, 341; and activist
burnout, 145; biographical sketch,
133; and community kinship, 102;
and economic development plan,
281–2; and RMC board, 309, 321; on
security concerns, 82, 133–7, 148; and
youth programs, 127
Manzo, L. D.: on place-based power
relations, 10
Marshall, George, 244; betrays SASNC,
239–40; criticizes Huels, 236–7; as
president of SASNC, 232
McCain, Alberta: and othermothering,
97; and resident management,
302
McCarthy, D.: on importance of
community size, 77–8
McKinney, Bertha, 354; and community
kinship, 102; and convenience store,
203–4; and food sharing, 103–4,
105, 106; and homeplace attachment,
85; and laundromat, 194; moves
to Wentworth Gardens, 72, 75;
and norm setting for youth,
109–110; on security concerns,
82
McMiller, Dorothy: and activist
burnout, 144, 325; and laundromat,
189–90, 193, 196; moves to
Wentworth Gardens, 70–1, 73; on
community, 77
Milano, Mary: as legal advisor to
SASNC, 235, 237; sides with
homeowners, 241, 243–4
Millennial Housing Commission,
352
modernist architecture. *See* public
housing developments: design
Monti, D. J., on community
development, 292; on resident
management, 300, 305–6,
316
Moore, William, Jr.: on public housing,
7
mothering. *See* community
othermothering
Myers, Susie: as SASNC officer,
223; settles with ISFA, 240

Naples, Nancy: on in-depth interview
methodology, 14; on motivation for
community work, 147
Nathalie P. Voorhees Center: as source
of technical assistance, 207
National Commission on Severely
Distressed Public Housing, 51–2
Naughton, Jack: and economic
development plan participatory
design workshop, 267, 268
Nemo, Mary: on slums, 42
New Urbanism, 350

othermothering. *See* community
othermothering
O'Brien, Patricia: on activists as heroes,
342; on public housing activists, 8

Pacyga, D., on Armour Square
problems, 218
Pader, Ellen: on public housing
activists, 8
Peace Fund: and economic
development plan, 279
Perry, Lucille: and RMC board,
319; on limits of community
household, 111
Perteet, Faye: and RMC board, 319;
on Amey as community organizer,
167, 168, 169; on limits of community
household, 111; and othermothering,
96–8; on security concerns, 80, 81–2
Peterman, William: and field house
repair campaign, 207; and resident
management, 302, 328–9, 333; and
White Sox battle, 231
Pied Piper preschool program, 181–2
place attachment: and grieving loss of
home, 247–8; as motivation for
community organizing, 225–9;
theory of, 66–8; at Wentworth,
84–8
poverty: feminization of, 18–20,
343
Powell, Melinda: and "Mothers in
Transition," 354
Power, Anne: on public housing,
348

Prim, Teresa: and economic development plan, 275

Progressive Baptist Church: role of, in White Sox Battle, 225, 232, 237

Prohansky, H. M., 187

Pruitt-Igoe (St. Louis housing project), 53

public housing developments: dilapidated condition of, 4, 6, 48, 49–50, 51–3; funding and management of, inadequate, 45–6, 48; high-rise design and construction problems, 44–5, 46; stigma of, 44. *See also* Chicago Housing Authority developments

public housing, federal programs, 57–8; demand for, 25–6, 68–72; and Chicago urban renewal, 39–43, 48; design and construction of, 26, 36–8; disinvestment in, 53–7, 295; for elderly, 53 (*See also* T. E. Brown Apartments); funding of, inadequate, 25, 45–6, 48, 50, 52, 79–80; Homeownership and Opportunity for People Everywhere (HOPE), 55–6; and National Commission on Severely Distressed Public Housing, 51–2; opposition to, 27, 29, 52, 57; origins of, in Depression, 26–30; privatization of, 53–7; Public Works Administration Neighborhood Composition Rule (NCR), 29; rent policies, 48–9; resident management (*See* Wentworth Gardens resident management); Section 8 rental assistance vouchers, 54–7; site selection for, 25, 29–30, 35–6, 43; social and recreational services in, 26

public housing laws and policies, federal: Brooks Amendments, 48; Federal Housing Act (1949), 41; Housing Act (1965), 48; Housing and Community Development Act (1974), 54–7; Housing and Community Development Act (1987), 300; National Housing Act (1954), 41; National Recovery Act (1933), 28; Wagener Steagall Act (1937), 28

public housing laws, Illinois, 39

public housing tenants: demonstrations by (*See* Coalition to Protect Public Housing); displaced by redevelopment, 55–7; family size in high rises, 43; and homeplace attachment, 60–2 (*See also* homeplace attachment: and Wentworth); racial and income composition of, 25, 30, 35n21, 41–2, 50; and tenants' rights, 49

Putnam, Robert: on social capital, 114, 170–1

racial segregation: Chicago Black Belt, 32–4; blockbusting, 33; patterns of in public housing 41–2

racism: and opposition to public housing, 29–30, 30–4; in housing site selection, 39–40, 42–3; and white flight, 42; in Armour Square neighborhood, 180, 216–18; and siting of White Sox stadium, 213, 220–1; and violence against African Americans, 33, 180, 216–18

Radford-Hill, Sheila: as Alinksy style organizer, 223–4; and Amey's use of bridging social capital, 173, 174, 175; and economic development plan, 259, 260, 263, 267, 273, 275, 276–7, 280, 283–4, 288, 290; assists field house repair campaign, 205–8; on place-based activism, 9; and resident management, 305; and White Sox battle, 214, 228, 234–5, 237, 238, 243, 245, 246, 254, 255

Rainwater, Lee: on St. Louis public housing, 7

Ramsey, Evelyn: on Amey as community organizer, 160; and activist burnout, 144–5; on limits of community household, 110–111; and community kinship, 101; and convenience store, 198, 200, 202–3,

204; and; repair campaign, 208; and food sharing, 104, 105; involvement in LAC, 122, 124–6, 148; moves to Wentworth Gardens, 69–70; and norm setting for youth, 108–9

Ramsey, Monica: and community kinship, 100; and special events organizing, 140; as second generation activist, 146–7

real estate industry: opposition of, to public housing, 27, 29

religion: influence of, on activists, 98–9, 155; and spiritual development center, 193–4

resident management. *See* Wentworth Gardens resident management

Resident Council. *See* Wentworth Gardens Resident Council

resistance: appropriating homeplace as, 342–3; and empowerment, 344–7; theory, 11–12; transgressive, 258, 335–6, 345, 346, 351; everyday, 346; limits of, 347–51

Reynolds, Thomas: as head of ISFA, 233

Rias, Mary: as creator of community household, 91–3; and community kinship, 102; on deteriorating condition, 80; and laundromat, 194; moves to Wentworth Gardens, 77; and RMC board, 309

Riger, S.: on empowerment, 334–5

Robert S. Abbott Elementary School: Amey's involvement with, 157; inferior education at, xi–xii; Local School Council, xii

Robert Taylor Homes. *See under* Chicago Housing Authority housing developments

Robinson, Carol: on community life, 77; on deteriorating condition, 80; and resident management, 311, 323, 326; on security concerns, 81

Robnett, Belinda: on women leaders, 152, 153, 178

Rohe, W. M.: on security concerns, 83

Sacks, Karen Brodkin: on centerwomen leadership, 152, 153, 156

Saegert, S., 93, 316; on community household, 94–5, 113; on importance of community size, 77–8; on homeplace attachment, 87–8

Salisbury, Harrison: on New York public housing, 7

SASNC. *See* South Armour Square Neighborhood Coalition

Save Our Homes Neighborhood Coalition (SOH): formation of, 225–9; strategies of, 229–32. *See also* South Amour Square Neighborhood Coalition

Save Our Sox (SOS): as ally of SASNC, 229–30, 235

Sawyer, Eugene: and SASNC, 237, 254

Scott, Geraldine: on Amey as community organizer, 167–8; moves to Wentworth Gardens, 72–3; and RMC board, 319

Seabrook, Gloria: on Amey, 169; and Wentworth RMC, 296, 301, 302, 307; on RMC/LAC conflict, 304; and RMC bureaucracy, 309, 311, 314, 315, 316; and dual management, 327, 328; and full management, 329, 332

Section 8 rental assistance, 54–7

security concerns, 77–8, 81–3, 132–3, 136–7; and CHA tenant patrol, 324; fear of retaliation, 134–6; liaison with police, 133–6; and youth programs, 136

Shah, Henrietta: and laundromat, 193

Sidel, Ruth: on rise of female-headed households, 19

Simkovitch, Mary: and early housing reform movement, 26

Small, Stephen: on collaboration between researcher and subjects, 14

Smith, Gloria: as second generation activist, 146, 147

social capital. *See* bonding social capital; bridging social capital

social reproduction, 343

South Armour Development Company, 245

South Armour Square Neighborhood Coalition (SASNC), 254–6; and Alinsky style organizing, 221–4, 250, 252–3, 254; attempts to gain concessions, 244–8; early tactics of, 233–7; formation of, 224–5, 232–3; confronts ISFA on environmental issues, 249–53; lawsuit, 242, 248–9; and legislative defeat, 238–9; and Save Our Homes, 225–9; split and betrayal of, 239–44

space appropriation: defined, 184–5; and economic development plan, 267; of homeplace, 185–7; obstacles to 187–8; power of, 209–10. *See also* Wentworth Gardens resident initiatives

spiritual development center. *See under* Wentworth Gardens resident initiatives

Spring, Melvin: on effectiveness of Wentworth LAC, 121

Stall, Susan: on community organizing, 117

Stoecker, Randy: community organizing, 117, 261, 290, 293–4

T. E. Brown Apartments: participation of, in White Sox stadium battle, 214, 225, 245, 246–7, 249

Taylor, Mae: and laundromat, 191

Taylor, Robert: as chairman of CHA, 30; tries to integrate CHA housing, 40

Thompson, James: role of, in White Sox stadium battle, 219–21, 231–2

Tillman, Dorothy, 277–8, 279–80, 288

transgressive resistance. *See* resistance: transgressive

urban renewal: in Chicago, 39–43; and National Housing Act (1954), 41

Vale, L. J.: on homeplace attachment, 86

Venkatesh, Sudhir Alladi: on CHA policies, 42; on public housing design, 57

Volunteers in Service to America (VISTA): and youth programs, 127

Walkins, Vincent: on Amey, 162

Warner, Lloyd: on gift giving and community, 106

Washington, Harold: role of, in White Sox stadium battle, 219–21, 224, 230, 231, 254

Washington, Sharon: on Chicago Plan Commission meeting, 246; and economic development plan, 259, 267, 270–2, 279–80, 284, 286, 289, 291; on importance of neighborhood, 255–6; on racism in Armour Square neighborhood, 228–9; as SASNC officer, 223

Weathersby, Lottie: and activist burnout, 145; and community kinship, 102; and events organizing, 140–2, 148; and gossip, 107; and homeplace attachment, 84, 87; on limits of community household, 110; residential autobiography, 62–6, 73; and stadium protests, 252

Weinstock, Jacquelyn: on recruiting activists, 165–7

Weisman, Leslie Kanes: on feminization of poverty, 19–20

welfare reform: Personal Responsibility and Work Opportunity Act (1996), 344n1

Wentworth Gardens: current conditions, 352–5; design of buildings, 36–8; deterioration of, 3–4, 64–5, 78–84, 296, 347; landscaping, 74–5, 287, 313–14, 324, 354; management of, by CHA, 76–7; memories of early days of, 72–8; site selection, 34–6; security concerns, 81–3, 133–7, 148, 353; social services inadequacies, 83–4

Wentworth Gardens Local Advisory Council: daily activities of, 115–16;

establishment of, 119–21; and event planning, 132–43; office as private/public space, 122–6; as site of women-centered organizing, 116–19; and conflict with RMC, 303–5; and tenant security, 132–7; and youth programs, 126–32. *See also* Wentworth Gardens resident initiatives

Wentworth Gardens resident initiatives, 345–6; community gardens, 184, 353–4; convenience store, 182, 197–205, 345, 179–82, 205–9, 223–4; field house, 179–84, 205–9, 345, 354; laundromat, 189–97, 345, 353; special events, 132–43, 323, 345 182, 189–97; Pied Piper preschool, 181–2; Spiritual Development Center, 193–4, 353; and youth programs, 129, 131 345

Wentworth Gardens resident management, 331–2; decision to pursue, 295–8; historic context of, 298–300; activists' capacity for, 301–3; HUD/CHA support, limits of, 305–7; establishing bureaucratic structure for, 307–18; community organizing in support of, 318–27; and empowerment, 333–7

Wentworth Gardens Resident Council: Amey as president of, 158; and LAC, 119–20, 354; and laundromat, 190–2

Wentworth Gardens Resident Management Corporation (RMC), 353; board members, 319, 325–7; board training, 309–12; and Community Advisory Board, 303; corporate office of, 316–17; and dual management, 327–31; and full management, 329–31; and LAC, collaboration with, 324–5; and LAC, conflict with, 303–5; resident participation, 321–5; staff hiring and training, 310–11, 312–14;. *See also* Wentworth Gardens resident management

Wentworth Gardens Residents United for Survival, 214

White Sox stadium, 213–14, 346; Alinsky-style organizing by opponents, 221–4; Bess plan for alternative site for, 239–40; and Illinois Sports Facility Authority (ISFA), 219–20, 230, 233, 238, 239–44, 254; impact of, on neighborhood, 250–2; and monopoly power of team owners, 219–20; power brokers, 218–21; protests against, 230, 233–5, 237, 238–9. *See also* Illinois Sports Facility Act; Save Our Sox (SOS); South Armour Square Neighborhood Coalition

Whittaker, David: on Amey as community organizer, 161, 174–5, 176–7

Wieboldt Foundation: and Amey's use of bridging social capital, 176

Wilkins, Craig: and economic development plan, 272–3

Wolfe, M.: on place-based power relations, 10

Woliver, L. R.: on value of modest victories, 209

women-centered leadership: defined, 152; traditional leadership compared to, 152–3, 177; and cultivation of social bonds within community, 159–70; and building social bridges to external resources, 170–76

women-centered organizing: defined, 117–19; LAC as site of, 116–17; and social networks, 123–4; combined with confrontational style in SASNC, 232

Wood, Edith Elmer: and early housing reform movement, 26–7, 28

Wood, Elizabeth: on design of public housing 44; as CHA executive secretary, 30; supports integration of CHA housing, 40; and Wentworth Gardens, 34, 35

Woods, Rose: as SASNC officer, 223

Wormeley, Melville: and economic
    development plan, 276
Wright, Gwendolyn: on Depression
    origins of public housing, 28; on
    segregation and urban renewal,
    41
Wright, Mary: and economic
    development plan, 258
Wright, Patricia: as technical advisor to
    SASNC, 247; and economic
    development plan, 259, 263, 264, 265,
    272, 274, 275, 281–2, 282–4, 286–7,
    290, 293
Wright, Timothy: and SASNC, 231, 240,
    246

Yotaghan, Wardell (head of CPPH),
    59–60
youth programs, 180–1, 345: and CAP,
    172, 173; and delinquency problems,
    108–9; in economic development
    plan, 265; and LAC, 116, 126–32